Europe on the move

Manchester University Press

Cultural History of Modern War

Series editors   Ana Carden-Coyne, Peter Gatrell, Max Jones,
Penny Summerfield and Bertrand Taithe

Already published

Carol Acton and Jane Potter   *Working in a world of hurt: trauma and resilience in the narratives of medical personnel in warzones*

Julie Anderson   *War, disability and rehabilitation in Britain: soul of a nation*

Lindsey Dodd   *French children under the Allied bombs, 1940–45: an oral history*

Rachel Duffett   *The stomach for fighting: food and the soldiers of the First World War*

Christine E. Hallett   *Containing trauma: nursing work in the First World War*

Jo Laycock   *Imagining Armenia: orientalism, ambiguity and intervention*

Chris Millington   *From victory to Vichy: veterans in inter-war France*

Juliette Pattinson   *Behind enemy lines: gender, passing and the Special Operations Executive in the Second World War*

Chris Pearson   *Mobilizing nature: the environmental history of war and militarization in Modern France*

Jeffrey S. Reznick   *Healing the nation: soldiers and the culture of caregiving in Britain during the Great War*

Jeffrey S. Reznick   *John Galsworthy and disabled soldiers of the Great War: with an illustrated selection of his writings*

Michael Roper   *The secret battle: emotional survival in the Great War*

Penny Summerfield and Corinna Peniston-Bird   *Contesting home defence: men, women and the Home Guard in the Second World War*

Trudi Tate and Kate Kennedy (eds)   *The silent morning: culture and memory after the Armistice*

Spiros Tsoutsoumpis   *The People's Armies: a history of the Greek resistance*

Laura Ugolini   *Civvies: middle-class men on the English Home Front, 1914–18*

Wendy Ugolini   *Experiencing war as the 'enemy other': Italian Scottish experience in World War II*

Colette Wilson   *Paris and the Commune, 1871–78: the politics of forgetting*

Centre for the Cultural History of War

www.arts.manchester.ac.uk/subjectareas/history/research/cchw/

Europe on the move

Refugees in the era of the Great War

~

EDITED BY PETER GATRELL AND LIUBOV ZHVANKO

Manchester University Press

Copyright © Manchester University Press 2017

While copyright in the volume as a whole is vested in Manchester University Press, copyright in individual chapters belongs to their respective authors, and no chapter may be reproduced wholly or in part without the express permission in writing of both author and publisher.

Published by Manchester University Press
Altrincham Street, Manchester M1 7JA, UK
www.manchesteruniversitypress.co.uk

British Library Cataloguing-in-Publication Data is available

ISBN 978 1 7849 9441 9 *hardback*
ISBN 978 1 5261 3935 1 *paperback*

First published by Manchester University Press in hardback 2017

This edition first published 2019

The publisher has no responsibility for the persistence or accuracy of URLs for any external or third-party internet websites referred to in this book, and does not guarantee that any content on such websites is, or will remain, accurate or appropriate.

Typeset by Servis Filmsetting Ltd, Stockport, Cheshire

Contents

List of illustrations	*page* vii
List of maps and tables	viii
Notes on contributors	ix
Preface	xii

	Introduction – *Peter Gatrell*	1
1	Population displacement in East Prussia during the First World War – *Ruth Leiserowitz*	23
2	'A mass which you could form into whatever you wanted': refugees and state building in Lithuania and Courland, 1914–21 – *Klaus Richter*	45
3	Refugees from Polish territories in Russia during the First World War – *Mariusz Korzeniowski*	66
4	'Human waves': refugees in Russia, 1914–18 – *Irina Belova*	88
5	Ukrainian assistance to refugees during the First World War – *Liubov Zhvanko and Oleksiy Nestulya*	108
6	'Cities of barracks': refugees in the Austrian part of the Habsburg Empire during the First World War – *Martina Hermann*	129
7	Between refugees and the state: Hungarian Jewry and the wartime Jewish refugee crisis in Austria-Hungary – *Rebekah Klein-Pejšová*	156
8	Beyond the borders: displaced persons in the Italian linguistic space during the First World War – *Marco Mondini and Francesco Frizzera*	177

Contents

9 Belgian refugees during the First World War (France, Britain, Netherlands) – *Michaël Amara* — 197

10 Citizenship on the move: refugee communities and the state in France, 1914–18 – *Alex Dowdall* — 215

11 *Golgotha*: the retreat of the Serbian army and civilians in 1915–16 – *Danilo Šarenac* — 236

12 The refugee question in Bulgaria before, during and after the First World War – *Nikolai Vukov* — 260

13 From imperial dreams to the refugee problem: population movements during Greece's 'decade of war', 1912–22 – *Emilia Salvanou* — 284

14 Becoming and unbecoming refugees: the long ordeal of Balkan Muslims, 1912–34 – *Uğur Ümit Üngör* — 304

Index — 328

List of illustrations

1.1 'Vertrieben' (The Expellees), medal by Ludwig Gies, 1915 © DACS 2017, photo © The Trustees of the British Museum.   35
6.1 Refugees arriving through the front gate of camp Gmünd. Courtesy of Stadtarchiv Gmünd.   137
6.2 A Habsburg propaganda event staged at the summer theatre of camp Gmünd. Courtesy of Stadtarchiv Gmünd.   140
6.3 Paula Czapka, Baroness Winstetten, the wife of Gmünd's camp director, distributes sweets to the camp's orphans. Courtesy of Stadtarchiv Gmünd.   142
8.1 Semantic analysis of diaries written by Trentino refugees in Austria-Hungary. Source: FMST, ASP; AAVV, Scritture di Guerra 4–5, Trento-Rovereto, 1995–96.   189
11.1 Military and civilian wagons in Prokuplje, photograph by Samson Tchernoff. Courtesy of National Library of Serbia.   240
11.2 The Serbian army in Rugova gorge, Peć, photograph by Samson Tchernoff. Courtesy of National Library of Serbia.   243
11.3 Serbian pupils in London, Saint Sava's Day 1918, photograph by Samson Tchernoff. Courtesy of National Library of Serbia.   251
11.4 Kosovo Day poster by Bernard Partridge. Courtesy of National Library of Serbia.   254

List of maps and tables

Maps

1.1	The First World War in East Prussia.	25
4.1	The Eastern Front, 1914–17.	92
6.1	Austria-Hungary during the First World War.	132
8.1	Italy's refugees during the First World War. Source: Ministero per le Terre Liberate, Censimento dei profughi di Guerra, Roma, 1919, pp. 218–19.	184
10.1	Location of refugees from four departments in France, September 1918.	219
11.1	Serbia during the First World War.	237
12.1	Bulgaria and its neighbours during the First World War.	261
14.1	The Ottoman Empire during the First World War	306

Tables

6.1	Camps in Cisleithania during the First World War with more than 500 inmates.	139

Notes on contributors

Michaël Amara is Chef de service aux Archives générales du Royaume, National Archives of Belgium. He is the author of *Des Belges à l'épreuve de l'Exil: les réfugiés de la Première Guerre mondiale: France, Grande-Bretagne, Pays-Bas, 1914–1918* (Brussels: Éditions de l'Université de Bruxelles, 2008).

Irina Belova is a professor in the Department of National History of Konstantin Tsiolkovsky Kaluga State University, Kaluga, Russian Federation. Her latest book is *Vynuzhdennye migranty: bezhentsy i voennoplennye Pervoi mirovoi voiny v Rossii. 1914–1925 gg.* [Forced Migrants, Refugees and Prisoners of War in Russia, 1914–1925] (Moscow: AIRO-XX, 2014).

Alex Dowdall is a temporary lecturer in the cultural history of modern war at the University of Manchester. His article, 'Civilians in the combat zone: Allied and German evacuation policies at the Western Front, 1914–1918' appeared in *First World War Studies* in 2015. He is currently completing a monograph on civilian communities under fire at the Western Front.

Francesco Frizzera is affiliated with the University of Trento where he completed a PhD on refugees during the First World War. He is currently preparing this for publication. In 2013–15 he was a member of the research team, 'World War I 1914–1918' at the Italian-German Historical Institute in Trento.

Notes on contributors

Peter Gatrell is Professor of Economic History at the University of Manchester. His books include *A Whole Empire Walking: Refugees in Russia during World War 1* (Bloomington: Indiana University Press, 1999), and *The Making of the Modern Refugee* (Oxford: Oxford University Press, 2013).

Martina Hermann is the Director of the Austrian Cultural Institut, Bern, Switzerland. She is the author of 'Fremd im eigenen Staat? Zur Perzeption der Kriegsflüchtlinge und -evakuierten im Barackenlager Gmund während des Ersten Weltkrieges', in Stefan Karner and Philipp Lesiak (eds), *Erster Weltkrieg: Globaler Konflikt – lokale Folgen* (Innsbruck: StudienVerlag, 2014).

Rebekah Klein-Pejšová is Associate Professor of History and Jewish Studies at Purdue University. She is the author of *Mapping Jewish Loyalties in Interwar Slovakia* (Bloomington: Indiana University Press, 2015). Her current research concerns postwar Jewish displacement, dispersion, and contact across the Iron Curtain.

Mariusz Korzeniowski is a professor of history attached to the Institute of History at the Maria Skłodowska-Curie University (UMCS) in Lublin. His latest monograph (co-authored with M. Mądzik, K. Latawiec, D. Tarasiuk) is *Polacy na wschodniej Ukrainie w latach 1832–1921* [Poles in Eastern Ukraine in the years 1832–1921] (Lublin: Wydawnictwo UMCS, 2012).

Ruth Leiserowitz is the Director of the German Historical Institute, Warsaw. Her many publications include *Sabbatleuchter und Kriegerverein: Juden in der ostpreussisch-litauischen Grenzregion 1812–1942* (Osnabrück: Fibre, 2010).

Marco Mondini is a researcher at the Italian–German Historical Institute in Trento and Adjunct Professor in Contemporary History at the University of Padua. His latest book is *La guerra italiana: Partire, raccontare, tornare 1914–1918* (Bologna: Società editrice il Mulino, 2014).

Oleksiy Nestulya is Rector of Poltava University of Economics and Trade. His many publications include *Ohorona pamjatok istoriji i kulturi v Ukraini (1917–1919 rr.): Zbirnik dokumentiv i materialiv* [The Defence of Historical and Cultural Memorials in Ukraine, 1917–1919] (Kyiv, 2008).

Klaus Richter is a lecturer in history at the University of Birmingham. His publications include *Antisemitismus in Litauen. Christen, Juden und*

Notes on contributors

die *'Emanzipation' der Bauern, 1889–1914* (Berlin: Metropol, 2013), and a chapter on population politics in Lithuania, 1916–23, in Tomas Balkelis and Violeta Davoliūtė (eds), *Population Displacement in Lithuania in the Twentieth Century: Experiences, Identities and Legacies* (Leiden: Brill, 2016).

Emilia Salvanou teaches European history at the Hellenic Open University. She has been a post-doctoral fellow at the University of Athens working on refugee memory during the interwar period and a research associate at the Act Aristeia studying the historiography of the First World War.

Danilo Šarenac is a research fellow at the Institute of Contemporary History, Belgrade. In 2014 he published the monograph, *Top, vojnik i sećanj: Srbija i Prvi svetski rat, 1914–2009* [Cannon, Soldier and Memory: Serbia and the First World War 1914–2009] (Beograd: Institut za savremenu istoriju, 2014). He has also co-edited with Vladimir Tomić a photo-monograph: *A City Surprised. Belgrade in the Great War 1914–1915* (Belgrade: Muzej grada Beograda, Institut za savremenu istoriju, 2015).

Uğur Ümit Üngör is Associate Professor at the Department of History at Utrecht University and Research Fellow at the Institute for War, Holocaust, and Genocide Studies in Amsterdam. In addition to *The Making of Modern Turkey: Nation and State in Eastern Anatolia, 1913–1950* (Oxford: Oxford University Press, 2011), he has recently published *Genocide: New Perspectives on its Causes, Courses and Consequences* (Amsterdam: Amsterdam University Press 2016).

Nikolai Vukov is Associate Professor at the Institute of Ethnology and Folklore Studies in Sofia and also teaches at the universities of Sofia and Plovdiv. Among his recent publications is 'Resettlement waves, historical memory and identity construction: the case of Thrace refugees to Bulgaria', in H. Vermeulen, et al. (eds), *Migration in the Southern Balkans: from Ottoman Territory to Globalized Nation States* (Amsterdam: Amsterdam University Press, 2014).

Liubov Zhvanko is Professor of History and Cultural Studies at the O.M. Beketov National University of Urban Economy, Kharkiv, Ukraine. Among her many publications is *Bizhentsi pershoi svitovoi viini: ukrains'kii vimir, 1914–1918 rr.* [Refugees of the First World War: the Ukrainian Reality, 1914–18] (Kharkiv: Apostrof, 2012).

Preface

The editors wish to thank the British Academy for generous funding that enabled most of the contributors to take part in workshops, first in Manchester and then in Poltava. Other support was forthcoming from the Jean Monnet Fund, University of Manchester, and from BASEES, the British Association for Slavonic and East European Studies. We are also grateful to staff at the University of Manchester and the Poltava University of Economics and Trade for providing the necessary facilities. We are indebted to Betty-Ann Bristow-Castle for her assistance in arranging the two workshops so efficiently.

We received helpful advice from anonymous reviewers at the start and end of the research process. We are also grateful for additional advice and support at various stages from Tomas Balkelis, John Horne, John-Paul Newman, Kaja Širok, Matthew Stibbe, Petra Svoljšak and Julie Thorpe. The two workshops were made more productive by the conscientious work of several interpreters, including Anna Biba.

The maps were drawn by Nick Scarle, Cartographic Unit, School of Environment, Education and Development, University of Manchester.

Finally we should like to thank Emma Brennan and the team at Manchester University Press for steering this volume through from its inception to completion.

Introduction

Peter Gatrell

The English writer and critic John Berger regarded the twentieth century as 'the century of departure, of migration, of exodus, of disappearance: the century of people helplessly seeing others, who were close to them, disappear over the horizon'.[1] Berger's characterisation of 'helplessness' invites us to consider not only how people were rendered liable to sudden and involuntary displacement, but also how those processes were represented at the time and subsequently. Global conflicts, revolutions and civil wars have played a major part in these processes of movement and loss, exposing combatants and non-combatants to personal risk. Civilians have frequently been the chief actors in the dramas of 'departure' and 'disappearance'. Massive displacement has not necessarily entailed movement across state borders, although it is only relatively recently that policy-makers have taken into account the large numbers of internally displaced persons in different parts of the world.[2] For their part, historians have been slow to address these questions.[3]

What, precisely, brought about the mass displacement of civilians in the twentieth century, and to what extent were they rendered 'helpless'? The answers to these questions requires us to consider specific episodes and contexts. Unquestionably, one of the most fundamental moments was the First World War.[4] Key sites of displacement extended from Belgium to Armenia, taking in France, Italy, Austria-Hungary, East Prussia, the Russian Empire, Bulgaria, Greece, Turkey and Serbia. The German army's occupation of Belgium, France, Poland and Lithuania prompted the mass flight of civilians, as did Russia's invasion of East Prussia in 1914. Jewish, Ruthenian and Polish civilians in the Habsburg Empire fled their homes or were deported by the military to distant locations. Following Italy's attack on Austria-Hungary in May 1915, the Habsburg authorities ordered around 100,000 Slovenian subjects of the empire to leave the battle zone on the frontier marked by the Isonzo/Soča River; a further deportation took place in May 1916. The Austrian and Bulgarian invasion of Serbia brought about a humanitarian catastrophe as civilians and the remnants of the Serbian army sought safety elsewhere (see Danilo Šarenac's chapter). The onslaught on Romania in 1916 led civilians to seek a place of relative safety in Moldova. Much of this history remains unknown or poorly understood. In the UK, for example, public knowledge of the war has tended to be informed by images of stalemate on the Western Front and the combination of terror and boredom that trench warfare induced.[5] In eastern Europe and the Balkans, by contrast, armies and civilians were regularly on the move, but the tribulations of refugees have barely registered in the literature.

The contributors to this book have adopted a flexible approach to the chronology of wartime displacement. Mass flight of civilian refugees did not begin in 1914 nor did it come to an end in 1918. In the Balkans in particular, the appearance of refugees needs to be set in a broad historical context. Nikolai Vukov emphasises that Bulgarians' experience of displacement stretched back to 1878.[6] Greece and Turkey too were already in the throes of a refugee crisis before the world war erupted: Uğur Ümit Üngör shows that Muslim refugees fled to the relative safety of Anatolia in order to escape violent persecution by Bulgarian and other forces during the Balkan Wars on 1912–13, and Emilia Salvanou unpicks the complex movements of population between Greece, Bulgaria and Turkey before 1914. Nor did the formal cessation of hostilities in 1918 bring about peace. The complex process of repatriation and resettlement affected soldiers and civilians alike and rarely took place in stable or peaceful circumstances.[7] The disintegration of the Russian Empire was followed by an extended civil war, which left few parts of Russia untouched, and which engulfed the population of the borderlands in the Baltic States, Poland, Ukraine, the Caucasus, Central Asia and the Far East. Short-lived regimes faced an almost impossible task to address the ongoing refugee crisis, which was exacerbated by political instability and uncertainty. The end of the Ottoman Empire and the creation of the Turkish Republic did not signal an end to demographic and social upheaval in the Balkans and in Anatolia.[8]

There were, as the American Red Cross official Homer Folks lamented in 1920, 'refugees all over Europe', adding that 'for five years it had seemed that almost everybody was either going somewhere else or expected to do so soon, and, meanwhile, was living in a makeshift fashion'.[9] Folks calculated that the war displaced nearly seven million refugees in western Europe, the Balkans, East Prussia and Armenia, but his estimate omitted the number of refugees in Austria-Hungary, Romania and the Russian Empire. A more accurate figure is likely to be closer to 14 or even 15 million.[10] The causes and consequences of the refugee crisis and its aftermath, and the attempts to understand its significance, constitute the subject of this book.

In the long twentieth century, it is clear that the omnipresent figure of the refugee not only testifies to multiple and extended conflicts but also directs attention to the emergence of an international refugee regime. Following the Second World War, the United Nations agreed upon a definition of refugees, to whom certain basic rights were accorded, above all the right not to be returned against their will to the country that had persecuted them and caused them to flee in the first place. At the same time, however, sovereign states retained the power to determine their eligibility and therefore to admit them.[11] This refugee regime did not emerge in an institutional vacuum: there were administrative and legal antecedents. During the 1920s the new League of Nations embarked on a programme to assist Russian, Armenian and Assyrian refugees who had, in the contemporary formulation, 'lost the protection' of the state when they fled from Soviet Russia and Turkey. Ukrainian diplomats in 1918 were already proposing an international forum to address the 'refugee problem' through organised repatriation (see the chapter by Liubov Zhvanko and Oleksiy Nestulya).[12] The political, social, cultural and economic implications of such efforts constitute an important element of each of the following chapters.

Berger's powerful metaphor of 'horizon' demands that we attend to other questions that are easily overlooked in discussions of violent conflict and international legal convention. What did refugees find over the horizon? Were their horizons restricted, or did new vistas open up, and of what kind? In what ways did they engage with governments as well as non-governmental organisations? What capacity did they have to express themselves, and what did they say? Historians frequently struggle to gain access to refugees' voices, particularly from the distant past. But there are surprises in store, as we shall see. Jewish refugees in the Habsburg Empire submitted petitions to officials; French refugees published their own newspapers, as did Muslim refugees from the Balkans who settled in Anatolia and the Armenian refugees who found sanctuary in Aleppo. This material yields insights into refugees' emotional responses to displacement.

Introduction

Although most informed observers anticipated a short war, the First World War lasted more than four years. European armies were expected to engage in military manoeuvres without substantial costs for civilians. This vision quickly evaporated. Civilians no less than military personnel experienced war as displacement, as they were caught up in the fighting across large swathes of territory on the European mainland, but also because the fraught conditions of prolonged war predisposed states to engage in the mass deportation of civilians who were believed to threaten freedom of military manoeuvre and to undermine the war effort more directly through espionage or other subversive activities. The Austro-Hungarian authorities targeted ethnic Ruthenian, Bosnian Serb, Slovenian and Italian-speaking minorities on the grounds of their imputed disloyalty. In 1914, as Ruth Leiserowitz shows, Russia's military commanders deported from occupied East Prussia many of the German population who had not already fled westward to the German interior. In the following year the Russian High Command launched an offensive on Jewish, Polish, Latvian and other subjects of the tsar, including German colonists who had been resident in the empire since the time of Catherine the Great.[13] Armenian men, women and children in the Ottoman Empire were deported and then murdered, punished for their purported sympathy for the enemy; survivors sought sanctuary on Russian soil.[14]

These practices opened up a whole series of troubling issues, including the interpretation that contemporaries placed on mass migration. Was the mass movement of refugees to be understood as civilians who simply tried to save their skins? If so, what did this imply for the physical and psychological well-being of refugees who appeared to have lost control over their lives? Might a more positive interpretation be placed on their actions, such as their wish to contribute to the war effort and avoid being made to work for the enemy? Had refugees, in fact, made the greatest sacrifice of all? If, on the other hand, displacement derived primarily from direct military intervention, what did this suggest about attempts to mobilise the 'nation', for example by targeting groups that were deemed not to belong? These are not prosaic questions. They had potentially profound consequences for the conduct of politics at the local, national and international level.

Closely linked to motives were issues of numbers, government policies and refugees' entitlement to assistance. These were fundamentally questions about politics. Who counted the number of displaced persons and how reliable were these calculations? This was a hotly contested topic with implications for central and local government budgets and responsibilities.¹⁵ Did the wartime refugee crisis open up new possibilities for critics of government competence, and if so how might such a critique be handled? How far should the central government accept responsibility for managing refugee relief, and what powers might be devolved on to voluntary agencies? To what extent might overseas communities become involved in assisting distant kin who suffered displacement and persecution? What scope did refugees themselves – particularly female refugees – have to manage their predicament, and what form did self-help measures take? Should displacement be understood as pure misery, or might it rather constitute a kind of opportunity, for example to mobilise the displaced in a new 'national cause'? Finally, what options became available as the war ended: how feasible was it to return and, if return was not an option, what other kind of provision existed for displaced persons in the aftermath of the war?[16]

The lexicon of displacement did not come ready made in 1914, but had to be assembled during the course of the war. This too was a political issue. Italian officials and public opinion deployed a variety of terms (*profughi*, *sfollati*, *rifugiati*), none of them politically neutral. Belgian and French propaganda portrayed refugees as victims of German barbarism, 'martyred' in the cause of 'civilisation', and these ideas informed the work of British relief committees acting on behalf of Belgians who reached the UK. French authorities distinguished between civilians who were displaced by the enemy invasion, those who had been evacuated from the front under official instruction, and foreign refugees. Habsburg officials initially drew a distinction between refugees (such as Jews who fled the Russian occupation of Galicia in 1914) and 'internees' (such as Ruthenians) who were believed to threaten the security of the state. But, as Martina Hermann indicates, this distinction evaporated quite quickly. Contemporary parlance in the Russian Empire distinguished 'forced migrants', who had been compelled to leave their homes by the actions of the Russian army, from refugees who were deemed to have fled 'spontaneously', responding to rumours of impending enemy attack. As in Austria-Hungary, these distinctions soon lost their meaning. Some displaced people were characterised as *skital'tsy* ('wandering folk'), a term in widespread popular usage before the war. Other distinctions also emerged. A well-informed observer attached to the Russian High Command argued that:

> those who 'ran' [*bezhali*] were the propertied classes, whereas the masses were chased away by force from their farms and hearths, deprived of

everything. Refugees managed to bring along their capital assets, enabling them to live a new life [whereas] the forcibly displaced (*vygontsy*) crawled along with half their family, having buried the others along the way; they are empty-handed, hungry and sick.[17]

In each country, refugees had to negotiate a legal-bureaucratic minefield as well as social uncertainty and cultural confusion, even in countries such as Turkey, which made formal provision for Muslim refugees from the Balkan Wars.

The scale and suddenness of population displacement, and the human anguish that it entailed, prompted the need to consider the assistance that might be offered to refugees who were caught up in the maelstrom. What form should this support take and how would it be resourced? There was no easy answer to these questions. The refugee studies literature pays considerable attention to the formation and operation of the modern 'refugee regime'. Elsewhere I have argued for a broad conceptualisation of the term.[18] What kind of regime operated during the First World War? In Russia in the first instance, the arrangements for assisting refugees were hastily devised: without any precedent to follow, improvisation necessarily characterised the initial phase of war. By the second year of war, however, more formal institutional provision began to be devised.[19] Generally speaking, arrangements elsewhere tended to be more ad hoc, with a combination of central and local government provision, along with non-governmental assistance and private charity, as emerges clearly in the case of refugees from East Prussia, where they themselves raised funds through mutual aid organisations. In Italy, the government only contemplated the formation of a central administration for refugee relief in late 1917, but voluntary bodies, including Catholic and socialist organisations, continued to do most of the hard practical work.[20] The same is true of the Habsburg Empire. Generally speaking, the main variable was not the political form of the state – authoritarian and democratic states all struggled to cope – but the scale of population displacement in relation to available resources. From this point of view, economically backward societies were particularly badly hit.

Whether we trace the contours of the wartime refugee in its early, improvised incarnation or its more systematic guise, we need to allow for the fact that power did not necessarily flow in one direction, from government officials at the centre or the locality down to refugee groups. Refugees developed strategies for articulating their own wishes and sense of purpose. Rebekah Klein-Pejšová describes how one determined Jewish skilled craftsman petitioned the authorities to allow him and his family to remain in Hungary rather than being transferred elsewhere, so that he might continue to work for the war effort.

Arrangements for transporting and resettling refugees did not conform to a common pattern. Although many were obliged to move in organised convoys, other refugees followed their own routes in seeking a place of safety. The connections and accumulated knowledge that resulted from the long history of migration of Jews between Galicia and Hungary before 1914 enabled some refugees to make their own arrangements, even if the journey itself was arduous in the extreme. In Russia, where it has been said that 'in two short years the movement of refugees and evacuees was as considerable as it had been during the migration to Siberia' in the quarter century before the war, officials struggled to organise the movement of refugees. This was partly because of shortages of rolling stock, the claims of the army on the rail transport system, and government efforts to evacuate industrial assets from the threatened western borderlands of the Russian Empire, and partly because provincial governors and municipal authorities were keen to offload refugees on to other jurisdictions at the earliest opportunity. Contemporary depictions of overcrowded railway stations where refugees were frequently a visible presence, as well as stories of crime, damage to property, and infectious disease gave hard-pressed officials the ammunition they needed to claim that they could not cope.[21] The same happened in Romania and in Hungary, where refugees were hurriedly moved on lest they spread disease to soldiers stationed nearby. By October 1914 the authorities in Berlin had already closed the city to new arrivals from East Prussia.

Incarceration was the exception rather than the norm. To be sure, camps were used to hold civilians who were thought to constitute a political threat, as in the Habsburg Empire where deportees from the Italian borderlands and from Galicia were transported to the interior to be kept under close surveillance in camps at Bruck an der Leithe, Wagna, Steinklamm, Mittendorf and Gmünd.[22] Polish and other refugees spent several weeks in Russian-administered camps in Kobrin and other villages in the tsar's western borderlands.[23] Belgian refugees were sometimes despatched to designated camps in Holland and forced to live in squalid conditions in camps at Gouda, Nunspeet and elsewhere (see the chapter by Michaël Amara).[24] Armenian refugees were resettled by the Egyptian Red Cross from the Ottoman province of Alexandretta to a refugee camp in Port Said, where their movement was closely controlled.[25] Around 100,000 Belgian and other refugees moved in and out of a large refugee camp organised by the Metropolitan Asylum Board in Earl's Court, London.[26] Impoverished Jewish, Ukrainian and Polish refugees who fled from Russian-occupied Galicia found it difficult to reach Austria but, as Klein-Pejšová and Hermann point out, those with means (*bemittelt*) were able to move more freely.

Relatively impoverished states, such as Russia and Turkey, already overwhelmed by the scale of the refugee crisis, shifted much of the responsibility for maintaining refugees on to public organisations and private charitable bodies, leaving the central government to concentrate on funding the direct war effort (see the chapters by Zhvanko and Nestulia, Belova, and Üngör). Italy did the same. Local villagers bore the burden of hosting refugees, as happened in Italy and with 'self-settled' refugees in Austrian-occupied Albania. This is a crucial dimension of the war: the growth of local and non-governmental organisations, largely at the behest of central governments that were overwhelmed by the crisis.

In the Habsburg Empire refugees were expected to 'put something back' by working for the war economy as well as supporting themselves, whether in camps or in urban centres. Jewish refugees from Galicia, exposed to hostility as they arrived in Hungary, reminded people that their sons were loyally serving in the Habsburg army. Polish refugees in Russia made the same point. Alex Dowdall explains how the French state acknowledged the sacrifice incurred by refugees, by offering them the same level of financial compensation as the families of soldiers. Italian refugees deployed a similar rhetoric.[27] The emphasis on refugees' 'contribution' took other forms as well. Julie Thorpe has shown how, a year into the war, Austrian officials devised an exhibition of refugee art in which pride of place was given to handmade dolls in national costume and to model farmhouses, the purpose being to highlight this 'transaction between refugees and the state' and to advertise refugees' hard work.[28] The tsarist authorities planned something along the same lines, although the February Revolution intervened before the exhibition was ready to open, and nothing came of it.[29]

The chapters in this book provide plenty of evidence of a dynamic cultural life among communities of refugees and its broader political and social import. Michaël Amara indicates that Belgian refugees formed choirs, theatre groups and sports clubs, not merely to pass the time but to sustain a sense of connection to their homeland. This is an important finding, because it suggests that refugees proved to be more than mere vectors of government propaganda about enemy brutality. Elsewhere, refugees found themselves living cheek-by-jowl with ethnic communities of long standing, and this posed questions about their sense of national identity. In his chapter, Mariusz Korzeniowski points out that refugees encountered Polish colonies in Moscow, Petrograd and parts of Siberia, where the descendants of Polish rebels were living half a century after the great revolt of 1863. Klaus Richter shows that the Lithuanian patriotic intelligentsia bemoaned the fact that established groups of exiles had become 'living corpses of the nation' who needed to rediscover their national pride. The political purpose behind these initiatives is not hard to detect. As Amara puts it, 'anxious to prevent the refugee population from permanently settling in their host countries, the Belgian authorities in exile attached great importance to promoting a strong sense of national identity among the refugees'. Education, too, reminded parents of their obligation to ensure that children should not 'assimilate' into the host communities, but rather think of themselves as sustaining a strong affiliation with Belgium, something that has been advocated in many other contexts over the course of the twentieth century.[30]

Issues around identity also emerge in France, Italy and Austria-Hungary. Dowdall offers a subtle account of the ways in which refugees' associations in unoccupied France preserved a strong sense of the *petite patrie*. Something of the same occurred in Italy where elite refugees spoke of the 'little homeland' (*patria*) they had left behind in Friule and Veneto, as Marco Mondini and Francesco Frizzera point out.[31] In Austria-Hungary, impoverished refugees were directed to camps according to their nationality. But this was only one aspect of Habsburg practice. Julie Thorpe has suggested that 'traditions, languages and artefacts were transported to the empire's hinterland via the refugees and packaged for "national" consumption in the empire's capital'; in a striking phrase, she refers to them as 'ambassadors'. Displacement allowed the emperor's subjects to know each other and enabled refugees to become more familiar with imperial space. Martina Hermann adds that the authorities in camp Gmünd invested in German-language provision for that purpose. Yet the project to promote a kind of imperial solidarity around the figure of the bereft and miserable refugee (a project in which Austrian journalists were enlisted during a series of staged visits to the refugee camps) did not always yield the anticipated results: Austrian citizens were quick to vent their dislike of 'dirty' and 'uncultivated' Jewish, Ukrainian and Polish newcomers. In seeking to reaffirm imperial solidarities, the Habsburg state 'nationalised those encounters at the same time'.[32] These expressions of 'national' identity did not dissolve other kinds of identity nor did they necessarily testify to a unity of purpose. In Budapest, for example, the

Jewish elite looked with some distaste upon co-religionists who arrived from the shtetls of Galicia. In the Baltic provinces, too, refugee relief committees were divided between conservative and clerical elites, on the one hand, and more progressive voices on the other that sought to engage with plebeian refugees. Class clearly mattered.[33]

What impact did the presence of large numbers of refugees have on local life in the towns and villages in which they settled? Contemporary officials feared that the encounter between refugees and non-refugees had the potential to generate antagonism, and indeed there are signs of this in Austria-Hungary. How might relations between refugees and non-refugees be managed in order to maintain a degree of stability as well as wartime morale, given that (as happened in Kaluga, according to Irina Belova) the presence of refugees might encourage defeatist talk? What would happen when refugees entered 'foreign' space whose residents spoke a different language or professed a different faith? How might the crisis be managed in such a way as to alleviate local disquiet and preserve social order in the localities that refugees reached? Would refugees be a drain on local resources, contributing to a sense that the burdens of war reached into the far corners of society? Would they be at the mercy of local predators who sought to turn a quick profit who might hope to exploit refugees for sex work? These questions resonate for the modern reader, but they were already being asked by contemporaries for whom refugees during the First World War constituted a new and unexpected 'problem'.

It would be simplistic to assume that reserves of sympathy at the outset were eventually exhausted, as if there were a well of charity that emptied over time. There is plenty of evidence of impatience and intolerance at the first sight of refugees but they were also an object of curiosity and fascination, as well as a source of information. They brought news from the front line. The presence of Belgian and French refugees on French soil constituted at least indirect evidence of German 'barbarism'. Nor did antagonism necessarily increase over time. In practice, dire predictions of social unrest failed to materialise. In provincial Russia, for example, local residents expressed sympathy for the 'victims of war' and urged officials not to add to the stress of refugees who 'had already endured a great deal'. Partly, this response reflected the fact that refugees – whether Belgians in the UK or Lithuanians, Poles and others in Russia – contributed to the local economy, either as agricultural labourers or in factories. Partly, too, it reflected the strenuous efforts by refugees to manage their own affairs without calling extensively upon external support. Furthermore, the presence of refugees and their interaction with non-refugees could yield more positive results, for example introducing new ways of working to economic backwaters. Refugees might be thought of as *Kulturträger* rather than as a burden or as the object of local greed.[34] Ruth Leiserowitz indicates that refugees from towns in East Prussia were twinned with towns in the German interior that were remote from the front line, in a policy clearly designed to elicit both sympathy and a sense of imperial solidarity.

We should be careful not to paint too rosy a picture of the relations between refugees and locals. For instance, refugees in Kaluga told of inflated rents. Attitudes appear to have hardened as civilian suffering became widespread. In France, for example, after the first rush to assist Belgian refugees, 'every family confronted loss and encountered grief [and] refugees found themselves accused of excessive comfort, idleness and grim opportunism'.[35] As already implied, relations between Jewish refugees and locals were particularly acrimonious, reaching a nadir in Hungary where Jews who fled Galicia were portrayed as shirkers and profiteers. Muslim refugees from the Balkans who moved to Anatolia faced a difficult time at the hands of some local officials and tradesmen. Everywhere, female refugees in particular ran the risk of being exploited and abused, whether at the point of departure or arrival.

Cultural representation expressed the new social and political landscape. The Slovenian artist Fran Tratnik (1881–1957) sketched dramatic and heart-rending scenes of refugees fleeing from the Isonzo/Soča Valley.[36] Newspapers in most belligerent countries favoured the evocation of women and children suffering in order to elicit donations for refugee relief. More broadly, the category of the refugee became part of the common currency of public opinion during the First World War. Russian observers acknowledged that 'the word "refugees" signifies a numerous body of people, of any age, sex and social status', and by 1915 the multiple mainsprings of displacement had been wrapped up in a single word, 'refugeedom' (*bezhenstvo*).[37] To be labelled as a refugee had demeaning consequences, stripping away attributes of social distinction to leave oneself exposed to a sense of pure deprivation. A Belgian refugee spoke from the heart when he summed up his feelings: 'One was always a refugee – that's the name one was given, a sort of nickname (*sobriquet*). One was left with nothing, ruined, and that's how people carried on talking about "the refugee". We weren't real people any more'.[38] It is difficult to overstate the importance of this kind of amalgamation and occlusion of difference, whether structured around class, gender or ethnicity.

Introduction

Yet, if prevailing images tended to homogenise the refugee, creating a single category of difference, nationality offered a means of drawing distinctions between refugees. Refugeedom contributed to the intensification of a sense of national identity, not because one ethnic group had been singled out – after all, displacement affected more than one nationality – but because it created the prospect that the 'nation' might be permanently displaced, uprooted and scattered. In the Russian Empire, newly minted national organisations claimed the refugee for themselves. Refugees had been forced to abandon their homeland, but this did not deprive their lives of purpose. They had a responsibility to the nation, which in turn would not shirk its responsibilities to the refugee. Refugees belonged somewhere after all.[39] A similar process occurred in other theatres of war. Tormented yet valiant Belgian refugees came to stand for the country as a whole and could trade on their valorisation. Refugees from East Prussia embodied the sacrifice of German people as a whole (see the chapter by Leiserowitz). Italian subjects of the Habsburg Empire, deported and placed in internment camps, became a ready-made audience for patriotic Italians attempting to disseminate nationalist propaganda, as Mondini and Frizzera suggest in their chapter. They usefully deploy the concept of an 'Italian linguistic space' in lieu of misleading territorial divisions to characterise common experiences of displacement and incarceration. Serbian refugees, as Danilo Šarenac points out, symbolised the travails of an entire people waiting for their country's deliverance from enemy occupation. These tropes also helped activate diaspora organisations, notably in North America where Polish-American relief committees and the American Joint Distribution Committee collected money and helped raise the international profile of Polish and Jewish refugees respectively.[40]

This is not to say that new states necessarily showed much appreciation of this fact when the war came to an end. Refugees were frequently hidden from the officially sanctioned narratives. Post-war governments drew a veil over the circumstances of mass displacement, particularly if they portrayed the state in an unfavourable light. Mussolini had no interest in talking about the mass exodus of Italians following the debacle at Caporetto in 1917, preferring instead to associate his regime with the glories of ancient Rome (although in private, families certainly did talk about their wartime experiences). In Russia the Bolsheviks derived their legitimacy from the Russian Revolution and relegated refugees to the political margins. Successor states such as Poland, Latvia and Lithuania devoted little attention to the history of refugees during the war, being more preoccupied with the immediate legacy of 'wars after the war' and with forging the new state than with encouraging commemoration of the refugee crisis in the First World War; indeed, it appears that only to the extent that the relief effort helped the careers of certain politicians did the history of wartime displacement get much of a mention. Though the experience of refugees might be slotted into a narrative of national salvation and deliverance, political leaders trod quite carefully lest they simultaneously draw attention to the wartime chaos and encourage refugees to claim compensation. Public opinion in Belgium and France had little to say about refugees, although popular memories of the crisis in 1914 were revived during the crisis of 1940 which afflicted the same regions and indeed often affected the same people, and the same is true of Germans who hastily fled East Prussia in 1944.[41] The new Turkish Republic sought a rapprochement with Greece, partly to make a common cause against Bolshevism. On the other hand, in Hungary, Armenia and Serbia mass displacement – and in Armenia's case, deliberate mass murder – contributed to the cultivation of new states and the diaspora of memories of national calamity. (Things were more complicated in respect of Hungarian Jewish refugees, however.) A Serbian teacher who taught refugee children in France during the war in France asked his pupils to write an assignment entitled: 'My departure from the fatherland and arrival in France'. He published the results in 1923, in a book entitled *The Hopes of the Serbian Golgotha*. It comes as no surprise that it was re-issued in Serbia eight decades later or to learn that other stories of suffering were revived in Belgrade in the late 1980s and 1990s, helping to legitimise nationalist claims as communist rule in Yugoslavia collapsed.[42] Here the refugee crisis during the First World War touched a political nerve long after the events had faded from direct memory. But this was the exception rather than the rule.

Repatriation rightly occupies an important place in the refugee studies literature.[43] It might be considered a purely technical or administrative matter, but an exclusive focus on logistical and related issues – important though these are – misses out many dimensions of refugees' experience. Repatriation raises questions around 'home' and 'homecoming', including relations with those who originally stayed put. The First World War and its aftermath demonstrated the difficulties around repatriation.

Certainly, displacement and repatriation might be construed in quite positive terms. In Vienna, for example, Habsburg officials hoped that by encouraging cultural activity and discouraging idleness among refugees, they would prepare the ground for their eventual repatriation. As the organisers of the 1915 exhibition put it, 'the noble cultural mission' would be complete by the return of refugees to their homes 'with broadened horizons and education, and an increased capacity to work'.[44] More prosaically, repatriation implied a wish to alleviate the heavy burden on host communities. Efforts to return Galician Jewish refugees to their original homes continued until 1918, although these efforts did not always succeed (see the chapter by Klein-Pejšová).

After the First World War these issues were further complicated not only by the reconfiguration of territory and the creation of new states but additionally by the raising of the political stakes as a consequence of the Bolshevik Revolution. In Russia, the new regime hoped to conscript able-bodied refugees into the Red Army, but many of them opted instead to make their way home by whatever means they could, until the civil war, the Allied intervention and war with Poland made this virtually impossible. Officials on all sides deplored such 'spontaneous' behaviour.[45] In the newly independent Baltic states, as Richter points out, political leaders discriminated against ethnic minorities in the pursuit of a strong and homogeneous national identity. This had implications not only for Latvians, Lithuanians and Poles, but also for Jews, Germans and Russians.

Returning to one's original place of residence and securing one's former property was made even more difficult by the devastation wrought by the war: homes had been destroyed, and farmland required months of backbreaking labour to bring under cultivation. In the dramatic words of Homer Folks, 'hordes of famished refugees [were] returning to the bare ruins of non-existent villages'.[46] Hitherto thriving industrial centres had been laid waste. Plans for economic reconstruction were hastily devised and implemented, and programmes to accommodate displaced people were incorporated in ideas about modernity. One such indication was the creation in early 1918 of a refugee colony for 2,000 Italian refugees outside Pisa, partly as a means to garner additional publicity for the American Red Cross. The refugee 'colony' was designed to be a showcase of a 'modern American city', with the emphasis on light and air to promote hygiene. A replica of the Piazza San Marco in Venice would add to the general sense of 'happiness and safety' provided by gardens, a community kitchen, a church and so on. The Armistice in November 1918 put paid to the programme, because the refugees returned to their homes. Nevertheless, it testified to ambitious plans for economic development against the backdrop of mass population displacement.[47] The situation in the Near East was even more complicated. Tens of thousands of Armenian and Assyrian refugees gathered in camps in Mesopotamia, until they could be 'repatriated' to the new socialist republic of Armenia in the early 1920s, where the government welcomed the efforts of the new League of Nations to invest in irrigation and other projects.[48]

Questions arose about the entitlement of refugees and returnees to be treated as citizens by the new state. In Germany, thousands of ethnic Germans took advantage of organised 'repatriation' to leave Russia or the lost lands of West Prussia and Posen for good. The *Berliner Volkszeitung* told its readers that 'we must not forget those who have been torn from their homes and livelihoods by fanatical Poles; they have neither committed a crime nor bear any other responsibility for their fate, but have rather been persecuted only because they are German'. These questions were linked to their ideological beliefs, which were tested by border guards and other figures of authority. German border authorities were expected 'to carefully sift through and observe all those who seek to enter Germany'. The German Red Cross operated temporary quarantine camps in order to forestall a public health crisis, and also filtered out those who were ethnically Polish and who (if they were adult males) were sent to concentration camps.[49]

The camp at Obeliai on the new Soviet-Lithuanian frontier was another notorious example of a concerted attempt to assess the 'character' of the returning refugee population. Jews were particularly exposed: many of those who fled violent onslaughts in Ukraine in 1918 were met with a hostile reception when they showed up at the frontier with Poland or Romania.[50] The cultural and political uncertainties around repatriation emerged in the observation of a Lithuanian journalist in 1922:

> Among the refugees conversation is conducted in all languages, or to be more precise, in a mixture of all languages … Having lived for so long in foreign lands, our countrymen intermarried with the Ukrainians; the majority are bringing their wives from Ukraine to Lithuania … [and they] don't understand a word of Lithuanian. An entire Lithuanian family speaks to itself in Russian.[51]

We should therefore look beyond the immediate circumstances of war and consider the 'violent peacetime' that ensued. Again the scale of displacement is striking, especially in the conflict zones of eastern Europe and the Caucasus. The end of the First World War did not deliver peace to war-weary populations. The dissolution of long-established imperial polities created fresh instability as a result of political and ideological conflicts, economic uncertainty and inter-ethnic confrontations in the successor states of central and eastern Europe. Korzeniowski emphasises the degree of upheaval in the Polish-Ukrainian borderlands. In the Baltic lands, as Richter makes clear, there was no return to the status quo ante, given the extent of political and social upheaval and the rearrangement of territorial borders. In the Balkans, European diplomats sought to bring an end to a decade of conflict between Greece and Turkey by engineering an organised transfer of population. In both countries, as Üngör and Salvanou explain in their chapters, the process itself was extremely complicated and the results on the ground proved to be profoundly unsettling.[52] After 1918, refugees from Bulgaria's 'lost' western borderlands pressed for their 'recovery' (see the chapter by Vukov). Hungarian refugees, too, were active in irredentist politics.[53]

Other states, notably France, Belgium and Italy, survived more or less intact and provided a greater degree of security to their citizens. Serbia formed part of an entirely new polity, the Kingdom of the Serbs and Slovenes. Germany and Hungary, as defeated states, were left to address an enormous humanitarian crisis when refugees crossed into their territory to seek what shelter they could. Many Hungarians lived for months or even years as 'railway dwellers' (*vagonlakók*) in carriages in the sidings of train stations, where emergency aid from Herbert Hoover's American Relief Administration helped to prevent mass starvation.[54] In Weimar Germany, hundreds of thousands of mostly impoverished anti-Bolshevik Russian émigrés and Jewish refugees escaping pogroms sought and received – grudgingly, in the case of the *Ostjuden* – sanctuary from the violent civil war.[55] Their numbers were swollen by the exodus of Armenian and Assyrian refugees. As indicated above, governments practised discriminatory policies towards those who did not belong to the titular majority, as for example with Jews and other non-Germans in post-war Austria, Poland and other successor states, whose leaders regularly described them as unwelcome 'invaders'.[56]

Did the First World War establish any kind of precedent or pattern? The speed and size of displacement encouraged an emergency response that eventually gave way to more formal institutional provision. It would be simplistic to suppose that there was a straightforward trajectory that led from improvisation to the systematic relief and 'rehabilitation' of refugees. Rather, the evidence suggests that each successive displacement was construed as a fresh 'refugee crisis' that gave rise to improvised action. The growth of bureaucratic administration during the war did not lessen but rather enhanced the importance of efforts by private or semi-official organisations to address the consequences of population displacement, in ways that became familiar in other times and in other places.[57] Likewise, the First World War provided new opportunities for training professional experts who were employed by governments and by voluntary agencies. Austrian doctors and epidemiologists regarded the refugee camp as a site of experimentation as well as a facility for treating the sick. These features, too, became part and parcel of the twentieth-century refugee regime.[58]

Non-governmental organisations, including faith-based groups such as the Quakers, who had devoted themselves to the relief of civilians in earlier conflicts, and women from various backgrounds who voluntarily performed dangerous work on behalf of the Scottish Women's Hospitals operated across the continent, along with well-resourced newcomers, such as Near East Relief and the American Red Cross. Their efforts did not come to an end in 1918.[59] Although relief efforts had an emergency character, they mattered in ways that were not always evident at the time. Some individuals drew upon their experience of wartime displacement to commit themselves to the relief of refugees elsewhere and on other occasions. Aid workers described their wartime activity in terms of 'romance' and 'adventure', in sharp contrast to their perception of refugees as inert and traumatised figures lacking in self-control.[60] The final word should belong to a Russian woman by the name of Vystavkina who wrote in 1915 in terms that speak powerfully and directly to a modern audience as it confronts another 'refugee crisis':

> Not so long ago, these people lived a full and independent working life. They had the right to be just like us, that is, indolent, rude and ungrateful. Now they have lost this prerogative; their poverty and helplessness oblige them to be meek and grateful, to smile at people they don't like, to answer each and every question without the right to ask questions of their own, to submit to the authority of people they don't respect and have no wish to know, to accept disadvantageous terms from those who wish to take advantage of their poverty and misfortunes.[61]

Her empathetic response goes some way towards mitigating the troubling manifestations of war and displacement that figure prominently in the contributions that follow.

Notes

1 Quoted in Geoff Dyer, *The Missing of the Somme* (Harmondsworth: Penguin, 1995), p. 128.
2 Roger Zetter, 'Unlocking the protracted displacement of refugees and internally displaced persons: an overview', *Refugee Survey Quarterly*, 30, no. 4 (2011), 1–13.

Introduction

3 Michael Marrus, *The Unwanted: European Refugees in the Twentieth Century* (New York: Oxford University Press, 1985; new edn, 2002); Tony Kushner and Katharine Knox, *Refugees in an Age of Genocide: Global, National and Local Perspectives During the Twentieth Century* (London: Frank Cass, 1999). Still valuable for the later period is the work of Joseph Schechtman, *The Refugee in the World: Displacement and Integration* (New York: Barnes, 1963). The global perspective emerges in Aristide Zolberg, Astri Suhrke and Sergio Aguayo, *Escape from Violence: Conflict and the Refugee Crisis in the Developing World* (Oxford: Oxford University Press, 1989), and Peter Gatrell, *The Making of the Modern Refugee* (Oxford: Oxford University Press, 2013).

4 Although there is no book devoted exclusively to the refugee crisis during the First World War, works with relevant contributions include Bruna Bianchi (ed.), *La violenza contro la popolazione civile nella Grande Guerra: deportati, profughi, internati* (Milan: Edizioni Unicopli, 2006) and Matthew Stibbe (ed.), *Captivity, Forced Labour and Forced Migration in Europe During the First World War* (London: Routledge, 2009). See also Marlou Schrover, 'Migration and mobility', in *1914–1918 online: International Encyclopedia of the First World War*, Freie Universität Berlin, 2014-10-08. DOI: http://dx.doi.org/10.15463/ie1418.10332.

5 See the report prepared on behalf of the British Council for the centenary of the outbreak of the war, *Remember the World as Well as the War* (London: British Council, 2014).

6 Theodora Dragostinova, *Between Two Motherlands: Nationality and Emigration Among the Greeks of Bulgaria, 1900–1949* (Ithaca: Cornell University Press, 2011).

7 Beryl Nicholson, 'Accommodating the internally displaced in south-central Albania in 1918', *New Issues in Refugee Research*, no. 267 (Geneva: UNHCR, 2013), draws upon a census carried out by the Austrian occupation regime in 1918 to trace the impact of population displacement as far back as 1912 as a result of Greek attacks on southern Albanian territory, the effects of which were compounded by Austro-Hungarian occupation in 1916.

8 Peter Gatrell, 'War after the war: conflicts 1919–23', in John Horne (ed.), *Blackwell Companion to the First World War* (London: Pearson, 2008), pp. 558–75; Willard Sunderland, *The Baron's Cloak: a History of the Russian Empire in War and Revolution* (Ithaca: Cornell University Press, 2014); Robert Gerwarth and Erez Manela (eds), *Empires at War, 1912–1923* (Oxford: Oxford University Press, 2014).

9 Homer Folks, *The Human Costs of the War* (New York: Harper, 1920), p. 250. Homer Folks (1867–1963) was a social worker and public health expert who headed the ARC's Department of Civil Affairs in France from July 1917.

10 Other work in progress on the wartime refugee crisis includes studies of Belarusian refugees (by Lizaveta Kasmach), Romanian refugees in Moldova (by Adrian Vițalaru), and Slovenian refugees (by Petra Svoljsak). Vițalaru

(personal communication) calculates that between 800,000 and one million Romanians were displaced as a result of the war.
11 There is an extensive literature on this topic, including Sylvia Benhabib, 'Critique of humanitarian reason', text of a lecture delivered in Cologne, 19 May 2014, available at www.eurozine.com/articles/2014-07-18-benhabib-en.html [accessed 2 August 2016].
12 On the post-1918 refugee regime, see Claudena M. Skran, *Refugees in Inter-War Europe: the Emergence of a Regime* (Oxford: Clarendon Press, 1995). A compelling introduction to the situation in the post-Ottoman Middle East is Dawn Chatty, *Displacement and Dispossession in the Modern Middle East* (Cambridge: Cambridge University Press, 2010). See also Najwa Al-Qattan, '*Safarbarlik*: Ottoman Syria and the Great War', in Thomas Philipp and Christoph Schumann (eds), *From the Syrian Land to the States of Syria and Lebanon* (Würzburg: Ergon Verlag, 2004), pp. 166–73, for a discussion of the Turkish word that denoted both 'mobilisation' and mobility ('to go away and never come back'), but which, she says, became 'a catchword for all the calamities and suffering experienced by civilians' in war-ravaged Syria.
13 Peter Gatrell, *A Whole Empire Walking: Refugees in Russia During World War I* (Bloomington: Indiana University Press, 1999), pp. 22–6.
14 New research on Armenian refugees in Russia is currently being undertaken by Asya Darbinyan, PhD candidate, Clark University, USA. In its session on 3 October 1915, the Special Council for Refugees spoke of 'foreign nationals' to whom Russia had a 'moral obligation'. Rossiiskii gosudarstvennyi istoricheskii arkhiv (RGIA), fond 1322, opis' 1, delo 1, ll. 25–7ob.
15 Not only in relation to the First World War: see Andrew Shacknove, 'Who is a refugee?' *Ethics*, 95, no. 2 (1985), 274–84; Roger Zetter, 'More labels, fewer refugees: remaking the refugee label in an era of globalisation', *Journal of Refugee Studies*, 20, no. 2 (2007), 172–92.
16 Hannes Leidinger and Verena Moritz, 'Flüchtlingslager in Osteuropa im Ersten Weltkrieg: Erschliessung, Positionierung und Skizzierung einer halb erkundeten Themenlandschaft', in Christoph Jahr and Jens Thiel (eds), *Lager vor Auschwitz: Gewalt und Integration im 20. Jahrhundert* (Berlin: Metropol Verlag, 2013), pp. 177–96.
17 M. Kh. Lemke, *250 dnei v tsarskoi stavke* (Petrograd: Gosudarstvennoe izdatel'stvo, 1920), p. 265.
18 Gatrell, *Making of the Modern Refugee*. For a survey of the state of the field, see Elena Fiddian-Qasmiyeh, et al. (eds), *The Oxford Handbook of Refugee and Forced Migration Studies* (Oxford: Oxford University Press, 2014).
19 In addition to reference in the chapter by Irina Belova, see Gatrell, *A Whole Empire Walking*, pp. 49–72; Anastasia Tumanova, 'The public and the organization of aid to refugees during World War I: institutional and legal aspects', *Russian Studies in History*, 51, no. 3 (2012), 81–107; Olga Pichon-Bobrinskoy, 'Action publique, action humanitaire pendant le premier conflit mondial:

les zemstvos et les municipalités', *Cahiers du monde russe*, 46, no. 4 (2005), 699–718.
20 Matteo Ermacora, 'Assistance and surveillance: war refugees in Italy, 1914–1918', *Contemporary European History*, 16, no. 4 (2007), 445–60.
21 Gatrell, *A Whole Empire Walking*, pp. 18–19, 52–3; Violetta Thurstan, *The People Who Run: Being the Tragedy of the Refugees in Russia* (New York: G.P. Putnam's Sons, 1916); Eugene Kulischer, *Europe on the Move: War and Population Changes 1917–1947* (New York: Columbia University Press, 1948), p. 32.
22 Paolo Malni, *Fuggiaschi: il campo profughi di Wagna 1915–1918* (San Canzian d'Isonzo: Consorzio Culturale del Monfalconese, 1998). For an excellent overview, see Pieter M. Judson, *The Habsburg Empire: A New History* (Cambridge, MA: Harvard University Press, 2016), pp. 408–13. The French authorities meted out the same treatment to 'Austro-Germans' and 'Alsaciens-Lorrains'. See Jean-Claude Farcy, *Les Camps de concentration français de la première guerre mondiale, 1914–1920* (Paris: Anthropos, 1995).
23 E.A. Nikol'skii, 'Bezhentsy v velikuiu voiny 1914–1918gg.' (unpublished manuscript, Hoover Institution, 1934), pp. 242–6.
24 Francesca M. Wilson, *In the Margins of Chaos: Recollections of Relief Work in and Between Three Wars* (London: John Murray, 1944), p. 6.
25 Keith David Watenpaugh, *Bread from Stones: The Middle East and the Making of Modern Humanitarianism* (Berkeley, CA: University of California Press, 2015), p. 15, citing work by Dr. M. Salbi, first published in 1919. Elsewhere, contemporary photographs of the Armenian refugee camp in Port Fouad, opposite Port Said, next to the Shell Oil Company's headquarters on the Suez Canal, reveal a gridded pattern of uniform refugee tents of a kind that became ubiquitous in subsequent years. See Valeska Huber, *Channelling Mobilities: Migration and Globalisation in the Suez Canal Region and Beyond, 1869–1914* (Cambridge: Cambridge University Press, 2013).
26 G.A. Powell (comp.), *Four Years in a Refugee Camp: Being an Account of the British Government War Refugees Camp, Earl's Court, London, 1914–1919* (London: Baynard Press, 1920). Powell reports on the creation of a 'resident population', mostly working class, in addition to the 'birds of passage' who moved quickly on to more comfortable accommodation. In Earl's Court he observed 'a government of benevolent firmness' in this 'township', adding that the camp bore little resemblance to the camps he visited in Holland (pp. 30, 52). By 1917 it had become a temporary home to a multinational population including Russians, Armenians and 'swarthy gypsies of the genuine nomadic type' who moved from Romania to Russia and thence to the UK (p. 56).
27 Ermacora, 'Assistance and surveillance', 457.
28 Julie Thorpe, 'Displacing empire: refugee welfare, national activism and state legitimacy in Austria-Hungary in the First World War', in Panikos Panayi

and Pippa Virdee (eds), *Refugees and the End of Empire: Imperial Collapse and Forced Migration in the Twentieth Century* (Basingstoke: Palgrave, 2011), pp. 102–26 (here pp. 112–13).
29 Gatrell, *A Whole Empire Walking*, p. 94. The Latvian refugee committee in Moscow organised its own art exhibition to raise money and to draw attention to Latvian settlements throughout the empire. See *Beglu kalendars 1917 gadam* (Peterpils, 1916), pp. 85–8.
30 Julie Peteet, *Landscape of Hope and Despair: Palestinian Refugee Camps* (Philadelphia: University of Pennsylvania Press, 2005).
31 See also Ermacora, 'Assistance and surveillance', 453.
32 Thorpe, 'Displacing empire'.
33 Andrea Griffante, 'Making the nation: refugees, indigent people, and Lithuanian relief, 1914–1920', in Tomas Balkelis and Violeta Davoliūtė (eds), *Population Displacement in Lithuania in the Twentieth Century: Experiences, Identities and Legacies* (Leiden: Brill-Rodopi, 2016), pp. 21–41.
34 Gatrell, *A Whole Empire Walking*.
35 Pierre Purseigle, '"A wave on to our shores': the exile and resettlement of refugees from the Western Front, 1914–18', *Contemporary European History*, 16, no. 4 (2007), 427–44 (here p. 442).
36 Alojzij Res, *Ob šoči: vtisi in občutja iz mojega dnevnika* (Trst: Štoka, 1916). I owe this reference to Kaja Širok.
37 Gatrell, *A Whole Empire Walking*, pp. 96–7.
38 Sophie de Schaepdrijver, *La Belgique et la Première Guerre Mondiale* (Frankfurt: Peter Lang, 2004), pp. 104–5.
39 Gatrell, *A Whole Empire Walking*, chapter 8.
40 A committee in Argentina also collected funds on behalf of Belgian and French refugees (María Inés Tato, personal communication).
41 Hanna Diamond, *Fleeing Hitler: France 1940* (Oxford: Oxford University Press, 2007).
42 John Paul Newman, personal communication.
43 Richard Black and Khalid Koser (eds), *The End of the Refugee Cycle? Refugee Repatriation and Reconstruction* (Oxford: Berghahn Books, 1999).
44 *Neue Freie Presse*, 15 December 1915, quoted in Thorpe, 'Displacing empire', p. 112.
45 See the contributions in Nick P. Baron and Peter Gatrell (eds), *Homelands: War, Population and Statehood in the Former Russian Empire, 1918–1924* (London: Anthem Press, 2004).
46 Folks, *The Human Costs of War*, p. 2.
47 Julia Irwin, *Making the World Safe: the American Red Cross and a Nation's Humanitarian Awakening* (New York: Oxford University Press, 2013), p. 134.
48 Jo Laycock and Peter Gatrell, 'Armenia: the "nationalization", internationalization and representation of the refugee crisis', in Baron and Gatrell (eds), *Homelands*, pp. 179–200.

Introduction

49 Annemarie Sammartino, *The Impossible Border: Germany and the East, 1914–1922* (Ithaca: Cornell University Press, 2010), pp. 42, 96–102.
50 Tomas Balkelis, 'In search of a native realm: the return of World War I refugees to Lithuania, 1918–1924', in Baron and Gatrell (eds), *Homelands*, pp. 74–97.
51 Mikų Dėdė, 'Lietuvos tremtiniai iš Ukrainos', quoted in Tomas Balkelis, 'Forging a "moral community": the Great War and Lithuanian refugees in Russia', in Balkelis and Davoliūtė (eds), *Population Displacement in Lithuania*, p. 50.
52 In addition to the works cited by Üngör and Salvanou, see Elisabeth Kontogiorgi, *Population Exchange in Greek Macedonia: the Rural Settlement of Refugees 1922–1930* (Oxford: Clarendon Press, 2006); Gatrell, *Making of the Modern Refugee*, pp. 62–72.
53 István I. Mócsy, *The Uprooted: Hungarian Refugees and their Impact on Hungary's Domestic Politics, 1918–1921* (New York: Columbia University Press, 1983).
54 Friederike Kind-Kovács, 'The everyday of statelessness: Hungarian railway dwellers after the Great War', *Geschichte und Gesellschaft*, forthcoming.
55 Sammartino, *The Impossible Border*, pp. 120–5, discusses German officials' febrile attempts to control the flow of refugees in 1919.
56 Skran, *Refugees in Inter-War Europe*; Mark Mazower, *Dark Continent: Europe's Twentieth Century* (London: Allen Lane, 1997); Lucien Wolf, *Russo-Jewish Refugees in Eastern Europe* (London: Joint Foreign Committee, 1923).
57 Homer Folks suggested that American towns might 'adopt' a village or town in France, Serbia, Poland or Armenia. Folks, *The Human Costs of War*, p. 255.
58 From an extensive literature, see in particular Jennifer Hyndman, *Managing Displacement: Refugees and the Politics of Humanitarianism* (Minneapolis: University of Minnesota Press, 2000).
59 Michelle Tusan, *Smyrna's Ashes: Humanitarianism, Genocide, and the Birth of the Middle East* (Berkeley, CA: University of California Press, 2012); Bruno Cabanes, *The Great War and the Origins of Humanitarianism, 1918–1924* (Cambridge: Cambridge University Press, 2014).
60 Rather alarmingly, Francesca Wilson spoke of having 'tasted blood' in 1914 at the start of her career as a relief worker. Wilson, *In the Margins of Chaos*, p. 2.
61 E. Vystavkina, 'Ikh dushi', *Sputnik bezhentsa*, no. 1, 22–23 September 1915.

Population displacement in East Prussia during the First World War

Ruth Leiserowitz

Introduction

As a region bordering the Russian Empire, East Prussia was, apart from Alsace-Lorraine, the only part of the German Empire to be directly affected by the military operations of the First World War. There had been no military actions in this region since the Napoleonic wars. Forced migration was hitherto unknown, and the refugee crisis in 1914 found everyone totally unprepared. In August 1914 two distinct waves of forced migration took place in opposing directions. In the first of these the population of various provincial towns fled westwards, away from the advancing Russian army. Most of those who sought refuge returned to East Prussia by 1916. The second movement concerned German civilians who had remained in the region but who were subsequently seized by the occupying Russian forces and taken to provinces in the interior of Russia, close to the Volga and Yenisei rivers. There they were housed together in the vicinity of prisoner of war camps. These deportees only began to return to their homes in 1919, but their repatriation came to a standstill during the Russian revolution and the ensuing civil war.

At the beginning of the war, the population displacements and resulting drama were broadly publicised in the media, provoking a surge of solidarity among the German public. By 1916, the media further promoted East Prussia as the only German region touched by the war. At this point, material reconstruction came to the fore, whereas the fate that befell human beings faded from view.

As yet, there exists no research regarding the flow of refugees from East Prussia. This neglect reflects the fact that these events were overshadowed by the far greater and more enduring consequences of the Second World

War. Although the Königsberg historian Fritz Gause had published a book in 1931 about the Russian occupation, such accounts were completely overlaid by the developing myth of the 'Battle of Tannenberg', the first great success of the German army in the First World War.[1] This myth, alongside the hero worship of Paul von Hindenburg, allowed no room for the subject of refugees. Besides, Germany was flooded with postcards showing the cities and communities that had been rebuilt, thereby crowding out any other images. The refugees of the First World War appeared marginally in the work of Andreas Kossert and other scholars.[2] As to those East Prussians who were transported to Russia, except for contemporaneous publications, only a memoir with an introduction and commentary by Lothar Kölm is available.[3] There is likewise a lack of an appraisal of the reaction in German politics to the events of 1914. What, for example, caused the government to transfer the then governor of the province, Ludwig von Windheim, to Hannover in September 1914 and replace him with Adolf von Batocki?

This is not to say that extant sources are unavailable. There are the records from the State Commissioner for Refugees (*Staatskommissar für Flüchtlinge*), along with contemporary writings from Albert Brackmann to the head of the Königsberg Archive, as well as articles from numerous periodicals. With the help of these sources, questions regarding the representation of displacement, assistance to refugees and their return may be answered. On such a basis, this German refugee group can then be placed within the context of broader European displacement events in the First World War.

The causes and dynamics of population displacement

To the great surprise of the German supreme command, by the middle of August, Russian troops – the Neman army under General Paul von Rennenkampf and the Narev army under General Aleksandr Samsonov – had already advanced on the East Prussian territory.[4] The German army failed to halt the Russians at the battle of Gumbinnen and the enemy soon stood only 40km from Königsberg. On 18 August, the governor announced that 'movement into Königsberg from without may not be possible', and advised that the sick, elderly and children should be evacuated, because finding adequate nourishment could be difficult in case of a siege.[5] A few days later, on 22 August, came the official order to send harvested grain and livestock to the western bank of the Vistula or to military collection points at Heiligenbeil, Wormditt and Mohrungen. This helped

Population displacement in East Prussia

Map 1.1 The First World War in East Prussia.

to encourage the mass movement of civilians in a largely uncontrolled fashion, but some saw no possibility of leaving East Prussia in good time, while others deliberately lingered, in part to defend their assets.[6]

In the first wave of attack the remaining local residents were generally spared systematic persecution by the Russian occupying forces. The rural population to the north of the Neman river and in the south-east of East Prussia fared worse; at least a thousand people were taken to Siberia.[7] At the end of August, the Eighth Army under command of Hindenburg and his chief of Staff, Erich von Ludendorff, defeated the Russian forces at the Battle of Tannenberg. Accordingly, the first group of displaced residents returned to their homes. In October, Russian troops once more advanced on East Prussia, and this assault provoked the rapid departure of approximately 350,000 people in the wake of systematic abuse.

Between November 1914 and January 1915, peace prevailed on the Eastern Front. The winter battle of February 1915 in Masuria culminated in the defeat of the Russian army, bringing a close to the hostilities in East Prussia. Most refugees delayed returning. It should not be forgotten that other civilians had lost their homes as a result of the fighting but remained in the province; many of them were in need of aid for a number of years and had to wait until long after the war for their houses to be rebuilt.

In short, there were two main waves of flight in the direction of the west, taking place in August and October of 1914. Each was accompanied by smaller movements within the province, and by two waves of deportation to Russia.

What explains this state of affairs? The local civil administration and the German army utterly underestimated the emergency situation. No arrangements were made for an orderly evacuation of the border districts, and calls for the removal of livestock were seldom observed. The commander of the XX Army Corps, General Friedrich von Scholtz, made the following announcement on 10 August:

> Among the population, the view is widely held that the Russian soldiers, upon entering Prussian land, will plunder and pillage. It has been made known with certainty here that the Russian command authorities have given a strict order, as long as the inhabitants leave their localities in peace, neither to plunder nor to set the settlements alight … It must therefore be assumed that the Russians have the sincere will to carry out war according to conventions for civilised peoples. Consequently I direct to the non-fighting population a serious appeal to prudence, and hope that this announcement will contribute to stemming the headlong flight from the approaching Russian troops and other panic actions, which have unfortunately already come to light.[8]

However, a series of hasty directives during the second half of August fomented fear and panic in the population, and led ultimately to a sort of domino reaction. The governor of the province of East Prussia, Ludwig von Windheim, who held office until September 1914, was not mentioned in this context at all. His successor, Adolf von Batocki, the former president of the Chamber of Agriculture in the province, was appointed in October and immediately embarked on numerous efforts to regulate the issue of the refugees and the later re-building of the province. As

Russian forces invaded anew, von Batocki and his officials were determined to call a halt to the flight of refugees and hoped that unfavourable winter weather would deter them. The East Prussian administration were particularly concerned that the refugees would not return, potentially leading to a depopulation of the province. They also took the view that the refugee movements were 'gravely detrimental in moral respects' as they promoted the 'unscrupulous transfer of moveable property'.[9]

Nonetheless, the flow of refugees could not be stemmed. In total, according to one contemporary observer, 'more than 870,000 people … during the [Russian] invasion left house and home … followed by some 300,000 during the second invasion. They needed to be housed outside the province of East Prussia in temporary accommodation'.[10] Many of them were taken on special trains to Pomerania, Schleswig, Lüneburg, Frankfurt/Oder, Potsdam, Osnabrück and Westphalia.[11]

Adding to the dire situation was the fact that East Prussia was a markedly agrarian province. In some districts affected by the invasion of the enemy army, the percentage of those working in agriculture reached 70 per cent, many of whom were farmers for whom livestock was a crucial resource.[12] The aforementioned appeal on 22 August to drive the livestock to safety, that is to the other side of the Weichsel, encouraged the owners to accompany their valuable animals. If farmers initially thought that the cows or goats would make the journey more tolerable because they had milk available to them along the way, it soon became clear that the flight was made significantly more difficult, indeed actually hindered by the livestock. The *Königsberger Volkszeitung* (26 August 1914) carried a story headed 'The flight of the country residents of East Prussia', in which an eyewitness reported that he had seen 'a vast line of wagons and carts, with livestock and horses driven along. From time to time one could see lambs and foals that had got separated from their mothers and were now astray'.[13]

It is not at all surprising that, prior to the second wave of refugees, a yellow placard carried the following message from the provincial governor: 'I ask the residents of the districts of East Prussia now under threat from the enemy, in order to avoid significant losses, to immediately and carefully read what follows and to take note of it before they make up their minds'. There followed a list of instructions 'to act with a clear head and calm deliberation' as well as cautioning refugees not to load the wagons too heavily. The instructions also expressly forbade them to bring their livestock with them.[14] When they encountered refugees who refused to give up their horse-drawn wagons, refugee commission officials insisted that in view of the current weather conditions at least the women and children should be sent on ahead by train.[15]

The areas where the refugees were sent had limited capacity to accommodate livestock and horses, and consequently the owners had to be prompted to part with their animals before departing, something that they were not prepared to do. The governor von Batocki therefore tasked the Chamber of Agriculture to take ownership of the animals on behalf of the East Prussian farmers, who received for them a written receipt. Around 80,000 cattle and 20,000 horses were kept in the province in this way. The owners were often unable to pay for the maintenance of the horses from their own pocket and therefore applied for what was called a financial pre-compensation to cover the costs, which later, when a final determination of the losses from the war was made, would be offset. Owners were permitted to receive no more than 5 marks per diem and in total no more than 75 marks for a horse for the entire duration of the war, as pre-compensation for feed.[16] Naturally this arrangement addressed only a fraction of the total number of horses in East Prussia.

Staying behind

One group of refugees in East Prussia that needed assistance was the Russian citizens of the Jewish faith, including those who were being cared for as patients in the Königsberg clinic, those visiting health spas in the seaside resorts, and those travelling from the west who discovered the Russian border was closed. They were interned in their hundreds in the Königsberg palace and looked after by the 'Jewish Aid Committee 1914' set up by the local Jewish community. Dietary restrictions meant that they could not receive the food aid that was being distributed generally, and instead the community was given a grant of money in order to have appropriate meals cooked for them.[17]

Various Evangelical pastors in the province, both in the city and in the countryside, declared in the face of the threat that they would stay, sharing their decision with their congregations and setting an example for their parishioners. The bishop of Ermland reminded his clergymen that they had a canonical residency requirement, and were only to leave their assignment if they received a command from a higher authority. They were, meanwhile, expected to be responsible for the care of the church, the parish buildings and the parishioners. This exposed them to considerable risk from the Russian authorities. One pastor was deported to Voronezh along with several members of the congregation. Another, in the district of Lyck, survived a series of investigations into his alleged spying activity during the occupation. A third, along with a number of members of his congregation, was less fortunate and was summarily executed by the Russians.[18]

What motives the Russian military had to carry off civil servants cannot be precisely determined, owing to missing sources. Over 10,000 people were deported to Russia, among them six clergymen, three of them with their entire family, two superintendents, and one 73-year-old with his elderly wife. Little is known about the support for the civilian detainees in Russia. They did, however, receive some assistance through the International Committee of the Red Cross. Lithuanians in the Russian Empire also organised assistance for the internees from East Prussia.

Residents in those rural communities that did stay behind, particularly during the episode of mass displacement, often had to provide for the refugees making their way through the area. They were followed by the Russian troops, who because of the weather conditions, did not bivouac as they would have done in the summer, but instead billeted themselves in local houses. In the cities and small towns, the Russians frequently imposed war levies and seized furnishings, clothing and goods from homes and businesses. There were reports of plunder, the wanton destruction of provisions, and of the resulting shortages and starvation. Numerous complaints surfaced about the rape of women.[19] Yet the worst things experienced were the arbitrary shooting of people and the deportation of others to the distant interior of Russia (see below).

Refugees, the German public, the state and non-governmental organisations

Very quickly there was a clear appreciation on the part of German society of the situation emerging in East Prussia and of the difficult circumstances for the population that resulted from it. Specifically, the reports that appeared in the press about Russian atrocities directed the attention of the Germans to the theatre of the war, as Alex Watson has remarked.[20] But even when one considers, as Watson has also underscored in this context, that the First World War was a media war, it is striking that photographic depiction of the war atrocities were generally eschewed. For one thing, the authorities dramatically limited the activities of the photographers in the province; for another thing, the main focus of the photographic representations was placed on the refugees and the destruction of buildings.[21] In view of the central pictorial representation of the East Prussian refugees while they were fleeing or returning, the question arises as to why the reception of the refugees in Germany found such limited visual resonance in the press. Given that the majority of the refugees were housed in private homes, there was limited motivation for a significant media representation of life in the refugee barracks, food distribution and so on.

Meanwhile, aid for the East Prussian refugees was swiftly perceived as a matter of national importance. First and foremost, it was necessary to provide administrative assistance, to direct the flow of refugees. This proved relatively successful outside of East Prussia. On the other bank of the Vistula, in the adjacent administrative region of Danzig, the district president permitted the admission of refugees, including arrangements for their distribution to districts in West Prussia. Likewise, government commissioners arrived in Dirschau on 28 August in order to evaluate the accommodation of evacuees from Vieh, some 300,000 in total. Other refugees were sent to Pomerania und Brandenburg.[22] At this juncture a single point of contact and determination for refugees in the entire affected region was established: Governor (*Landeshauptmann*) von Berg in Königsberg assumed the role of commissioner of the senior president (*Kommissar des Oberpräsidenten*). From 24 September 1914, he was to organise evacuation options for the refugees and to co-ordinate these. Consequently, to prepare for the second wave of refugees, officials were sent to designated assembly points and were to arrange for the refugees' evacuation by train.[23] Medical orderlies and nurses attended the trains. Meals were arranged in part by the 'fatherland' women's associations, and in part by the military. Within the commissioner's remit was communication with the military regarding the approval for refugees to return to the province and organisation of the necessary transport. His office remained open for business until the middle of August 1916.[24]

Financial support was also badly needed. A decree of the Prussian State Ministry in 1914 had already established a refugee fund which by 17 October had already accumulated 433,924 marks. These sums were initially intended for refugees who found themselves outside the province. Only a few days later, the Finance Ministry announced that an additional 500,000 marks would be made available for the procurement of essential lodgings for those within East Prussia who found themselves outside of their home districts. As of the beginning of November, when it was clear that no immediate return for refugees would be possible, the Ministry of the Interior determined that those who provided accommodation for refugees would be reimbursed. As long as their return remained impossible, adult refugees would be given 1 mark per day, with half that amount for children under 14 years.[25]

Appeals to assist refugees came from citizens in various cities in Germany. In Frankfurt, an 'Appeal for East Prussia' referred to the last real experience of war in the region and thereby constructed an idea of continuity:

> The East Prussian towns have continued to suffer even into this very century from the material pressure of the war contributions that were imposed on them in Napoleonic times over 100 years ago! Slowly and with difficulty the area has been able under its own power to overcome the losses it suffered. We must be sure that this time the sister provinces, who experience on our behalf hardship at first hand, receive in ample and quick measure our assistance and support.[26]

Numerous private aid organisations and initiatives quickly sprang up. In Berlin, they included: the War Office of the Police headquarters (subsidised by the state); the Central Committee of the German Associations of the Red Cross, Department XI for Refugee Relief (East Prussians and German expatriates); the East Prussian Support Association; the Society of Friends of East Prussian Refugees; the National Women's Service; the Patriotic Women's Association; and the Committee of East Prussian Refugees.[27] Most of these organisations financed themselves through donations, and although they attempted to obtain and distribute state funds, the government rebuffed them.[28]

One of the largest associations was the Munich East Prussia Aid, founded in March 1915. This association donated home furnishings or even entire rooms based upon designs produced and exhibited in carpentry shops in Bavaria. The most important organisation was founded in March 1915 by Baron Bernd von Lüdinghausen, the police chief from Berlin and the previous East Prussian district commissioner, who launched an appeal for refugees. He took the imaginative step of twinning towns in East Prussia with those in other parts of Germany. Later on this contributed considerably to economic reconstruction of communities in East Prussia. Alongside these there were also self-help organisations, such as the Committee of East Prussian Refugees, based in Berlin, in which the author, Richard Skowronneck, played a prominent part.[29] Regular gatherings of East Prussian refugees took place in the New Philharmonic Hall, at 96–97 Köpenickerstrasse, in which aid was organised and claimed, and which provided them with information about conditions back home.[30]

Within the province, the 'East Prussian Refugee Care' (*Ostpreussische Flüchtlingsfürsorge*) was primarily responsible for material support. It also catered for the needs of refugees who, out of necessity, stayed at other locations within the province. At Christmas 1914 a great array of donations was on display, and among other things, 37 wagon-loads of clothing were distributed among the needy.[31]

In summer 1915, support was withdrawn for refugees who did not wish to return.[32] Conversely, there was yet another string of 'scattered refugees', mainly in the Ruhr district, who received some assistance. In autumn 1915, the East Prussian authorities declared that it might not be possible to complete a return journey in the winter without detriment to refugees' health. It was suggested that 'all refugees, who at the moment still obtain state assistance, as long as no change occurs in their personal circumstances, should leave by 30 April 1917, as the start of the warmer season in East Prussia can be expected in May'. It was estimated that the strain would be kept to moderate limits. Certificates of assistance were issued to 461 adults and 525 children from 91 districts. The projected aid for the period from 1 December 1916 to 30 April 1917 totalled 105,000 marks, a relatively low sum.[33] By this stage, the number of refugees awaiting return had also decreased.

Refugees and non-refugees

Various provinces lent themselves to receive refugees in August 1914, such as West Prussia, Pomerania, Hannover, Brandenburg and Mecklenburg-Schwerin, which received around 250,000 to 300,000 persons. Many refugees, however, preferred large cities as places of residence. Some 20,000 to 30,000 refugees found themselves in Berlin in the autumn of 1914. On 3 October, the Ministry of the Interior was already attempting to prevent further refugees from settling in Berlin and sent a telegram to this end.[34] On 23 October the ministry announced that the city was officially barred for the arrival of new refugees.[35] Königsberg attempted to keep the tally of refugees as low as possible, while the district town, Tilsit, sheltered over 9,000 refugees in December 1914.[36]

Towns in western Germany had reached their capacity. As the district president of Stade reported to the governor of East Prussia in January 1915, 'with the arrival of 500 refugees from East Prussia, the region of Stade will soon be full. Request indication whether to reckon with a larger number of additional refugees'.[37] Two weeks later, on 28 January 1915, the senior mayor of Altona wrote in the same vein:

> Toward the end of August 1914, under my chairmanship, a committee was established in Altona for the support of the needy East Prussian refugees. The appeals, supported by well-respected Hamburg citizens, and announced in all the Hamburg, Altona, and Wandsbek newspapers, resulted in such generous donations of money and clothing, that the committee was initially able to support adequately all the refugees who arrived in Hamburg, Altona and Wandsbek. After the evacuation of large masses of inhabitants from the province of East Prussia, however, the increase in the number of refugees in the towns named here grew so extraordinarily that not just the greatest thrift was demanded, but also at that point a reduction in the disbursements had to be considered.[38]

Many refugees did not take up the state's offer of accommodation, but rather sought quarters on their own, for example staying with acquaintances or relatives. In Westphalia, whither many workers had fled from East Prussia in previous decades, there was a large concentration of refugees. The fact that state-sponsored support was only available in regions officially designated to take in refugees contributed to this process.[39]

Social solidarity between refugees and the host population in Germany appears to have been strong. One small but telling example is an incident that occurred in Berlin in early February 1915, when a comedian in the Metropol-Kabarett decided to recount a series of jokes about East Prussia. Loud protests ensued, as if the audience decided that it was inappropriate to make fun of East Prussian customs at such a difficult time for the region and its inhabitants.[40]

As to the details of refugees' life in German towns and cities, relatively little information was recorded. For example, not much is known about the experiences of children. A report from Stettin in the middle of December 1914 indicated that in Anklam, more than half of the 1,080 refugees housed in the district were under 14 years of age. In the district of Rügenwalde, 920 refugees out of a total of 2,074 were under 14 years old. The same applied in Ückermünde.[41] One can only assume that these refugee children were simply sent straightaway to local schools to continue their education. Certainly women and children predominated among the refugee population, because husbands and fathers had to fulfil their obligations on the front or to work as civil servants in other locations.

Refugees were predominantly from districts with a pronounced evangelical population. As mentioned earlier, the evangelical church authorities in East Prussia instructed priests to care for the refugee groups.[42] The region housed only a small Jewish minority. Jews who did not hold

German citizenship were not interned (although consideration had initially been given to internment), but were nevertheless subject to special police oversight, especially in Königsberg and Memel.

The Ministry of the Interior anticipated that displaced civil servants among the first wave of refugees would return as quickly as possible, and the government issued a directive in the press to public employees along these lines. The authorities were instructed in case of emergency to furnish these returnees with free travel.[43] One consequence was that scores of families were wrenched apart. After the second wave of displacement, many civil servants from the Russian-occupied rural districts were relocated. Those from Pilkallen and Stallupönen found themselves in Stettin, those from Oletzko in Berlin, those from Lyck in Königsberg, and those from Johannisburg in Sensburg.[44] In February 1915, the Ministry of the Interior reported that it was urgently desired 'that those in the not-yet-vacated districts take their positions as provincial, regional and local officials, including municipal jurymen and teachers, for the time being without their families'.[45] A further separation of families followed, and this was often perceived as more disruptive than the temporary loss of their homes.

Many people went missing in these turbulent times. At the beginning of February 1915, the Provincial Organisation of the Patriotic Women's Association in Königsberg established an information and news office. It was overwhelmed with information, and issued up to 1000 separate disclosures daily. The sudden interruption of railway and postal service made family members worried, and they hastily turned to these and news services. The information office issued over 93,000 cards in all, on which approximately 300,000 refugees were listed. But it transpired that many apparently missing persons had never fled in the first place.[46]

Representations of displacement

Between autumn 1914 and February 1915, the topic of the East Prussian refugees was never absent from German newspapers and journals. They were portrayed as having made a sacrifice on behalf of the entire German people. Accounts of the flight from East Prussia made a regular appearance. Photos were much less frequent, but graphic art was very popular. Illustrations appeared in specialist periodicals such as a series of lithographs by Ernst Bischoff-Culm that were reproduced in *Wachtfeuer*, depicting 'Refugees from Memel'. 'Christmas celebration of the East

Population displacement in East Prussia

Figure 1.1 'Vertrieben' (The Expellees), medal by Ludwig Gies, 1915.

Prussian refugees' was particularly calculated to have an emotional impact on the journal's readership.[47] These images emphasised that refugees were far from home, and that the territory of East Prussia had been badly damaged. Another poignant and dramatic image was the medal designed by Ludwig Gies that showed a refugee family (*Die Vertriebene*) struggling through the snow with their belongings, including a young child holding on to a large kettle.[48]

By the second half of 1915, less emphasis was being given to the circumstances and motives for flight, and was replaced by the representation of the possibility of return to East Prussia. Now the focus turned to the reconstruction effort in the province. Copious numbers of postcards were distributed, showing new, neat buildings. They drew attention to the fact that 39 towns and cities and nearly 1,900 villages had been badly affected by the war in East Prussia. At the same time, and in the midst of war, a state-funded reconstruction programme had commenced with the fervent support of the entire German population. The message was repeated again and again that 'the distant province of East Prussia, with its casualties, devastation and triumphs [enters into] the national consciousness of the entire empire'.[49]

Starting with the liberation of the province, publications such as *The East Prussian War Journal* were launched in order to put on record the experience of the events of the war and the rushed departure. As early as January 1915, the upper presidium of the province had begun to seek reports 'as documentation of the events of the East Prussian war'. They looked to 'educated men' who were capable of writing reports.[50] (Evidently they did not trust the East Prussian women among the refugees to give a compelling report.) District president Adolf von Batocki formulated it in a more nuanced way: 'at my request, numerous educated and trustworthy men and women interviewed those refugees who were housed near them as to [their] experiences during the first Russian period, and then put their statements in writing. The extensive material received was the primary stuff out of which the *East Prussian War Journal* was drawn'.[51]

When viewed this way, one can speak here about this being a very early 'oral-history project'. The introduction to one of the texts composed in July 1915 states that it 'should illustrate the history of the province of East Prussia during the current war. It has grown out of the conviction that the generation now alive is obliged to record these major and almost unprecedented events in world history, and to give a truthful portrayal of them'.[52] This exceptional perspective of the East Prussian writer, which assumes the uniqueness of the events, had to be significantly revised in later years when the deeds committed by the Germans in Belgium and in other places became generally known. This may also explain why these publications ceased to be issued.

Homeward bound? Return and material support following the liberation of East Prussia

Government officials in East Prussia feared that the refugees would remain in their new locations rather than return to their homes. The region had survived a major rural exodus since the 1870s. The agricultural labour market had witnessed large-scale internal movements of people before the war. In some East Prussian districts up to two-thirds of those born between 1870 and 1908 had emigrated to the west of Germany; put differently, the annual exodus from the province averaged 30,000 people.[53] The district president, in his announcement before the second wave of refugees (the yellow placard mentioned above), explicitly asked people to return, expressing the following: 'All of you, even if you plan to flee, continue to hold dear your East Prussian homeland, come back home as soon as the circumstances allow, and help therewith our dear East Prussia after a victorious peace treaty to bloom again'.[54]

Misgivings about this situation are reflected in correspondence between the Jewish councillor in Insterburg, Otto Eichelbaum, and the senior president of the province, von Batocki in late October 1914:

> All these occurrences in history of flight, as warranted as they perhaps seemed at the moment, suggest that many displaced East Prussians are not returning to their soil … It is advisable, among other official measures, to make a public appeal, that it is every individual's duty not to faithlessly abandon his native soil, that it is also the duty of the employer not to hold on to workmen accepted for temporary aid and employment.[55]

The senior president replied that 'the danger you describe is grave … The remuneration for war damages should be regulated only in their native towns. I hope that in this way, after the commencement of secure conditions, most refugees will arrange for their return. Already now, refugees from reasonably secure districts who refuse to return are not granted assistance'.[56] The state authorities thus fixed their sights on the matter of finance, which was governed by the War Provision Law.

As soon as the weather conditions allowed, refugees were instructed to repatriate to the openly available areas. Concessions were also offered as an inducement. The Minister of Public Works and chief of the Reich Office for the Administration of Imperial Railways issued a circular on 11 January 1915, stipulating that refugees who could document their special circumstances should be carried free of charge.[57] Farmers in particular desired to cultivate their land. Ignoring temporary prohibitions, they set out for home, only to be sent back by the police. They received no financial contribution upon their return.[58] Fragmented families – that is, women and children whose husbands and fathers were serving in the army or in government offices – delayed their return, as most of them knew that they would find no roof over their heads in their homeland.[59]

By the autumn of 1915 it was announced that 'the return of East Prussian refugees is generally possible, provided of course that they are able to procure accommodation in their home. They must satisfy themselves that accommodation is available for them, and should therefore contact in advance the mayor of their home city, or, if they had lived in the country, their district administrator'.[60] The expectation was that most refugees would be back home by the autumn. Financial support was again imperative, and at times the local administration was overwhelmed by the task of disbursing remuneration payments, which also required a claims assessment.[61]

In the summer months support was withdrawn for the remaining refugees who expressed no wish to return. There were still a number of 'scattered refugees', particularly in the Ruhr valley. For the time being, they continued to receive support. In the autumn, the East Prussian authorities determined that returning in winter would be detrimental to one's health. Accordingly, the proposal was made that 'the refugees still present who are still receiving state support, to the extent that no other change happens in their personal circumstances, should continue receiving support until 30 April 1917' when the weather would improve. It was calculated that the financial liability would stay within modest limits.[62]

After the liberation of East Prussia, when the return of the refugees was taking place, it seemed that the authorities were in fact of the opinion that enough private money had been donated. What remained uncertain was the extent to which refugees would be compensated from public funds. Richard Skowronnek, who involved himself significantly for his Masurian fellow countrymen and who had written several articles for the press, wrote about this in May 1915:

> Governor von Berg, with whom I spoke during his time in Königsberg, took the view that private charity had now been generally stirred enough; but after all the severe misery that I have seen in my home area, I could not concur. Private charity can indeed never be stretched far enough, because what the state of things will be with full compensation from public funds no-one knows. And who will replace for our poor countrymen the loss of things with sentimental value which can never be restored by any claim for compensation?[63]

Most return journeys took place by train. A written certification from the respective district administrator was imperative. Based on this, refugees could obtain a free travel voucher. The Ministry of the Interior and the High Command issued instructions to the police to oversee the trains in this regard.[64]

As mentioned earlier, a large percentage of the houses and dwellings had been destroyed. The owners had to attend to the reconstruction of the destroyed buildings themselves, although the authorities simplified and adapted the building regulations in the province, and provided experts to give advice on construction. Nevertheless, the construction work took time. In the interim, things looked bleak. Barracks were not set up as a rule, because the current models in use were too expensive to purchase.

The building administration suggested emergency accommodation in the ruins of the damaged buildings. Otherwise, for the summer and until a part of the new structure was built, 'simple sheds or burrows with simple roofs (using the model of field defences) would have to serve the purpose'. The administration emphasised that 'as many structures be completed in the countryside as were necessary for the cultivation of the fields'.[65]

The funds for reconstruction were at first only granted as a pre-compensation, that is, from the funds the *Landtag* had granted for the restoration of the province first time round. From this it can be inferred that the first summer of the return was filled with great strain. When refugees returned, the loss of the animals was clearly noted, even though in April 1915 orders had been given for the speedy return of milk cows from Potsdam and horses from Pomerania.[66] At the beginning of September, the district administrator of Darkehmen asked the chamber of agriculture 'to immediately bring in 200 milk cows for the Darkehmer district'. He suggested buying them in other districts and underscored that the returning residents suffered real misery and hardship, particularly the children who were not getting any milk. The chamber of agriculture estimated that around 120,000 horses over three years of age had ended up in the hands of the Russians or else had died during the flight through the forests. It imported 40,000 horses into the province, mostly from the occupied areas of Russia, but a further 40,000 horses were needed in order to till the fields and complete the winter sowing. A remedy had to be found urgently so that in the coming spring it would be possible to cultivate all available acreage: Poland seemed the obvious choice.[67]

Many structures intended for communal purposes were built with help from the afore-mentioned twinning partnerships created through East Prussia Aid.[68] As mentioned earlier, von Lüdinghausen had begun to link west German communities and organisations with the East Prussian districts and towns destroyed by the war. City districts in Berlin, Wilmersdorf and Grunewald took on the sponsorship for Gerdauen as well as Nordenburg. These building projects were mostly completed in 1916. The success of these expenditures was widely documented in a flood of postcards and became a secure fixture in the collective memory.

Civil internees in Russia were the last to be able to return home. They returned relatively late, between 1919 and 1921, and occasionally found great difficulties in being accepted back into their rural or small-town communities.

In January 1918, the upper presidium of East Prussia applied for financial support from the Ministry of the Interior on the grounds that in spring 1915 the state had promised to cover the bulk of the expenses for the refugees. The costs of clothing, medical care and education for all refugees, whether self-supported or in the state refugee assembly areas, were to be financed out of a so-called 'collected fund', that is from donations. The presidium established that it had fulfilled this obligation. But it maintained that proper state refugee relief had only been introduced on 1 November 1914, and what had not been taken into consideration by the settlement conference were the costs prior to that date. These amounted to accommodation and provisions from 10 October to 1 November 1914 (250,000 marks); expenditure from districts and communities for accommodation and provisions prior to 1 November 1914 (164,000 marks); and clothing and medical care (853,000 marks), all of which had been procured from donations.[69] For its part, the ministry decided that according to the settlement from March 1915, all outstanding bills had in fact been settled. The author of the rejection notice could not deny himself a further postscript. He wrote, in convoluted bureaucratic prose:

> I would not want to leave unmentioned, however, that in my representation of your matter, I encountered one voice that was very adversely influenced by the dismissive response of the East Prussian provincial administration in relation to the defraying of the general relief of refugees returning from distant areas.

The author closed with the sentence that one would assume that the province of East Prussia, for which so much has been done on the part of the German state, would hardly shirk from this responsibility as a matter of honour.[70] In clearer language, this meant on the one hand that the state saw no reason to provide financial support when it could rely upon private contributions. On the other hand, it was clear that, so far as the Prussian Ministry of the Interior was concerned, the situation in East Prussia had been resolved. Other problems now required urgent attention.

Conclusion

The flow of refugees from East Prussia in the autumn of 1914 was felt by all parts of Germany, and led to extensive services from a number of private and state bodies. Once the area had been liberated, the state commissioner for refugees was recalled in August 1916. The state regarded the refugee question as settled for the most part, and turned its attention elsewhere.

But the population displacements remained anchored in the memory of the population. Above all, women and children, as well as being far from their home, often had to manage without the support of male family members. Residents who fled in 1914 mostly belonged to the same groups who again fled in 1944, and, owing to their personal experiences, pressed for their rapid departure. What revived many memories in the summer of 1944 were the events of August 1914 when the residents of the Memelland district were first taking flight, but then were called back for six weeks in order to bring in the harvest. Whereas the German authorities then had sought to disperse the fleeing population as much as possible over the whole state territory in order to achieve a broad mobilisation of the population, in late autumn 1944 the Nazi state wanted to deter a large refugee trail from settling elsewhere in the Reich, on the grounds that German people should not be exposed to evidence that the perils of war were moving closer to home. This purely propaganda-based decision cost many human lives, because the advance of the Red Army and the order eventually given by the East Prussian administration of the National Socialists to evacuate the localities happened during extremely cold weather.

Numerous sponsorship groups that arose between East Prussian and west German cities during the occupation and reconstruction of the province in 1914–15 were revived after the Second World War, when the bulk of the East Prussian population fled to the territories of the later Federal Republic of Germany and were supported for many years. After the 1970s the historical context that has formed the bulk of this chapter disappeared from view, and scarcely anyone could explain the geographical ties to the former Prussian region and their historical background. The centenary of the First World War provided an opportunity to shed new light on a forgotten chapter of history and to re-evaluate the long forgotten processes of population displacement and 'replacement'.

Notes

1 Fritz Gause, *Die Russen in Ostpreussen 1914/15, im Auftrage des Landeshauptm anns der Provinz Ostpreussen* (Königsberg: Gräfe und Unzer, 1931).
2 Andreas Kossert, *Damals in Ostpreussen: Der Untergang einer deutschen Provinz* (München: Deutsche Verlags-Anstalt, 2008); Andreas Kossert, *Ostpreussen: Geschichte und Mythos* (München: Pantheon, 2007). See also Alexander Watson, '"Unheard-of brutality": Russian atrocities against civilians in East Prussia, 1914–1915', *Journal of Modern History*, 86, no. 4 (2014), 780–825.

3 Christian Grigat, *Unter russischer Knute im deutschen Gebiet nördlich der Memel: Erinnerung an d. Zeit d. beiden Russeneinfälle in den nördl. Teil d. Kreise Ragnit u. Tilsit* (Reyländer, 1916); Karin Borck and Lothar Kölm, *Gefangen in Sibirien: Tagebuch eines ostpreussischen Mädchens 1914-1920* (Osnabrück: Fibre, 2001).
4 The military actions have been variously described in great detail. There are, however, still major gaps relating to daily life during the war. Stig Förster, 'Einführende Bemerkungen', in Gerhard Paul Gross (ed.), *Die vergessene Front der Osten 1914-15: Ereignis, Wirkung, Nachwirkung* (Paderborn: Schöningh, 2006), pp. 29-34.
5 Albert Brackmann, 'Aus der Fluchtbewegung', in Brackmann (ed.), *Die Fluchtbewegung und Flüchtlingsfürsorge* (Berlin: Fischer, 1915), pp. 7-27.
6 F. Simon, 'Der ostpreussische Handel während des Krieges', in Albert Brackmann (ed.), *Die zweite Besetzung Ostpreussens und die Wirkung des Krieges auf Landwirtschaft und Handel der Provinz* (Berlin: Fischer, 1916) pp. 52-3.
7 From Schmalleningken and Wischwill around 500 persons apiece were deported according to Grigat, *Unter russischer Knute*, p. 32; H. Schöttler, 'Kriegsnot und Kriegshilfe in Ostpreussen', in *Ostpreussenhilfe: Zeitschrift für den Wiederaufbau und die Neubelebung östlicher Marken*, 4, Heft 1915, 37-40.
8 Brackmann, ed., *Die Fluchtbewegung*, pp. 7-8.
9 Geheimes Staatsarchiv Preussischer Kulturbesitz in Berlin (GStA, Berlin): *Flüchtlingsfürsorge: Verkehr mit den Flüchtlingskommissionen, 1914-1923*, pp. 39-40.
10 Schöttler, 'Kriegsnot', p. 39.
11 Gause, *Die Russen in Ostpreussen*, pp. 69-70.
12 Dieter Hertz-Eichenrode, *Politik und Landwirtschaft in Ostpreussen 1919-1930: Untersuchung eines Strukturproblems in der Weimarer Republik* (Wiesbaden: VS Verlag für Sozialwissenschaften, 1969).
13 Brackmann, ed., *Die Fluchtbewegung*, p. 14.
14 Brackmann, ed., *Die Fluchtbewegung*, pp. 17-19.
15 Landesrat Meyer, 'Staatliche und private Flüchtlingsfürsorge', in Brackmann, ed., *Die Fluchtbewegung*, pp. 36-7.
16 GStA, Berlin, *Flüchtlingsfürsorge und Verkehr mit dem Flüchtlingskommissar*, 23 December 1914-4 February 1915, p. 177; Meyer, 'Staatliche', pp. 36-7.
17 Vogelstein, Dr. Rabbiner in Königsberg, 'Die Flüchtlingsfürsorge in den jüdischen Gemeinden', *Die Fluchtbewegung*, p. 101.
18 Dr. Gerhard Matern, 'Die Fluchtbewegung und Flüchtlingsfürsorge in den katholischen Gemeinden Ostpreussens', *Die Fluchtbewegung*, pp. 79-83.
19 H. Schöttler, 'Aus der Kriegsarbeit der evangelischen Kirche Ostpreussens', *Die Fluchtbewegung*, pp. 69-84; Albert Brackmann, 'Aus der Zeit des zweiten Russeneinfalls', *Die Fluchtbewegung*, pp. 9-18.
20 Watson, '"Unheard-of brutality"', p. 813.

21 Watson, '"Unheard-of brutality"', p. 815.
22 Brackmann, 'Aus der Zeit', pp. 16–17.
23 Meyer, 'Staatliche und private Flüchtlingsfürsorge', pp. 34–7.
24 GStA, Berlin, *Flüchtlingsfürsorge*, 1914–23, pp. 32–3; GStA, Berlin, *Flüchtlingsfürsorge und Verkehr mit dem Flüchtlingskommissar*, July 1916–June 1917, p. 57.
25 GStA, Berlin, *Flüchtlingsfürsorge*, 1914–23, pp. 62, 91–3, 124.
26 GStA, Berlin, *Unterstützung der durch den Krieg geschädigten Bevölkerung: Allgemein* (August 1914–May 1915), p. 43.
27 GStA, Berlin, *Flüchtlingsfürsorge*, July 1916–June 1917, p. 225.
28 Rechtsanwalt Rohr, 'Ostpreussische Flüchtlingsnot und -fürsorge', *Der Tag*, 24. January 1915.
29 GStA, Berlin, *Flüchtlingsfürsorge*, 1915, p. 101.
30 Eduard Kenkel, 'Vorwort', in *Mitteilungen und Nachrichten herausgegeben vom Ausschuss der ostpreussischen Flüchtlinge in Berlin*, no. 1, 11 February 1915.
31 GStA, Berlin, *Flüchtlingsfürsorge*, July 1916–June 1917, p. 261; GStA, Berlin, *Flüchtlingsfürsorge*, 1914–23, pp. 309–12.
32 GStA, Berlin, *Flüchtlingsfürsorge*, July 1916–June 1917, p. 22.
33 GStA, Berlin, *Flüchtlingsfürsorge*, July 1916–June 1917, pp. 38, 125–7.
34 GStA, Berlin, *Flüchtlingsfürsorge*, 1914–23, p. 318.
35 Rohr, 'Ostpreussische Flüchtlingsnot'.
36 Pfarrer Tribukait, 'Die Flüchtlingsnot in unserer Stadt', *Tilsiter Allgemeine Zeitung*, 1915, p. 4.
37 GStA, Berlin, *Flüchtlingsfürsorge*, 23 December 1914–4 February 1915, p. 114.
38 GStA, Berlin, *Flüchtlingsfürsorge und Verkehr mit dem Flüchtlingskommissar*, 5 February–25 March 1915, p. 75.
39 Meyer, 'Staatliche und private Flüchtlingsfürsorge', p. 39.
40 Kenkel, 'Vorwort', p. 4.
41 GStA, Berlin, *Flüchtlingsfürsorge*, 1914–1923, p. 298.
42 GStA, Berlin, *Flüchtlingsfürsorge*, 1914–23, p. 318.
43 GStA, Berlin, *Flüchtlingsfürsorge*, 1914–23, pp. 8–9.
44 GStA, Berlin, *Flüchtlingsfürsorge und Verkehr mit dem Flüchtlingskommissar*, 1914–1915, p. 137.
45 GStA, Berlin, *Flüchtlingsfürsorge*, 1914–23, p. 130–1.
46 GStA, Berlin, *Flüchtlingsfürsorge*, 1914–23, p. 118.
47 Ernst Bischoff-Culm, 'Aus Ostpreussens schlimmen Tagen: in Ankläger', *Wachtfeuer*, 1 (1914); 'Weihnachten, ostpreussischer Flüchtlinge', *Wachtfeuer*, 11 (1914); 'Die Flüchtlinge von Memel', *Wachtfeuer*, 28 (1915).
48 Gies produced other medals, including 'The Russian Bear' and 'Totentanz'.
49 Von Batocki, 'Vorwort', *Die August- und Septembertage 1914* (Berlin: Fischer, 1916), p. 7.
50 GStA, Berlin, *Flüchtlingsfürsorge*, 23 December 1914–4 February 1915, p. 82.

51 Von Batocki, 'Vorwort'.
52 Von Batocki, 'Vorwort', p. 6.
53 Schöttler, 'Kriegsnot', p. 40. See also Klaus J. Bade, 'Politik und Ökonomie der Ausländerbeschäftigung im preussischen Osten 1885–1914: die Internationalisierung des Arbeitsmarkts im Rahmen der preussischen Abwehrpolitik', *Geschichte und Gesellschaft*, Sonderheft (1980), 273–99; Hans Linde, 'Die soziale Problematik der masurischen Agrargesellschaft und die masurische Einwanderung in das Emscherrevier', *Soziale Welt*, 9, nos. 3–4 (1958), 233–46.
54 Albert Brackmann, 'Aus der Fluchtbewegung', in *Die August- und Septembertage 1914*, p. 19.
55 GStA, Berlin, *Flüchtlingsfürsorge*, 1914–23, pp. 105–6.
56 GStA, Berlin, *Flüchtlingsfürsorge*, 1914–23, p. 107.
57 GStA, Berlin, *Flüchtlingsfürsorge*, 1914–23, p. 88.
58 GStA, Berlin, *Flüchtlingsfürsorge*, 1914–23, pp. 130–1.
59 'Kriegserlebnisse eines ostpreussischen Bürgermeisters', in Brackmann, ed., *Die Fluchtbewegung*, pp. 110–13.
60 'Umschau in Ostpreussen', Berlin, 15 September 1915, *Ostland*, Jahrgang 1, Heft 1 (1915), p. 11.
61 GStA, Berlin, *Flüchtlingsfürsorge*, 5 February–25 March 1915, pp. 99–100.
62 GStA, Berlin, *Flüchtlingsfürsorge*, July 1916–June 1917, pp. 22, 38, 50.
63 GStA, Berlin, *Unterstützung*, August 1914–May 1915, pp. 290–1.
64 GStA, Berlin, *Flüchtlingsfürsorge*, 5 February–25 March 1915, pp. 130–1.
65 Geheimer Baurat Fischer, 'Die Massnahmen der Staatsregierung für den Wiederaufbau Ostpreussens', *Zentralblatt der Bauverwaltung*, 46 (1915), 297–8.
66 GStA, Berlin, *Königliches Ober-Präsidium von Ostpreussen Wiederaufbau der Provinz: Pferdeversorgung*, 1 August 1914–5 October 1915, p. 51.
67 GStA, Berlin, *Wiederaufbau der Provinz*, pp. 52–3, 341.
68 Fischer, 'Die Massnahmen', p. 298.
69 GStA, Berlin, *Unterstützung*, January 1919, pp. 14–19.
70 GStA, Berlin, *Unterstützung*, January 1919, p. 10.

2

'A mass which you could form into whatever you wanted': refugees and state building in Lithuania and Courland, 1914–21

Klaus Richter

Introduction

When refugees made their way from Russia back to their homes in Lithuania and Latvia at the end of the First World War, they returned to entirely different countries. Ravaged by destruction and the deportation of one-third of the population, the region was barely recognisable. Moreover, what were once provinces on the periphery of the Russian Empire had now been transformed into independent states, striving for international recognition and the security and consolidation of their borders. This rapid transformation over the course of the First World War still lacks detailed research, with most imperial narratives ending in 1914 and national narratives picking up in 1918.

However, for the history of refugees, this transformation is crucial. Deportations led to profound long-term changes in the social structure of the populations of Lithuania and Latvia. Lithuanian and Latvian peasants fled the advancing German army. The Polish nobility in the German military occupation zone of Ober Ost was politically marginalised and the Baltic German nobility in Latvia was deported. For the Jewish population in Lithuania, most of them urban, the war brought the most significant changes, reducing their share in the population by a half and irrevocably changing their social structure.[1] The situation was similar in the province of Courland, the southernmost of the Baltic Provinces of the Russian Empire, covering roughly the southern half of today's Latvia. Here, the population reduced from almost 800,000 to just 250,000 during the war. Even after the most intensive phase of repatriation, the size of the Jewish and German population of Latvia stood at around half of its pre-war total: Jews numbered fewer than 80,000 compared to

142,000 in 1914, and the number of Baltic Germans fell from 120,000 to around 58,000.[2]

Thus the First World War and repatriation that began during the war and lasted well into the 1920s led to the disentanglement of the multi-ethnic population of Lithuania and Latvia. Whereas such processes of 'unmixing' are commonly associated with expulsions and 'population exchanges' such as those in the Balkans and Turkey, they seem to have taken place much more covertly in the Baltic lands.[3] They were woven into much broader crises such as the punitive arrangements made under the terms of the Brest-Litovsk treaty and the all-engulfing Russian civil war, and for this reason have remained largely hidden.

Looking at developments from the beginning of the First World War until the early 1920s, this chapter considers the impact of ethnic belonging on the treatment of refugees and the changes in ethnic policies over the course of the war and the first years of independent statehood. The focus is on Lithuania and Courland for two reasons, firstly because they both formed part of Ober Ost and therefore shared many of the consequences of occupation. However, displacement and repatriation differed quite significantly between the two regions. In the second place, Courland and Lithuania had a similar social structure in the sense that there was a substantial Jewish population and the nobility was increasingly perceived as foreign (Polish in the case of Lithuania and Baltic German in the case of Courland). The latter differentiated Courland from Livonia province, which was occupied at a later stage of the war. The southern part of Ober Ost, namely the Grodno-Białystok region (today part of Poland and Belarus) will be referred to as well, as it shared many features of the refugee crisis in Lithuania and Courland.

In general, research on refugees from the Baltics is still sparse – particularly with regards to transnational studies.[4] The most substantial research on the Latvian and Lithuanian cases is that of Aija Priedīte[5] and Tomas Balkelis,[6] who focus mostly on the formation and consolidation of national communities and identities among refugees in inner Russia by examining national relief associations and refugee experience. Balkelis also considers the process of repatriation and emphasises that refugees 'had to be persuaded or forced to abandon their divergent and multiple identities'[7] in order to become citizens of the newly established independent nation state. This chapter will build on this research and provide an additional perspective on refugees who were not considered part of the new titular nations, thus highlighting the entangled history of ethnic groups between imperial and national policies: Russian policy backed some groups but not others; Jews, for example, had no imperial support. As Peter Gatrell puts it, imperial policies targeted entire communities that were perceived as disloyal, and post-war national policies 'created even more favourable conditions for the persecution of minorities who did not meet the criteria for political membership'.[8] The implications of this approach for the different ethnicities in Lithuania and Courland are at the core of this research.

Wartime evacuations from Lithuania and Courland, 1914–15

When the First World War broke out, the tsarist government put the front zones under the direct control of Russian generals who proceeded to 'evacuate' between 500,000 and one million people suspected of harbouring sympathies for the enemy.[9] On 3 October 1914, all Germans, including Baltic Germans living in Latvia and Estonia, were ordered to prepare for deportation. This order was extended to all Jews in January 1915.[10] Evicted persons had between three hours and one day to pack what they could carry and then to leave forthwith.[11]

Lacking systematic support, some refugees managed to find shelter in abandoned (mostly Jewish) houses; most, however, stayed in camps or in the open, exposed to disease and hunger.[12] Particularly during the first short-lived incursion of German troops into southern Lithuania in autumn 1914, there was no infrastructure in place for refugees. For example, Jews from Vilkaviškis who set out for Mariampolė in October found themselves in the middle of a five-hour long gun battle. Spending the night in a forest, they headed towards Kaunas, but learned that its Jewish inhabitants were currently being deported and that no-one was allowed to enter the city. After spending a night on a farm near Birštonas, they headed further via Žiežmariai to Kaišiadorys, where they had to leave an elderly woman behind, before eventually reaching Vilnius.[13]

The deportees or 'evacuees' ended up as refugees in inner Russia, although many preferred to stay close to home, hoping to return as soon as possible. Jewish community leader Shaul Lipschitz recounted that at the outbreak of the war Jews from Ventspils (Windau) were assigned to five provinces for resettlement, but they decided to resettle to Orsha in Mogilev province: 'there was actually no reason whatsoever to choose Orsha, other than it being the least distant point from Kurland'.[14]

Baltic Germans in Courland were prone to being libelled by Latvians, because the existing social antagonism between German landowners and Latvian peasants sharpened still further during the war.[15] As evacuations assumed the character of deportations, families were regularly torn apart. The pregnant wife of a Baltic German estate owner recalled that her husband was drafted into the army at the beginning of the war, while she stayed behind. In December 1915, her father, who had two imperial German sons-in-law, was charged with treason and deported to Irkutsk. After the October Revolution, Red Army soldiers abducted her husband, who had just returned home, and her sister. She herself fled the estate shortly after.[16]

The local population perceived the massive deportations, which led to a significant long-term change in the regional demographics, as something unimaginable, as refugee trails of apocalyptic proportions moved through the countryside.[17] A peasant woman recounted that Jews 'ran as if into Babylonian slavery',[18] while their property was seized by soldiers and townspeople. As Lipschitz pointed out, Jewish evacuees did not regard themselves as 'refugees', because they had not chosen to flee but had instead been expelled by force.[19]

During the course of 1915, the German army pushed on as far as the river Daugava, where the front stabilised for the following two years. While retreating through Courland and Kovno provinces, the Russian army evicted members of the Latvian and Lithuanian intelligentsia along with skilled workers, resulting in a massive depopulation of the cities.[20] The German offensive uprooted hundreds of thousands of people who abandoned their homes out of fear of violence from the advancing troops. At first they too tried to stay as close to home as possible, seeking shelter with relatives or simply in nearby forests, where they waited until it was safe to return home, not wanting to abandon farmsteads and harvests to looters. In Kaišiadorys, between Kaunas and Vilnius, only the landless peasants fled, while most landowners decided to stay.[21] Many people thus did not join the long columns of refugees, but rather retreated no more than a few kilometres.[22] Fifteen thousand peasants from the Suvalkija region fled to Vilnius, waiting for news that it was safe enough to return home.[23] When it turned out that the German army would not be pushed out of Suvalkija in a hurry, many peasants, anxious about what would happen to their land and cattle, tried to make their way through the Russian and German positions, but were usually arrested by Russian soldiers.[24]

The main refugee crisis happened further away from the front, where thousands of refugees and deportees often waited in a single locality to receive food and information about the possibility of returning home, frequently without any indication of whether their home was still under

Russian rule or already occupied by the German army. Wealthier people managed to stay in towns, closer to relief points, while poorer refugees had to stay in the countryside, regularly sleeping in fields or forests. Locals were often reluctant to help, because they feared that refugees carried contagious diseases.[25] A Baltic German reported that the road from Kūldiga to Jelgava was filled with exhausted refugees and livestock.[26] By summer, the number of people on the move and those who were waiting to see what would happen had multiplied. Around 150,000 refugees had passed through Oshmyany (Vilnius province) by September 1915, and some 5,000 refugees were leaving Kovno and Courland provinces via Daugavpils every day. There were reports of up to 20,000 people living in the forest of Rudninkai, south of Vilnius. In addition, 30,000 refugees roamed the districts of Kuronis, Daršūniškis and Pakuonis, 16,000 in Jeznas district, 3,000 in Naujadvaris, and 10,000 in the districts of Eišiškės, Trakai and Valkininkai.[27]

Refugees who reached a place of safety were viewed with a mixture of compassion, suspicion and curiosity. They brought news from the front when all other channels of communication had broken down. In Riga, the Tatiana committee urged refugees to report acts of violence against civilians perpetrated by the German army, so that 'the barbarity and insidiousness of the enemy can be pinned down for future historical depictions'.[28] Peasants from Suvalkija pressed newly arrived refugees for news about the damage caused to their home region and about epidemic diseases.[29] The inhabitants of Illūkste in Courland province learned from refugees who fled Jelgava that the Germans had placed mines at the outskirts of the town.[30] Sometimes refugees contributed to the spreading of sensationalist rumours, in turn causing other refugees to try to make it back to their farms. Refugees reported that the Germans were allegedly threatening all those who abandoned their farms with confiscation of their land, which would then be handed over to German colonists.[31] As the German army made its way further into Lithuania and Courland in summer 1915, refugees from the region around Kaunas reported on alleged German plans to unite Prussian and Russian Lithuania along with Latvia into a single Kingdom.[32]

When Riga, the largest and by far the most economically important city in the region, was evacuated in autumn 1915 along with its main factories, 96,000 workers were forced to retreat with the army.[33] The Livonian industry was also evacuated in anticipation of a further German advance. When the offensive came to a halt just before Riga, almost 35,000 refugees remained in the city and a further 120,000 in

Livland.³⁴ By October 1915, Riga had become a huge hub, distributing tens of thousands of refugees to the adjacent provinces and inner Russia, as the *Rigasche Zeitung* reported:

> The majority are still in Riga and besiege the police offices to receive new passports, as they left their old ones at home or lost them on the way, or because they want to obtain a second one for free, knowing that a 'real' passport is a well-paid commodity in Russia … The rush for the municipal savings bank has become so immense that 145 persons set up their sleeping place on the street after the gates closed, in order to be the first ones to be admitted next morning.³⁵

Refugee policies in Ober Ost, 1915–18

When German soldiers advanced into Lithuania and Courland, they encountered a desolate landscape. Roughly one third of the Lithuanian population and fully two thirds of the population of Courland province had been forced into the Russian interior.³⁶ Three quarters of the population had already left Kaunas when they heard of the advancing German army.³⁷ Many of them fled to Vilnius (Vilna), only to find that 200,000 local residents were awaiting evacuation. Thieves plundered or occupied abandoned houses.³⁸ As Vejas Liulevicius has pointed out, German soldiers and the administrators of Ober Ost perceived the sick and bedraggled refugees and residents alike as characteristic of the entire region.³⁹

To be sure, the German administration acknowledged that the Baltic region had been transformed by displacement. They calculated that a mere 2.9 million people were left in the territory of Ober Ost, as opposed to 4.2 million inhabitants before the war. The administration introduced a number of symptomatic measures aimed at reviving an economy that felt the effects of the 'evacuation' of skilled workers, farmhands and estate owners. Residents in Kaunas were hired to guard the property of deportees.⁴⁰ Special units of 'house guards' were established in Vilnius to look after houses at night time.⁴¹ Peasants were put in charge of cultivating the small holdings abandoned by their neighbours. Large and profitable estates of the Baltic German gentry in Courland, as well as of the Polish gentry in Lithuania, were given to German officers.⁴²

It took more than half a year to resettle the majority of refugees within Ober Ost territory. In autumn 1915, 20,000 Jewish refugees from Courland and Kovno province were still in Vilnius along with 10,000 refugees from other localities.⁴³ An initial order went out on 13 October for these refugees to return home within twelve days, provided their homes were intact, but it was a sign of the times that several months later at least 7,000 refugees still remained in the city, most of them professional people.[44] The military administration relied heavily on national relief committees, which reflected the multi-ethnic composition of Vilnius, where a Polish Refugee Relief Committee worked alongside a Jewish Relief Committee, a Lithuanian Society for War Relief and a municipal evacuation commission.[45] By May, the number of refugees in Vilnius finally dropped to 1,500.[46]

The first wave of repatriations – mostly of Baltic Germans – from Russia to Courland took place in autumn 1917 after German troops had managed to cross the Daugava and occupy Riga. In October, the *Libausche Zeitung* reported that refugees used the chaos among the dissolving Russian army to return home, where they encountered the improvised and opaque Ober Ost administration of abandoned properties and its misappropriation by 'disloyal people, relatives, friends and former servants … even foreign usurpers', who had ruined the farms.[47]

Systematic repatriation finally became possible with the signing of the peace treaty of Brest-Litovsk in March 1918, which envisaged the exchange of refugees and POWs and the establishment of (formally) independent states. The fledgling Lithuanian national government immediately demanded that the German military administration revoke its notorious restrictions on movement that hindered commerce and economic organisation and hampered arrangements for repatriation. Meanwhile, two trains were expected to run weekly via Riga, Daugavpils and Minsk into Ober Ost in order to repatriate refugees.

The peculiar and rigorous movement policy (*Verkehrspolitik*), which was enforced by sealed internal borders within Ober Ost, posed a significant obstacle for returnees. Aleksandras Stulginskis, head of the Lithuanian repatriation commission and future President of Lithuania, argued that repatriates were unaccustomed with German occupation policy and demanded that all restrictions should be removed.[48] In April 1918, the Taryba (Lithuanian Council) proposed organising repatriation on its own account and enlisting local Lithuanian committees, unhindered by the Ober Ost authorities. The Taryba took the line that only refugees 'from Lithuania' should be repatriated, but left open whether this meant ethnic Lithuanians only.[49]

The Brest-Litovsk system finally 'nationalised' the question of repatriation. Before March 1918, the national aspect of the refugee question had been restricted to the work of national relief associations working with refugees in Ober Ost and inner Russia. Now, the connection of repatriation to newly independent states in the former borderlands turned it into a powerful tool for German imperialists as well as providing an opportunity for national activists to impart a national character to territory and population. The German administration was reluctant to return estates close to the German border to their owners, whom the German military had taken hostage as reprisals for the 'evacuation' of Baltic Germans at the beginning of the war.[50]

Courland rapidly became an imperial project. The increasing conviction among conservatives that the region should be annexed to the German Empire meant that the new border with Bolshevik Russia would need to be closed to returning refugees of ethnic Latvian origin.[51] The treaty of Brest-Litovsk included a clause that stated that only Latvians currently residing in Courland could gain citizenship, thus preventing a return of Latvian refugees and shifting the demography in favour of the Baltic Germans – a plan already discussed in early 1917.[52]

The significance of these imperial plans for Latvia's national future was reflected in partly sympathetic and partly derogative views of their unfortunate neighbours held by Lithuanian and Estonian nationalists, who alleged that Latvia's development had been cut short by the refugee crisis and German occupation policies. An Estonian national activist claimed in the *Neue Zürcher Zeitung* that the devastations of the war had

> damaged Latvia and the Latvian people to such an extent, that the consequences cannot even be measured. The sticking point is whether the national-Latvian culture will have the possibility of developing any further at all ... The longer the war continues, the fewer the number of evacuees and refugees who will return, and Germany will want to settle the conquered region with German colonists.[53]

In 1918, the Jewish-Latvian Social Democrat Alexander Lipschütz said the German government intended to colonise Courland by keeping its Latvian inhabitants out, by force if necessary. However, Lipschütz claimed that the return of Latvian refugees was the necessary prerequisite for any plans to ally a future Latvian state with Germany, lest the Baltics otherwise become 'a new Balkan peninsula'.[54]

After the sudden German defeat in November 1918, the Latvian Provisional National Council (*Latviešu Pagaidu Nacionālā Padome*) declared all annexation plans void, and claimed it was the only legitimate authority to solve repatriation until all Latvian refugees had returned.[55]

Repatriation polices of the new nation states after 1918

With Germany's defeat in the west, the system of Brest-Litovsk collapsed, and the responsibility for repatriation at last fell into the hands of national activists. Repatriation remained complicated, as the Eastern Front, which had been peaceful since March 1918, became a zone of power vacuums that different emerging states aimed to fill. Over the course of 1919, the Red Army advanced deep into Latvia and Lithuania, opposed by national units as well as German Freikorps and White Guards, which obstructed the organised transport and support of returnees.[56] At the same time, these wars resulted in new refugee crises, as Russians fleeing the Bolsheviks poured into Latvia. On a smaller scale, the Lithuanian-Polish conflict over the Vilnius region also led to further refugee crises. Continuing warfare and food requisitions conducted by all competing factions – Germans, Lithuanians, Latvians and Poles – made it difficult to provide for returnees who had no land to reclaim. The nascent Lithuanian authorities demanded that German officials impose a monopoly on trade in food to prevent its export from Ober Ost and urged that a proper inventory of refugee estates be maintained to prevent unauthorised sales.[57]

Returnees who owned land outside the area of conflict could be repatriated quickly, but those who lived in the war zone or whose property had been expropriated or taken over by squatters often had to spend months in temporary housing or in quarantine camps established in 1919 and 1920. The worst conditions prevailed in the region stretching from central Latvia to eastern Lithuania, which had formed the Russo-German front line for more than two years. Here most homes and farm buildings had been destroyed, and the returnees lived in dugouts, basements and trenches. Three years after the German defeat, some 2,000 repatriates had no other option but to occupy former trenches in the town of Smarhon (Smorgon) near Grodno, now being fought over by opposing forces in the Polish-Soviet war.[58] A similar situation prevailed in Ikšķile, where the Latvian Riflemen had defended a small island in the river Daugava (later called *Nāves sala* – the 'Island of death') for six months. After visiting the area, a worker for the organisation Save the Children recounted:

> Nearly all the houses are completely destroyed, over an area covering several hundred miles, and the people are living in dug-outs, and temporary wooden huts, one of these built by two boys of 14 and 16 years for their mother and sister. Close by, I saw two men piling together stones to make a house, one can hardly say build, and I congratulated them that they would

have a roof over their heads for the winter, and they replied 'it is not for ourselves, but for our cows'. They showed me where they were living underground, like other families.[59]

Refugees belonging to minorities-in-the-making had the greatest difficulty reclaiming land. Around 500 Russians who had bought land in a colony near Vilnius in the late nineteenth century returned to their homes, only to find that the German occupation authorities had sold their land to various buyers. Unable to reclaim their plots, they were forced to live in sheds. Many such returnees contracted with typhus, leading to at least a dozen deaths. Vilnius became a gathering point for many more returnees who could not move into their former homes. A health commission appointed by the Polish parliament reported that refugees 'absolutely do not know what to do with themselves or where to go, so for the time being they are staying at the *étape*, and when they are evicted almost with physical force, they probably suffer the same fate as the [erstwhile] inhabitants of the trenches'.[60]

Ethnic conflict between Poles and Lithuanians in the Vilnius region further complicated the process of repatriation. At the same time, the increasing control and impermeability of the new borders perpetuated the status quo of displacement. Lithuanian refugees from Ukraine who attempted to enter Lithuania from the south became stranded in Vilnius. The Polish administration blamed the Lithuanian authorities, who allegedly refused to grant these refugees passports, thus forcing Polish officials to provide the refugees with food. Lithuanian officials in turn complained that the Polish authorities were using repatriation as a means of ethnic homogenisation, in so far as they barred Lithuanians and Belarusians from returning to the Vilnius and Grodno regions and prevented Jews from coming back at all.[61] Belarusian activists complained that the Polish army, which now occupied the eastern parts of Ober Ost vacated by the retreating Germans, deliberately pushed returnees into Bolshevik Russia, where civil war raged.[62] Belarusian refugees from the Białystok and Grodno regions, now part of the Polish republic, found that their farms had been given to Polish soldiers.[63] According to Lithuanian nationalists, the Polish government was polonising Vilnius by sending Poles from Warsaw and other cities there under the guise of being refugees from the Vilnius region.[64]

In order to organise repatriation, but also to deal with the new waves of refugees from Bolshevik Russia, the emerging Lithuanian and Latvian states established refugee camps at their borders. Latvia set up quarantine stations in Rēzekne and Daugavpils. As the border between Poland and Lithuania was closed, the Latvian and Lithuanian governments signed a treaty in 1921, which stipulated that Lithuanian repatriates also had to pass through the Latvian stations before they reached Obeliai, the main quarantine station on Lithuanian territory.[65] For similar reasons, refugees from the Vilnius region had to pass through Polish-administered quarantine stations in Baranaviči (Baranovichi) and Smarhon.[66] The purpose of these stations was not only to prevent the spread of epidemic diseases, but also to screen refugees for 'dangerous' political views and to ascertain their nationality. The Latvian-Soviet and Lithuanian-Soviet peace treaties of 1920 specified that only refugees who could prove that they had been registered in the territory of the new states before the First World War could become citizens.[67] In practice, however, as Tomas Balkelis has shown in the case of Lithuania, refugees confirmed as ethnically Lithuanian had a significantly higher chance of being repatriated than others: whereas only 27 per cent of all applicants were Lithuanians, they formed 60 per cent of all those allowed to return. On the other hand, Jews made up 30 per cent of all applicants but accounted for only 11 per cent of total returnees.[68]

Around 245,000 Lithuanian refugees managed to return in 1918 and 1919, and another 345,000 returned before 1924. Around 185,000 refugees could not or did not want to return at all.[69] Some 85 per cent of all Lithuanians returned to the new republic, but only 70 per cent of all Poles, 50 per cent of all Jews, and fewer than 40 per cent of Russians.[70] In the south of the disintegrating Ober Ost, subsequently part of interwar Poland, the British relief mission to Poland estimated in 1919 that no more than 20 per cent of the pre-war population was still living there and that only half could be expected to return.[71]

The new states made significant efforts to get back those people whom they considered part of the new titular nations. In June 1919, the Latvian Committee for Refugee Relief in Ekaterinodar complained that many of the 10,000 Latvian refugees in southern Russia had been drafted into the white armies, although they should have been considered citizens of Latvia in accordance with the de facto recognition of the state by the western powers. The committee made it clear that these refugees were needed to strengthen the Latvian army.[72] On the other hand, wealthier Baltic Germans found it difficult to enter the new state, often being charged high sums for making the journey from Rēzekne to the Latvian interior. One returnee reported that he and fellow Baltic Germans were only issued provisional residence permits, which they could only exchange for passports after paying an exorbitant fee: 'we had not expected such a welcome in our home country'.[73]

Initially, because Latvia and Lithuania refused to allow non-Latvian and non-Lithuanian citizens to transit their territories, thousands of refugees from Bolshevik Russia were stranded at the Latvian quarantine stations. Konstantin Arabazhin, a Russian nobleman from Poltava, came to Latvia to escape the Russian civil war. In January 1921 he urged Russians to commit to the new Latvian state: 'It is time to carry on, to begin with constructive, honest work on the creation of a class of citizens and the preservation of Russian culture. We have every possibility to do that. We are not refugees; we, the Russians, are present here in all social layers'. But there was much work to be done to secure the future of Russians as a national minority in a nationally fragmented order: 'We do not even know how many of us there are in Latvia, who we are, what we are, what we occupy ourselves with, in what condition of health the Russian population is, how big their power and knowledge for creative and productive work are – we don't know anything about ourselves'.[74]

In fact, the Russian community in Latvia at this point was almost 40 per cent smaller than it had been before the war.[75] Thousands of Russian refugees waited at the border, where they received emergency supplies from local relief groups and international associations such as Save the Children. By summer 1921, the situation in Daugavpils had become so hopeless that Russian refugees began to return to famine-struck Russia, 'convinced that they are more likely to perish if they remain', wrote Muriel Paget, director of Save the Children in the Baltic region.[76] The war that had raged at the gates of the city turned Daugavpils into a wasteland, reducing its population from 250,000 before the war to 30,000 in 1922. Most houses had neither windows nor roofs, and flooding had exacerbated the terrible housing conditions.[77] Nonetheless, refugees kept pouring in, many of them starving and in very poor health.[78] For refugees without knowledge of Latvian, it was close to impossible to find work, and families with children often shared massively overpriced rooms without furniture.[79]

Due to the closed Lithuanian-Polish border and the rigid Latvian policies against Russian refugees in Rēzekne and Daugavpils, Lithuania never suffered the same refugee crisis as Latvia. Relatively few Russian refugees found their way into the repatriation camp established near Obeliai in December 1920, five months after the Soviet-Lithuanian peace treaty had provided for the exchange of refugees. Transit through the camp gathered speed, after a mere 2,114 repatriates registered in January 1921;

a total of 42,859 refugees were registered in Obeliai as of August 1921. Lithuanians formed the largest group with 13,032, closely followed by 12,081 Jews. Russians comprised the third largest group at 5,217. Fewer than 1,000 Poles were registered, along with 500 Belarusians. The Ministry of Defence complained that refugees had wildly different papers, with some arriving only with blank documents. In May 1921, the Lithuanian Ministry for Interior Affairs ruled that refugees in Russia had to register in provincial or district centres with proper documents, either old passports, registration slips issued by the Russian imperial police, or new passports issued by refugee relief committees in Russia. Alternatively, relatives who had stayed in Lithuania could attest to their identity. If none of this applied, they would be regarded as citizens of Russia.[80] This excluded from repatriation a large number of refugees who had no family in Lithuania.

Refugees who could not provide proper documents or did not meet the criteria for Lithuanian citizenship were declared 'undesirable', unless they had professional skills classified as 'productive' by the Foreign Ministry. Already under German occupation, the Taryba favoured skilled workers over people who were 'not occupying themselves with any productive work' with regards to repatriation.[81] At 10 per cent of the total, skilled workers did indeed form the largest group of people granted permits to stay in Lithuania, whereas farmhands and merchants accounted for only 5 per cent between them. Particularly exposed were repatriates who had worked in the tsarist administration as teachers, Orthodox priests, writers, accountants, estate economists and estate supervisors: they were declared 'undesirable'.[82] Most of them were Russians, who rarely received permits for return. In late summer 1921, the situation of Russian refugees in the camps became so dire that the Ministry of the Interior considered granting them temporary residence permits.[83] But Lithuanian newspapers reported that gangs of criminal Russians operated in the Obeliai camp, and this did nothing to persuade public opinion of the plight of ordinary Russians.[84]

Jewish organisations who tried to help refugees get into Lithuania – mostly from Bolshevik Russia, but also from pogrom-ravaged Ukraine – were frequently accused of bringing ever more 'unproductive elements' into the country. This was the case with international organisations such as the Comité Executive de la Conférence Universelle Juive de Secours (Jewish World Relief Conference), which helped refugees from Ukraine and southern Russia to settle in neighbouring countries.[85] In addition, the Lithuanian Ministry of Jewish Affairs, which employed a special plenipotentiary to contact all Jewish repatriates at all refugee camps in order to provide social, religious and legal assistance was, from the outset, regarded as working not merely in favour of Jews, but also to the detriment of Lithuanians.[86] One employee of the ministry was criminally prosecuted for trying to get as many Jewish refugees as possible (including those considered 'undesirable' by the Lithuanian government) from Latvia via Obeliai into Lithuania. The Lithuanian plenipotentiary in Rēzekne stated that this Jewish official had 'never learned how a Lithuanian should love his fatherland; I cannot stand such people, who constantly blather about the honour of the fatherland and its wellbeing but harm it in all kinds of ways behind its back'.[87] Mirroring similar grievances in other parts of east central Europe, the Lithuanian government considered the dedicated food rations given by international organisations and the Ministry for Jewish Affairs to Jewish refugees as not conducive to maintaining harmony between Jews and Lithuanian refugees who suffered from malnutrition.[88] In 1921–22, the opposition frequently attacked the Lithuanian government for letting too many Jews into the country.[89] On the other hand, supply points organised by local Jewish organisations to feed refugees from the Vilnius region were often praised by the Lithuanian army as reliable suppliers.[90]

Attempts to use repatriation to achieve an ethnically more homogenous country corresponded quite closely to the strategies employed in south-eastern Europe and the former Ottoman Empire (see chapter 14). Nationalisation was designed to disentangle populations allegedly mixed together by imperial policies. The absence of large numbers of refugees at the Lithuanian border enabled the government and the local authorities to homogenise formerly multi-ethnic towns such as Tauragė, a town with a population of 14,000 before the war, which had been almost completely destroyed during the advance of the German army. Some 1,500 refugees who returned in the second half of 1918 had begun to build huts in the outskirts of the town. As district chief Stanislovas Kuizinas recounted later:

> From a national perspective, this was a mass which you could form into whatever you wanted. And before the war, this had been a real Babel, because real Lithuanians lived in the city [along with] Polonised Lithuanians, Germanised Lithuanians, Russians, Jews, Germans, Russophile Jews and Germanised Jews and all those mixed peoples that we connect with trade and smuggling. The occupying power had wanted to Germanise a significant part of the population for good ... The refugees returning from Russia, however, were influenced by the spirit of Russification and Bolshevisation. We had to work steadily and diligently to explain the idea of the declaration

of independence, its meaning and its necessity and also its usefulness. Thus we toiled from early morning until night-time; after all, we had to make Lithuanians of all this mass of people.[91]

The practice of distributing people to those parts of Lithuania where land was available was not always welcomed by the returnees, who included people of Lithuanian origin who had been exiled long before the war and had made a successful, if modest living in Russia. In the early 1920s, a number of families of Lithuanians deported after the Polish uprising of 1863 chose to leave Soviet Russia for Lithuania along with the crowds of returning refugees. After waiting for two years for a permit and having been promised the return of family land that had been seized by the tsarist authorities, they ended up with thousands of war refugees in the camp at Obeliai. Having liquidated their holdings in Russia, they were disappointed to learn that the new government of Lithuania intended to relocate them in unfamiliar districts with poor soil. In 1925, spokesmen for 100 such families complained that their communities had been torn apart in the process of repatriation and they now found it much more difficult to make a living than in Russia.[92]

Moreover, the refugee crisis did not only concern the process of repatriation, it also included the question of how to deal with those refugees already living in the new nation state as a result of the events of the war itself and the new outbreak of fighting between 1918 and 1921. In a report in August 1921, Save the Children reported that that 9,688 people, most of them Russians, from a total of 16,800 refugees currently on Latvian territory had no Latvian passport, making them vulnerable and their future uncertain.[93] In Lithuania, 6,239 people lacked citizenship in 1923, and it is safe to assume that the figure had been significantly higher in 1921.[94]

Conclusion

The refugee crisis of the First World War and ensuing repatriation irrevocably changed the ethnic fabric of Latvia and Lithuania. The share of Jews and Russians in the population slumped significantly, as did the numbers of Baltic Germans in Courland and Poles in Lithuania. This was a result not only of deportation but also of the politics of repatriation. The pronounced congruence of ethnicity and social function in imperial Russian society meant that all ethnic groups were affected to differing degrees by the refugee crisis. Under Ober Ost, the German military occupation strongly differentiated between Lithuanians and Latvians, perceiving Courland to be an ideal territorial addition to the empire, thus preventing the repatriation of displaced Latvians. After the Armistice in November 1918, repatriation gained momentum, while at the same time new refugee crises emerged, with refugees of the Russian civil war trying to pass through Latvia and Polish-Lithuanian (para-)military clashes displacing the population at the new border.

The refugee crisis and both imperial and national repatriation policies are crucial when looking at the transformation from an imperial to a national order. Lithuania and Latvia not only had different borders and different governments after the war, but also different populations. Repatriation was not merely a reaction to expulsions, but a policy with its own strategic purpose, with aims that went far beyond a return to the status quo ante 1914. In the case of Courland, the repatriation policy of Ober Ost turned the region into an imperial project, which aimed at transforming it into a German colony by barring Latvians from returning to their 'empty' homeland. Post-war national repatriation policies aimed to resettle as many Latvians and Lithuanians as possible, while preventing refugees from other regions – particularly Russians fleeing the civil war – from entering the territory. At the same time, refugees originating from Lithuania and Latvia could be kept outside the borders if the group they were ascribed to was allegedly 'unproductive' or opposed to the empowerment of the new titular nationality. This meant that although the logic of how people became refugees (because the Russian imperial authorities considered them disloyal) was similar to the logic according to which refugees were barred from repatriation (because they were considered disloyal towards the new titular nations), its different inflections meant that repatriation could and was not intended to 'right' the 'wrongs' of 1914–15. Repatriation thus contributed significantly to the fundamental political, social and economic changes wrought in the Baltic region at the end of the war.

Notes

1 'Memorandum', Lietuvos centrinis valstybės archyvas (LCVA), undated, f. 1129, ap. 1, b. 32, l. 23–30, here l. 26; Monographie über die ökonomische Lage der litauischen Juden, May 1920, LCVA, f. 1129, ap. 1, b. 32, l. 31–44 a.p., here l. 35; 'Memorandum', 12 November 1923, LCVA, f. 1129, ap. 1, b. 32, l. 17–22, here p. 19.
2 'Latvija', *Trimitas*, 33 (1921), pp. 19–25.

3 Peter Gatrell, *The Making of the Modern Refugee* (Oxford: Oxford University Press, 2013), pp. 62–72.
4 Vital' Karnyalyuk, 'Faktary historyka-demahrafičnyh zmen u skladze nasel'nictva Belarusi u 1913–1918 gg.' [Factors in the historical-demographic change in the composition of the population of Belarus in the years 1913–1918], PhD dissertation, State University of Belarus, Minsk, 2001; Tatjana Bartele and Vitālijs Šalda, 'Latviešu bēgļi Petrogradā, 1915–1920' [Latvian refugees in Petrograd, 1915–1920], *Latvijas arhīvi*, 1 (2002), 83–99; Vida Pukienė, 'Voronežas: Lietuvių švietimo židinys Rusijoje Pirmojo pasaulinio karo metais' [Voronezh: the hearth of Lithuanian education in Russia during the First World War], *Istorija. Mokslo darbai*, 70 (2008), 17–27.
5 Aija Priedite, 'Latvian refugees and the Latvian nation state during and after World War One', in Nick Baron and Peter Gatrell (eds), *Homelands: War, Population and Statehood in Eastern Europe and Russia, 1918*–1924 (London: Anthem, 2004), pp. 35–52.
6 Tomas Balkelis, 'The return of World War One refugees to Lithuania', in Baron and Gatrell (eds), *Homelands*, pp. 74–97.
7 Balkelis, 'Return', p. 96.
8 Gatrell, *Making of the Modern Refugee*, p. 3.
9 Eric Lohr, *Nationalizing the Russian Empire: the Campaign against Enemy Aliens During World War 1* (Cambridge, MA: Harvard University Press, 2003), p. 138.
10 Joshua Sanborn, 'The genesis of Russian warlordism: violence and governance during the First World War and the Civil War', *Contemporary European History*, 19, no. 3 (2010), 195–213 (p. 203).
11 *Lietuvos ūkininkas*, 24 July 1915, 189–90; J. Pikčilingis, 'Pergyventos valandos' [The hours survived], *Karo archyvas*, 3 (1926), 90–111; Kauno apskrities archyvas, f. I-50, ap. 2, b. 481, l. 1, 14–31.
12 *Lietuvos ūkininkas*,15 July 1915, p. 215.
13 Flüchtlinge, *Libausche Zeitung*, 6 October 1914.
14 Shaul Lipschitz, 'Jewish communities in Kurland', in M. Bobe et al. (eds), *The Jews in Latvia* (Tel Aviv: Association of Latvian and Estonian Jews in Israel, 1971), pp. 276–84.
15 'Lebenserinnerungen Margarethe von Gersdorff (15.5.1889–9.7.1974) geschrieben von 1955–1969', *Dokumentensammlung Herder Institut*, 140 Balt 617, p. 20; Toivo U. Raun, 'Violence and activism in the Baltic provinces during the revolution of 1905', *Acta Historica Tallinnensia* (2006), 48–59, here p. 50.
16 'Lebenserinnerungen Margarethe von Gersdorff', pp. 20–4.
17 Pikčilingis, 'Pergyventos valandos', p. 104.
18 Ona Gudliauskaitė, 'Biržų apskrities: nuo maro, bado, ugnies ir karo' [Biržai district: of disease, hunger, fire and war], in Petras Ruzeckas (ed.), *Lietuva Didžiajame kare* [Lithuania during the Great War] (Vilnius: Wydawnictwo Vilniaus Žodis, 1939), pp. 259–67.

19 Lipschitz, *Jews of Kurland*.
20 *Lietuvos ūkininkas*, 3 July 1915, p. 162; Daina Bleiere, *History of Latvia: the Twentieth Century* (Riga: Jumava, 2006), pp. 76–7.
21 'Musų pabėgėliai' [Our refugees], *Lietuvos žinios*, 18 February 1915.
22 Nemakščia, Ras. apskr. ['Nemakščia, Raseiniai district'], *Lietuvos žinios*, 25 February 1915.
23 'Musų pabėgėliai', *Lietuvos žinios*, 8 March 1915.
24 'Lietuvių neatsargumas' [Lithuanian carelessness], *Šaltinis* 7–14 (1915).
25 'Musų pabėgėliai', *Lietuvos žinios*, 18 February 1915.
26 'Als deutscher Balte aus Sibirien nach Libau', *Libausche Zeitung*, 26 October 1915.
27 'Karo aukų globojimas' [Reflief for war victims], *Lietuvos žinios*, 18 September 1915.
28 'Rigaer Kriegschronik', *Rigasche Zeitung*, 25 May 1918.
29 'Vokiečiai Lietuvoje' [The Germans in Lithuania], *Šaltinis* 17–18 (1915), 123–5; 'Užkrečiamosios ligos ir kova su jomis' [Contagious diseases and how to fight them], *Šaltinis*, 19–20 (1915), p. 130.
30 'Auf dem Südufer der Düna', *Libausche Zeitung*, 1 January 1916.
31 'Vokiečių nežmoniškumas' [The inhumanity of the Germans], *Šaltinis*, 29 (1915).
32 'Dar apie teikiamąjį Lietuvai karalių' [More on giving Lithuania a king], *Šaltinis* 30 (1915).
33 Paul Bräunlich, *Kurländischer Frühling: Persönliche Eindrücke* (Berlin: Verlag der Täglichen Rundschau, 1917); Priedite, 'Latvian refugees', p. 37.
34 'Rigaer Kriegschronik', *Rigasche Zeitung*, 4 October 1918.
35 'Rigaer Kriegschronik', *Rigasche Zeitung*, 9 August 1918.
36 Georg von Rauch, *The Baltic States: the Years of Independence: Estonia, Latvia, Lithuania, 1917–1940* (London: Hurst, 1987), p. 25; Vejas Gabriel Liulevicius, *Warland on the Eastern Front: Culture, National Identity and German Occupation in World War I* (Cambridge: Cambridge University Press, 2000), pp. 19–20.
37 Marius Pečiulis, 'Pirmojo pasaulinio karo veiksmai vakarų Lietuvoje – Vokietijos ir Rusijos pasienyje – 1915 m. pradžioje', *Karo archyvas*, 26 (2011), 44–80; Theodore S. Weeks, 'Vilnius in World War I, 1914–1920', in Joachim Tauber (ed.), *Über den Weltkrieg hinaus: Kriegserfahrungen in Ostmitteleuropa, 1914–1921* (Lüneburg: Nordost-Archiv, 2009), pp. 34–57, here p. 39.
38 *Lietuvos ūkininkas*, 15 July 1915; *Lietuvos ūkininkas*, 24 June 1915.
39 Liulevicius, *Warland*, pp. 89–90.
40 Pikčilingis, 'Pergyventos valandos', p. 104.
41 'Bekanntmachung vom 29. November 1911', Martyno Mažvydo Biblioteka (MMB), UDK 351. 74.
42 Wiktor Sukiennicki, *East Central Europe During World War I* (Boulder: East European Monographs, 1984), p. 157.

43 'Lokales', *Libausche Zeitung*, 14 October 1915.
44 'Bekanntmachung vom 13. Oktober 1915', MMB, UDK 351.74; 'Aus dem besetzten Gebiet', *Libausche Zeitung*, 7 February 1916.
45 'Bekanntmachung vom 12. Januar 1916', MMB, UDK 325.1 (474.5).
46 'Aus dem besetzten Gebiet', *Libausche Zeitung*, 15 May 1916.
47 'Aus dem besetzten Gebiet', *Libausche Zeitung*, 11 October 1917.
48 'Taryba an Chef der Militärverwaltung Litauen', 18 May 1918, LCVA, f. 1014, ap. 1, b. 16, l. 8.
49 'Kommission der Taryba für Rückführung, geleitet von A. Stulginskis an die Militärverwaltung Litauen', 15 April 1918, LCVA, f. 1014, ap. 1, b. 16, l. 6–7.
50 'Tatbestand über die Angelegenheit des Grafen W. v. Polenta-Wolmer, Grossgrundbesitzer von Wiesajcie/Litauen', 2 August 1918, Archiwum Akt Nowych (AAN), 473, sygn. 21, pp. 181–3.
51 Karl-Heinz Jassen, 'Die baltische Okkupationspolitik des Deutschen Reiches', in Jürgen von Hehn et al. (eds), *Von den Baltischen Provinzen zu den Baltischen Staate: Beiträge zur Entstehungsgeschichte der Republiken Estland und Lettland 1917–1918* (Marburg: Herder Institut, 1971), pp. 217–54 (here p. 227).
52 'Rückwanderungen', 31 March 1917, Bundesarchiv, R 704/50, pp. 12–15.
53 'Lettische Gegenwarts- und Zukunftsfragen', *Neue Zürcher Zeitung*, 24 March 1916.
54 'Germany and the Baltic provinces', press cutting, *Vorwärts*, 22 April 1918, Estonian National Archives (Rahvusarhiivi), 1583. 1. 174.
55 'Der Protest des Lettischen Nationalrats gegen die Annexion Kurlands', in *Dokumente und Materialien zur ostmitteleuropäischen Geschichte: Themenmodul Lettland in der Zwischenkriegszeit* www.herder-institut.de/no_cache/bestaende-digitale-angebote/e-publikationen/dokumente-und-materialien/themenmodule/quelle/901/details.html [accessed 18 July 2016].
56 'Polnische Flüchtlinge in Libau', *Libausche Zeitung*, 26 July 1920.
57 'An Seine Exzellenz, den Herrn Chef der Zivilverwaltung für Litauen', 18 November 1918, LCVA, f. 392, ap. 1, t. 2, b. 76, l. 2.
58 'Sprawozdanie dla Sejmowej Komisji Zdrowia', 29 November 1921, AAN, 15, sygn. 90, p. 14.
59 'Muriel Paget to Mr Golden', 4 July 1921, Cadbury Research Library, Save the Children Fund (CRL/SCF), A401, EJ 73.
60 'Sprawozdanie dla Sejmowej Komisji Zdrowia', pp. 15–16.
61 Balkelis, 'Return', p. 90.
62 'Gudų memorandumas' [Belarusian memorandum], *Karys*, 6 October 1921, p. 474.
63 'Žinios iš okupuotojo krašto', *Trimitas*, 50 (1921), p. 36.
64 'Ruošiasi apsispręsti' [Preparing for a decision], *Karys*, 25 November 1920, p. 444.

65 'Dogovor mezhdu Litvoi i Latviei o perevozke litovskikh bezhentsev cherez territoriiu Latvii ot granitsy Rossii do granitsy Litvy' (Riga, 22 iiulia 1921g.)', in Pranas Dailidė (ed.), *Lietuvos sutartys su svetimomis valstybėmis, 1919–1929* (Kaunas: Užsienio reikalų ministerijos leidinys, 1930).
66 'Do Pana Ministra Zdrowia Publicznego i Naczelnego Nadzwyczajnego Komisarza w miejscu', 16 January 1922, AAN, 15, sygn. 90, p. 21; Emigracja, 1922, AAN, 15, sygn. 1654, p. 21.
67 'Latvia and Russia. Treaty of Peace, done at Moscow, and completed and signed at Riga, August 11, 1920', *League of Nations Treaty Series 67*, p. 218. [www.worldlii.org/int/other/LNTSer/1920/63.html]; Lithuania and Soviet Government of Russia. Peace Treaty and Protocol, signed at Moscow, July 12, 1920, League of Nations Treaty Series 94, p. 127 [www.worldlii.org/int/other/LNTSer/1920/2.html].
68 Balkelis, 'Return', pp. 83–4.
69 Priedite, 'Latvian refugees', p. 49.
70 Balkelis, 'Return', p. 92.
71 Reports on the districts of Volkovysk, Pinsk, Slonim, Grodno, 3 May 1919, The National Archives, UK, FO 608/223/11.
72 'Comité letton de secours aux réfugiés en Ekatérinodar', 13 June 1919, The National Archives, UK, FO 608/203/28, p. 539.
73 'Unbillige Behandlung von Flüchtlingen aus Russland', *Rigasche Rundschau*, 30 March 1921.
74 K.I. Arabazhin, 'Nezavisimost' Latvii i russkoe naselenie', *Segodnya*, 31 January 1921
75 'Latvija', *Trimitas*, 33 (1921), p. 22.
76 'Muriel Paget to Mr Golden, 4 July 1921', CRF/SCF, A401, EJ 73.
77 'Latvia', 21 April 1922, CRF/ SCF, A401, EJ 70.
78 'Monthly Report, Dvinsk Welfare Centre, 30 November 1921', CRF/SCF, A401, EJ 72.
79 'Paget Mission Latvia, Monthly Report, Dvinsk Welfare Centre', 31 December 1921, CRF/ SCF, A401, EJ 72.
80 'Vidaus Reikalų Ministerijai', 10 May 1921, LCVA, f. 377, ap. 5, b. 9, l. 43.
81 'Kommission der Taryba für Rückführung, geleitet von A. Stulginskis an die Militärverwaltung Litauen', 15 April 1918, LCVA, f. 1014, ap. 1, b. 16, l. 6–7.
82 Pranas Baronas, 'Obelių karantinas 1919 metais', *Istorija*, 57 (2003), 45–50.
83 'Užsienių Reikalų Min-jos Europos Centro Departamentui', 13 August 1921, LCVA, f. 383, ap. 7, b. 216, l. 7.
84 'Obeliai', *Darbininkas*, 12 January 1922.
85 'Conférence universelle juive de secours, Paris 1924; Comité Executive de la Conférence Universelle Juive de Secours to the Cabinet of Ministers', 16 September 1921, LCVA, f. 377, ap. 5, b. 10, l. 1.
86 'Instruktsii o pravakh i funktsiiakh polnomochennykh ENS na Litve po delam reevakuatsii bezhentsev', 1921, LCVA, f. 1129, ap. 1, b. 49, l. 36–7.

87 'Prano Daugirdo pranešimas', 14 July 1921, LCVA, f. 377, ap. 5, b. 12, l. 87.
88 'Makausko byla', 6 August 1921, LCVA, f. 377, ap. 5, b. 12, l. 78-80; 'Šidlauskaitės pranešimas', 29 July 1921, LCVA, f. 377, ap. 5, b. 12, l. 81-3. See also Rebecca Kobrin, *Jewish Białystok and its Diaspora* (Bloomington: Indiana University Press, 2010), p. 142.
89 Balkelis, 'Return', p. 91.
90 'Žydų Reikalų Ministerija, spaudos skyriaus žinios', 1920, LCVA, f. 1129, ap. 1, b. 45, l. 143.
91 'Pirmasis kariuomenės paradas Žemaičiuose'[The first military parade in Žemaitija], *Karys*, 16 February 1928, pp. 149-51, here p. 149.
92 'Prašymas. Nuog. tremt. 1863 metu grižusijų iš Rusijos 1922 met. Lapkričio men. iš 100 Šeimynu, apsigivenusijų: Kedainių, Rokiškio, Utenos, Biržų - Pasvalio, Šaulių, Šakių, Vilkavyškio ir Maryampolio apskričiose', 25 March 1925, LCVA, f. 392, ap. 1, t. 3, b. 2201, l. 384-5.
93 Report Concerning Russian Refugees in Latvia, 18 August 1921, CRL, SCF, A401, EJ 77.
94 *Statistikos biuletenis*, 1 (1923), p. 14.

3

Refugees from Polish territories in Russia during the First World War

Mariusz Korzeniowski

Introduction

Warfare on Polish soil in 1914–15 caused huge material losses, as well as the impoverishment and deprivation of the local population.[1] The war also led to mass displacement, much of it involuntary, involving people living in the territories of the Kingdom of Poland, a constituent part of the Russian Empire, and in Galicia, belonging to Austria-Hungary. Migration began in the first weeks of the war but acquired a mass character only in the latter half of 1915. The exodus of civilians was prompted by the actions of the Russian military. At the beginning of June 1915, General Nikolai Ivanov, Commander-in-Chief of Russia's South-Western Front which now extended into Austria-Hungary, ordered the expulsion of all Galician peasant men of military service age, along with their families, to the Russian interior. The Russian occupation regime also decided to deprive Galicia of the entirety of its stock, crops and livestock. These orders were subsequently extended to the North-Western Front which ran across the Kingdom of Poland, leading directly to the forced migration of the population from this area.

The scale of the exodus exceeded the expectations of the decision-makers who, under the pressure of Polish public opinion, sought – to no avail – to limit the scale and the negative consequences of this migration, which increased with every day of the Russian retreat, as well as the enormity of the damage caused by the military operations and the scorched earth tactics employed by the Russians.[2] The fate of the people, as well as the likeliness of saving the property, crops and livestock from being destroyed, depended on how individual commanders interpreted the orders they received.[3] It is worth adding that the delayed revocation of some orders by the Russian High Command may have been an attempt to create the impression that its 'orders were misunderstood and misapplied by the authorities here [i.e. in the Kingdom of Poland]'.[4]

Exodus

Capturing the onset of this mass migration of civilians into the interior of Russia is extremely difficult, as eye-witness accounts and memoirs are not numerous. The conclusion reached by Bruno Rappaport, author of one such memoir, is particularly interesting: he noticed that 'the first hour on the clock of the Great Emigration' struck when the German army took Warsaw in August 1915. Rappaport acknowledged that, even though forced migration had already occurred much earlier, the takeover of the city, symbolising the severing of the refugees' ties to their patrimony, could be seen as its formal beginning. When refugees became separated from Warsaw by the front line moving westwards, they became 'a part of the national organism which had been cut off and deprived of the head'.[5]

Władysław Glinka, a landowner from Susk Stary in the Ostrołęka region, noted in his memoir that 'in spring 1915, the retreating Russian army began to evict people from their homes. The populace was first forced out of the villages directly endangered by the battle, but then the army, having apparently acquired a taste for this activity, began to evacuate all the villages. Gender and age made no difference'. Moreover, he noted that the thought of leaving one's ancestral land became a reality at the moment when thousands of refugees appeared in 1915 'from beyond the Narew [river]', that is from the territories of the Łomża governorate north of the river. Some of them, namely people from territories 'near the border [with the German Empire, MK] and from Przasnysz county' had already been exiled in 1914. According to Glinka, that was the point when local people understood that they too could be destined to become refugees and 'live like these homeless people do'.[6] The inhabitants of Warsaw had the same impression when they saw refugees passing through the city. At the beginning of March 1915, Maria Lubomirska, the wife of Zdzisław Lubomirski, chairman of the Citizens' Committee for the City of Warsaw, described how the figures moving through the streets of Warsaw on carts or on foot had 'a mournful countenance (especially the women) which would make any man collapse under the burden of injustice which surrounds them, and which they can neither prevent nor alleviate'.[7]

When writing about the onset of the forced mass migration, contemporary authors pointed out that people were often pressured to make decisions in a hurry. They also noted how people adopted an opportunistic approach to the realities of war. Glinka emphasised that the preparations undertaken by his family 'dejected [them] so much' that nothing but compulsion could drive them to leave their ancestral seat. Likewise, he mentioned the determination not to move any further on the part of refugees from Kurpie who ended up on his property and its environs.[8] However, this conviction did not prevent the Russians from expelling people from their patrimony. Of course, forced exile affected many more people than Glinka and his neighbours, and engulfed thousands of inhabitants of the 'Polish' governorates. The Cossack whip – symbol of oppression – together with the destructive momentum of the retreating Russian forces, compelled people to flee.[9] The more far-sighted among their number tried to prepare for their departure. Glinka wrote that 'we could not wait until the very last moment; even if the regular [Russian] army would leave us alone for the time being, they would certainly take away all our horses as they retreated; and if the Cossacks then used their whips to drive us out, we would have to go into the world on foot and without any possessions'.[10] However, rational behaviour was not characteristic of most refugees; rather the opposite.

The expulsion of the population often took place in circumstances that stuck in the memory of those most directly affected. A memoir by Maria Lubomirska is very compelling in this regard:

> Maławieś is surrounded by a ring of fire, the villages around are burning, and sparks are flying, filling us with great fright. They [the Russians] chase the desperate people ahead with brutal cold-bloodedness. Łęczeszyce will soon cease to exist; the church, stripped of the roof, is to serve as a fortress. Goliany is to be dismantled, crops are being mown, potatoes are grabbed from the soil, probably not even ripe yet.[11]

The author was not alone in her realistic presentation of the circumstances under which the exodus of the population further into the interior of Russia began. General Józef Dowbor-Muścicki also evoked the exodus vividly in his memoirs. The testimony of this professional military officer showcases the emotions of the author as he watched the effects of the withdrawal of Russian troops:

> No pen can describe what was happening at that time. A mass of frightened and starved villagers were walking behind me, with me and before me, driving their livestock. The Cossacks marching alongside the regiment were

setting fire to villages and fields. I was walking among an immense sea of fire and people, hearing moans and crying everywhere. I watched terrifying scenes [...] Corpses of horses and people filled the roads; there were fresh graves everywhere, marked with crosses made from scraps of timber.[12]

The cruelty of its perpetrators led observers such as Glinka to conclude that the refugees would never forgive the Russians for this suffering, and that not the material, but the moral aspect was the most flagrant, namely 'treating the Polish nation as a herd of cattle'.[13]

From the outset, the scale of the migration took the Russian authorities by surprise. Eyewitnesses mentioned thousands of refugees clogging the roads, even in the Kingdom of Poland. Landowner and social activist Michał Stanisław Korwin-Kossakowski who, at the time of the withdrawal, found himself with his 82nd Division of the Russian Red Cross in the back of the Russian Army in the Lublin region, claimed that he passed at least 8,000 carts with 55,000 refugees on the road from Chełm to Włodawa. But the author himself conceded that even these estimates could be low because 'the lines were double in some places, and, in addition to those on the main road, innumerable carts drove beside it, and there were thousands of camps in every wood; I believe that there were at least 200,000 people scattered over a distance of 44 versts [47 kilometres]'.[14]

The main routes followed by the refugees once they left the borders of the Polish governorates ran through present-day Belarus and Ukraine. Masses of people walked down the Brest-Moscow roadway that cut across Belarus, but also from Białystok, via Vawkavysk and Slonim towards Baranovichi, the latter being also the destination of those taking the path from Pruzhany to Slonim. The itinerary led further towards Minsk, Mogilev, Roslavl and Smolensk. Some refugees took the road usually leading from Vilnius to Polotsk. Thousands more were forced into the interior via Ukrainian governorates, particularly Volhynia, Podolia, Kiev and others further east. One of the main routes ran through Rivne and Sarny. Many converged in Kiev, which for most was merely a stage in a much longer journey further into the interior of Russia.[15]

The routes which ran through Belarusian lands were taken mainly by the inhabitants of Lublin, Chełm, Łomża and Płock governorates, as well as those from the western part of the Grodno Governorate and Lithuanian governorates. Refugees from the Lublin and Chełm regions also journeyed through the Ukrainian territories. Among the refugees were also inhabitants of other Polish governorates: Kalisz, Kielce, Piotrków, Radom, Suwałki and Warsaw.

Drama and suffering

The memoirs illustrating the everyday realities of the exodus depict a frightening picture of human dramas taking place with indifference or lack of opposition from fellow victims. The latter often witnessed irreversible decisions. In his book *Na wschodnim posterunku*, Zygmunt Wasilewski quotes an eyewitness who saw a man bury his wife who had died during childbirth; his surviving children looked on as he did so. A 'group of onlookers' gathered at the scene but had 'no words either of comfort or reprimand for this tragic man'.[16] A similar reaction was described by Korwin-Kossakowski, when a refugee jumped from a bridge with his two children into the waters of the Berezina river after the death of his wife. Desperation, the will to save one's life, but also indifference: these were some of the reasons that incited parents to abandon their children, who then found refuge at the sanitary ward for which Korwin-Kossakowski was responsible.[17]

With each passing day, the refugees' hope of being able to return home soon, which they had carried since the beginning of the exile, gave way to doubt, increasing disbelief in a potential improvement of their situation, and ever growing pressure. Some expellees interpreted their tragic situation as God's punishment for their past life or their failure to appreciate their possessions or quality of life hitherto.[18] Ryszard Wójtowicz cited the appearance and mental condition of the refugees who received help from the Central Citizens' Committee of the Provinces of the Kingdom of Poland (*Centralny Komitet Obywatelski guberni Królestwa Polskiego*; CKO); according to Wójtowicz, a CKO activist and memoirist, within a matter of weeks, they had become paupers begging for any sort of help, devoid of hope that they would ever see their homeland again.[19]

The drama was deepened by the deaths of thousands of refugees, which resulted in cemeteries emerging in all places of their stay and crosses in roadside ditches alongside the paths of their journey. Korwin-Kossakowski, Rappaport and Wójtowicz mention tens, hundreds and thousands of graves along the Zhytomyr-Kiev tracts, near Lyakhavichy or around Baranovichi in Belarus. Infant mortality increased due to infectious diseases, starvation and exhaustion. The tragic position of the youngest refugees was deepened by being orphaned or separated from their parents. The elderly suffered acutely too. Due to their advanced age they could not cope with the toil of the road. Those who managed to survive often had to face the fate of living in a poorhouse or being at the mercy of other people.[20]

Within a few weeks, this perceived dehumanisation and moral decay no longer caused outrage among most refugees. Wasilewski wrote that refugees who joined the 'way of the cross' forfeited dignity and hope. They also committed acts that were incompatible with the ethical precepts of Christianity.[21] However, not all refugees were affected by what might be termed a 'refugee syndrome'. The diaries that are available to us also acknowledge that some refugees refused to succumb to negative feelings. Despite their harsh situation, they attempted to surmount the drama of displacement.[22] They might do so by departing for the Russian interior in an organised fashion. This more disciplined behaviour was acknowledged by Jerzy de Moldenhower who inspected the activities of CKO in August 1915 as a representative of the Council of the Assemblies of the Polish Relief Organisations for Victims of War (*Rada Zjazdów Polskich Organizacji Pomocy Ofiarom Wojny*, RZ POPOW), as well as by W. Grabski, Plenipotentiary of CKO and future Prime Minister of the Second Polish Republic.[23]

Refugees attempted to maintain their dignity. They demonstrated a sense of their national, cultural and linguistic distinctiveness, something that was felt not only by landowners and members of the bourgeoisie and the intelligentsia, conscious of their Polishness, but also by the more enlightened peasants and workers.[24]

Numbers

The number of refugees from the Kingdom of Poland is extremely difficult to establish, mainly because the registers are incomplete, but also due to the fact that an unknown number were not recorded in the Polish, Russian and other registers created by the humanitarian organisations. Various correspondents of the Polish press in Russia, authors of memoirs or reports from refugee paths for humanitarian organisations spoke of thousands of exiles, clogged roads and large concentrations of people in nearby towns important for communication. A huge camp with about 200,000 people was established near Kobrin in August 1915. Between 87,000 and 120,000 people of different nationalities lived as nomads in nearby Roslavl. Other camps were located in the region of Bobruisk and nearby Rahachow, Baranovichi, Sinyavka and Stare Dorohi. Between 60,000 and 150,000 refugees congregated in these three towns prior to their migration into the Russian interior.[25]

Indirect confirmation of the presence of thousands of refugees comes in the unpublished memoirs of Józef Kożuchowski, who estimated that

715,000 people of different nationalities passed through Smolensk.[26] Other accounts and reports stated that 400,000 refugees were moving towards Minsk. Nearly 30,000 people were marching from Rivne into Ukraine, and 20,000 people passed through Slutsk (Belarus) every day.[27] There were also estimates of the number of inhabitants of the Polish territories who reached the interior of Russia. They ranged between 850,000 and one million refugees. Some 150,000 state officials, railwaymen, tradesmen and industrialists evacuated from the Polish provinces and Galicia could have ended up inside European Russia.[28] These estimates broadly corresponded to the statistics generated by Polish humanitarian organisations. The CKO claimed to have records for 744,319 individuals by the beginning of 1916. The Polish Relief Association for Victims of War (*Polskie Towarzystwo Pomocy Ofiarom Wojny*, PTPOW) estimated the number of refugees from the Kingdom of Poland at about 850,000. The Council of Assemblies acknowledged around 808,000 registered refugees in the first quarter of 1916; in contrast, the Commissariat of Polish Affairs (*Komisariat do Spraw Polskich, Komisariat Polski*), which operated beside the Bolshevik People's Commissariat of Nationalities, claimed that Polish humanitarian organisations helped 948,554 refugees in the second half of 1917 and the first quarter of 1918. The Department of Repatriation, subordinate to the Commissariat of Polish Affairs, brought this number up to 1,005,610 persons.[29] It is conceivable that the total stood even higher: according to Wasilewski, the number of refugees from Polish lands may have reached 1.5 million people.[30]

It is clear that Polish refugees made up a significant proportion of the total number of refugees who ended up in Russia. The Tatiana committee for the relief of refugees concluded that there were 3,113,400 refugees of different nationalities in Russia at the beginning of 1917, of whom more than 606,000 hailed from the Kingdom of Poland. In fact the number of refugees from the Polish lands was probably much higher. According to official Polish sources, 1.5 million persons from a total of five million refugees in Russia in 1918 were of Polish nationality, or around 30 per cent of the total. However, this figure is certainly an exaggeration, because it included not only refugees and deportees but also civilian prisoners and demobilised soldiers.[31] W. Grabski and Antoni Żabko-Potopowicz estimated that one-quarter of all refugees were 'Polish exiles and refugees'.[32] As a general order of magnitude, it is reasonable to agree with Walentyna Najdus who concludes that the Russian Empire was home to around one million refugees from the Polish lands during the First World War.[33]

Profiling refugees

The findings of Grabski and Żabko-Potopowicz raise another issue, namely how many refugees from the Polish lands were of Polish nationality. According to the data from late 1916 gathered by the Special Council for the Refugees at the Russian Ministry of Internal Affairs, there were over 576,000 ethnically Polish refugees in tsarist Russia. The Tatiana committee put the total at more than 483,000 in February 1917.[34] On the other hand, the CKO maintained that nearly 750,000 of the refugees registered by the Polish Relief Organisations were Poles.[35]

What of the social origin of refugees from the Polish lands? As already indicated, Wasilewski stated that the vast majority of refugees were 'common people'. B. Rappaport agreed that 'the core of the emigration in 1915 was an enormous mass of peasants who suddenly became landless, a small percentage of the working population and an even smaller of artisans and intelligentsia'.[36] These conclusions are reflected in the press and the statistics of Polish relief organisations. Preliminary estimates made during the war emphasised the preponderance of the peasant population. In November 1915, *Głos Polski* described 400,000 refugees 'from the peasant population' of the Kingdom of Poland; *Ognisko Polskie* offered a figure of 450,000. The historiography comes to similar conclusions.[37]

Nevertheless, the intelligentsia constituted a noticeable group among the refugees and gained special attention from the relief organisations. Its involvement in the forced migration was confirmed by the measures taken by relief organisations, which sought to create decent living conditions for intelligentsia during the 'emigration', in the hope that they would support the development of Polish national life in Russia. However, the exact figures are difficult to specify. The doctoral dissertation of Alicja Głaz underlines the fact that the intelligentsia played a very significant part in this displacement out of all proportion to their actual number. Certainly the intelligentsia made up a considerable number of those Poles who returned to Poland after the war, and they would have included people who fled to Russia in 1915.[38]

Among the refugees were workers who had not been evacuated eastwards along with the industrial plants. It is not easy to determine their number either, particularly because many among the workers and their families already lived and worked in Russia before the mass evacuation from the Kingdom of Poland and the part of Galicia occupied by the Russians.[39] As indicated earlier, landowners, the middle class and the bourgeoisie also became refugees, forced by the aforementioned decisions of the Russian authorities, the events of war and the wish to avoid its consequences.

The forced migration involved all social classes of the Kingdom of Poland. Not only its mass character but also the diversity of those affected appeared to distinguish it from the migration of Poles during the nineteenth century. As Wasilewski put it:

> The conditions of this 'eastern exile' were very different from those familiar to us from western emigration after 1830. Emigration due to this war is greater in number, and affects all social classes, the common people in particular, while the previous migration to the west attracted mainly members of the intelligentsia. The latter ended up in an environment of higher civilisation, while in this case people reach an environment that is significantly lower than the one at home.[40]

Early relief measures

The arrival of refugees in the deep interior of Russia put the tsarist authorities and relief organisations in a very difficult position. Worsening weather conditions in the autumn and winter of 1915 made it imperative to resettle them as soon as possible. In the case of refugees from Polish lands, the criteria used by Polish relief organisations also proved to be important. In addition to the conditions described above, the relief organisations hoped to avoid the dispersal of Polish refugees across the immense territory of the Russian Empire. Therefore they tried not only to influence the refugees' route but to protect them against the inclination of the tsarist government to move the refugees further into the Russian state.

Polish organisations sought to ensure that the majority would remain in provinces close to the Polish lands. In any case, they insisted that the resettlement of refugees should not reach further than the river Volga. The aim of settling refugees in European Russia, and, above all, in Belarus and Ukraine, was based also on the assumption that it would be easier for Polish committees to organise help based on the Polish natives who lived in these regions, and to make use of the high social status and material resources of their members. It should be noted that Poles living in this territory owned estates and industrial enterprises. Finding accommodation for refugees as quickly as possible was supposed to show that relief organisations had shifted from half-improvised actions undertaken during the evacuations to more permanent and systematic programmes of assistance. In general, the resistance of relief organisations to the attempt by Russian officials to use refugees to colonise and contribute to the economic development of the tsarist state reflected a strong desire to maintain control over the refugees and prevent their denationalisation.[41]

The decisions made confirm the assumptions of the Polish relief organisations, but at the same time, they point out that Polish refugees were to be found in almost every province of the Russian Empire, including large concentrations in Kiev, Ekaterinoslav, Mogilev, Moscow and Petrograd.[42]

Refugees, especially Polish peasants, who entered Belarusian, Ukrainian, and subsequently Russian, provinces faced more than just material difficulties and poor health. They also came face to face with a local population that spoke a different language, had a different culture, adhered to different religious beliefs, used distinctive farming practices and so on. The standard of living in Russia was also generally lower than the one which they had been used to. Furthermore, they now came face to face with Poles who had been living in towns and provinces (including those on Belarusian and Ukrainian territories) for several generations. This too was a new experience for the refugees.

So far as we can tell, the relationship between Poles and non-Poles was strained from the outset, largely because of the economic status of Polish refugees. For thousands of refugees the situation only began to ease, and their relations with the local populace became less awkward, when they started to pay rent for their housing, often with the help of humanitarian organisations, and began to work in order to support themselves.[43]

Encounters

Mutual prejudice and aversion was combined with friendly feelings and sympathy towards refugees on the part of local people. There is no doubt that the wave of refugees moving eastwards and their tragic situation filled many native people with compassion and made them eager to help. Thus, refugees could find support both in the manor houses, mostly Polish ones, and in the homes of local peasants. However, the attitude defined by Korwin-Kossakowski in his diaries is striking. His entry for 13 September 1915, when the forced migration process attained its apogee, read as follows:

> One now comes across fewer and fewer Polish people on the roads – they have already left for the interior of Russia. How will they be received there? I do not talk about the organisation of a reception, but I am asking this: Will this people haunted with misery actually encounter an 'open heart

and brotherly outstretched hands with which, according to the words of the Appeal, the Great Russia[44] was supposed to stride towards us?' What I hear around sounds ominous. To the disdainful name of fugitives now are added terms of hate: 'It is a scourge! They are like locusts coming to exploit Russia! They are bringing about demoralisation and destruction! The state should devise the means of protecting us from this invasion before this scourge drains everything out of Russia by living at its expense'. All these are words and sentences that I have heard many times, and among them there were false voices, as if showing understanding, but in fact sounding more like a sneer. After all they are wives and children of our soldiers, some Russian romantics admitted. During the free distribution of bread it was easy enough to distinguish a farmer type from Lublin region among the numerous crowds, and one's ear could catch the hateful words addressed to him: Begone you Polish fool!'[45]

Kossakowski's opinion found confirmation in the reflections of B. Rappaport who observed that 'even the most ignorant Polish peasant in emigration expressed amazement when the political wiseacres tried to convince him that the Russian nation looked kindly on him'. On the contrary, the Polish peasant refugee was oppressed by the police and the military authorities, as well as by the Russian peasantry. The epithet quoted by Kossakowski was supposed to be the favourite and the most popular one, and according to Rappaport it described 'the attitudes of Russians to our entire nation, not only to Poles in emigration'. He explained these aversions and attitudes by cultural differences and the superiority of western culture towards Russians who hated a 'latinist'.[46] R.M. Wójtowicz believed that the hostility of Russians reflected their jealousy of what they took to be the cleverness of the Polish peasant, his ability to manage in difficult situations, his capacity for hard work, his agility, his tidiness, and the wealth of possessions he brought from the Kingdom of Poland.[47]

The negative attitude towards refugees from Polish lands was probably also shared by the local Polish population, especially landowners. Wójtowicz described in his memoir the resettlement of refugees from Belarus and indicated that one Jan Lenkiewicz, owner of Berezovka, was somewhat exceptional in believing that refugees were not 'a gang of thieves as many others did'. He wrote bitterly that in many cases local Poles were indifferent and even hostile to the fate of Polish refugees.[48]

Reciprocal distrust was deepened by the fact that the majority of the refugees did not speak the language of the local population, making for mutual incomprehension. In the following period, the situation was intensified by the differences (in case of Polish refugees) which arose from conflicting habits and attitudes towards religion, and also because the local population was treating refugees as intruders. Furthermore, the attempts of landowners (Poles too) and tradesmen to exploit the difficult situation of refugees in order to multiply their profits made for disharmony. For example, the owners and tradesmen bought their properties on the cheap and offered a low price for their work. Another cause of rising hostility was the fact that refugees who frequently worked more efficiently took the jobs of local workers, thereby depriving them of sources of income.[49] This situation was exacerbated by the growing economic and political crisis.

Local people were interested in the refugees but at the same time showed their ignorance of even elementary knowledge about the world. Wójtowicz, who reported on his travels to Yelets and Livny communes in the Orel province, wrote that local peasants and even intelligentsia did not understand so-called 'tribal difference'. He noticed that Poles were identified as Jews, and that the Russian peasantry regarded the Catholic custom of making the sign of the cross as un-Christian. Over time, when a priest started to visit the Polish refugees, their interest in the Catholic religion increased.[50]

There is no doubt that the new circumstances induced refugees to make observations and express their opinions about new realities which they encountered during the forced migration and their stay in Russia during the war. Much attention was given to the towns, through which refugees from Poland passed through or stayed in, and their inhabitants. These memories tend to underline the colossal differences between the conditions in the provinces of the Kingdom of Poland on the one hand, and the encountered Belarusian, Ukrainian, Russian and Siberian ones on the other. Very critical remarks tended to be made about Belarusians, who were portrayed as a perfect type of slave, as a result of the 'work' done by Polish landowners and Russian officials. Also the inhabitants of Siberia encountered in Tobolsk province failed to make a good impression on Rappaport. Although he underlined their good-naturedness and hospitality, he nevertheless emphasised their rudeness, their dishonesty in attempting to expand their assets, and their lack of pity for the weaker ones. He also criticised the places in which the local population lived. It seems that the peasant's remark quoted by Wójtowicz, saying that a farmhand in the Kingdom of Poland lived in better conditions than Belarusian or Russian farmers, perfectly illustrated this point. They described in critical terms the primitive methods of husbandry and low agrarian culture of the local Belarusian and Russian population, as well as their resistance to adopting better ways of exploiting the land to increase crops and thereby profits.[51]

The attitude of local people towards refugees was shaped not only by their own experience, but also by the stance of local Russian authorities, which did not act according to central government directives received from Petrograd, ordering them to support the refugees. The thousands of refugees arriving in the first months of forced migration paralysed the decision-making of the central authorities regarding the types and methods of assistance. The helplessness and chaos on migration routes, enhanced by the evacuation orders of the tsarist administration (in Kiev, for instance), only partially justify their behaviour. This draws attention to the explicit efforts of getting rid of the refugees, and consequently of the related problems, from the various administrative regions, by encouraging them to migrate further into Russia.[52] Russian relief organisations were supposed to be the solution for the refugee issue, but they did not meet the expectations of the authorities, and even less those of refugees, at least in the first phase of their activities. Only when humanitarian activities stabilised did they play an important part in assisting refugees, although the state remained the main distributor and organiser of aid.[53]

Systems of support

The influx of refugees encouraged the efforts of Polish organisations bringing support to war victims. The Central Citizens' Committee of the Governorship of the Kingdom of Poland contributed greatly to this field and to the development of all the aspects of national activity. This organisation, based in Petrograd, took over the apparatus established in the empire's Polish provinces in the second half of 1914. It coordinated the activities of several hundred local citizens' councils founded as a result of grass-roots initiatives by locals. The formation of CKO on the Neva took place in August 1915. Its main initiator was W. Grabski who was entrusted by the Warsaw authorities of this organisation with assisting refugees from the Kingdom of Poland.[54] He shared this function with Seweryn Światopełk-Czetwertyński – landowner, social activist and politician – and Stanisław Wojciechowski, future President of the Second Polish Republic.

Another Polish institution which looked after the refugees was the Polish Relief Association for Victims of War (*Polskie Towarzystwo Pomocy Ofiarom Wojny*, PTPOW). Thanks to the involvement of the representatives of the old emigration, the native Polish population and (from 1915 onwards) refugees, the PTPOW established and maintained 247 divisions with a considerable degree of internal autonomy under the formal supervision of the main committee in Petrograd. Its foundation in 1914 was inspired by the news regarding the constant worsening of the living conditions of inhabitants of the Kingdom of Poland. The activities of the PTPOW were managed by Władysław Żukowski (engineer, economist and politician), Stanisław Łopaciński (landowner, lawyer and politician), General Aleksander Babiański and others.[55]

The autonomous Sanitary-Alimentary Section (*Sekcja Sanitarno-Żywnościowa*, SSŻ) of PTPOW worked in Belarusian provinces, Pskov and Petrograd, two counties of Chernihiv and Vilnius provinces, and in Riga. It was founded in August 1915 on the initiative of landowners and Polish intelligentsia in Lithuania who were affected by the tragic situation of the refugees. Bolesław Jałowiecki (landowner, army general and politician) played a major role.[56]

The Polish Relief Committee for the Victims of War under the Roman-Catholic Charity Association (*Komitet Polski Pomocy Ofiarom Wojny przy Towarzystwie Dobroczynności*) must be given credit for its work with refugees and Polish inhabitants of Moscow during the war. It began operating in the first months of the war, but started acting as an independent institution only in July 1915. The chairman Aleksander Lednicki (lawyer, politician and social activist) contributed greatly to its activities.[57]

Also worth mentioning are the activities of the Polish Committee of Sanitary Help (*Polski Komitet Pomocy Sanitarnej*, PKPS). Established in Warsaw in 1914, it was reorganised one year later since some of its activists were exiled to Russia. The reorganisation allowed the PKPS to continue assisting wounded soldiers, as well as bringing support to the refugees. Franciszka Woroniecka and Marian Lutosławski (mechanical engineer, social activist) played important roles in the work of the organisation.[58] Another institution looking after the refugees, more precisely those originating from Galicia and Lviv, was Polish Rescue Committee of Lviv (*Polski Lwowski Komitet Ratunkowy*, PLKR). Its operation was reactivated in Kiev in August 1915 on the initiative of Professor Stanisław Grabski (economist, politician).[59] It is necessary to mention as well the emergence in summer 1915 of the idea of creating a relief organisation, which, according to the intention of the circles gathered around A. Lednicki, would co-ordinate the activities of Polish organisations of relief to war victims. The Council of Assemblies of Polish Relief Organisations for Victims of War was established in Moscow in 1915 during a congress of about 200 representatives of Polish organisations in Russia. Lednicki became its chairman.[60]

The activities of these Polish institutions looking after refugees came to an end in 1918. The basis for their liquidation was the decree of Bolshevik authorities in July.[61] Before their activities ceased, thousands of refugees benefited from their help. In the years 1915–1918, CKO, PTOPOW and SSŻ supported, respectively, 333,794, 198,715 and 27,526 persons, while PLKR supported 9,000 refugees from Galicia.[62]

The arrival of thousands of refugees in Russia compelled relief organisations to verify prior forms of activity and, at the same time, to expand their scope and define new directions. Since the beginning of the migration, the organisations were – besides temporary activities – registering refugees, working towards the stabilisation and regular provision of support, and developing various forms of the latter. The refugees received material assistance (food, accommodation and clothing), financial, sanitary, legal, religious, cultural and educational support, as well as help in finding work.

The huge needs of refugees required large financial sums. These were mainly at the disposition of the Russian authorities, who disbursed funds to Polish organisations via the Special Council for Refugees and Russian relief organisations such as the Tatiana committee, local authorities and zemstvos. Additional support came from Polish institutions operating outside the empire, from Poles living in Russia and from profits of relief organisations. The Council of Assemblies claimed that it received and spent more than 90 million rubles on their activities between 1915 and the end of 1917.[63]

However, the Russian revolution in 1917 turned everything upside down. The fall of tsarism and the weakness of the Provisional Government, the Bolshevik seizure of power and the resulting anarchy and intensification of the economic crisis led to a drastic decline in the living standards of refugees and their hosts, mainly due to the loss of pensions and work, which were their sources of income.

Refugees and Polish national identity

The presence of the refugees definitely contributed to an increase in activity of the native Polish population and the 'old emigration' in different fields of national work. Among the refugees were members of intelligentsia, landowners from the Kingdom of Poland and Galicia who actively participated in the charity work of Poles in Russia in years 1915–1918, as well as their cultural, educational, journalist, economic and political activities. Various publishing initiatives, the aim of which was to fulfil the increasing needs of Polish schools and readers, also gained momentum and recognition among refugees. According to the findings of Jacek Kuszłejko, Polish textbooks, prose and socio-political literature were published in Russia during the war.[64]

The development of the Polish press also demonstrates the increased activity of Poles in Russia. Social and political activists and members of the exiled Polish intelligentsia from the Kingdom of Poland and Galicia played a prominent role in founding new newspapers, writing for existing ones, and working for publishing houses. They improved the quality of newspapers that were being published before the war and that already enjoyed an acknowledged reputation, such as *Dziennik Kijowski*. The new titles were addressed to readers representing various political options: right wing, democratic, socialist and communist (*Echo Polskie, Gazeta Polska, Głos Robotnika i Żołnierza, Sprawa Polska* and *Trybuna*). We should also mention professional periodicals directed to doctors and teachers, such as *Polski Miesięcznik Lekarski* and *Przewodnik Oświatowy*. Among those who largely contributed to the development of the Polish press – as much before as during the war – were its founders, editors and columnists such as A. Lednicki, Joachim Bartoszewicz (politician), Z. Wasilewski, Eugeniusz Starczewski (columnist), Joseph Hlasko (columnist), Bohdan Wasiutyński (columnist). We should also add that many of them later left Russia to continue their work in the reborn Polish Republic.[65]

Relief organisations, organisations for refugees and committees of local Polish populations registered a big success in relation to educational initiatives, the aim of which was to strengthen ties between Poles. However, the true objective was to arouse and reassert the national consciousness of the local Polish population and to protect them, along with the youngest generation of refugees, from denationalisation, but often also from demoralisation and losing their lives. Numbers prove the scale of the educational initiative: the main relief organisations founded 2,084 educational facilities for 116,546 children, including 25 high schools and extra-curricular lessons for almost 6,500 students. One outstanding achievement was the Polish University College in Kiev. During the first year, 718 students attended this institution (527 of whom were female).[66]

The appearance of Polish political activists from the Kingdom of Poland and Galicia caused not only the rise of the consciousness and patriotism of Poles who had lived in the tsarist state for several generations, but also led to the revival and significant polarisation of the local

Polish political scene. Dariusz Tarasiuk has described the activities of the Polish nationalist intelligentsia in Russia in 1917–18. It should be noted that Polish right-wing, democratic and left-wing circles were all active, especially after the fall of tsarism.[67]

Repatriation

From the very beginning, refugees did not abandon the thought of a swift return to their homeland. This issue became one of the most important problems discussed by Polish relief organisations. Near the end of 1915, CKO decided to create a special Repatriation Fund (*Fundusz Powrotu do Kraju*), and two years later a discussion began regarding plans of return in the initiative of S. Wojciechowski. However, serious efforts of supporting institutions did not start until the regime change in Russia.

One of the projects, prepared by Adolf Świda (an activist of CKO), became the basis for the elaboration of further plans for an organised return of refugees to their homeland. His plan entailed a division of Russia into three areas, one from the front line to Moscow, the second from Moscow to the Volga and the third on territory located east of the Volga. This proposed division was designed to prepare an orderly evacuation of about 730,000 refugees from their place of temporary settlement to resurgent Poland. Unfortunately, Świda's plan was not implemented due to the deepening of the economic and political crisis in Russia after the collapse of the tsarist regime.[68]

When the Bolsheviks seized power in Russia, the activities of CKO towards the preparation and the implementation of repatriation plans intensified. However, despite intense attempts, the Committee did not manage to realise the planned re-emigration of refugees to their country.[69]

The return of the refugees, together with other Poles who had taken up residence in Russia before the war, was managed by government officials. Examples include the Main Council for Repatriation through the Western Front (based in Minsk), and the Polish Central Committee for Repatriation in Ukraine, established in Kiev in March 1918.[70]

Despite the efforts to conduct an orderly repatriation of the refugees, many of them attempted to return without waiting for the approval or assistance of any re-emigration or relief organisation. They took advantage of the fact that the Central Powers occupied the Belarusian and Ukrainian lands in 1918. Many others returned after the end of the Polish-Soviet war, although some 476,000 refugees had already returned to Poland at the beginning of 1919.[71]

Conclusion

For many refugees, exile amounted merely to the attempt to survive a miserable displacement. For some, it also meant a period of intense effort to preserve national consciousness. By so doing they contributed to the revival, and often the revaluation and extension of the activities of the 'old emigration' and the Polish native population. This became possible not only due to their activities but, above all, to the immense efforts of Polish relief organisations which concerned themselves with the daily lives of refugees in Russia, and worked hard to arouse their national consciousness at the same time. They contributed thereby to the preservation of dignity and a sense of national distinctiveness on the part of many refugees and they certainly convinced refugees of the imperative to return to a restored Poland.

Notes

1. J. Pajewski, *Pierwsza wojna światowa 1914–1918* (Warsaw: Wydawnictwo Naukowe PWN, 2004); J. Dąbrowski, ed. *Wielka wojna 1914–1918*, parts 1–4 (Poznań: Wydawnictwo 'Kurpisz', 2000; 2001).
2. W. Najdus, *Polacy w rewolucji 1917 roku* (Warsaw: Państwowe Wydawnictwo Naukowe, 1967), pp. 24–6.
3. W. Glinka, *Pamiętnik z wielkiej wojny*, vol. 1 (Warsaw: Gebethner i Wolff, 1927), pp. 70–1, 90.
4. *Pamiętnik Księżnej Marii Zdzisławowej Lubomirskiej 1914–1918* (Poznan: Wydawnictwo Poznańskie, 1997), p. 204.
5. B. Rappaport, *Carat i rewolucja (trzy lata za frontem rosyjskim)* (Warsaw: Nakładem Kasy Przezorności i Pomocy Warszawskich Pomocników Księgarskich, 1919), p. 7.
6. Glinka, *Pamiętnik*, vol. 1, pp. 45–6, 54–5.
7. *Pamiętnik Księżnej Marii*, p. 142.
8. Glinka, *Pamiętnik*, vol. 1, pp. 62–3.
9. *Pamiętnik Księżnej Marii*, pp. 178, 199; Glinka, *Pamiętnik*, vol. 1, p. 63; Z. Wasilewski, *Na wschodnim posterunku: Księga pielgrzymstwa 1915–1918* (Warsaw: E. Wende i Spółka, 1919), p. 11.
10. Glinka, *Pamiętnik*, vol. 1, p. 63.
11. *Pamiętnik Księżnej Marii*, p. 208.
12. J. Dowbor-Muśnicki, *Moje wspomnienia* (Poznan: Zysk i S-ka Wydawnictwo, 2013), pp. 184–5; S. Dzierzbicki, *Pamiętnik z lat wojny 1915–1918* (Warsaw: Państwowy Instytut Wydawniczy, 1983), p. 54; M. Korzeniowski, M. Mądzik and D. Tarasiuk, *Tułaczy los: Uchodźcy polscy w imperium rosyjskim w latach*

pierwszej wojny światowej (Lublin: Wydawnictwo Uniwersytetu Marii Curie-Skłodowskiej, 2007), pp. 15–20.
13 Glinka, *Pamiętnik*, vol. 1, p. 64.
14 M.S. Kossakowski, *Diariusz 21 maja-31 sierpnia 1915*, ed. M. Mądzik, vol. 1, part 1 (Lublin: Wydawnictwo Uniwersytetu Marii Curie-Skłodowskiej, 2010), p. 177.
15 Korzeniowski et al., *Tułaczy los*, pp. 15–16.
16 Wasilewski, *Na wschodnim*, p. 162; see also Glinka, *Pamiętnik*, vol. 2, p. 18.
17 M.S. Kossakowski, *Diariusz 1 września 1915–4 lutego 1916*, ed. M. Mądzik, vol. 1, part 2 (Lublin: Wydawnictwo Uniwersytetu Marii Curie-Skłodowskiej, 2010), pp. 38, 67.
18 Kossakowski, *Diariusz*, vol. 1, part 2, p. 12.
19 R.M. Wójtowicz, *Społeczna praca ludowa w czasie wojny: Pamiętnik instruktora opieki nad wygnańcami Centralnego Komitetu Obywatelskiego, pisany na tułaczce w Rosji w latach 1915, 1916, 1917 i 1918* (Warsaw: Dom Książki Polskiej, 1936), pp. 13–14, 36.
20 Kossakowski, *Diariusz*, vol. 1, part 2, pp. 13, 27, 29, 31, 36–8, 46, 90; Rappaport, *Carat*, p. 15; Wójtowicz, *Społeczna*, pp. 19, 37–8.
21 Wasilewski, *Na wschodnim*, p. 160; Kossakowski, *Diariusz*, vol. 1, part 2, pp. 25, 31; Glinka, *Pamiętnik*, vol. 1, p. 109.
22 Kossakowski, *Diariusz*, vol. 1, part 2, p. 61; Korzeniowski et al., *Tułaczy los*, p. 18.
23 Archiwum Akt Nowych (AAN), Centralny Komitet Obywatelski Królestwa Polskiego w Piotrogrodzie (CKO), 94, Lustracja okręgów CKO. Raport z objazdu starszego instruktora CKO Jerzego de Moldenhowera, p. 76; W. Grabski, 'Sprawozdanie z objazdu drogi, którą wędrowali wygnańcy z Królestwa Polskiego z 8 X 1915 r', preface by A. Achmatowicz, *Studia z Dziejów Rosji i Europy Środkowo-Wschodniej*, 39 (1994), p. 87.
24 Korzeniowski et al., *Tułaczy los*, pp. 15–20.
25 AAN, CKO, 722, Sprawozdanie. Zebranie instruktorów CKO w Rosławlu z 23 IX 1915, p. 56; AAN, CKO, 16, List J. Dangla do W. Grabskiego z 29 IX 1915, p. 2; A. Głaz, *Repatriacja ludności polskiej z terenu byłego imperium rosyjskiego w latach 1917-24*, PhD thesis, Lublin 2001, p. 34; M. Mądzik, 'Z działalności Polskiego Towarzystwa Pomocy Ofiarom Wojny na Białorusi w latach I wojny światowej', *Zapiski Historyczne*, 61 (1996), z. 1, p. 62; Kossakowski, *Diariusz*, vol. 1, part 2, pp. 37–8; Wójtowicz, *Społeczna*, pp. 19–20; Korzeniowski et al., *Tułaczy los*, p. 20.
26 Biblioteka Uniwersytetu Warszawskiego (BUW), 1732/III, nr akc. 184–a, J. Kożuchowski, 'Dziennik z lat 1914–1920', manuscript, p. 40.
27 'Sprawozdanie z działalności Centralnego Komitetu Obywatelskiego wśród wygnańców w Rosji za czas od 1 sierpnia 1915 r. do dnia 1 października 1916 r', *Materiały i studia w sprawach odbudowy państwa polskiego*, vol. 1, part 1 (Petrograd, 1918), p. 14; Korzeniowski et al., *Tułaczy los*, pp. 20–1;

M. Korzeniowski, *Na wygnańczym szlaku ... Działalność Centralnego Komitetu Obywatelskiego Królestwa Polskiego na Białorusi w latach 1915–1918* (Lublin: Lubelskie Towarzystwo Naukowe, 2001), p. 113.
28 Korzeniowski et al., *Tułaczy los*, p. 21.
29 Korzeniowski et al., *Tułaczy los*, p. 22.
30 Korzeniowski et al., *Tułaczy los*, pp. 22–3; Z. Wasilewski, *Proces Lednickiego: Fragment z dziejów odbudowy Polski 1915–1924* (Warsaw: Księgarnia Perzyński, Niklewicz i Sp., 1924), p. 7.
31 Korzeniowski et al., *Tułaczy los*, p. 23; Najdus, *Polacy*, p. 46.
32 AAN, CKO, 285, 'Opracowanie statystyki wygnańców z Królestwa Polskiego podług ich pochodzenia i rozmieszczenia', p. 44; W. Grabski and A. Żabko-Potopowicz, 'Ratownictwo społeczne w czasie wojny', *Polska w czasie wielkiej wojny (1914–1918)*, vol. 2, *Historia społeczna* (Warsaw: Towarzystwo Badania Zagadnień Międzynarodowych, 1932), p. 65; Korzeniowski et al., *Tułaczy los*, pp. 23–4; Najdus, *Polacy*, pp. 44–6.
33 Korzeniowski et al., *Tułaczy los*, p. 24; W. Najdus, 'Uchodźcy polscy w Rosji w latach 1917–1919', *Kwartalnik Historyczny*, 61, no. 6 (1957), p. 26; Z. Łukawski, 'Polityka polskich organizacji w Rosji w sprawie powrotu uchodźców do kraju (1917–1918)', *Kwartalnik Historyczny*, 74, no. 3 (1967), p. 627; I. Blum, 'Polacy w Rosji carskiej i w Związku Radzieckim', *Wojskowy Przegląd Historyczny*, no. 3 (1966), 204–5.
34 Korzeniowski et al., *Tułaczy los*, pp. 25–6; Najdus, *Polacy*, p. 44.
35 AAN, CKO, 284, 'O organizacji wygnańców i powrocie do Kraju (streszczenie przemówienia na zgromadzeniu wygnańczym)', p. 1 (38).
36 The author of the memoir refers to the migration of Poles during the nineteenth century following unsuccessful uprisings against tsarist Russia. Most exiles were landowners and representatives of intelligentsia and bourgeoisie. See Rappaport, *Carat*, p. 5.
37 'Pomoc wygnańcom', *Głos Polski*, 15/28 November 1915, no. 46, p. 18; W. Bzowski, 'Jak sobie pomagamy wzajemnie na obczyźnie', *Ognisko Polskie*, 17/30, 1916, no. 2, p. 6; Korzeniowski et al., *Tułaczy los*, pp. 42–7.
38 Korzeniowski et al., *Tułaczy los*, p. 47; Głaz, *Repatriacja*, p. 223.
39 Korzeniowski et al., *Tułaczy los*, p. 48; Najdus, *Polacy*, pp. 8–23; Najdus, *Uchodźcy*, pp. 27–8.
40 Wasilewski, *Na wschodnim*, p. vi.
41 Korzeniowski et al., *Tułaczy los*, pp. 39–42; Regarding the Polish properties in the so-called Annexed Lands, see J. Bartoszewicz, *Na Rusi polski stan posiadania (kraj, ludność, ziemia)* (Kiev: L. Idzikowski, 1912); R. Jurkowski, *Ziemiaństwo polskie Kresów Północno-Wschodnich 1864–1904: działalność społeczno-gospodarcza* (Warsaw: Przegląd Wschodni, 2001); D. Beauvois, *Trójkąt Ukraiński. Szlachta, carat i lud na Wołyniu, Podolu i Kijowszczyźnie 1793–1914* (Lublin: Wydawnictwo Uniwersytetu Marii Curie-Skłodowskiej, 2005); T. Epsztein, *Polska własność ziemska na Ukrainie w 1890 r. (gubernia*

kijowska, podolska i wołyńska) (Warsaw: Wydawnictwo Neriton: Instytut Historii PAN, 2008).

42 Korzeniowski et al., *Tułaczy los*, pp. 31–42.
43 Korzeniowski et al., *Tułaczy los*, pp. 151–4, 158–60.
44 M.S. Korwin-Kossakowski made a reference to the 'Appeal of Grand Duke Nicholas Nikolayevich to Poles', published on 14 August 1914.
45 Kossakowski, *Diariusz*, vol. 1, part 2, p. 39.
46 Rappaport, *Carat*, pp. 33–4.
47 Wójtowicz, *Społeczna*, p. 70.
48 Wójtowicz, *Społeczna*, p. 40.
49 Korzeniowski et al., *Tułaczy los*, pp. 152–3, 189–92; Kossakowski, *Diariusz*, vol. 1, part 2, p. 24.
50 Wójtowicz, *Społeczna*, pp. 67–8.
51 Rappaport, *Carat*, pp. 22–3; Wójtowicz, *Społeczna*, pp. 21, 24, 40–1, 60–1, 65–6; Glinka, *Pamiętnik*, vol. 2, pp. 97–8, 169–171.
52 Rappaport, *Carat*, pp. 10–15; Kossakowski, *Diariusz*, vol. 1, part 2.
53 See the chapters by Belova, and Zhvanko and Nestulia.
54 Korzeniowski, et al., *Tułaczy los*, pp. 51–78; Korzeniowski, *Na wygnańczym*, passim.
55 M. Mądzik, *Polskie Towarzystwo Pomocy Ofiarom Wojny w Rosji w latach I wojny światowej* (Lublin: Wydawnictwo Uniwersytetu Marii Curie-Skłodowskiej, 2011); Korzeniowski et al., *Tułaczy los*, pp. 78–109.
56 Korzeniowski et al., *Tułaczy los*, p. 91; Grabski and Żabko-Potopowicz, *Ratownictwo*, pp. 89–91.
57 M. Mądzik, 'Komitet Polski w Moskwie w latach 1 wojny światowej: Struktura organizacyjna i początki działalności', *Res Historica*, 1997, z. 1; Korzeniowski et al., *Tułaczy los*, pp. 109–10.
58 A. Felchner, *Działalność Polskiego Komitetu Pomocy Polski Komitet Pomocy Sanitarnej (1914–1918)*, PhD thesis, Biblioteka Uniwersytetu Łódzkiego, Łódź 1976; Korzeniowski, et al., *Tułaczy los*, pp. 110–14.
59 Korzeniowski, et al., *Tułaczy los*, pp. 115–20.
60 Korzeniowski et al., *Tułaczy los*, pp. 120–9.
61 Grabski and Żabko-Potopowicz, *Ratownictwo*, p. 107.
62 Korzeniowski et al., *Tułaczy los*, p. 24.
63 Korzeniowski et al., *Tułaczy los*, pp. 135–46.
64 J. Kuszłejko, *Książka polska w Rosji na przełomie XIX i XX wieku* (Warsaw: Biblioteka Narodowa, 1993); Korzeniowski et al., *Tułaczy los*, pp. 185–8; M. Korzeniowski, *Za Złotą Bramą: Działalność społeczno-kulturalna Polaków w Kijowie w latach 1905–1920* (Lublin: Wydawnictwo Uniwersytetu Marii Curie-Skłodowskiej, 2009), pp. 446–56.
65 Korzeniowski, *Za Złotą Bramą*, pp. 253–364; A. Ślisz, *Prasa polska w Rosji w dobie wojny i rewolucji (1915–1919)* (Warsaw: Książka i Wiedza, 1968).
66 Korzeniowski, *Za Złotą Bramą*, pp. 143–251; Korzeniowski et al., *Tułaczy*

los, pp. 173–85; J. Róziewicz, L. Zasztowt, *Polskie Kolegium Uniwersyteckie w Kijowie (1917–1919)*, *Rozprawy z Dziejów Oświaty*, no. 34, 1991.
67 D. Tarasiuk, *Polski obóz narodowy w Rosji w latach 1917–1918* (Lublin: Wydawnictwo Uniwersytetu Marii Curie-Skłodowskiej, 2014); Najdus, *Polacy*; A. Miodowski, *Wychodźcze ugrupowania demokratyczne wobec idei polskiego wojska w Rosji w latach 1917–1918* (Białystok: Wydawnictwo i Drukarnia Libra, 2002).
68 Korzeniowski et al., *Tułaczy los*, pp. 211–21.
69 Korzeniowski et al., *Tułaczy los*, pp. 213–14, 221–7.
70 Korzeniowski et al., *Tułaczy los*, pp. 215–16; Korzeniowski, *Za Złotą Bramą*, pp. 582–4; Korzeniowski, *Na wygnańczym*, pp. 361–80.
71 D. Sula, *Powrót ludności polskiej z byłego Imperium Rosyjskiego w latach 1918–1937* (Warsaw: Wydawnictwo Trio, 2013), p. 107.

4

'Human waves': refugees in Russia, 1914–18

Irina Belova

Introduction

The mass movement of refugees from the western borders of the Russian Empire to the Russian interior was unprecedented in Russian history. Contemporary observers made an attempt to preserve this phenomenon for posterity by preparing studies of refugees' journeys and destinations, their number and socio-ethnic composition, the legislative basis of government refugee policy, and the arrangement for the relief of refugees by the state and non-governmental bodies.[1] These studies were hurriedly shelved and forgotten after 1917. A brief article about refugees in the first edition of the Big Soviet Encyclopedia vanished from subsequent editions.[2] Soviet works on the history of the First World War neglected the flight of refugees, although aspects of population displacement emerged in works devoted to other topics such as the rural economy and food procurement.[3] Soviet demographers occasionally referred to data on the number of refugees.[4] The most notable such contribution was made by E.Z. Volkov, author of one of the first historical-demographic studies. Volkov put the total refugee population at 7.42 million in 1917, adding that 'this figure is probably an under-estimate'.[5] Most historical demographers concur. Only since the late 1990s have studies of refugees during the First World War appeared in Russia and in other countries on refugees. They include studies of the political, social, economic and cultural consequences of mass population displacement.[6]

This chapter contributes a discussion of refugees from Russia's Western Front territories who reached the rear provinces of European Russia, namely Kaluga, Tula, Riazan, Orel, Kursk and Voronezh. This region was of considerable size and importance. At the beginning of the twentieth century it comprised half the territory of central European Russia, an area of 250,000 square kilometres with a population of about 16 million. During the First World War the tsarist authorities had to address quickly the difficult problem of placing some 450,000 people in this region, which displayed in microcosm the political, social and demographic processes associated with mass population displacement in the Russian Empire.

Many of the refugees who fled from the western borderlands originated from Grodno and Vilna provinces. For the most part they were ethnically Belarusians, who settled in Kaluga, Tula, Riazan and Orel, although their numbers included Polish and Jewish households. In addition, Ukrainian refugees from Volyn' and Kholm, as well as Grodno, tended to settle in Kursk and Voronezh. Finally, the mass migration eastwards included German colonists – like everyone else, subjects of the tsar – who were deported to the Russian interior.

In addition to official and semi-official published and unpublished material, this chapter draws on refugee testimony, including the memoirs of Belarusian Orthodox refugee families from Grodno province who settled in the Russian interior in the second half of 1915. The initiative for collecting their testimony derived from the Belarusian historical society in the Polish town of Bialystok/Belostok, with financial support from the Polish Ministry of Cultural and National Heritage. Refugees' testimony was collected between 1958 and 2000 by journalists at the newspapers *Niva* and *Belskii Gostinets*, as well as by historians and volunteers from youth groups. These memoirs cover the period from the refugees' mass departure in 1915 to their return home, by which time an independent Poland had come into existence. It is important to keep in mind the context in which this source material was collected.[7]

Another important source is the memoir of the Belarusian public figure, writer and historian F.A. Kudrinskii (1867–1933): a native of Vilna province, he was himself a refugee. He helped refugees in Rogachev, Mogilev province, through which around 700,000 refugees passed in the course of 1915. He recorded refugees' stories along with his personal impressions of the evacuation of Belarusian and Polish refugees, as well as German colonists. These were published in his book *Liudskie volny: bezhentsy* ('Human waves: refugees'), which first appeared in Petrograd in 1917. Eighty years later, his memoir was republished in the Belarusian magazine *Nyoman*.[8]

This chapter begins by describing the 'spontaneous' migration of the population of the Western Front areas of the Russian Empire at the outbreak of war in 1914 along with deportation of others, including Russian subjects. It examines the causes and consequences of mass movement of refugees that began in the summer of 1915, the efforts of the authorities to accommodate refugees in the rear and ensure their welfare. The chapter also addresses the activities of public organisations before and after February 1917 and the activities of the main Soviet organisation for refugees after the Bolshevik revolution. It concludes with a discussion of the Soviet apparatus for the repatriation of refugees in 1918.

The first phase

Although many people fled their homes at the outbreak of war in order to evade the incursions of the enemy, most returned at the earliest possible opportunity or settled temporarily in the vicinity of the front.[9] Simultaneously, the Russian army began to deport enemy subjects and German settlers of Russian citizenship who were suspected of co-operating with the enemy. German settlers were given five days to leave their homes.[10] Judging by the belongings they were able to take, they were relatively wealthy people. They spoke only German or Polish and reportedly said that Russia would never beat Germany. According to Kudrinskii, they looked upon the locals with disdain and hostility, and denied that Russia was a real state, since the tsar was 'not really Russian' but German, and that when Wilhelm conquered Russia, he would teach the people how to manage their economic affairs.[11]

Likewise, Russian Jews were deported from the immediate vicinity of the front to render them 'harmless'. Russian officials typically maintained that Jews sympathised with the enemy because of tsarist policies of discrimination and persecution, which the authorities thought Germany was likely to exploit.[12] According to the police in Grodno, Jews sought to persuade Russian peasants not to join the army. At the beginning of August 1914, for example, the Grodno gendarme department received information that a Jewish tenant had expressed his willingness to give half of his land to the Germans if they won. In September 1914, Abraham Tropp-Kranskii, a pharmacy owner in Grodno, insulted the Emperor, claiming that he was 'a fool and a dunce'.[13]

Public aid charities were created in the autumn for those other than Germans who had to leave their homes. They included a committee of temporary aid to war victims established on 14 September 1914, chaired by the tsar's daughter, Grand Duchess Tatiana Nikolaievna, which received a substantial government subsidy. The Tatiana committee also sought donations from the public. It remained the central body to protect the refugees until the formation of the special council on 30 August 1915 (see below). It paid lump sums to refugees, helped them to get a job and placed those unable to work in shelters and alms-houses.[14] Branches were created all over Russia. The committee subsidised new national organisations that supported refugees of a given nationality (again, this excluded German colonists). In September 1914 the Ministry of the Interior agreed to the formation of the Petrograd Jewish committee to aid victims of war, and offered it some finance support. Similar organisations to assist poor Polish families and other national groups also came into being, with the help of leading national public activists. Already, however, the emergence of these national committees began to generate complaints from Russian peasants that Polish refugees were being helped from the Tatiana committee, their national committees, and other organisations. This resentment did not diminish over time.

Mass displacement: journeys and destinations

In spring 1915 Germany and Austria-Hungary mounted a fresh attack. On the North-Western Front people had to decide whether to pack their bags hurriedly or hide in the forest until the enemy retreated. Catholic priests advised their Polish parishioners to stay put, on the grounds that the Germans were fighting Russians not Poles. By contrast, Orthodox priests urged their flock, predominantly Belarusian, to leave for the Russian interior. In June and July 1915 military commanders and government officials, as in Grodno, tried to move people to the rear, first to adjacent provinces and later on further east. But most refugees continued to remain near the front line in the hope of returning quickly.[15]

On 22 July 1915 (4 August, new style) the Russian army evacuated Warsaw and decided to move all civilians from the front to the rear. Refugees recalled the endless stream of overcrowded railway carriages moving slowly east, the journey time being delayed by the dearth of railway bridges and the resulting bottlenecks. Long queues built up when trains stopped for meal breaks at the open-air catering facilities, and fields were covered with excrement and rubbish.[16] A few better-off refugees travelled in some style, and attracted envious glances from the majority who could only make use of wretched carts. Contemporaries – non-refugees as well as refugees – commented on the fact that refugees from Kholm, Lublin and Lomzha looked healthy, neat and generally in good shape. Others were less fortunate and suffered from cholera and other epidemic diseases. From his vantage point in Rogachev, Kudrinskii

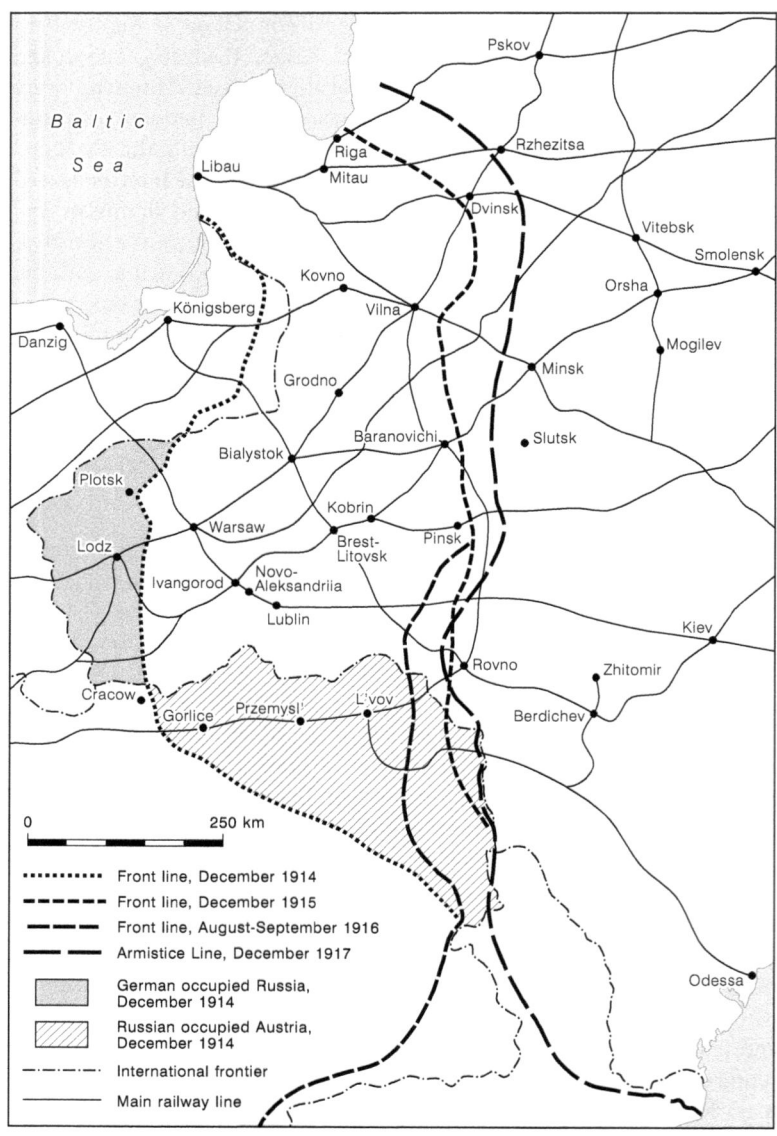

Map 4.1 The Eastern Front, 1914–17.

described how peasants from Grodno and Minsk were (in his words) 'depressed, drab and dirty'.[17]

In July 1915 two organisations were established by the tsarist government, Severopomoshch' (Northern Help) and Iugobezhenets (Southern Refugee), each of them with a chief commissioner appointed by the Ministry of the Interior. These bodies assisted with the evacuation of refugees from regions under military administration.[18] In conjunction with the military, the commissioners arranged for the transport of refugees to the rear of the country where provincial governors were expected to report about the number of refugees and the measures they proposed to take to preserve their health and find them work. It is important to add that the evacuation of people was accompanied by the evacuation of government institutions and enterprises; thus, public institutions in Grodno, Lomzhin and Vilno were evacuated to Kaluga, Riazan and Smolensk respectively.

In July 1915 the first contingent of 600 refugees arrived in Kaluga. They were provided with food and medical aid by the Tatiana committee which had already opened offices to assist refugees. The committee set up hospital and catering facilities in Kaluga and other stations in the province. Other assistance was provided by local branches of the All-Russian Zemstvo Union and the All-Russian Union of Towns. In August 1915 the number of refugees increased considerably, reaching 50,000 in Kaluga the following month. At this point the governor demanded that this influx be brought to a halt and that any further arrivals should forthwith be ordered to nearby Tula and Riazan.[19]

Difficulties continued to mount. In autumn 1915 new groups of refugees who were put on trains faced an arduous journey to a place of safety. Although some railway wagons were equipped with bunks and stoves, this was not always the case. Refugees were also held up for hours or even days at a time.[20] Often they were kept waiting for transport. For example, Jan Zinuk, a refugee from Grodno province, recalled that in August 1915 his family and fellow-villages were unable to find a berth because the train was overcrowded and crowds of refugees had already been waiting for their turn for more than two weeks. When he decided to take a cart to the station at Baranovichi station, he described seeing 'so many people that you couldn't squeeze between them'. The same was true of Bobruisk. People could only board the train in Roslavl, which lay in Smolensk province.[21] The numbers only began to abate in October 1915, as a result of improvement in the operation of the Russian railways.

Some of the challenges emerge in the personal accounts of refugees. These make it clear that many refugees could decide where to go only as they got to the place of departure. For example, Maria Lisovskaia, a refugee from Grodno province, said that her fellow-villagers, who reached Minsk by cart before catching a train, opted variously to settle in Smolensk, Samara, Ukraine and Siberia. People were split up, six families to a carriage. The railway carriages were packed but warm. Refugees described being given a quick medical examination before being allowed to proceed; those found to be sick were taken to hospital. Iosif Novitskii from Grodno province recalled being given food and money on the way to the departure station. On arriving in the Siberian city of Omsk, refugees were taken to temporary hostels until the following spring. These were equipped with a kitchen and bath; refugees were given hot meals and cash; those without warm clothes were able to obtain the basics. One refugee, Nikolai Panfiluk, in a subsequent interview, took the opportunity to praise the help given to refugees in transit, indicating that he and his friends recalled Russians as belonging to 'the best nation in the world'.[22] The editors of the volume in which this testimony appeared in 2000 were no doubt happy to hear this encomium. Other refugees such as Anton Kozlovskii from Belostok district of Grodno province readily acknowledged that the arrangements for transporting them to the interior were satisfactory.[23]

Non-refugees often had a different perspective on the mass exodus of refugees. A zemstvo doctor in Briansk noted with alarm the arrival of a 'flood' of refugees in his district. In a report to the local governor he wrote:

> At about 11 o'clock in the morning on 22 September [1915] a crowd of 700 refugees headed by a priest forced their way past the camp guard and settled themselves in a birch forest near the Pesochnia estate. They trampled down the crops, cut down the trees to make fire and grass for the cows. This group from Kholm province ravaged everything on their way to Briansk. Before that a group of 1,000 Polish refugees had gone through Pesochnia, but on that occasion everything was fine.[24]

It is unclear whether the doctor was more horrified by the damage done by refugees or the fact that they were undeterred by the presence of their priest.

The Tatiana committee established distribution points in provincial cities and towns, and hired local peasants to transport refugees from the railway station to towns and villages where billets awaited them.[25] The local police also took a hand in settling refugees, as did zemstvo officials at district (volost) level and the peasant commune. In the heavily industrial Briansk district in Orel province refugees were housed in factory buildings and in warehouses and other buildings owned by railways and town councils.[26] Local authorities did not hesitate to advertise the praise they received from some refugees.[27] This is in sharp contrast to evidence that local home-owners exploited refugees by letting out property at extortionate rents, a practice that some authorities attempted to stamp out by imposing fines.[28]

Local diocesan committees also did their bit by housing refugees in church buildings. These committees reminded parish priests that they had a duty to lift the spirits of refugees whether at railway stations or in their place of 'temporary' shelter.

The status of refugees and relief work in the Russian interior

The tsarist state issued an important law on 30 August 1915, 'On meeting refugee needs'. This law for the first time defined the term 'refugee'. According to Article one, refugees are those 'people who left territory which is under threat from the enemy or captured by the enemy, as well as those who were ordered to leave the territory of war operations by military or civil authorities'. It added, 'citizens of states opposing Russia are also recognised as refugees'. However, 'individuals who were deported from the territory of war operations are not recognised as refugees'.[29]

The legislation also specified that the Ministry of the Interior should have overall responsibility for the care of refugees, which was entrusted to a new special council for refugees, chaired by the minister himself. Later on, in November 1915 the empire was divided into 12 regions, each with a department under the chairmanship of a commissioner for refugee settlement.[30]

Meanwhile local responsibility for refugee relief was devolved on to provincial councils for refugee settlement, with some role anticipated for the zemstvos and municipal councils.[31] The Tatiana committee continued to look after refugees, as did the national committees mentioned above. A particularly important role was undertaken by provincial governors who combined their function as chair of the special council at provincial level with their duties as chair of the Tatiana committee, thereby bringing official, public and charitable relief work under the same umbrella. This represented a defeat for liberal parliamentarians in the State Duma, which had discussed entrusting public organisations (such as the zemstvo union) with all responsibility for refugee relief.[32] The zemstvo and town councils therefore stepped back from their plan to direct relief at the centre and in the localities.[33]

The special council provided refugees with a regular living allowance determined by law and designed to enable them to pay for their food and accommodation.[34] The state also provided money for medical treatment and hospital care. Local councils under the aegis of the special council helped refugees to find work. In addition, they were expected to find the means to assist elderly refugees and provide homes or shelters for orphaned refugees and for children who came from very large families which could no longer look after them. Besides food rations, refugees could expect to get extra allowances, clothes and footwear, education loans for secondary schooling (primary education was free), free or cheap meals in a canteen, firewood at a reduced price, and so forth. Despite these generous provisions, it proved impossible to provide all refugees with clothes and footwear.[35]

The law of 30 August also gave formal recognition to national refugee committees. In Tula, for example, this affected five different organisations: Lithuanian, Latvian, Jewish and two Polish committees.[36] They handed out rations, as well as opening and maintaining hostels, orphanages, homes for invalids, sewing workshops, public kitchens and other facilities. Polish groups were particularly active, organising cultural events such as plays, concerts, vocal music and family parties. For example, on 21 March the Voronezh branch of the Petrograd society for assisting Polish war victims arranged a concert of works by Polish composers, with the participation of Polish artists, such as violinist Josef Oziminskii and soloists of the Warsaw Opera.[37] Likewise, in Kaluga on 18 April 1916 the official Polish committee organised a performance in the Polish language at the municipal theatre, in support of Polish refugees.[38] Refugee youth groups took part in provincial social and cultural life, performing charity concerts, and publishing books and several periodicals in the Lithuanian language. A national charity, the West Russian Society for Refugee Aid also secured jobs for refugees from Kovno, and opened schools and hostels for students, as well as orphanages, alms-houses and hospitals in the central European Russian provinces. As with other bodies, it paid for schooling and provided refugees with clothes and linen.[39]

All this was calculated to ensure that refugees remained together in order to sustain a sense of 'national' identity. It was also important for the national committees to be able to claim that they used donations wisely in support of refugees. Hence committee leaders made a point of emphasising that no more than ten per cent of the funds they collected went on overhead costs. This was designed to enhance their legitimacy in the eyes of their members and of the Russian public at large.[40]

The provincial branches of the Tatiana committee were already in place in the spring and summer of 1915. The social composition of local branches was emphatically upper-class and bourgeois, comprising high-ranking officials, clergy, local government representatives, prominent local intellectuals, and 'honourable citizens' (*pochetnye grazhdane*). They dealt with the complex business of registering refugees, establishing orphanages and schools, and particularly looking after orphans and disabled refugees. Workshops produced warm clothes for refugees. The wives of provincial governors and other members of the elite handed out fresh linen, footwear and clothes. Cash grants ranged from 5 to 25 rubles. The Tatiana committee also channelled funds to diocesan committees and to national committees in provincial towns and cities.[41] Street collections were held in Russian towns and cities between 29 and 31 May 1915, timed to coincide with Grand Duchess Tatiana Nikolaevna's birthday. This alone generated more than two million rubles, a tidy sum when we consider that the monthly expenses of the Tatiana committee were running at half a million rubles in early August, and climbed to six million rubles in September.[42]

The All-Russian public organisation Zemgor (the union of towns and zemstvos) also drew on state funds to maintain canteens and hostels for refugees free of change.

Government funds for refugee relief began to decline during 1916 due to the growing costs of the war effort. The state calculated that most refugees had by this time settled in the interior and could become independent since jobs were relatively easy to come by. Government officials, including local representatives of the special council, began to look for ways to reduce expenditure. Governors were enjoined to carefully scrutinise refugees' claims for state allowances, to find jobs for unemployed refugees who were able to work, and to threaten them with the withdrawal of benefits if they refused to work without offering a good reason.[43] In June 1916 the special council ordered a reduction of 10 per cent in food rations in the countryside, and 15 per cent for refugees living in towns, on the grounds that 'refugees are no longer in a critical or helpless condition'. This is not to underestimate the total cost to the tsarist state of supporting refugees, which amounted to 510 million rubles between July 1915 and May 1917.[44]

It is important to emphasise that most refugees did not expect to be a charge on the state. This, together with the fact that the state allowance made it impossible to get by, ensured that refugees actively went in search of work.[45] Refugees worked in state and private enterprises, in sawmills, on the railways and in other industrial jobs. The Tatiana committee enlisted refugees in digging trenches, mending solders' clothes and sewing clothes for other refugees. In 1916, some 700 female refugees took jobs at a wage of one ruble for a nine-hour shift in the Bobruisk ordnance depot that had been evacuated to Kaluga.[46] Local newspapers advertised job openings. Local householders asked for nursemaids, housekeepers, cooks, hairdresser and seamstresses. Men advertised their technical services and offered to mend gramophones, sewing machines, stoves and musical instruments, or to work as painters and decorators, even though they had university qualifications. Some student refugees offered lessons in mathematics, Latin and Russian.[47]

By the end of 1916 refugee employment had begun to stabilise. In Riazan province, for example, around one in ten refugees performed some kind of agricultural labour, 14 per cent worked in other sectors, and 8 per cent were unemployed. Two out of three refugees were unable to work, either on grounds of age or disability, or because they looked after family dependents.[48] It is fair to say that the majority of refugees who wished to work, did so. They made a full contribution to the war effort and did not constitute a burden on society.

The majority of refugees dreamed of an early return to their homes, hoping to enlist the help of the state in this regard, not least to re-establish their farms. Refugees who were working for the war effort, often for good money, were regarded as particularly productive, since they had a vested interest in getting the job done and seeing the Russian army victorious.

Encountering refugees

The suddenness and intensity of the refugee crisis caught most ordinary Russians by surprise. By the beginning of 1916, the central European Russian provinces of Kaluga, Orel, Tula, Riazan and Voronezh had become home to at least 350,000 refugees (the figures only include registered refugees). According to official figures, by the beginning of 1916, refugees accounted for more than 4 per cent of the total population of Kaluga province. The proportion was much higher in towns and cities, where refugees accounted for around 12 per cent of the total. The proportions were slightly less in Orel and Tula.

Women, children and the elderly made up nearly three-quarters of the total. Most of them received some kind of assistance from the state.

One-third of all refugees settled in towns.[49] In terms of ethnic composition, most refugees were counted as 'Russians', by which was meant Belarusians and Ukrainians, who together accounted for 72 per cent of the total. The remainder were Polish (12 per cent), Latvian and Lithuanian (5 per cent). Jews made up barely 3 per cent of the total in these provinces.[50]

Numbers alone do not explain the reaction of local authorities to the presence of refugees in the Russian interior, or the reception they received at the hands of local people. We have already mentioned the variety of responses to the arrival of refugees, from heartfelt sympathy, to the opportunity to make a quick profit at their expense. But cultural interaction was as important as socio-economic relations.

As indicated above, reports circulated of the damage that refugees inflicted on Russian property. Other kinds of damage were no less threatening to social stability. According to provincial Russian authorities, the mass arrival of refugees in autumn 1915 risked spreading rumours about the imminent threat from the enemy and the risk that local inhabitants too would be confronted with the need to flee their homes. Reports began to circulate that people were getting alarmed and were withdrawing their savings from the banks. Sometimes locals accused refugees of harbouring Germanophile sentiments. The police duly investigated. One instance concerned Frantz Rudkovskii and his daughter Salome, refugees from Riga, who took refuge in Sapozhok, a small town in Riazan province. They were overheard supposedly maintaining that Germans would occupy Riga (as they eventually did in 1917) and that this would open the way to Petrograd. The result of the investigation was that neither Rudkovskii nor his daughter had any sympathy for Germans or for Germany, and that they posed no threat to state security.[51]

Relationships between locals and refugees did have more positive connotations and outcomes. Some accounts indicate that ordinary people liked refugees and were happy to engage them in conversation. There are plenty of instances of locals and refugees getting together to socialise or to watch their children play together. Local people shared food and clothes with refugees. New friendships sometimes culminated in marriage between refugees and locals.[52] Newspapers wrote that the refugees made themselves 'at home' and were keen to attend the theatre and cinema – although these reports were tinged with a degree of unease that refugees had become 'nearly the prevalent part of the public'. But refugees were not passive spectators. They expressed astonishment at the untidy yards, the dirty snowdrifts that hampered movement on the street, and the piles of sewage near important architectural sights.[53]

Certainly, some locals complained that refugees were receiving undue care and attention. But most people felt sorry for refugees and believed they should be treated sympathetically. A district police officer who attended a local meeting about drafting men for defence work reported that the peasants opposed sending refugees to undertake difficult and potentially dangerous jobs, because 'they had already endured a great deal'. It is this kind of underlying attitude that helps explain why Russians continued to donate money to support refugees, at least until the outbreak of the revolution in February 1917.[54]

The 'democratisation' of refugee relief in 1917

After the change of power in February 1917 and the general democratisation of political life, refugee committees, including national committees, were reformed to include an elective element. Mass meetings took place in which active, educated refugees informed other refugees about the political situation in Russia and the programme of the new government. Refugees elected new executives to enable closer co-operation with the new Provisional Government relating to various aspects of refugee life.

In November 1917, following the Bolshevik revolution, the Second All-Russian Congress of Refugees announced its readiness to co-operate with Soviet power in setting up refugee soviets (councils) on 'democratic' principles. New leaders were elected to the All-Russian Refugee Soviet.[55] The congress announced a broad programme of state aid to refugees in Russia and when they returned to their homes. Provisional arrangements were agreed about the process of 're-evacuation'. The congress anticipated that refugees would be able to return to their homes as soon as military demobilisation got under way. The state was expected to take care of the detailed arrangements including the provision of food and medical assistance during the journey. On returning to their 'ruined hearths' refugees were to be given state allowances of food, clothes and footwear, 'until they had settled down properly'. Financial support was likewise the responsibility of the state, which would distribute funds via local offices of the refugee soviet. Meanwhile the congress drew the attention of the Soviet government to the need to allow refugees to use the plots of land where they currently lived, because refugee families were clinging on to bare life: they were in a 'disastrous state'.[56]

Between January and April 1918 refugee soviets were established at provincial and volost levels. They provided refugees with an allowance, subsidised schools and orphanages, and food, using funds left over from the previous organisations. Most importantly, they also made travel arrangements for refugees who hoped to move to the fertile grain-growing regions of western Siberia and in Russia's south-east. However, the plans for re-evacuation came unstuck once the Soviet government pulled out of the war. It now became necessary for the refugee soviets to try and restrain the 'spontaneous' movement of refugees to the west, which was likely to occur as a result of the dire economic situation in Russia.

Few of these plans were realised. By the summer of 1918, democratisation was a thing of the past.[57]

Brest-Litovsk and refugee resettlement from Soviet Russia

After signing the Brest-Litovsk peace treaty in March 1918 the Soviet government was obliged to prepare for the re-evacuation of prisoners of war and refugees on its territory. Many refugees soon started to return home. This was no great surprise. The People's Commissariat of Internal Affairs announced that state allowances paid to refugees would come to an end. Since most refugees in the countryside were unable to obtain farm tools and seeds, this was devastating news. The main reason was Bolshevik economic policy, which made it impossible to employ refugees on peasant farms. In the opinion of refugees, peasant farmers suffered because the government constantly robbed them. Everyone was doomed to starvation. Nor were any jobs to be had in Russia's towns and cities.[58]

The business of re-evacuation was entrusted to a 'central commission for prisoners of war and refugees' (*Tsentroplenbezh*), which came into being at the end of April; local departments followed two or three months later. In July 1918, under the terms of Brest-Litovsk, individuals from the territories that were not by this stage already part of the new Soviet republic were entitled to request a change of citizenship; however, they had to submit this request within one month. Refugees protested the lack of time they were given, and the time period was continually extended. By the end of 1918 it was no longer possible to renounce Soviet citizenship. Anyone who had not opted to change their citizenship received equal rights with Russians. These refugees were not allowed to return but were instead conscripted into the Red Army or expected to work for the state in some other capacity.

What were the results? In the region under consideration, around 200,000 refugees, half the total living in six central provinces left the country on their own or with the help of the pre-Soviet refugee committees before the district departments of the Tsentroplenbezh were set up in 1918. Some 71,000 refugees from the remaining 200,000 either left the territory under their own steam or died of illness or hunger in the terrible winter of 1918. Tsentroplenbezh itself managed to 're-evacuate' only 15,000 refugees, usually those who advanced a claim on the basis of being in a 'really serious state of affairs'.

With the abrogation of the Brest-Litovsk treaty in November 1918, the re-evacuation of refugees came to a halt. It resumed in 1920 after agreements were signed between Soviet Russia and its neighbours. The process continued until the middle of 1925.

Conclusion

The mass flight of people from the front line to the rear of the empire in the second half of 1915 came about as a result of military defeat. Notwithstanding the efforts of the tsarist government to organise this evacuation, it did not take place without loss of life. However, the greatest loss of life among refugees in transit occurred in the Soviet period.

The central region was home to around 350,000 refugees by the beginning of 1916. Three quarters of refugees were adopted by wealthy farmers, who provided them with jobs. Refugees in cities, given the shortage of workers, also had an opportunity to work in a variety of occupations, including white-collar jobs. In 1915 the state intervened to provide assistance for refugees; local authorities also got involved. As a result refugees received government food and housing rations, medical treatment, as well as help in finding work.

Refugees faced privation, of course, but this chapter offers support for the view that the life of refugees in the Russian interior was relatively comfortable compared to the situation after the October Revolution. Certainly there is some evidence that refugees acknowledged the support they received from the tsarist authorities, from the indigenous population, and from various relief organisations. Returning to the first-hand testimony of refugees that was referred to in the introduction to this chapter, we can detect plenty of expressions of gratitude to local people and the authorities alike in European Russia. In the accounts they provided in the late communist period and following the collapse of communism refugees emphasised the warm welcome they received, contrasting it with their struggle to survive during the first months of Soviet power. The following extracts provide a flavour of this testimony:

> We were very pleased. We would not have returned if there had not been a Communist regime under which people were starving.

> Russians are very good people. If anybody had come to our place, they would have died of hunger. We were welcomed warmly even though the local people weren't very wealthy.
>
> Local hosts and refugees lived together very well before the Revolution, there was everything we needed in the shops, the local folks brought us food and clothes. Each of us got three rubles, as well as linen, exercise books and other items free of charge.
>
> We would never forget how Russians were good to us. If so many people had come to Poland, they would have been turned out. The Poles and Belarusians care only about themselves, they don't care about other people.
>
> All refugees remember Russians who are the best nation in the world. People in Russia are not like us, they are kind and simple. If so many people had come to our place, the locals would not even look at them, we would have told them to live as best they could. But both Russian authorities and the locals helped us.[59]

However, these arrangements, as well as the ability of refugees to organise their own self-help, came to an end with the establishment of Soviet power. The Bolsheviks scrapped the most valuable features of tsarist relief work. One consequence of Bolshevik agricultural and food procurement policy was a shortage of food, which prompted a mass movement of people including refugees, around the country in search of food. For refugees in particular, the looming food crisis meant that decisions to return home acquired extra urgency. In this endeavour they were assisted by Tsentroplenbezh which embarked upon the organised re-evacuation of refugees in August 1918. But most refugees made their own arrangements to return home. Those who could not or did not return had to remain on Soviet soil for at least five more years. They were expected to submit to Soviet power and to serve the new state. These people experienced a great deal more deprivation and loss of freedom than they had done under tsarist rule.

Notes

1 *Otchet o deiatel'nosti Osobogo otdela Komiteta Ee Imperatorskogo Vysochestva Velikoi kniazhny Tat'iany Nikolaevny* (Petrograd, 1916); *Spisok organizatsii, vedaiushchikh delo pomoshchi bezhentsam na 1 maia 1916 g.*, vypusk 1, Evropeiskaia Rossiia (Moscow, 1916); Ia. Kersten, *Litovskie bezhentsy v Tule* (Tula, 1917); N.I. Kustov, *Kratkie ocherki o deiatel'nosti natsional'nykh i blagotvoritel'nykh organizatsii, okazyvavshikh pomoshch' bezhentsam v g. Moskve* (Moscow, 1917); Kh. Braude, *Evreiskoe naselenie g. Voronezha: dannye perepisi 1917 goda* (Moscow, 1918).

2 A.D. Kirzhnits, 'Bezhenstvo', *Bol'shaia sovetskaia entsiklopediia*, vol. 5 (Moscow, 1927), cols 176–8.
3 A.M. Anfimov, *Rossiiskaia derevnia v gody pervoi mirovoi voiny* (Moscow: Nauka, 1962), pp. 106–7; T.M. Kitanina, *Voina, khleb i revoliutsiia* (Leningrad: Nauka, 1985).
4 L.I. Lubny-Gertsyk, *Dvizhenie naseleniia na territorii SSSR za vremia mirovoi voiny i revoliutsii* (Moscow, 1926); Iu. A. Poliakov, *Sovetskaia strana posle okonchaniia grazhdanskoi voiny: territoriia i naselenie* (Moscow: Nauka, 1986).
5 E.Z. Volkov, *Dinamika narodonaseleniia SSSR za 80 let* (Moscow-Leningrad, 1930), p. 72.
6 A.N. Kurtsev, 'Bezhentsy Pervoi mirovoi voiny v Rossii (1914–1917)', *Voprosy istorii*, no. 8 (1999), 98–113; A.N. Kurtsev, 'Bezhentsy Pervoi mirovoi voiny v Kurskoi gubernii, 1914–1917 gg.', *Kurskie tetradi, Kursk i kuriane glazami uchenyh*, vypusk 1 (1997), 33–64; V.M. Lavrent'ev and V.V. Khasin, 'Migratsionnye protsessy v Rossii v Pervuiu mirovuiu voinu', *Voenno-istoricheskie issledovaniia v Povolzh'e: sbornik nauchnykh trudov*, vypusk 1 (1997), 139–50; Peter Gatrell, *A Whole Empire Walking: Refugees in Russia During World War I* (Bloomington: Indiana University Press, 1999); N.V. Lakhareva, *Reevakuatsiia bezhentsev Pervoi mirovoi voiny s territorii Kurskoi gubernii (1918–1925)* (Kursk, 2001). For a survey of recent work, see N.V. Surzhikova, N.A. Mikhalev and S.A. P'iankov, 'Rossiiskoe bezhenstvo 1914–1922 godov v kontekste noveishikh otechestvennoi i zarubezhnoi istoriografii', *Vestnik Permskogo universiteta*, 20, no. 3 (2012), 140–52, available at http://cyberleninka.ru/article/n/rossiyskoe-bezhenstvo-1914-1922-godov-v-kontekstah-noveyshih-otechestvennoy-i-zarubezhnoy-istoriografiy.
7 Vital' Luba (ed.), *Bezhanstva 1915 goda* (Belastok: Niva, 2000); V. Cherepitsa, *Shchast'e zhit' dlia drugikh: Zapadnobelorusskie posledovateli religiozno-filosofskogo ucheniia L.N. Tolstogo (1921–1939)* (Grodno, 2007); P. Sjaÿruk, *Nebyccja ne isnue: nevjadomyja staronki belaruskaga nacyjanal'naga ruhu* (Garodnja-Wrocław, 2008).
8 F.A. Kudrinskii, 'Liudskie volny: bezhentsy', *Njoman*, no. 6 (1997), 79–193.
9 For example, Jan Tsybulsky, a dweller of the edge Suwalki province, and his wife were told about Germans approached by the shepherds but actually it turned out to be Russians. The family left and came back to their home village several times. During their last leaving they stayed for a while in Grodno province where they were until the middle of 1915, and then went south-east. Kudrinskii, 'Liudskie volny', p. 96.
10 S.G. Nelipovich, 'Repressii protiv poddannykh tsentral'nykh derzhav: deportatsii v Rossii 1914–1918 gg.', *Voenno-istoricheskii zhurnal*, no. 6 (1996), 32–42 (here p. 41).
11 Kudrinskii, 'Liudskie volny', pp. 82–7.
12 G.Z. Ioffe, 'Vyselenie evreev iz prifrontovoi polosy v 1915 g.', *Voprosy istorii*, 9 (2001), 85–97; Eric Lohr, *Nationalizing the Russian Empire: the Campaign*

against Enemy Aliens During World War 1 (Cambridge, MA: Harvard University Press, 2003).
13 V.N. Cherepitsa, *Gorod-krepost' Grodno v gody Pervoj mirovoi voiny: meropriiatiia grazhdanskikh i voennykh vlastei po obespecheniiu oboronosposobnosti i zhiznedeiatel'nosti* (Grodno, 2006), p. 148.
14 *Sbornik vazhneishikh zakonopolozhenii i rasporiazhenii, deistvuiushhikh s iiulia 1914 g. po 1 ianvaria 1916 g., vyzvannykh obstoiatel'stvami voennogo vremeni* (Petrograd, 1916), p. 47.
15 Cherepitsa, *Gorod-krepost' Grodno*, pp. 274–5, 277–8; Kudrinskii, 'Liudskie volny', p. 96; *Bezhanstva 1915 goda*, pp. 47, 66, 254.
16 Cherepitsa, *Gorod-krepost' Grodno*, pp. 277–8; *Bezhanstva 1915 goda*. pp. 86, 104–5, 116, 121, 256.
17 Kudrinskii, 'Liudskie volny', pp. 101–7, 115–17, 134–5, 141, 143, 147–8, 153, 154, 158, 161, 165.
18 The chief commissioner of Severopomoshch' was S.I. Zubchaninov. Prince N.I. Urusov headed Iugobezhenets. See *Bezhentsy i vyselentsy* (Moscow, 1915), p. 20.
19 Gosudarstvennyi arkhiv Voronezhskoi oblasti (GAVO), fond I-20, opis' 1, delo 9894, list 1; Kurtsev, 'Bezhentsy Pervoi mirovoi voiny v Kurskoi gubernii', p. 44.
20 O.V. Sheveleva, 'Sel'skohoziaistvennoe razvitie velikorusskoi provintsii i stolypinskaia agrarnaia reforma v gody Pervoi mirovoi voiny', kandidatskaia dissertatsiia (Tula, 2008), p. 186. On the arrhythmia of refugee trains, see Kurtsev, 'Bezhentsy Pervoi mirovoi voiny v Kurskoi gubernii', p. 42.
21 *Bezhenstvo 1915 goda*, pp. 86–7, 135–7.
22 *Bezhenstvo 1915 goda*, pp. 90, 138–41, 160–4, 176, 256.
23 A. Kozlovskij, 'Brali nas narashvat', *Bezhenstvo 1915 goda*, p. 103.
24 Gosudarstvennyi arkhiv Brianskoi oblasti (GABO), f. 374, op. 1, d. 204, l. 64.
25 *Bezhenstvo 1915 goda*, p. 121.
26 GABO, f. 4. op. 1, d. 5384, l. 34; d. 5342, l. 13.
27 *Bezhenstvo 1915 goda*, p. 74.
28 Gosudarstvennyi arkhiv Kaluzhskoi oblasti (GAKO), f. 784. op. 1. d. 1195.
29 On the law of 30 August on providing refugee needs, see *Zakony i rasporiazheniia o bezhentsakh* (Moscow, 1916), p. 2.
30 *Pravitel'stvennyi vestnik*, 1915, no. 260.
31 In autumn 1915 provincial councils of refugees chaired by governors were set up. The membership included representatives of local administrative boards at provincial and county level, together with the chief commissioner on refugee settlement, representatives of the provincial administration of one of the evacuated provinces in the rear, the chairman of the provincial Tatiana committee. Gosudarstvennyi arkhiv Riazanskoi oblasti (GARO), f. 29, op. 396, d. 6, ll. 31–2 ob.
32 The Constitutional Democratic Party (Kadets) was a major left-liberal political party in Russia, founded in October 1905. It played a decisive

role in the Fourth State Duma, in the organisations of the zemstvo and city unions, and the war-industry committees. Initially it supported the policy of the government in the First World War, but in 1915 helped launch the Progressive Bloc. The party acted under patriotic, but radically anti-government slogans.

33 *Bezhenets*, 23 December 1915; F.A. Gaida, *Liberal'naia oppozitsiia na putiakh k vlasti (1914–vesna 1917 g.)* (Moscow: Rosspen, 2003), pp. 108, 172.
34 Each person was given 15–20 kopeks for food, and 1.2–2 rubles for rent (*Rukovodiashchie polozheniia po ustroistvu bezhentsev, 2 marta 1916 g.* (Petrograd, 1916).
35 GAKO, f. 599, op. 1, d. 4, l. 106; f. 648, op. 1, d. 620, l. 113; f. 783, op. 1, d. 1192, l. 178; f. 1025, op. 2, d. 2, l. 89.
36 Gosudarstvennyi arkhiv Tulskoi oblasti (GATO), f. 90, pp. 1, d. 39813, ll. 68–9 ob.
37 B.A. Firsov, *Polozhenie bezhentsev v Voronezhe v gody Pervoi mirovoi voiny*, http://vrnlib.ru/polozhenie-bezhencev-v-voronezhe-v-gody-pervoj-mirovoj-vojny/ [accessed 25 May 2015].
38 I.B. Belova, *Pervaia mirovaia voina i rossiiskaia provintsiia, 1914–fevral' 1917 g.* (Moscow: AIRO-XX, 2011), p. 267.
39 Gosudarsvennyi arkhiv Orelskoi oblasti (GAOO), f. 4, op. 1, d. 5384, l. 29–30.
40 Zhurnal Gubernskogo soveshhaniia po delam bezhentsev g. Riazan', 2 May 1916, GARO, f. 29, op. 396, d. 6; *Kaluzhskii sanitarnyi obzor*, 1915, nos. 10–12; Rossisskii Gosudarstvennyi Voenno-istoricheskii arkhiv (RGVIA), f. 13273, op. 1. d. 209, ll. 4–5.
41 Diocesan committees started their work in August 1915 on the order of the Holy Synod. They were closed by order of Sovnarkom and the Commissariat of Justice in 1918.
42 *Letopis' voiny 1914-1915-1916 gg.*, no. 107, pp. 11–17.
43 GATO, f. 90, op. 1, d. 39813, l. 95.
44 Gosudarsvennyi arkhiv Rossiiskoi Federatsii (GARF), f. R-3333, op. 2, d. 1 a, l. 54.
45 *Bezhenstvo 1915 goda*, p. 152.
46 GAKO, f. 599, op. 1, d. 4, ll. 130–4, 382.
47 *Polozhenie bezhentsev v Voronezhe*.
48 Counted according to information in GARO, f. R-547, op. 1, d. 1, l. 117.
49 *Otchet o deiatel'nosti Osobogo Otdela Komiteta EIV VK Tat'iany Nikolaevny*, p. 40; GAOO, f. 4, op. 1, d. 5304, l. 22.
50 GAKO, f. 594, op. 1, d. 5, ll. 203–203 ob; GATO, f. 90, op. 1, d. 39813, l. 95; GAOO, f. 4, op. 1, d. 5304, l. 22; Kurtsev, 'Bezhentsy Pervoi mirovoi voiny v Kurskoi gubernii', p. 5.
51 GAKO, f. 783, op. 1, d. 1204, l. 638.
52 GARO, f. 1292, op. 1, d. 988, ll. 11–11 ob; op. 2, d. 175, l. 22; GAKO, f. R-2019, op. 1, d. 22 (no pagination).

53 *Kaluzhskii kur'er*, 18 August 1915; *Kaluzhskii kur'er*, 21 November 1915; *Kaluzhskii kur'er*, 22 January 1916; *Kaluzhskii kur'er*, 28 February 1916.
54 Belova, *Pervaia mirovaia voina*, pp. 107–11.
55 The All-Russian Union of Refugees was established by the First All-Russian Congress of Refugees that took place in Petrograd from 1 to 12 September 1917.
56 GAKO, f. R-2019, op. 1, d. 1, ll. 6–12.
57 I.B. Belova, 'Bezhentsy Pervoi mirovoi voiny v rossiiskoi provintsii: sovety bezhentsev 1918 g.', *Vestnik Brianskogo gosudarstvennogo universiteta: istoriia, literaturovedenie, pravo, iazykoznanie*, no. 2 (2011), 26–30. www.brgu.ru/bank/zhurnal/vestnik_2.pdf [accessed 27 March 2014].
58 *Bezhenstvo 1915 goda*, pp. 29–30, 46, 99–100, 103, 110, 153–4.
59 *Bezhenstvo 1915 goda*, pp. 28, 46, 83, 121, 131, 161, 176, 219, 250.

5

Ukrainian assistance to refugees during the First World War[1]

Liubov Zhvanko and Oleksiy Nestulya

Introduction

The impact of war has been widely felt in modern Ukraine. The First World War acutely affected ethnic Ukrainians who lived under tsarist and Habsburg rule. This chapter concentrates on the impact of war on displaced Ukrainians before and after the collapse of tsarism in February 1917, whose lives were beset by political uncertainty, economic deprivation and social conflict.

Tsarist Russia was a faltering giant with a backward economy and an ineffective communications system, and as a multinational empire it faced a number of dilemmas relating to ethnic minority groups. Despite its many problems and shortcomings, the Russian Empire was nevertheless a functioning polity. The war turned everything upside down. Ukraine became a battleground and Ukrainian territory, particularly western Ukraine, was severely damaged as a result of the war. From the outbreak of war, Galicia, Volhynia and (to a lesser extent) the central Ukrainian provinces were turned into major theatres of war. Other Ukrainian provinces in the rear of the empire accommodated a significant number of refugees, organised hospitals for the wounded, managed POW camps, and helped meet the growing needs of the imperial army. Many Ukrainians became refugees, while others helped to shelter their brethren.[2]

Further upheaval followed the disintegration of the Russian Empire and the formation of new states. The February Revolution made possible the establishment of a Ukrainian Central Rada in Kiev on 4 March 1917, with the well-known historian Mikhail Hrushevsky as its leader. The Rada published a series of four legislative acts or 'Universals', regulating changes to Ukraine's legal status; the Fourth Universal (22 January 1918) proclaimed the creation of an independent Ukrainian People's Republic (*Ukrains'ka Narodna Respublika*; UNR). On 9 February 1918 the new government signed a peace treaty at Brest-Litovsk. It preserved Ukrainian independence, and agreed to supply food to Germany and Austria-Hungary in exchange for military support against Soviet Russia. Failing to deliver on its promises, Austria-Hungary and Germany supported a change of government in Ukraine, and on 29 April 1918 a Hetmanate was proclaimed by a former tsarist general Pavlo Skoropadskyi. The Hetmanate provided a measure of internal stability and began to address the economic and health crisis as well as to assist prisoners of war, war invalids, orphans and refugees. However, the regime faced a challenge from peasants and workers, and a new republic was proclaimed in December 1918. With the defeat of Germany and Austria-Hungary, Ukraine was exposed to Soviet military occupation, and to a prolonged period of political and military conflict, the eventual outcome of which was the formation of the Ukrainian Soviet Socialist Republic.

At least one million refugees were to be found on Ukrainian lands between 1915 and 1917. A further increase in the number of refugees took place as a result of revolutionary events in 1917, the outbreak of civil war and the 'red terror' in Russia. Paradoxically, at the same time, in the middle of 1918 Ukraine was considered to be an oasis of stability that offered shelter to the displaced.[3] It thus served as a transit territory through which various ethnic groups sought to flee from the chaos in Russia.

Population displacement and relief efforts

In summer 1915, as the mass movement of refugees gathered pace, the Russian media began to publish articles on the causes of the crisis. At the beginning of August, an Odessa newspaper stated: 'this phenomenon may be seen as a result of panic, but in most cases it is the result of the evacuation ordered by the authorities'.[4]

'Panic' certainly contributed to displacement. Escape seemed the only means of saving one's skin. Russian propaganda cleverly played on these psychological aspects by depicting pictures of the atrocities inflicted by German and Austrian troops, indirectly encouraging civilians to think of escape from 'Teutonic barbarism' before it was too late. As eye-witnesses testified, Russians and others retreated as the enemy approached. People did not know whether to flee to the Russian interior or to hide in the woods and marshes until the front line moved on. Cossacks rode from village to village, with tales of rape and mass executions. However, contemporary journalists were right to say that the crucial factor was the actions of the imperial military command, which in order to 'cleanse' the territory on the principle of 'scorched earth', forcibly removed civilians from front-line provinces. These orders took effect in summer 1915 and triggered a gigantic movement of people.

Refugees travelled across the territory of Ukraine by road and rail. They were instructed to follow prescribed routes, either one of thirty highways or one of eight railway lines, and to cross the rivers Dnepr, Desna, Zdvyzh and Prypyat at a number of points, chiefly Kaniv, Cherkasy and Kremenchug. However, refugees frequently ignored instructions. As a leading Russian military figure wrote: 'when moving by railway or by road [they] avoided or missed the defined routes and moved in all kinds of different directions, embracing wider and wider regions'.[5] This 'spontaneity' reflected the lack of resources and the fact that officials failed to co-ordinate refugees' movement. In addition, refugees more often than not changed their route themselves in order to feel safer. Matters were not helped by poor transport infrastructure. Railway stations were so overcrowded that local committees were simply unable to assist refugees satisfactorily. Officials bemoaned what they saw as chaos.[6]

In the first months of the war the Russian authorities failed to understand the scale and the challenge posted by mass displacement. Guided by the experience of previous wars, they shifted the care of refugees to charitable organisations such as the committee of her Imperial Highness Grand Duchess Tatiana Nikolaevna for the provision of temporary assistance to the victims of war. However, it was impossible to solve the knot of the most complicated refugee problems on the basis of public charity, even when backed by the authority and resources of the Russian imperial family and the tsarist state.

The Ukrainian lands were of course subject to Russian legislation and jurisdiction, chiefly the law providing for the needs of refugees, promulgated on 30 August 1915, legislation that outlined the concept of 'refugee'. Further legal clarification came in the guidelines on refugee settlement issued on 2 March 1916. These documents outlined the legal status of refugees, guaranteeing them a number of rights in the evacuation and in the places of resettlement, and outlining the responsibilities of government and society for arranging for the social protection of refugees (see chapter 4).

Following this legislation, the welfare of refugees became the responsibility of the state, in the shape of a Special Council for Refugees under the auspices of the Ministry of the Interior. In Ukraine, as throughout the

Russian Empire, provincial councils were established and chaired by provincial governors who co-ordinated the arrangements for refugee relief. In addition, two commissioners or plenipotentiaries were appointed to manage the settlement of refugees on the North-Western Front (Sergei Zubchaninov) and the South-Western Front (Nikolai Urusov). In addition, public organisations played an important part in refugee relief work, notably the All-Russian Union of Zemstvos and the All-Russian Union of Cities. Throughout the entire period an important role in assisting refugees was played by organs of local self-government – provincial, district zemstvo and municipal council.

Supporting refugees in their place of temporary residence raised difficult issues which neither officials in the Russian Empire nor their successors were fully able to address. One reason was the recurrent lack of sufficient funds. The main source of funding for refugee assistance was the state budget, supplemented by the resources of local authorities. However, budgets did not stretch very far. Consequently an important source of support was the funds generated by private charity. Fundraising evolved throughout the course of the long war. To begin with one could observe universal euphoria and enthusiasm caused by the desire to help, in what was described as a 'spontaneous outpouring of selfless generosity'. The pages of newspapers were full of appeals by Grand Duchesses Tatiana. In crowded venues special banners advertised the need for donations of money, clothes and food for refugee needs.[7] As to the scale of fundraising it is possible to distinguish all-Russian from local fundraising and the numerous donations of private individuals. The Tatiana committee attracted funds from the autumn of 1914. On the local level zemstvos and municipalities, local committees for refugee assistance, national committees and the clergy all raised money through subscription lists, concerts and other performances, mass festivities, tea parties, deductions from employee salaries, and the sale of books, handicrafts, flowers and lottery tickets, as well as lectures and discussions. By 1916, however, the press reported a degree of apathy, a 'general tiredness and reluctance to raise funds'.[8] Charitable fundraising continued under the UNR and the independent Ukrainian state, but once again there were difficulties in maintaining commitment.

Refugees in Ukraine

The precise ethnic composition of refugees is difficult to establish. Officials normally referred to Russian, Ukrainian and Belarusian refugees as 'Russian refugees'. Only after the February Revolution did they begin to express their national identity. Polish refugees outnumbered them all.⁹ In total, refugees on Ukrainian soil belonged to 20 different national groups, including Ukrainians, Russians, Belarusians, Poles, Germans, Latvians, Lithuanians, Estonians, Czechs, Slovaks, Moldavians, Rumanians and Serbs.

From the beginning of the war a wide network of 'national' committees operated on Ukrainian territory to cater for the needs of specific ethnic minority groups. These included the Central Public Committee of Polish Kingdom Provinces, the Polish Central Committee on Assistance to Victims of War, the Society to Assist Poor Polish Families, the Polish Committee of Sanitation Aid, the Polish L'viv Assistance Committee, the Latvian Central Committee to Assist Refugees, and the Central Committee of Lithuanian Society to Assist War Victims. The Jewish community in Ukraine likewise established refugee aid committees under the aegis of the Central Jewish Committee on Rendering Assistance to War Victims.[10]

Government officials thus sought to shift the burden of refugee care on to local authorities as well as the established ethnic minority communities and new national committees. The war demonstrated the strength of ethnic solidarity, as local Poles, Lithuanians, Latvians, Jews and others shared their homes and donated money, clothes and footwear, as well as giving their time and sympathy to geographically distant but spiritually close refugee compatriots who shared a common motherland. Leaders of new refugee national committees, as well as local residents of non-Russian ethnicity, prided themselves in offering a degree of spiritual warmth and a means of overcoming a sense of common homesickness. For example, Poles in Kharkiv actively helped their fellow refugees, opening shelters for children, collecting funds for refugees, and providing them with food and clothing.[11]

Ukrainian institutions were separately listed among these national committees. Their official approval was beset by significant difficulties. Although the tsar had promised autonomy to the Poles and supported dedicated Polish relief organisations, he would not entertain anything comparable for Ukrainians. Nor is it surprising that there was no charitable body at an all-Russian level to cater for Ukrainian refugees and be represented on the Special Council. Ukrainian political and cultural activity was severely constrained under tsarist rule. Peter Gatrell rightly describes Ukrainian refugees as 'awkward refugees' in so far as Russian chauvinists opposed any attempt to draw attention to refugees of Ukrainian nationality.[12]

Nevertheless, Ukrainian organisations did begin to mount a relief effort on their own account. The first such public organisation was the 'Society to support the population of the South [sic] affected by the war', which came into being in spring 1915. In addition, from the outset, Ukrainian women and clergy of various denominations took an active part in the organisation of assistance to refugees by setting up 'ladies' and diocesan committees. Later on, during the revolution, it was renamed the 'Ukrainian association to assist victims of war'. In general, provincial Ukrainian towns and cities became the focus of official, non-governmental and private activity on behalf of refugees. Local committees reported to them in turn.

Refugees constituted a changeable population that was in constant flux, and this made it difficult to collect objective data. Natural demographic factors (births and deaths) influenced refugee numbers, with the added complexity of movement from one area to another, along with conscription, family reunion, and so forth. The best estimate is that refugees on Ukrainian territory numbered more than 400,000 in November 1915, increasing to about one million in the winter of 1918. In autumn 1915 some 220,000 refugees sheltered in Ekaterinoslav province, making it home to the largest number in the Russian Empire. Naturally these data can only be considered tentative. Following the February Revolution an uncontrolled movement of refugees took place from Russia to Ukraine which they regarded as a place of transit. Additional contingents of refugees included Romanian refugees who fled German occupation of their country. Nearly 900 such refugees were sent to Kremenchuk, Poltava, and the Poltava district in the first three months of 1917. Others found temporary shelter in Ekaterinoslav and Kherson provinces.[13]

Most registered refugees were women and children who belonged to farming families. Local committees distinguished 'intellectual and semi-intellectual refugees' from those of a non-professional background.

We can distinguish three periods in the activities of the institutions charged with the care of refugees. The first period was characterised by meeting the everyday needs of refugees in the course of their evacuation. The second involved settling them in new locations. The third period was dominated by refugees' repatriation or (as it was called) their 're-evacuation'.

During the first year of the war the relocation of refugees to the rear provinces took a predominantly random form. Most refugees moved under their own steam using horse-drawn wagons covered with tarpaulins and loaded with their most precious belongings. Contemporary newspaper reports provided a vivid picture of this mass movement:

> Province after province is on the move. You can distinguish one province from another. Here is Kholm province: you recognise it by the women's hairstyle – under their kerchiefs you can see their curls of hair. [...] People from Kholm left the earliest and they are the angriest. Their women are quarrelsome and cry hysterically on any pretext. Their nerves were entirely frayed. Meanwhile people from Grodno province look dignified in their reddish jackets. You can recognise them by their carts covered with striped and check cloths. The same cloth is used for the aprons that women wear on holiday. This is all very fashionable.[14]

Those who witnessed events in Volyn' province described how refugees packed their wagons with clothes, towels and fabrics, a bread bin, a shovel to put bread into the oven, a barrel of pig's fat, a sack of flour, a spade, an axe and a saw. There was no room for anything else. Each horse-drawn wagon was protected against rain. When it was dry everyone commented on how the wagons creaked. The list of belongings suggests that refugees expected to rely upon their own resources by taking supplies of food and work tools suitable for use by men and women. Female refugees anticipated that somewhere en route it would be possible to find an oven in which to bake bread and remove it with one's own bread shovel, as they was accustomed to doing at home. Even in unfamiliar surroundings they expected to carry out the same tasks as 'at home', and to maintain a familiar life-style as far as possible.[15]

One outcome was a degree of 'antisocial' behaviour on the part of refugees, who understandably sought to survive as best they could. To take one example, on 15 October 1915 the head of the police department of Slaviansk telegraphed the provincial governor of Kharkiv complaining that, 'driven to extremes, and getting no fuel from anyone, women refugees along with their children openly steal coal from railway wagons at the station and along the length of the railway line'.[16]

Probably the most difficult period for refugees came at the outset when they were supported only by some public organisations and a handful of well-disposed people. Later on, in summer and autumn 1915, around 500 'support stations' had been established on Ukrainian territory lands, including feeding points and paramedical facilities providing vaccinations, disinfection, medicines and so on. Other facilities included baths and laundries, as well as forges where horses could be shod and refugee carts mended. At meal stations refugees received hot meals and children were given milk once a day. Daily rations were described as follows: 'The refugee receives one meal: a soup with onion fried with pig's fat, or meat stock or porridge and then bread and tea. Bread is rationed to half a pound per person per day, pig's fat – a quarter of a pound, sugar – three lumps. Meals are issued twice a day.[17] Having covered hundreds and sometimes thousands of kilometres, on foot, by cart, in overcrowded carriages, and having undergone the trial of hunger and diseases, extremes of heat and cold, often spending a night in an open field, exhausted psychologically and physically, refugees then found that their problems did not end once they reached a place of safety in the Russia interior.

One very difficult task for central and local government and for refugee committees was to provide housing. The diverse refugee population comprised large families, as well as orphans and children lost in transit, the elderly, the disabled and the sick, all of whom required a different approach. Single girls and young women were potential victims of sexual violence, and were often provided with sheltered accommodation. By late summer 1915 local authorities imposed a greater degree of control. Governors of Ukrainian provinces ordered local people to accommodate refugees, and in exchange refugees paid a monthly rent, so-called 'apartment money'. This became progressively worthless with the increase in inflation. Due to the lack of funds on the part of the UNR, refugees largely ceased to receive this payment by spring 1918. Furthermore local people and refugees, constantly experiencing psychological tension, got tired of each other. These and other negative factors explain why refugees were increasingly evicted by landlords. By the time the Hetmanate came to power the scale of eviction had become rampant. Accordingly on 29 May 1918 the Refugee Department of the Ministry of the Interior issued an order instructing local authorities to intervene, and in early June the government ordered them to protect refugee families from eviction. The results were, however, quite modest.

Clergymen took an active interest in the resettlement of refugees, and placed monastery premises, other church buildings, and parish schools at their disposal. In addition, priests used their personal authority to appeal to parishioners to accommodate refugees. National committees also involved themselves in matters of housing. Their scope was extensive. For example, the Central Public Committee of Polish Kingdom Provinces, which operated in the Kharkiv region, resettled over 12,000 Polish refugees in Ukraine and paid for their housing and heating. Kharkiv province opened 35 shelters, mostly for Poles but also for Lithuanians and Jews. A small number were able to locate relatives and friends with whom they could share accommodation.[18]

Given the shortage of available housing refugees were also accommodated in specially built temporary barracks at railway junctions. In Ekaterinoslav the provincial committee of the All-Russian Union of Zemstvos began to build a refugee barracks at the end of August 1915. It was called 'Pokrovske town', after the name of the railway station square, where it was located. The municipal council in Poltava placed refugees in special camps, since it had no other housing at its disposal. One such camp lasted for two months and provided temporary shelter for around 1,200 refugees. After which they were resettled elsewhere in the province.

One of the most difficult problems proved to be the task of providing refugees with adequate food. Refugees received food at specially arranged canteens or cafeterias. These stations became places for mutual exchange of information between compatriots, and here we can begin to see the impact of the war on people's lives and character. In August 1916 the correspondent of a Kyiv newspaper described one establishment that he visited as follows:

> It is lunch time. A dense grey crowd. Senior citizens, teenagers, children – but the majority are women. Grey 'Little Russian' [Malorossiia] coats, jackets, city coats, Galicia fur hats. The nuns who bring meals are scarcely able to make their way through the crowd. Refugees eat at long tables, others are waiting their turn, and some are receiving rations to take away. On one side there are the tables of inquiry offices: Russian, Polish, Jewish.[19]

In addition, they received monthly cash, 'food aid', to purchase their own products. On average, this amounted to six rubles per month per adult which corresponded to the amount recommended by government guidelines. Thirdly, non-Ukrainian refugees were given food to prepare meals according to their own cuisine. Refugee rations were uniform, differing from province to province only in the amount allocated, and this depended on local opportunities to purchase food. These practices, as well as the problems associated with them, persisted under the UNR and the Ukrainian state.

Providing refugees with employment entailed a complex web of different factors – economic, social and psychological. The situation was perceived differently by authorities, society and refugees themselves. Non-refugees tended to adhere to the view that refugees were reluctant or simply unable to work:

> One cannot call it 'idling' when refugees have lived through the destruction of their homes, the loss of the fruit of numerous years of labour, and after having survived separation, illnesses or the death of their relatives and close friends. They are really ill, physically, morally and spiritually.[20]

In fact most refugees managed to find work in agriculture, in the coal and iron ore mines in the Donbass and Kryvyi Rih (Krivoi Rog), and in newly created workshops. Some refugees managed to find a job for which their qualifications made them suitable. By September 1916, 2,500 men worked in the coal and anthracite mines of Ukraine. In turn, the imperial authorities sought to use refugees dispersed in rural areas to substitute for peasant men who had been conscripted. The expectation that refugees should work, especially in agriculture, was embodied in the guidelines on refugee settlement. Taking jobs in agriculture if asked to do so served as a condition for receiving food rations. Many Ukrainian provinces established workshops employing refugees to produce clothes, shoes and other items for their own needs. Refugees received remuneration according to their gender and qualifications, and whether or not they provided their own meals.[21]

Some potentially employable refugees found work harder to come by, particularly when the overall level of unemployment began to rise. Local farmers sought out cheaper labour where possible. For example, businesses in Kharkiv sought to employ refugees, but offered them less than the going rate for the job. One leading locomotive factory paid refugees only half the wage that local workers received.

At the same time, refugees' growing awareness of the possibility of re-evacuation, not to mention a degree of spiritual fatigue, made them reluctant to seek work.[22] They expressed anger with the government: 'the government brought us into poverty, and kept us there'. There was also a sense of dissatisfaction with the local population: 'we have lost property, and here you are sitting quietly and not offering to give us even a penny'.[23]

Throughout the war, as well as during the revolution and civil war, refugees who settled in Ukrainian towns and villages were given free medical care as outpatients, or in hospitals and tents. The main burden of care of evacuees was shouldered by rural and city councils that provided free medicine when presented with a refugee certificate from a local refugee committee. The vast majority of evacuees needed urgent medical attention to deal with outbreaks of typhoid, cholera and smallpox, which of course posed a danger to local people as well. Unfortunately, refugees in general suffered from poor health as a result of their prolonged displacement, malnutrition and exposure to violence. Despite all the efforts of local authorities, it was quite difficult to provide all evacuees with proper medical care. In the spring of 1918 local authorities faced a serious threat from infectious diseases. The complex epidemiological situation in Ukraine was linked to global and cyclical epidemics, aggravated due to the influence of negative external factors. In this regard the fight against epidemics gained national importance. Where refugees were constantly moving from place to place, officials organised vaccination against smallpox, cholera and typhoid fever.[24]

An extremely important area of assistance from government bodies and the public in Ukraine was the social care of vulnerable refugee children of all ages, different class backgrounds and ethnicities who shared the misfortune of adult refugees but who had specific needs. From autumn 1915 the Tatiana committee assumed overall responsibility for the care of children, supported locally by its own staff, by public organisations and national committees. Thanks to public and charitable donations in Ukraine a network of orphanages and kindergartens was established. School-age children were able to attend school, and special classes provided instruction by refugee teachers in their mother tongue. For example, one parish school in the bishopric of Poltava enrolled 400 refugee children. Thanks to the charitable donations organised by the Orthodox Church, refugees in Kremenchuk and Kobeliatsk districts received free clothing, footwear, writing implements and textbooks. In general, the social protection of refugee children reflected the general trends of humanitarian policy. It was carried out in difficult circumstances and did not always provide appropriate conditions for their development.[25]

Finally, the spiritual needs of refugees could not be overlooked. This was especially true for the people evacuated from the Polish and Baltic lands where worship had to be conducted in their own language. Again, however, this was easier said than done. Often priests were unavailable to offer a service for the dead, to baptise babies, or to support desperately unhappy people of all ages. To do this, the Holy Synod, the supreme church authority in the Russian Empire with support from high commissioners Zubchaninov and Urusov, as well as commanders of the Russian army, ordered Orthodox priests to remain with their parishioners, including joining them on the journey eastwards. In autumn 1915 a commission on meeting refugees' spiritual needs made provision for those of Catholic faith. From late November 1915 Catholic and Protestant priests visited the locations of their respective flock. Orthodox priests did likewise, and met refugees at railway stations where they read prayers, had pastoral conversations, and handed out gospels, prayer books and crosses.[26]

Thus, on Ukrainian lands during the First World War arrangements were made for the resettlement of refugees, for a network of shelters, and for the supply of food, clothing and footwear, well as health care in rural and urban hospitals. In addition, refugees had an opportunity to continue their education. Adults were able to find work. These measures improved their prospects and enabled some of them to adapt to local society.

The psychological world of refugees

Refugees cannot be unequivocally and categorically perceived as an amorphous mass lacking the capacity to evaluate their situation and to take care of themselves. It is not surprising that among them there were those who found it difficult to adapt to new conditions. Over time the refugee phenomenon ceased to be an extraordinary event, and the refugees, along with the local population, got used to their conditions. One could almost say that the refugee phenomenon (*bezhenstvo*) had become part of everyday life. Most refugees settled reasonably well and managed to adapt to their new circumstances. Some of them started their own businesses while others found manual or office jobs and adjusted to a kind of ordinary, sedentary way of life.[27] Notwithstanding numerous hardships, refugees were becoming part of the society that had offered them shelter. As we shall see, however, this did not preclude a wish to return to their place of origin.

Women and children faced particular hardship, including a degree of psychological trauma. Refugee women not infrequently had to bury their children or elderly parents, and the route to the Russian interior was marked by graves. They were consumed by the need to find out about husbands, lovers, brothers and fathers. They had to find food for their children, who were sometimes lost in the chaos of flight. Women experienced displacement as a fearful process: fear of the enemy; fear of spending the night in dark forests or ditches; fear of contracting disease after drinking from dirty pools; fear of strangers; fear of losing their belongings; fear of being tricked by merchants and landlords; fear of being raped by soldiers; and fear of never seeing their homes again and dying in a foreign land.

Contemporary commentators pointed to the predicament of female refugees, noting how horror was imprinted on the face of refugees:

> What a gloomy picture these people presented: upset, impoverished, old, middle-aged, women, children, exhausted, yellow-faced ... Tears flowed when listening to people's stories about the terrible destruction of their homes, about the enforced departure, separation of husbands and wives, parents and children.
>
> Their circumstances were made worse by the spread of false rumours. For example, when a number of refugees from Volyn arrived in Kherson, they were afraid to leave the railway wagons because someone repeated a story that the refugees had drowned in the sea. Women repeated the rumour: 'They will take us to the sea and drown us there!'[28]

In autumn 1915 journalist Timofei Emtsev, a former village teacher, related the horrible story of an eye-witness who had visited a refugee shelter in Kherson district:

> Day and night a baby was sobbing its heart out. It shouted itself hoarse and having turned blue, it was swinging its lean greenish worm-like legs and moaning like an adult. Its mother with tormented face full of tears put her empty breast to its mouth and faltered ... 'Die! I've got no milk! O! Die! I cannot!' She clasped her head and moaned ... Ah! I cannot take any more! God, take it! I cannot'.
>
> At night the baby suddenly died. It did not cry anymore and did not swing its worm-like legs and its mother was sitting and striking her head against the wall.[29]

An uncertain future also preoccupied refugees. 'What awaits her tomorrow, whether it would be news of her husband's death, her children's illness, or if a local refugee committee would refuse to give refugees "rations", or if she would be evicted by the owners?' Female refugees had to take responsibility for the family at the time when men were at war, in captivity or even worse without any news about them at all. Their social role changed, turning them from passive 'hearth keepers' into the family breadwinners. Although the war destroyed the patriarchal foundations of family life, nevertheless women found that the lack of security and a sense of not being in control negated any sense of inner tranquillity or empowerment.[30]

Children were exposed to a whirlwind of displacement, though those who remained with their parents or relatives suffered less than others. Contemporary observers expressed amazement at the large number of children:

> Almost every carriage disclosed dozens of fair-haired children who lifted their bright eyes to meet yours and looked up with a serene gaze. And they

are smiling: what are they up to? They may be glad to travel, they are certainly glad … And sometimes children are forgotten at stations amidst all this noise and bustle.[31]

Meanwhile orphaned children suffered from deep psychological wounds, since they had lost their loved ones in the course of an inexplicably long journey to a foreign realm where they encountered the unknown. And all this filled them with dread. A representative of the Ekaterinoslav committee for refugee aid described being introduced to a young orphan sitting on a bench in the open air:

> From the stories of the people surrounding her it became clear that her mother had died some days before and she did not have a father. So this six-year-old girl was living alone. She is a nice and clever girl. Her blue eyes look wise, her hair is done well, she is neat and does not resemble the children I have just seen. She is sitting with her feet covered by her mother's jacket. After her mother died all she had was nine rubles in cash and her mother's jacket.[32]

Elderly people also suffered from torments which filled their days with dread. They were afraid to die in a foreign land and never again see their homeland. They lamented the fact that the priest would never read the burial service. Refugee men who were unable to find work felt powerless to support their familes.

Revolution and repatriation

In 1917 the Ukrainian Central Rada and thereafter the UNR took charge of policy towards refugees on Ukrainian territory. On 28 December 1917 the General Secretariat of the Rada approved 'Temporary regulations for the management of aid to refugees in Ukraine', which had the status of a law and regulated all aspects of UNR policy in managing refugees. Among them were the areas of financing assistance to refugees, organisation and re-evacuation of refugees, and support for ethnic committees.[33]

The Ukrainian government introduced various legal measures relating to the provision of assistance to refugees, and the extension of refugee legislation to Ukrainians beyond the borders of Ukraine. The main achievement of the Rada/UNR legislation in the sphere of the refugee problem was to seek to 'upgrade' to a matter of international diplomacy. In January 1918 during the Brest-Litovsk negotiations, the Ukrainian delegation introduced for the first time in European diplomatic practice the concept of inter-state agreement to repatriate refugees. The fact that the well-known Polish politician Stanislav Moskalevsky (1876–1936) was included in the Ukrainian delegation as adviser on refugees testifies to the importance that Ukraine attached to this issue. On 2 February 1918 he submitted a special memorandum to the Ukrainian delegation supporting the idea of creating a joint commission with Germany and Austria-Hungary to solve the 'problem of re-evacuation of those who had been taken to Ukraine as hostages, deportees or refugees to their homeland: to the pre-war areas of Volyn' and Podolia as well as Halychyna [Galicia] and Poland; taking into account the positive attitude of the Ukrainian People's Republic to the need for an imminent return to their homes of these innocent people mostly expelled by force'. According to the Ukrainian proposal, Kyiv was to become the headquarters for international missions to arrange for repatriation, due to its position as the epicentre of wartime displacement. Under this proposal, Ukraine would have occupied a central place in solving this complicated international problem.[34] However, European diplomats took a different view, and Ukraine was left on its own to face the problems posed by the presence of hundreds of thousands of refugees.

During the Rada period several Ukrainian government agencies for refugee assistance came into being, and the jurisdiction of the district conference on refugees was now extended to Volyn', Kyiv, Podolia, Poltava and Chernihiv provinces. The basic legal act, designed to regulate refugee problems in the new Ukrainian state was the 'Law on the Department and National Conference for Refugees'. This document legally cemented the chain of command of the Ukrainian state in the sphere of refugees entrusting the refugee department with management of the above.

The Hetmanate did not introduce any radical changes to the local administration on the refugee question lest this lead to the destruction of the entire local system of social protection. Experts kept their offices regardless of their political affiliation. The network of national committees continued to operate with government support. In addition, special structures were created to deal with the co-ordination of repatriation. These included a Latvian Central Committee in Ukraine as well as a 're-emigration department' of the Polish Ministry of the Interior and the re-emigration bureau of the Polish Civil Commissariat. Their agencies operated in Kyiv, Odessa, Kharkiv, Lutsk and Kovel'.[35] Finally, a 'Belarus Refugee Organisation' was established in Kyiv in summer 1918 to co-ordinate the activities of all existing Belarusian societies to assist refugees.

Refugees dreamed of returning home as soon as possible no matter how warmly they had been welcomed in a new place. At the beginning of 1918 the Ukrainian delegation in Brest proposed a conference with the representatives of the General Secretariat and the Austro-Hungarian monarchy to discuss how refugees, hostages and deportees might be released through the front line. Kyiv was to be the headquarters of international missions to handle this repatriation. However, Germany and Austria-Hungary, along with Turkey and Bulgarian officials, did not support the humanitarian proposals of the Ukrainian delegation. Ukraine was left alone to deal with the problem of re-evacuating hundreds of thousands of refugees.

Notwithstanding these obstacles, in April 1918 the UNR Ministry of the Interior approved a plan of repatriation. The practical implementation of this plan was entrusted to government authorities, but officials were hampered by the huge volume of work. They had to collect statistics, including the ethnic origin of refugees, and then plan appropriate and safe routes and develop mechanisms to transport them, as well as set up checkpoints and arrange for quarantine, food and medical facilities.[36]

Travel by refugees across Ukrainian territory could take place only with the permission of the Ministry of the Interior. Refugees now needed a special document, the so-called 'vigilant ticket' (*bditel'nyi talon*), which enabled provincial conferences to maintain a record of repatriates. The movement of refugees from the Austro-Hungarian occupation zone to the German zone had to take place under the permission of the German authorities. The latter also issued orders on refugee re-evacuation abroad from its sphere of influence. In the first instance plans were made to concentrate refugees from the northern and south-eastern regions of Ukraine in Kiev/Kyiv before moving them on to Volyn' and Podilia provinces, to Poland, Germany, Belarus, the Baltic States and other countries. Train schedules had to be worked out and approved. As in 1915, some refugees had their own means of transportation and they were able to return to their homes by themselves. In July 1918 the occupation authorities opened the border to let them pass.

In late May 1918 customs checkpoints for foreign refugees were opened in Radyvyliv, Volochys'k, Husyatyn, Zbarazh, Rozhyshche and later in Manevichi and Luninets. There refugees were registered, received documents and were transported home. A separate category of stations were so-called 'quarantine stations', where refugees were subject to medical inspection and disinfection after their long journey to the border. Each station had one or several washing stations and disinfection chambers for clothing. Doctors and nurses provided medical care and vaccinated refugees.[37] Railway stations also had quarantine and sanitation areas as well as canteens – by autumn 1918 there were around 50 of these. Canteens providing food for up to 6,000 people were normally situated at large junctions. Refugees waited for transportation in camps that were set up as temporary facilities, as at the railway station Rivne (20,000 persons), Homel (6,000), Bakhmach (6,000), Kyiv (5,000), Katerynoslav (5,000), and Kharkiv freight station (5,000 persons). These stations were fenced and had checkpoints.

In the first place the re-evacuation of foreign refugees took place under the auspices of the Ukrainian state. However, Austro-Hungarian and German military administrations, despite their declarative statements, were reluctant to permit certain ethnic groups to leave, particularly Lithuanian and Polish Jews. At the same time, the new governments of Poland, Lithuania and Latvia procrastinated, on the grounds that their compatriots had been 'infected' by Bolshevism. As of mid-November 1918 at the railway stations of Shepetivka, Lutsk, Zdolbuniv, Kivertsi, Holoby and Kyiv there were around 16,000 Polish refugees in 700 railway carriages. In addition, about 3,000 refugees gathered in camps in Rivne and Holoby. Nevertheless, Ukraine managed to organise repatriation of a significant number of Poles, Lithuanians, Latvians and representatives of other ethnic groups, insisting on the establishment of a special 'open corridor' in the open front section for the refugees to be sent home as soon as possible. Ukrainian authorities adhered strictly to the principle of the 'open corridor' whereby refugees were able to cross the existing South-Western Front at a place designated by the international treaties, rather than through distant Sweden, as was the case with the refugees returning home from Bolshevik Russia.[38]

Resettlement of Ukrainian refugees from the east to the west of the country began in the second half of July 1918. This too did not proceed smoothly. The governments of Germany and Austria-Hungary did not always give consent for the trains to pass through their occupation zones. Due to the spread of infectious diseases, they required refugees to undergo lengthy quarantine measures. Refugees' determination to return to their homes as soon as possible found its expression in their uncontrolled movement. All these factors led to numerous traffic jams at junctions. Refugees had to wait for days before being allowed to leave.

Ukrainian refugees' return from Bolshevik Russia was regulated by the provisions of the preliminary peace treaty signed in Kyiv on 12 June 1918 between the Ukrainian state and Bolshevik Russia. Given the food crisis in Russia, Ukraine took responsibility for providing refugees with food. On 13 July 1918 a conference was held in Moscow where the conditions on refugee transportation through the demarcation line to the Ukrainian territory were discussed. Unfortunately, the Bolsheviks failed to comply with any of its promises.

In November 1918 there was an attempt to return Ukrainian refugees from Soviet Russia with the assistance of the Swedish Red Cross which brokered a draft agreement between the Soviet government of Russia and the Ukrainian state. However, the political conditions at the time made it impossible to put this agreement into effect. The change of the political system in Ukraine in December 1918 called into question the possibility of any further systematic return of refugees to their homes, because the UNR Directory proved unable to consolidate the political forces of Ukrainian society and to end the mounting anarchy. This affected a large number of the refugees who had not yet managed to return to their homes. However, the overwhelming majority of them, thanks to the efforts of the Ukrainian Central Rada and the Ukrainian state, felt that they were well treated.[39]

The fate of those refugees who remained in Ukraine was different. In 1919–20 the Bolsheviks embarked on their policy of incorporating Ukraine into the Soviet sphere of influence and subjecting Ukrainian organisations to Bolshevik control, including those in the sphere of refugee social security.

In the years 1920–25 the Bolsheviks strengthened their control over refugee repatriation. Soviet policy was determined by domestic political interests and by relations with the receiving states, Poland, Latvia and Lithuania. In 1920 Soviet Russia concluded bilateral agreements with these countries in which, among other things, Polish, Latvian and Lithuanian refugees' re-evacuation was regulated. However, in reality, Soviet power hindered the re-evacuation of intellectuals, specialists such as engineers and doctors, some categories of qualified workers and employees, as well as Ukrainian peasants.[40] The tragic fate of those refugees who failed for whatever reason to prove that in 1915 they had been forced to leave their homes by order of tsarist military authorities was sealed by the directive of the People's Commissariat of Internal Affairs dated 5 May 1925. This stipulated that the repatriation of all refugees had come to an end and that the refugees who had by then failed to depart were to be regarded as Soviet citizens. Ultimately they felt the full consequences of the Great Terror when many Poles, Latvians and Lithuanians perished in Stalin's prisons and in the Gulag.[41]

Conclusion

The refugee phenomenon during the First World War was a new social phenomenon that embraced the European continent. It produced moral and psychological damage on a large scale. It shattered the lives of millions of people, deprived them of shelter and a family life, and radically altered attitudes towards life, religion, and cultural and spiritual values. Ukraine found itself at the centre of military events and thus became an epicentre of mass displacement. Nevertheless, having set up its own state institutions, Ukraine was able to organise an impressive degree of social protection for refugees, to exemplify sacrifice and to demonstrate that Ukrainian public opinion was sympathetic towards refugees from a different ethnic background.

The agreements between the Ukrainian party and Austrian-Hungarian, German, Polish and Russian representations concerning refugee repatriation became the forerunner of international regulation of the new humanitarian problem after the end of the First World War. These agreements were amongst the first to be agreed in the twentieth century. Many of those who originally fled from the empire's western provinces lived as refugees until they were able to return home in the mid-1920s. Successive state systems – the Russian Empire, the Ukrainian People Republic, and the Ukrainian state adopted different approaches to the refugee problem. In sum, attitudes to the refugee problem depended on the nature of the political regimes under whose rule refugees had to exist. The volatile situation brought about by war, revolution and civil war displaced hundreds of thousands of people and turned them into refugees. But having fled their homes as subjects of Tsar Nicholas II they eventually returned as citizens of newly born states.

Notes

1 This chapter was translated into English by Sergei Shcherbina.
2 Liubov Zhvanko, *Bizhentsi Pershoi svitovoi viini: ukrains'kii vimir (1914–1918 rr.)* (Kharkiv: Apostrofe, 2012), p. 26.
3 See the discussion in Herman Hummerus, *Ukrayina v perelomni chasy: shist' misyatsiv na choli posol'stva u Kyyevi* (Kyyiv: Kyyivs'kyy universytet, 2004), p. 57.
4 'Po povodu "potoka bezhentsev"', *Odesskii listok*, 6 August 1915.
5 Vasilii Gurko, *Voina i revoliutsiia v Rossii: memuary, 1914–1917* (Moscow: Centropoligaf, 2007), p. 157.
6 Zhvanko, *Bizhentsi Pershoi svitovoi viini*, p. 178.

7 'Rossiia razorennyim okrainam!', *Zemskaia mysl'*, 6 June 1915.
8 'Na pomoshch' razorennym brat'yam', *Volchanskii zemskii listok*, 15 August 1915.
9 Walentina Najdus, 'Uchodzcy polscy w Rosji w latach 1917–1919', *Kwartalnik Historyczny*, 26, no. 6 (1957), 24–40.
10 Polish historians estimate that there were 115 branches on Ukrainian soil in 1914–1916. Mariusz Korzeniowski, Mariusz Mandzik and Dariusz Tarasyuk, *Tułaczy los: Uchodźcy polscy w imperium rosyjskim w latach pierwszej wojny światowej* (Lublin: Wydawnictwo Uniwersytetu Marii Curie-Skłodowskiej, 2007), pp. 89, 93–4, 226.
11 Liubov Zhvanko, 'Pol's'ka hromada Kharkova i pol's'ki bizhentsi Pershoyi svitovoyi viyny: rodynna turbota', *Vydatni polyaky Kharkova: materialy mizhnararodnoho naukovoho sympoziumu, Kharkiv, 7 hrudnya 2011* (Kharkiv: Maydan, 2012), pp. 86–7.
12 Peter Gatrell, *A Whole Empire Walking: Refugees in Russia During World War I* (Bloomington: Indiana University Press, 1999), p. 64.
13 'Bezhentsy rumynii v Ekaterinoslave', *Rodnoi krai*, 12 January 1917; 'Evakuatsiia rumyn v Kherson', *Rodnoi krai*, 19 August 1917.
14 'Krestnyi khod', *Odesskii listok*, 15 October 1915.
15 Zhvanko, *Bizhentsi Pershoi svitovoi viini*, p. 46.
16 Zhvanko, *Bizhentsi Pershoi svitovoi viini*, p. 179.
17 'Pomoshch' bezhentsam', *Izvestiia Glavnogo komiteta Vserossiiskogo Zemskogo Soiuza*, 15 October 1915, pp. 128–31.
18 'Litovskii komitet', *Iugobezhenets*, 1 November 1915.
19 'Deiatel'nost' Volynskogo i Kievskogo otdelenii Komiteta ee Vysochestva', *Izvestiia Komiteta Ee Imperatorskogo Vysochestva Velikoi Kniazhny Tatiany Nikolaevny*, 6, 15 August 1916, 6–7.
20 'Punkt po raspredeleniiu bezhentsev i Biuro Truda Vserossiiskogo Soiuza Gorodov v gorode Khar'kove', *Izvestiia Vserossiiskogo Soiuza gorodov*, 15 January 1916, 80–2.
21 'Bezrabotnye bezhentsy', *Odesskii listok*, 13 August 1915.
22 'Khotiat li bezhentsy rabotat?' *Iuzhnii krai*, 19 November 1915.
23 Zhvanko, *Bizhentsi Pershoi svitovoi viini*, p. 229.
24 Liubov Zhvanko, *Sotsial'ni vymiry Ukrayins'koyi Derzhavy, kviten' – hruden' 1918* (Kharkiv: Prapor, 2007), p. 89.
25 Zhvanko, *Bizhentsi Pershoi svitovoi viini*, p. 238.
26 Zhvanko, *Bizhentsi Pershoi svitovoi viini*, p. 237.
27 'Sredi besprizornykh detei', *Poltavskii den'*, 2 August 1916.
28 Liubov Zhvanko, 'Zhenshchina-bezhenka Pervoi mirovoi voiny: shtrikhi k psikhologicheskomu portretu (na primere ukrainskikh gubernii)' www.spbiran.nw.ru/files/zvanko.pdf.
29 Timofei Emtsev, 'Obezdolennye', *Izvestiia Khersonskogo uezdnogo zemstva*, 9 October 1915.

30 Zhvanko, *Bizhentsi Pershoi svitovoi viini*, p. 56.
31 'Na Volyne', *Nezhinets*, 29 August 1915.
32 'Sredi bezhentsev', *Ekaterinoslavskaia zemskaia gazeta*, 25 September 1915. The original text mentions 'karbovanets' rather than rubles.
33 Zhvanko, *Bizhentsi Pershoi svitovoi viini*, p. 276.
34 Zhvanko, *Bizhentsi Pershoi svitovoi viini*, pp. 280–1.
35 Korzeniowski et al., *Tułaczy los*, p. 226.
36 Zhvanko, *Bizhentsi Pershoi svitovoi viini*, p. 328.
37 'Ukrayinska telegrafna agentsIya povidomlyae iz Zhitomira', *Vilne slovo*, 22 June 1918.
38 Korzeniowski et al., *Tułaczy los*, p. 221.
39 Zhvanko, *Bizhentsi Pershoi svitovoi viini*, p. 429.
40 Liubov Zhvanko, 'Do problemy repatriatsiyi inozemnykh bizhentsiv z terytoriy kolyshn'oyi Rosiys'koyi imperiyi (1918–1925 rr.)', *Kyyivs'ka starovyna*, 2 (2011), 81–97.
41 Jörg Baberowski, *Scorched Earth: Stalin's Reign of Terror* (New Haven: Yale University Press, 2016).

6

'Cities of barracks': refugees in the Austrian part of the Habsburg Empire during the First World War

Martina Hermann

The unprecedented mass displacement of civilians during the First World War represents a crucial component of the seminal catastrophe of the twentieth century. All belligerent nations confronted issues generated by large population movements. However, while enemy aggression and the loss of territory were the primary factors causing refugees to flee, at the same time, the multinational Habsburg Empire forcibly evacuated its own nationals from border regions. In a programme devised by the Ministry of War and implemented by the army in Cisleithanian border regions, Ruthenians, Poles and Jews in Galicia and Bukovina, as well as the Serb-Croatian population of Bosnia and (after 1915) the Italian-speaking population of South Tyrol and Trentino, were evacuated and deported into other parts of the monarchy.[1]

This chapter introduces refugee/evacuee politics in Austria-Hungary, in particular Cisleithania, and then explores the approach of the Habsburg administration towards refugees. (For the sake of convenience, the term 'refugee' will be used throughout the remainder of this chapter.) Austrian officials established a network of large camps in seven administrative regions of Cisleithania. In reality, the daily life of the refugees, characterised by poor housing, inadequate nutrition and low standards of sanitation, as well as other constraints, created conditions that hardly differed from those of enemy aliens or prisoners of war, who were at least guaranteed minimal standards of treatment under international law.

The barrack camp in Gmünd in Lower Austria occupied a central position in the network of camps, since it was not only the largest camp on Austrian soil, housing predominantly Ruthenian refugees, but also served as a showcase camp for propaganda purposes between its creation in 1914 and closure in 1918. Gmünd therefore deserves closer scrutiny.

The scale of population displacement

Exact figures of internally displaced civilians in the Habsburg monarchy during the First World War are hard to come by. The reasons can be found mainly in improvised, unstructured and changing registration techniques. Refugees 'endowed with insufficient means' (*unbemittelt*) were not registered from 1915 on, whilst the registration of refugees 'with means' (*bemittelt*) was fragmentary due to their greater freedom of movement. Numerous people in the war zone evaded registration because they feared being sent to a camp; they preferred to remain in their homes, even if the village had been devastated. Furthermore, since state assistance required registration, refugees with financial means normally registered only when their funds had become depleted. This further complicated registration. Moreover, as soon as the situation on the Eastern Front became more favourable to Austria-Hungary, officials began to repatriate refugees; by the same token, people were re-evacuated as soon as the front line got closer.[2]

The first peak in the number of refugees occurred in early autumn 1914 when the Ministry of the Interior counted 350,000 people in Cisleithania who now depended on state aid. In October this figure jumped to 600,000. The Russian offensive on the Eastern Front in winter 1914 led to another dramatic rise in refugee numbers. Italy's entry into the war in 1915 added 150,000 deportees to that number; repatriation to the eastern parts of the empire probably countered that increase. The first large-scale repatriation waves took place in summer and autumn 1915, when Krakau/Kraków and Lemberg/Lviv were opened for repatriation. Official guidelines for repatriation were laid down in a decree of 11 July 1915 and divided reoccupied territories into zone A, open for general repatriation, zone B for limited repatriation and zone C, for which a special permit was required.[3]

On 1 October 1915, 382,577 refugees were receiving state aid, but this figure does not include persons with 'sufficient means', who were often not registered as refugees. Nor does it take account of refugees temporarily housed in Hungary.[4] With numbers falling slightly in spring 1916, the Russian Brusilov offensive generated a significant increase in the number of refugees in summer 1916: a total of 503,818 individuals received state aid in October 1916. Following favourable conditions for the empire on the Eastern Front and the separate peace treaty with Russia in late 1917, the number of refugees dropped. Austria-Hungary pursued repatriation to the east with added vigour. Even so, as of October 1918 the registered refugee population in Austria amounted to some 100,000 persons. Taking everything into account, it seems reasonable to conclude that there were around two million internally displaced persons in the monarchy during the First World War.[5]

Languages and legal frameworks

A clear-cut definition between different categories of internally displaced persons is extremely difficult in the Habsburg context. While one portion of the population certainly fled from the advancing front lines, others were forcibly removed from the war zone by the Austrian army because of their supposed political unreliability, or because the army was attempting to contain epidemic disease, or secure military supplies and basic necessities. The Habsburg authorities did attempt to maintain a distinction between refugees and evacuees. This distinction also evoked a moral dimension: refugees could be pitied for their plight, whereas evacuees were at least politically unreliable and suspected of unpatriotic tendencies. An additional category was constituted by individuals who were suspected of outright Russophile tendencies and were housed in separate camps. The Austrian authorities used the term 'Flüchtlinge' and 'Internierte' for the first two groups of people; however the latter group was also frequently referred to as 'Internierte' or 'Politisch Verdächtige'. In addition, 'Konfinierte' were refugees who had sufficient financial means to stay outside the camps, but with restricted freedom of movement.[6]

In truth, however, the categories of flight and deportation became blurred and defy simple categorisation. Moreover, even 'Russophiles' were sometimes housed together with refugees and evacuees. Camp Gmünd, for instance, accommodated both refugees and evacuees, and there is ample evidence of persons suspected of Russophile tendencies interned in Gmünd. Blurring categories even further, camp Gmünd was also briefly home to 'enemy aliens', namely civilians of Russian nationality from Volhynia.[7] This fact is striking, since nationals and enemy aliens were normally kept meticulously apart.[8] Like Gmünd, other camps such as Camp Wagna in Styria also housed Russian POWs, evacuees from Krain and Carinthia, and political suspects, in addition to refugees.[9] A clear-cut dichotomy between 'refugee' and 'evacuee' could not be

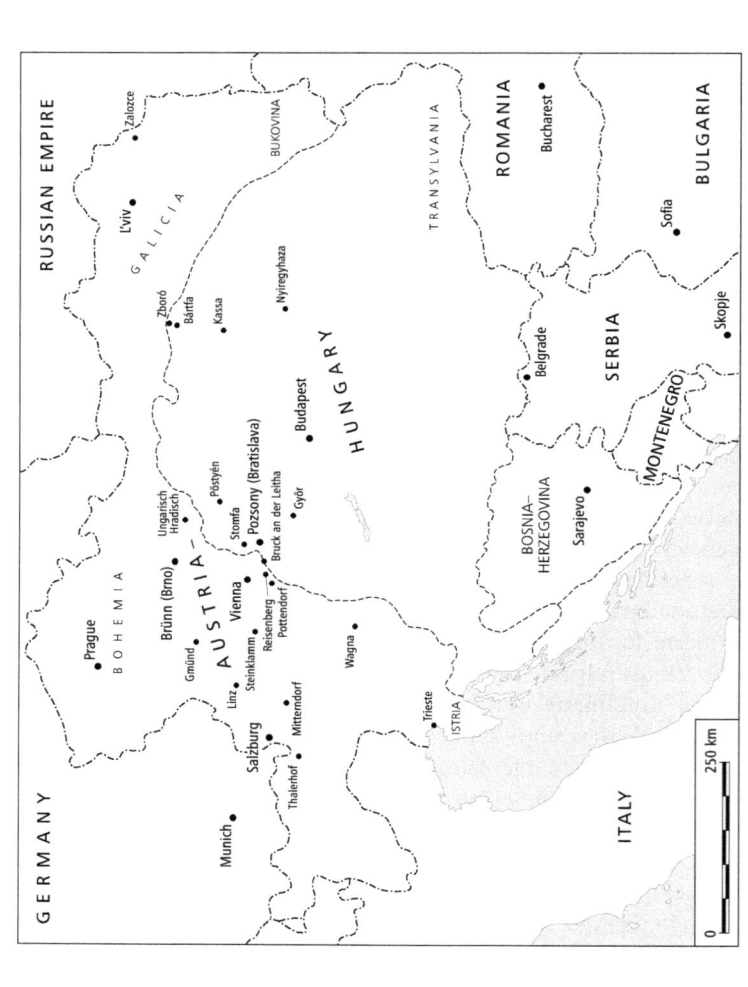

Map 6.1 Austria-Hungary during the First World War.

sustained even in the bureaucratic mind. Camp Gmünd was simultaneously referred to as 'Interniertenstation' and 'Flüchtlingsstation', and its inmates were likewise classified as refugees, internees and evacuees. The press too used both terms interchangeably.

One of the results of this variable terminology was that stereotypes such as 'political unreliability' came to be associated in the popular imagination with all displaced persons living in the hinterland of the monarchy, irrespective of the circumstances that contributed to their displacement. Before the arrival of the refugees, officials of the Gmünd district, for instance, were already claiming that the district was not fit for accommodating 'foreign deserters, refugees or other suspicious foreign persons', which shows that the categories were blurred evenbefore the refugees arrived.[10]

Civilians on the Eastern Front endured precarious conditions from the very outset. Here, as opposed to the Western Front, the situation was much more mobile and characterised by changing front lines. The region between Krakau/Kraków and Rzeszow/ Rzeszów, for instance, changed hands nine times during the war. Civilians often received little information and were obliged to leave their homes at short notice when the enemy approached. In addition to the devastation of the region brought about by the constant fighting, military requisitioning contributed to a shortage of food. Moreover, the systematic infringement of civil rights took place on a regular basis. As a result, flight and deportation from the north-west and central Galicia took place more or less continuously.[11]

Furthermore the Austrian army increasingly blamed civilians in the war zone for the heavy losses suffered on the Galician front. This attitude was informed by anti-Slavic sentiments and reinforced by anti-Russian war propaganda, as well as antisemitic stereotypes that have been shown to have had a long history in travel accounts of the region.[12] These clichés included notions of 'laziness' and 'cowardice' on the part of the 'filthy' local population in Galicia and Bukovina. The Ruthenian population in particular, speaking a Slavic language quite similar to Russian, was suspected of having Russophile tendencies. The resulting treatment of the civilian population in Galicia by the Austrian army is one of the darkest chapters in the history of the Habsburg Empire. Between 11,400 and 30,000 civilians, many of them women, were hanged or shot without trial, their execution being regarded as a deterrent.[13]

The Habsburg authorities forcibly evacuated nationals from the border regions, not only Ruthenians, but also the Serbian population in Bosnia, along with the Italian residents of South Tyrol and the Trentino.

As early as 1910, guidelines and regulations had been drafted to permit the removal of such nationals, curtailing the right of freedom laid down in the Austrian basic state law of 1867. These provisions allowed for the evacuation of so-called 'fortified places' (*befestigte Plätze*), mostly large cities in Galicia and Istria, which were important military strongholds.

Deportations of these 'fortified places' began in autumn 1914 in the wake of the considerable losses suffered by the Austrian army on the Eastern Front. Lemberg/Lviv was the first city in the north-east of the monarchy to be evacuated according to these pre-war regulations; at this stage the city was already full of refugees who had fled smaller villages to the east and found temporary lodging. The second city scheduled for evacuation was Czernowitz/Chernivtsy, from where around 40,000 inhabitants were expelled on 27 November 1914. These abrupt evacuations entailed the use of considerable force on the part of the military.

With the Russian army approaching, it became apparent that evacuations from fortified places alone provided insufficient room for manoeuvre. Accordingly, a further directive issued on 11 August 1914 extended the scope of action by providing for the removal of population from places other than these fortified towns. As a result, the evacuation and deportation of nationals became a ubiquitous practice, the only formal requirement being that evacuation had to correspond to cases of 'necessity' or 'suspicion'. Such vague wording offered ample scope for interpretation. The August directive constituted the basis for forced evacuation and deportation of civilians for the remainder of the war. Only in 1917, after parliament was recalled, did new refugee legislation take into account some of the insights and experiences of the refugee crisis.[14]

The law defined refugees as 'persons, who had either voluntarily or through official ordinance left their permanent abode or could not return there', thus also comprising deported persons. Moreover, a financial subsidy of a maximum of 500 crowns could be applied for, including retrospectively. As a result, people who had stayed in the war zone and who had not applied for a refugee subsidy could now also apply. In addition, participation of refugees in the camps was extended, for example by opening up certain areas, such as nutrition in the camps, to consultation with a group of refugee representatives. However, this development was not effective in many camps, such as Gmünd, as they were already being dissolved.[15]

In the meantime, however, the Austrian army made extensive use of the powers given to them in 1914.

Managing displacement: finance, transport and perlustration

The immense influx of refugees and evacuees over a short period of time necessitated a complex organisational system for transporting, supervising and housing them. The Ministry of the Interior and the tenth department of the Ministry of War were responsible for transport and accommodation of the refugees. The fact that the Ministry of War was involved in overseeing refugees already suggests the militarisation of the refugee issue in Austria-Hungary. Arrangements for accommodation modelled on military barracks, together with a rigorous daily schedule and meticulous surveillance, further reinforced a sense that the average refugee was treated more like a prisoner than a citizen of the monarchy.

The political framework for the transportation and housing of the refugees only came into being on 13 September 1914, by which time mass flight and deportations from the Eastern Front were already under way. According to the aforementioned guidelines, refugees were to be segregated on the basis of ethnic and confessional criteria, financial means and social status.

State welfare rested on a meagre financial basis, since refugees were only to be provided with housing and limited nourishment. Between 1914 and 1918 a total of 2.4 billion crowns was spent on refugee welfare, equivalent to 2.4 per cent of total war expenditure, although thanks to reporting restrictions and wartime propaganda, the chronic underfunding of refugee welfare did not reach the public.[16] To a large extent, refugee welfare within the Habsburg Empire rested mainly on private donations in support of multifarious committees, many of them founded at the outbreak of war. The committees were normally headed by a prominent individual such as a member of the royal family or a member of parliament. Financed by donations and staffed by volunteers, their main aim was to provide the refugees with adequate clothing and food. Most committees were organised along ethnic, confessional or professional lines.[17] In the absence of parliamentary sittings, the network of private relief agencies played the lead role in criticising the system of state welfare and lobbying for an improvement in living conditions in the refugee camps.

Refugees were transported in freight wagons that carried the inscription, '40 men or 6 horses'.[18] Trains were guarded, so as to hinder the refugees from getting off before they reached the prescribed destination. Some refugees had already completed tiring journeys by foot or wagon before reaching villages with rail connections. In the bigger towns and cities officials gathered the refugees together prior to transporting them towards the western regions of the monarchy via so called perlustration stations. By departure, police had already segregated refugees into people with sufficient and insufficient means. There were, however, no clear directives as to what was considered 'sufficient', since numbers ranging from 200 crowns to 500 crowns are mentioned.[19] In addition, family size and profession were taken into account. With the ongoing war economy, utilitarian considerations became prevalent. Since a work force was needed in an economy depleted of working men, authorities were more likely to declare somebody without sufficient means and direct them towards a camp, where adults could be 'reintegrated' into the working process. Another key consideration was the social status of the refugees: whereas those of 'high standing' and persons with sufficient means were allowed to travel without restriction, persons with 'insufficient means' were directed towards the perlustration stations.[20]

The rail infrastructure in the Habsburg Empire was not designed for the simultaneous transport of such large numbers of people. Since supply lines for the army were the priority, and military trains went in the opposite direction, rail transport for refugees was often delayed, and they were left waiting in the wagons without adequate food, clothing or sanitation. Moreover, the journey often took weeks and took a heavy toll on refugees' health. As a result, many refugees were already in a weak condition when they arrived in the hinterland, which rendered them more susceptible to disease and illness.[21]

The perlustration station occupied a central place in the logistical network surrounding the refugees. The biggest such stations were built in Ungarisch – Hradisch and Prerau. A perlustration station for Jewish refugees was erected in Gänserndorf; individual passengers were controlled in Lundenburg. In summer 1915, a perlustration station was built in Gnigl for refugees from the southern front. Additional stations were constructed in Odersberg, Teschen, Marchegg, Bruck an der Leitha and Ungarisch-Brod. Similar facilities were built alongside the main roads leading into the centre of the monarchy.[22]

Perlustration stations fulfilled a number of functions. They maintained direct contact with the central transportation direction (*Zentraltransportleitung*), which controlled the influx of refugees into the western parts of the empire, and had the power to close cities such as Vienna, Graz, Brno, Prague and Linz to refugees, as they did from autumn 1914 onwards.[23] The pre-segregated refugees were gathered into separate groups according to ethnicity and religious confession. Close scrutiny of their financial resources took place to determine whether

Refugees in the Austrian part of the Habsburg Empire

refugees were to be housed in particular districts or in camps. A security examination carried out by Landsturm units[24] and a medical examination were also normal practice. As a result, these stations functioned as kind of safeguard for the western half of the empire. So far as the refugees were concerned, however, conditions in the perlustration stations played havoc with their health since they were housed in overcrowded and unheated hovels, pigsties, factories and even in the open air.[25]

Managing refugees: the camp system

During the First World War, refugees were settled in seven crownlands of the monarchy: Lower Austria, Upper Austria, Bohemia, Moravia, Styria, Salzburg and Silesia. As indicated above, refugees were either interned in camps or lived in refugee districts according to their financial means and social status.

In refugee districts people were housed in spare accommodation, but also in workshops, brick factories, old castles, guest houses or schools. The refugees received a fixed allowance per day, starting with 70 Heller[26] and raised to two crowns in 1917.[27] These sums, however, were insufficient to provide for basic necessities. Even in these districts, refugees were limited in their mobility and threatened by transfer to a refugee camp if there were sufficient complaints by the regional population. Reasons for

Figure 6.1 Refugees arriving through the front gate of camp Gmünd.

transferring refugees into camps were, for instance, accusations of price driving, theft or indecent behaviour.

According to a decree of the Ministry of the Interior issued on 15 September 1915 refugees accused of price driving in refugee districts should be deported into a refugee camp. This provision was extended in November 1915 to also encompass refugees with 'sufficient means', thus broadening the possibilities of the local authorities. This reproach was frequently used against Jewish refugees.[28]

Another reason for transferal was 'indecent behaviour'. Ruthenian refugee Marie Gawiuk is an example of a transferal to a camp because of this reproach. She was transferred from refugee housing in Eggerding to camp Gmünd on 1 December 1916 because of her 'dissolute morals' and on grounds of upholding public morality.[29]

Following the closure of the monarchy's main cities for refugees, as well as the ongoing influx of refugees and evacuees into the hinterland of the monarchy, the Ministry of the Interior advocated the erection of refugee camps. The camps had to be located as far away as possible from the vicinity of fighting but also from relevant infrastructure, including larger cities and munitions factories as well as POW camps in the hinterland. Access to water and favourable traffic connections, especially to the monarchy's well developed rail system was essential for the transport of refugees, building materials and goods.

The first refugee camps in the monarchy were erected in autumn 1914. The last camp, at Braunau am Inn, was built in the summer of 1915. Overall numbers of camp inmates are very difficult to establish, since fluctuation of inmates in refugee camps was immense. Repatriations, which were linked to the changing front lines in the east, further blurred the picture. By the middle of 1915 around 100,000 refugees were housed in camps in Cisleithania. Table 6.1 gives an overview of the camps in the Austrian part of the Habsburg Empire and the predominant ethnicity in each one.

While separation based on ethnicity and confession was initially observed, logistical considerations soon prevailed over ethnic and confessional segregation. Especially at times of a large influx of refugees, inmates were frequently and repeatedly moved within in the network of camps according to available space. Moreover, the internees seldom adhered to a monolithic 'national' and confessional group. Even within a given 'nationality' and confession, there were heterogeneous subgroups, often organised along regional, professional or social criteria, which were perceived as being more important for identity than the arbitrary

Table 6.1 Camps in Cisleithania during the First World War with more than 500 inmates

Ethnic group	Camps
Jewish	Nikolsburg/Mikulov
	Phorlitz/Pohořelice
	Gaya/ Kyjov
	Mährisch-Trübau/ Moravská Třebová
	Deutschbrod/Havlíčkův Brod
	Padubitz/Pardubice
	Mitterndorf
Ruthenian	Gmünd
	Wolfsberg
	St. Andrä
	Thalerhof
	Bruck an der Leitha (Hainburg)
	Chotzen/Choceň
	Oberhollabrunn
Polish	Wagna bei Leibnitz
	Chotzen
	Oberhollabrunn
	Mitterndorf
Italian	Mitterndorf (Reisenberg)
	Pottendorf
	Braunau am Inn
	Wagna
	Pottendorf
Croatian, Slovenian	Steinklamm
	Gmünd
	Bruck an der Leitha
Romanian	Oberhollabrunn
Roma and Sinti	Hainburg

Source: Walter Mentzel, 'Kriegsflüchtlinge in Cisleithanien im ersten Weltkrieg', PhD dissertation, University of Vienna, 1997

'national' or 'confessional' selection by the authorities. These regional identities frequently led to clashes of camp inmates. In camp Pottendorf, for example, there were tensions between inhabitants from South Tyrol and those from eastern upper Italy.[30] Meanwhile, in camp Gmünd, Ruthenians from Bukovina demanded separate schooling and housing from Galician Ruthenians, in order to emphasise their 'distinct' identity.[31]

In contrast to the depiction of the refugee camps in war propaganda as showcase examples of public relief work, living conditions were dire. Camps were praised as 'model' cities for innovation and relief

Figure 6.2 A Habsburg propaganda event staged at the summer theatre of camp Gmünd.

achievements in newspaper articles and in the Viennese refugee exhibition of 1915, which was designed to propagate state achievements in refugee welfare to the monarchy's public.[32] Exhibitions were a favourite vehicle for influencing public opinion during the war, the most prominent example being the war exhibition open from July to October 1916 on the Viennese Prater Grounds.[33] The refugee exhibition, opened on 15 December 1915 similarly worked with entertainment and spectacle. It showcased miniature models of camps Gmünd, Pottendorf and Langegg, explained state relief and displayed craftwork deemed to be typically Ruthenian, including a complete farmhouse parlour.[34] The camp administration received a catalogue of exhibits to be sent in for the exhibition, also detailing the motives of the photographs of camp life.[35]

It would be more truthful to say that official attitudes towards the refugees in camps were characterised by pity and a 'colonial' attitude based on the stereotypes vis-à-vis the population from the imperial borderlands. These stereotypes, directed especially at populations in the east and south-east of the monarchy, can be tracked back to travel accounts, essays and letters in the early nineteenth century, which include anti-Slavic and frequently also antisemitic elements. Preconceived ideas included blanket allegations of laziness, cowardice, alcoholism, cultural backwardness, lacking civilisation, and associated Ruthenians in particular with a lack of hygiene standards.[36] These perceptions are also congruent with the Austrian mythos of Galicia, which stressed the civilising mission of the Austrian state vis-à-vis a backward 'colony' in the east. These stereotypes are found in military reports before and after the war.[37] Refugee camps served as a venue for social engineering and experimentation. The 'learning effects' of the administration are discernible in every aspect of the organisation in the camps. Basic rights of inmates were not respected.

Since the Austrian authorities believed the war likely to be of short duration, accommodation in the refugee camps was temporary and unfit for longer habitation. The provisional character of the refugees' housing was also a symbol for the refugees' temporal status within the 'foreign' western parts of the Habsburg monarchy, as well as the provisional character of refugee welfare as a whole. The first barracks in the camps were dark, wooden buildings, cold, chronically overcrowded and entirely unsuitable for ordinary social interaction. Since the majority of the camp inmates were women and small children, this first type of accommodation was especially inadequate. Although there were different variants of the barracks erected in the individual camps, they all shared the deficiencies mentioned above. In the next phase, the authorities tried to alleviate the catastrophic housing situation by introducing improvements to the basic type of barracks. Increasingly, there was also differentiation between different types of barracks for different subgroups within the refugee population, which shows that the administration began to take the heterogeneous composition of the camp inmates into account.[38]

Living conditions continued to cause problems for refugees. In camp Wagna, barracks were supposed to house 384 refugees, while in fact as many as 560 refugees often lived in each barrack.[39] In Gmünd, 250 persons were initially housed in one barracks, leaving approximately 1.6 square metres per refugee. Many barracks were even more overcrowded, housing as many as 280 refugees apiece. The first serious defects in Gmünd became apparent as early as March 1915, after four months of use, when rain entered through the roofs and the barracks sank because of the poor foundations.[40] Furthermore the barracks were increasingly difficult to heat because of a shortage of coal. Straw for bedding was also sparse.[41] The authorities tried to improve the housing conditions by introducing improvements such as larger windows and reducing the number of refugees per barrack. The basic barrack type was changed in order to provide a more welcoming appearance for refugee families.

Figure 6.3 Paula Czapka, Baroness Winstetten, the wife of Gmünd's camp director, distributes sweets to the camp's orphans.

Special barracks were erected for orphans and military personnel. The administration in Gmünd also had a few houses with gardens and bathrooms built, although they were reserved for 'high standing' families. Generally speaking the housing situation of most refugees remained precarious throughout the war, as numerous complaints testify.[42] A sanitary inspection of camp Gmünd in May 1917 even reported that living conditions in sections nine and ten (each section consisted of eight barracks and one kitchen) were so detrimental that 'a healthy person is bound to fall ill'.[43]

There is ample evidence as to the poor diet of refugees in the camps. It became increasingly difficult for officials to sustain a minimal level of nutrition even as they sought to prevent insurrections because of insufficient food. The diet of the refugees varied due to the individual internment camps, with camps like Wagna and Bruck an der Leitha becoming infamous for the poor quality of food they provided to the inhabitants.[44] Officials revised the dietary arrangements several times during the war. In Gmünd the private company 'Verpflegsgesellschaft' was responsible for the buying and stocking of ingredients, as well as cooking and serving the food. It also supplied other refugee camps in the county of Lower Austria, catering for a total of 50,000 refugees in Mitterndorf, Steinklamm and Reisenberg, as well as Gmünd.[45] However, as a result of rising costs and declining profit margins the company asked to be relieved from the contract. The result was that the monarchy effectively took over the supply of food. Refugees noticed little difference, and their diet remained insufficient, monotonous, tasteless, and not very nourishing, consisting of beans, cabbage, maize porridge (*mamaliga*) and barley (*tarhonya*).[46]

Despite the centralisation of the refugees' meals, as well as inspections of nutrition plans for the camps, refugees' diet deteriorated. By 1917, meat, beans, potatoes, flour and corn were no longer available. The administration in Gmünd reported frequent food crises and was finally forced to demand that some refugees be discharged from the camp because even minimal nutrition could no longer be guaranteed.[47] There were frequent complaints by the inmates of the camps concerning the food provided. In May 1915, Ruthenian refugees in camp Gmünd wrote as follows about the food they received in the camp:

> We Ukrainians in barrack camp Gmünd direct our pleas and complaints to the Ministry of the Interior and ask you to visit the camp, in order to confirm how we are treated and that we are kept hungry. Our rations mainly consist of water and green runner beans, in which there are also mice, rats, lizards, glass and other things. Our complaints have been unsuccessful and nobody cares about our pleas.[48]

Croatian and Slovenian refugees were used to a different diet. A letter written by the Croat Sandina Re in autumn 1915 and intercepted by the Croatian censorship unit describes how children especially were reluctant to eat the food in the camps: 'We are living badly here. Sixty children die every day. If there is no help from the Lord, we will all perish miserably. The children don't tolerate the food here, because it is worse that pig fodder. Little Beppo, even though nearly beaten to death, won't eat.'[49] The authorities rejected these reports and claimed the refugees were 'fussy' and spoiled.

The main priority of officials lay elsewhere, namely to address the concerns of local people who deemed the refugee population better cared for than themselves.

Work, discipline, surveillance and cultural policy

A basic motif in refugee politics was the need to find a means to 'occupy' the refugees, since, as Jochen Oltmer has pointed out, the utilisation of civilians is one of the most striking aspects of 'total war'.[50] The refugee camps in the hinterland of the monarchy became veritable reservoirs supplying the workforce desperately needed in the war economy. Apart from the instrumentalisation of the refugee for war economy, 'occupation' as a concept was also connected to cultural policy towards the refugees and had disciplinary functions.

It was an explicit aim of the administration that all adult refugees should be integrated into the war economy. This was achieved by sending refugees to work outside the camp and increasingly by providing employment within the camps. Most refugees working outside the camps left in spring and returned in autumn. The main jobs were in industries vital to war economy such as armaments and mining. Refugees also worked in agriculture, particularly helping with the harvest. Competition for their labour was fierce, as indicated by correspondence between the firms requesting refugees and the camp administration. In September 1915 the programme had to be discontinued due to a depletion of work population in the camps. Even so, the administration of camp Gmünd prided itself on having found jobs for 55,742 refugees outside the camp by mid-September 1917.[51]

Although applying for work was voluntary in Gmünd, there were strong incentives for taking up the jobs that were on offer, such as avoiding a reduced diet. In addition, the fact that refugees received remuneration helped to ease life in the camp during the harsh winter months. In other camps, however, refugees had no choice but to work. At the end of 1914 around 4,000 refugees from camp Wagna were, for example, taken to Serbia at night and were forced to assist the army with road and rail construction works.[52]

Apart from refugees working outside the camp, increasing employment opportunities could be found within the camps themselves. Gmünd hosted a complex system of workshops. Facilities included a shoe factory, a needlecraft studio, a forge, and workshops for carpenters, glaziers, decorators, wood carvers and tailors.[53] Gangs of workmen, including plumbers and roofers, were responsible for carrying out repairs and making improvements to the camp. By September 1917, around 800 refugees were working on construction, 673 worked in the camp's hospitals, and more than 1,300 were employed in other workshops. A similar pattern can be observed elsewhere.[54]

Moreover, the camps increasingly began to co-operate, splitting up the production process and organising labour in order to create a single economic entity out of scattered camps. Skilled workers were subcontracted to work temporarily in other camps: for example, refugees from Pottendorf were sent to help in camp Mitterndorf's shoe factory and tailoring shop. From May 1916 onwards camps Gmünd and Mitterndorf collaborated in the production of wooden shoes according to the Lichtenfeld system, with soles produced in Mitterndorf and other parts in Gmünd where the shoes were assembled.[55] These workshops manufactured goods for the inmates of the refugee camps, but also catered for 'external' demand. Many of them became lucrative and profitable enterprises, and in so doing were frequently criticised by professional associations that accused them of monopolising national markets.[56] In addition to the workshops, refugees were exhorted to follow so-called 'occupation courses'. These were aimed mainly at women and provided instruction in sewing, needlework, hat-making and basketwork. Additional courses provided skills in gardening, and fruit and vegetable farming. Most camps also rented agricultural plots that helped improve the meagre food supplies, and also became a showcase for modern agricultural techniques.

The cultural policy towards the refugees, including literacy and German courses, has to be seen in this context. The 'programme for religious, cultural and social refugee welfare' had been introduced by the Ministry of the Interior in January 1915.[57] It stressed the importance of occupation for the refugees, which also including 'educational' elements. Generally speaking, the priority of the camp administration was to improve literacy and to provide instruction in the German language.[58] Very fitting in this context is also the strong advocacy of the state for German-language courses, a measure which should not 'only strengthen economic relations between the hinterland and border regions' but also 'deepen the feeling of harmonious togetherness'. A decided aim of educational and cultural policy was to 'alleviate homesickness and pain' among refugees. This formed part of a general policy to 're-educate' the inmates of the camps and inculcate the virtue of 'love for state and country'.[59]

The German courses were flanked by patriotic events orchestrated by the camp authorities, which were meant to uphold the pro-Habsburg spirit of the camp inmates. Events were held for example on the 85th birthday anniversary of Emperor Francis Joseph, as well as on the day following the reoccupation of Przmysl.[60] These events were frequently instrumentalised to portray the monarchy's unity despite rising nationalism during the war. As a contemporary newspaper article phrased it:

> And soon the half melancholic, half passionate songs of the Ukraine can be heard ... The people's hymn is struck up and then everyone is singing 'Heil Dir im Siegerkranz' and the 'Wacht am Rhein' [patriotic songs] in

Ukrainian. More than ever the indissoluble pact is apparent, which has surpassed the languages and hearts of completely heterogeneous peoples. And a speaker who knows German more with the heart than with the tongue, stands up and enthusiastically praises German culture. War is destructive, but it reconstructs anew and more beautiful than before.[61]

Apart from refugees leaving the camp to work, the mobility of the refugees was limited to the premises of the camp. Permits were needed to enter or leave the refugee camps. The stipulated reason for restricting the refugees' mobility was the fear that disease and epidemics would be spread by the camp inmates (see next section). The 'military' character of the treatment of the refugees by the monarchy's administration was perpetuated within the camps. After disinfection and a period of incubation, during which the refugees were housed on the perimeter of the camp, inmates were given a designated place to sleep within a barrack. The frequency, quantity and preparation of their meals were regulated and the schedule of all age groups was tightly controlled.

The organisation of camp life was hierarchical, with the structure reminiscent of POW camps.[62] A barrack commander, chosen from among the refugees was responsible for the functioning of daily life. He oversaw the cleaning of the barracks, as well as the allocation of the meals. He prepared daily reports. In addition, the commander was responsible for resolving conflicts between inmates and for seeing that orders from the camp's administration were carried out. The barrack commanders were overseen by the section supervisors, who were in turn overseen by the camp inspectors. A chief inspector reported directly to the camp's administration.[63]

Camp Gmünd was surrounded by high fences on all sides. Moreover, the camp was guarded by both a reserve army group of about 200 men, as well as a police force within the camp. In addition, the direction of the railway services had been instructed not to hand out train tickets to the refugees.[64] Despite these restrictive measures, there are numerous cases of refugees escaping at night. In June 1916 the war surveillance bureau complained to the camp administration because a large number of refugees, thought to have escaped from Gmünd, had been seized in the restricted war area without travel documents. The direction of camp Gmünd blamed the unreliable 'Slavic' guards and promised to take adequate steps in the future to hinder refugees escaping.[65] Tight surveillance of the refugees did not prevent the outbreak of strikes and riots inside the refugee camps.

In camp Gmünd the various refugee groups differed in their ability to cope with the dire living conditions. Whereas the Ruthenian inmates generally accepted the conditions in the camp, the Croatian and Slovenian inmates frequently demonstrated because of the living conditions. Wasil Makowski, an envoy of the Ruthenian parliamentary club staying in camp Gmünd wrote frequently about the Slovenian and Croatian refugees in the camp. He adopted a rather biased tone:

> The Slovenians had frequent disputes with the Ruthenian refugees because of their quick temper and their aggressiveness. In order to calm the Slovenians, the camp administration needed 'special weapons', sometimes also firearms … They were used to fighting for their freedom. Their character was not as submissive as our refugees. If they could not bear something they screamed and screamed so loudly and terribly that it was heard in Vienna.[66]

As a result, this refugee group's rebelliousness was the declared reason why they had to leave camp Gmünd and be taken to other camps in early 1916.[67] Demonstrations in the camps were mainly directed against the immediate living conditions. Meagre food rations were the main reason for riots, as in camp Mitterndorf, where a demonstration on 12 July 1917 was motivated by insufficient rations, consisting of 1 part maize to 11 parts water.[68]

Although there were no causalities during the strikes that took place in camp Gmünd or Mitterndorf, an 11-year-old refugee was shot by a policeman in camp Wagna during a demonstration on 4 October 1917, when women and children demonstrated against the manhandling of refugees by two soldiers. This incident led to further demonstrations that turned violent. These were quickly suppressed by the camp authorities.[69]

Disease and epidemiology

A frequent fear of regional populations perpetuated by the authorities was that the refugees might pass on illness and disease. Discourses on epidemics linked to the eastern parts of the monarchy were already in evidence before the war.[70] In reality, however, epidemics such as typhus fever had been reintroduced by the army and had been transmitted to the Galician refugees.[71] Nevertheless, the catastrophic conditions of transportation, in perlustration stations as well as in the camps, encouraged the spread of illness and epidemics amongst the refugees. Moreover, basic sanitary regulations and precautions were disregarded in the camps. The frequent exchange of groups of refugees within the network of the camps led to aggravation by neglect. For example, typhus fever was introduced by a Ruthenian girl from camp Wagna to camp Gmünd in March 1915, triggering a large-scale epidemic in the spring.[72]

Most refugee and POW camps were affected by epidemics, which were difficult to control due to camp size and frequent turnover of refugees. Apart from typhus fever, dysentery and cholera, endemic epidemics of measles and scarlet fever led to a dramatically high infant mortality rate. This was particularly acute in Gmünd, Wagna and Pottendorf. Moreover, there are also recorded cases of pertussis, influenza and scabies. Mortality rates fluctuated according to conditions in the camps. While the mortality rate during an outbreak of typhus fever outbreak in Gmünd was 15 per cent and in Wagna 9 per cent, it rose to 29 per cent in Thalerhof.[73]

Refugee camps were also used as a site of medical study and experimentation. In contrast to hospitals on the front line (which also advanced medical progress during the war) the refugee camps were filled with a representative cross-section of society, a fact that rendered them especially interesting to those researching epidemiology. In camp Gmünd, medical director Dr Reder conducted a widespread study on typhus patients from 1914 to 1917, detailing his findings in a publication in 1918. In it, he specified the advantages of experimental study in the refugee camps: 'Our observations derive from a camp with civilians who fled. [This] human material differs from that in prison camps in that there are men, women and children of various ages'.[74] Reder studied three typhus epidemics in camp Gmünd, two in spring and autumn 1915 and another one at the end of 1916, investigating a total of 1,130 cases. He meticulously recorded fever curves, statistics as well as courses of the disease and offered findings on etiology, symptoms, diagnosis, epidemiology and prophylaxis, as well as suggesting possible therapeutic interventions. Since diagnosis of typhus fever was still in its infancy and the initial symptoms shared characteristics with measles, Reder frequently had healthy persons brought into the camp hospital, some of whom fell victim to the disease and subsequently died during quarantine.[75]

The camps also afforded an opportunity to test competing professional opinions on therapy or prophylaxis. In 1916, for example, such an argument developed between the doctors Cipanowskyj and Weiss regarding the treatment of the measles in camp Gmünd. In order to settle the dispute, a team of doctors visited camp Gmünd and condoned Weiss's method of treatment, while describing Cipanowskyj's views as incompatible with 'modern' medicine.[76]

The fact that the refugees tended to hide sick children rather than send them to the hospital seems understandable against this background.

According to a prevailing stereotype, refugees' distrust in medical treatment typified their 'uncivilised nature'. From autumn 1915 onwards, barrack reports were conducted in the presence of a doctor, who checked the barracks for sick refugees. In June 1916, the camp's director himself is reported to have discovered 126 sick children hidden in the barracks. They were promptly transferred to hospital for compulsory treatment.[77]

The camps proved an interesting venue not only for the study of epidemiology. Jakob Levy Moreno, founder of sociometrics, a psychological method in the empirical social sciences, cited the refugee camp in Mitterndorf as his first research venue. Sociometrics views the human being within its social fabric and examines relationships between members of groups. Group phenomena such as cohesion or structure constituted the basis for Moreno's therapeutic group work. His sociogramms and psychodrama are used in pedagogics, supervision, in theatre and cultural work.[78] Moreno worked sporadically in Mitterndorf as a doctor between 1915 and 1918. Responses of the inmates to Moreno's observations are not known. According to a book in which he describes his work, the closed structure of camp Mitterndorf gave him an opportunity to develop his theories:

> The first sociometric plan of a population was constructed by me between 1915 and 1918. The place of study was an Italian colony [sic] with a population of more than 10,000. It was during First World War when great numbers of peasants, Austrian citizens of Italian extraction ... were transplanted by the Austrian government to a place near Mitterndorf in close proximity to Vienna ... There was great unhappiness and friction among the population ... I studied the psychological currents they developed around varying criteria ... It was through this experience that the idea of a sociometrically planned community began to occupy me.[79]

Repatriation

Repatriation was fraught with difficulty. Ruthenian refugees, the first to be repatriated, returned to a region devastated by war. Destroyed houses and farmland, a lack of infrastructure, and shortages of food, water and heating materials were an everyday reality. Poor hygiene contributed to the spread of epidemic disease.[80] In addition to economic insecurity and these other risks, the refugees were returning to a region in political turmoil, where state borders had yet to be drawn. As a result, the authorities were interested in their swift repatriation to the successor states, where the entitlements of repatriated refugees were also frequently disputed.

These debates can be traced back as early as 1917, already demonstrating the ongoing battle for the distribution of resources between the crownlands in the monarchy. In autumn 1917 German National deputies demanded that 'either the refugees, whose home is free of the enemy are sent back at the earliest possibility or that the surplus lands are used to nourish the refugees'.[81]

As the monarchy fell apart, the stance towards the refugees radicalised. The Austrian republic, created in October 1918 following the dissolution of the Habsburg monarchy, perceived the remaining refugees, now attributed to the newly created independent nation states, as foreigners. Benefits to 'foreign' refugees were declared to be tradable by compensation payments by the successor states, preferable in the form of food. Repatriations were pushed from October 1918 onwards; in some regions, like Styria and the Czech Republic, even acts of aggression as well as 'wild' repatriations by the population were reported.[82]

Since the Ruthenian refugees had already been repatriated and the Italian and Slovenian refugees followed suit, the Jewish refugees in Vienna were targeted by new legislation. The amendment of the law on citizenship must be seen in this context. The respective law, adopted on 5 December 1918 declared all persons citizens of the new German Austrian state, who had been living on the current territory before the first of August. This also concerned immigrants, exempting those from Dalmatia, Istria and Galicia, where most Jewish refugees came from.[83]

Conclusion

The refugee camps set up in Cisleithania during the First World War were characterised by poor living conditions, isolation and the infringement of civilians' rights. They were designed to accommodate refugees and those from the borders of the empire who were suspected of political unreliability. These suspicions, which blended with accusations of laziness, a lack of 'civilisation', and a tendency towards filth and disease were reinforced by existing stereotypes and by anti-Slavic war propaganda that informed the state's treatment of the refugees during their deportation.

Against the backdrop of wartime mobilisation, these camps also served as labour reservoirs for the war economy. Microcosms containing a cross section of society, the camps served too as laboratories for medical research, and for social engineering and experimentation.

As the war dragged on, the administration demonstrated an increasing readiness to draw lessons regarding the structure and organisation of camps that were originally designed to be temporary facilities. This concerned the accommodation of the refugees, and the centralisation and nationalisation of nutrition, as well as the surveillance and control of the refugees. Under the heading of state-decreed 'occupation', a leitmotif in refugee politics, the administration created a nearly autonomous and interrelated economic system of camps, which coexisted and increasingly competed with the arrangements outside. In its policy aspects, 'occupation' was also designed to re-educate and civilise the internees by passing on virtues embraced by the state.

Notes

1 Following the Compromise of 1867, Cisleithania denoted the northern and western parts of Dual Monarchy, as opposed to Transleithania. Cisleithania consisted of current Austria without Burgenland, but with Krain, Görz and Gradisca, the city of Trieste, Istria, Bohemia, Moravia, Austrian Silesia, the Kingdom of Galicia and Lodomeria, dukedom of Bukovina and the Kingdom of Dalmatia.
2 Beatrix Hoffmann-Holter, 'Abreisendmachung': Jüdische Kriegsflüchtlinge in Wien 1914–1923 (Wien: Böhlau 1990), pp. 29–30, 283; Hermann Kuprian, 'Flüchtlinge, Evakuierte und die staatliche Fürsorge', in Klaus Eisterer and Rolf Steininger (eds), Tirol und der Erste Weltkrieg (Innsbruck/Wien, 1995), pp. 277–306 (here p. 286); Walter Mentzel , 'Kriegsflüchtlinge in Cisleithanien im ersten Weltkrieg', PhD dissertation, University of Vienna, 1997, pp. 4–6.
3 Mentzel, 'Kriegsflüchtlinge in Cisleithanien', pp. 388–419; Hoffmann-Holter, 'Abreisendmachung', pp. 52–60.
4 As Rebekah Klein-Pejšová demonstrates in chapter 7, the Transleithanian authorities regarded refugees from the Austrian administrative entities as Austrian citizens. Nevertheless, a large number of Austrian refugees stayed temporarily in Hungary.
5 Mentzel, 'Kriegsflüchtlinge', pp. 4–6; Hoffmann-Holter, 'Abreisendmachung', pp. 29–30; Julie Thorpe, 'Der rote Faden der Vertreibung: Österreich-Ungarns Flüchtlinge im Ersten Weltkrieg und ihre Darstellung in der Kriegshilfeausstellung von 1915', in Kathrin Pallestrang (ed.), Stick- und Knüpfmuster ruthenischer Flüchtlinge im Ersten Weltkrieg: aus der Sammlung des Volkskundemuseums Wien; Katalog zur Ausstellung (Wien: Österreichisches Museum für Volkskunde, 2014), pp. 31–46 (here p. 34), and Peter Gatrell, 'Refugees and forced migrants during the First World War', in Matthew Stibbe (ed.), Captivity, Forced Labour and Forced Migration in Europe During the First World War (London: Routledge, 2009), pp. 82–110 (here p. 85).
6 Matthew Stibbe, 'Enemy aliens, deportees, refugees: internment practices in

the Habsburg Empire, 1914-1918', *Journal of Modern European History*, 12, no. 4 (2014), 479-99.
7 Niederösterreichisches Landesarchiv, St. Pölten (NÖLA, State Archives of Lower Austria, St. Pölten), Präsidialaktenbestand (Pr), Pr2701PXIIa1916 and Pr336PXIb1919.
8 Matthew Stibbe, 'Civilian internment and civilian internees in Europe, 1914-1920', in Stibbe (ed.), *Captivity, Forced Labour and Forced Migration*, pp. 49-81. At the end of the war, the camp also briefly accommodated POWs. See Pr336PXIb1919, NÖLA.
9 Heimo Halbrainer, *Das Lager Wagna 1914-1935: die zeitweise drittgrößte Stadt der Steiermark* (Graz, Univeralmuseum Johanneum, 2014), p. 53.
10 PrZ70M4, NÖLA.
11 In addition to the flight of the population of Czernowitz/Chernivtsy, when Russian troops were already occupying the suburbs, another example is Przmysl', where only the departure of the regiment informed the civilian population of precariousness of the military situation. See Mentzel, 'Kriegsflüchtlinge', pp. 26-8, 33-7.
12 Anton Holzer, *Die andere Front: Fotografie und Propaganda im Ersten Weltkrieg. Mit unveröffentlichten Originalaufnahmen aus dem Bildarchiv der Österreichischen Nationalbibliothek* (Darmstadt: Böhlau, 2007), p. 201.
13 Hans Hautmann, 'Kriegsgesetze und Militärjustiz in der österreichischen Reichshälfte 1914-1918', in Erika Weinzierl and Oliver Rathkolb (eds), *Justiz und Zeitgeschichte*, vol. 1 (Wien: Jugend und Volk, 1995), pp. 74-8, and Brigitte Haman, *Der Erste Weltkrieg: Wahrheit und Lüge in Bildern und Texten* (München: Piper, 2004), p. 102.
14 Mentzel, 'Kriegsflüchtlinge', pp. 63-5, 85-91.
15 Gesetz vom 31. Dezember 1917, betreffend den Schutz der Kriegsflüchtlinge, unter: http://alex.onb.ac.at/cgi-content/alex?aid=rgb&datum=19180004&seite=00000081 [accessed 9 November 2016].
16 Mentzel, 'Kriegsflüchtlinge', pp. 355-9.
17 Hoffmann-Holter, 'Abreisendmachung', pp. 43-5; Mentzel, 'Kriegsflüchtlinge', pp. 347-55; and Walter Mentzel, 'Weltkriegsflüchtlinge in Cisleithanien 1914-1918', in Heiss Gernot and Oliver Rathkolb (eds), *Asylland wider Willen: Flüchtlinge in Österreich im europäischen Kontext seit 1914* (Wien: J&V, 1995), pp. 17-44 (here p. 28).
18 Manfried Rauchensteiner, *Der Erste Weltkrieg und das Ende der Habsburgermonarchie 1914-1918* (Wien: Böhlau, 2013), p. 840.
19 To put this amount into perspective, a worker could expect to earn 99 crowns per month, and a skilled worker 136 crowns. See Erik Eybl, *Von der Eule zum Euro, nicht nur eine österreichische Geldgeschichte* (Klagenfurt: Verlag Hermagoras, 2005), p. 145.
20 Hoffmann-Holter, 'Abreisendmachung', pp. 31-3.
21 Hoffmann-Holter, 'Abreisendmachung', pp. 26-9; Bruno Enders, 'Die

österreichische Eisenbahnen', in *Verkehrswesen im Kriege* (Wien: Hölder-Pichler-Tempsky, 1931), pp. 57–8.
22 Mentzel, 'Kriegsflüchtlinge', pp. 243–5.
23 Hoffmann-Holter, 'Abreisendmachung', pp. 35–40.
24 Landsturm units comprised men unfit for military service, either because they had been wounded at the front or because of their age.
25 Mentzel, 'Kriegsflüchtlinge', pp. 246–7; Pr1861PXIIa1916 und Pr1861PXIIa1916, NÖLA.
26 The author writes: 100 heller = 1 crown, In 1914 one kilo of bread cost 0.32 crowns, a kilo of beef 1,95 crowns, and one kilo of flour 0.44 crowns. Wartime inflation needs to be taken into account. This does of course not take inflation during the war into account. Eybl, *Geldgeschichte*, p. 145.
27 Mentzel, 'Kriegsflüchtlinge', pp. 231–2.
28 Pr974PXIIe1915, NÖLA.
29 Pr6700PXIIe1916, NÖLA.
30 Heidelinde Jasser and Hans Leopold, *Das Flüchtlingslager Landegg, NÖ von 1915 bis 1918* (Pottendorf: Jasser/Leopold, 2002), p. 34.
31 Manfred Dacho, Franz Drach and Harald Winkler, *Am Anfang war das Lager, Gmünd – Neustadt* (Weitra: Bibliothek der Provinz, 2014), pp. 65–6.
32 *Reichspost*, 16 December 1916.
33 Maureen Healy, *Total War and Everyday Life in World War I* (Cambridge: Cambridge University Press, 2004), pp. 87–121.
34 *Reichspost*, 16 December 1916.
35 Pr6913PXIIe1915, NÖLA.
36 Mentzel, 'Kriegsflüchtlinge', pp. 106–8; Holzer, *Die andere Front*, p. 201; Emil Brix, 'Galizien als "österreichischer Mythos"', in *Mythos Galizien: Ausstellungskatalog Wien Museum* (Wien: Wien Museum, 2015), pp. 59–66 (here p. 60).
37 Mykola Riabchuk, 'Die Neuerfindung Galziens', in *Mythos Galizien*, pp. 101–2; Maximilian Schönowsky-Schönwies and August Angenetter, 'Der russische Durchbruch im Juni 1916', *Aus der Geschichte des bestandenen k. k. Schützenregiments Wien*, Number 1 (Wien: Braumüller, 1919), pp. 13–21, with heavy racist and antisemitic undertones.
38 See the technical report of the construction of camp Gmünd in the city archives of Gmünd, Lower Austria, Pr345XIIb1915, Pr970PXIIa1917 and Pr7744PXIIa1915; also Georg Hoffmann, Nicole-Melanie Goll and Philipp Lesiak, *Thalerhof 1914–1936: die Geschichte eines vergessenen Lagers und seiner Opfer* (Budapest: Schäfer, 2010), p. 34; Halbrainer, *Das Lager Wagna*, pp. 30–1; Jasser and Leopold, *Flüchtlingslager Landegg*, p. 36.
39 Halbrainer, *Das Lager Wagna*, p. 31.
40 Pr1256PXIIb1915, NÖLA and TB.
41 See the list of complaints by inmates of the camp on 20 and 21 November 1915 and in December 1916. Pr970PXIIa1917 and Pr1992PXIIa1918, NÖLA.

42 Pr3775PXIIa1918, NÖLA.
43 Pr1121PXIIb1917, NÖLA.
44 Halbrainer, *Das Lager Wagna*, p. 23.
45 Pr159PXIIb1916, NÖLA.
46 Pr884PXIIb1919, NÖLA.
47 Pr970PXIIa1917, NÖLA.
48 Pr905/2PXIIa1915, NÖLA.
49 Pr3775PXIIa1918, NÖLA.
50 Jochen Oltmer, 'Krieg, Migration und Zwangsarbeit im 20. Jahrhundert', in Hans-Christoph Seidel and Klaus Tenfelde (eds), *Zwangsarbeit im Europa des 20. Jahrhunderts: Bewältigung und vergleichende Aspekte* (Essen: Klartext, 2007), p. 143.
51 Pr4150PXIIa1917, NÖLA.
52 Halbrainer, *Das Lager Wagna*, p. 17.
53 Pr4150PXIIa1917, NÖLA.
54 Pr4150PXIIa1917, NÖLA. In camp Pottendorf, 1,300 refugees were employed on 16 January 1917 out of a total refugee population of 5,200.
55 Jasser and Leopold, *Flüchtlingslager Landegg*, p. 27; Pr707PXIIb1917, NÖLA.
56 Hildegard Mandl, 'Galizische Flüchtlinge in der Steiermark zu Beginn des ersten Weltkrieges', in Fritz Posch and Gerhard Pferschy (eds), *Zeitschrift des Historischen Vereines für Steiermark* (Graz: Landesarchiv, 1986), p. 288.
57 Friedrich Wiser, 'Staatliche Kulturarbeit für Flüchtlinge', *Österreichische Rundschau* 45, no. 5 (1915), p. 3.
58 Pr66P1918, NÖLA.
59 Pr1786PXIIa1917, NÖLA.
60 *Die Neue Illustrierte Zeitung*, Vienna/Czernowitz, 15 September 1915; *Neue Freie Presse*, Vienna, 27 June 1915)
61 *Illustriertes Wiener Extrablatt*, 22 September 1915.
62 Herbert Brettl, *Das Kriegsgefangenen- und Interniertenlager Boldogasszony/Frauenkirchen* (Halbturn: Brettl, 2014), p. 18.
63 *Illustrierte Kronenzeitung*, 22 November 1915.
64 Pr2419PXIIa 1915 and Pr380PXIVa1915, NÖLA.
65 Pr5729PXIIe1915, NÖLA.
66 Manfred Dacho, Franz Drach and Harald Winkler, *Am Anfang war das Lager, Gmünd – Neustadt* (Weitra: Bibliothek der Provinz, 2014), pp. 61–2.
67 Pr1992PXIIa1918, NÖLA.
68 Pr1121PXIIb1917, NÖLA.
69 Halbrainer, *Das Lager Wagna*, p. 40.
70 Mentzel, 'Kriegsflüchtlinge', pp. 106–8, Holzer, *Die andere Front*, p. 201.
71 Mentzel, 'Kriegsflüchtlinge', pp. 160–72.
72 Josef Reder, *Das Fleckfieber nach dem heutigen Stande seiner Lehre und nach Beobachtungen in den Epidemien des k. k. Flüchtlingslagers Gmünd* (Leipzig-Wien, 1918), p. 83.

73 Pr654PXIIa1915, Pr1249PXIIa915 and Pr4050PXIIa1918, NÖLA, Jasser and Leopold, *Langegg*, p. 31, Reder, *Fleckfieber*, p. 76; Halbrainer, *Das Lager Wagna*, 36.
74 Reder, *Fleckfieber*, p. 86.
75 Reder, *Fleckfieber*, pp. 6–7.
76 Pr1367XIIa1916, NÖLA.
77 Pr109PXIIa1916, NÖLA.
78 Friederike Scherr, 'Jakob Levy Moreno im Flüchtlingslager Mitterndorf an der Fischa – eine Spurensuche', *Zeitschrift für Psychodrama und Soziometrie* (Wiesbaden, 2013), 3–126 (here, pp. 32–5).
79 J.L. Moreno, *'Who Shall Survive? Foundations of Sociometry, Group Psychotherapy and Sociodrama* (Beaon, 1953), pp. xxxxii–iii; Scherr, 'Jakob Levy Moreno', pp. 46–8.
80 Mentzel, 'Kriegsflüchtlinge', pp. 388–419; Hoffmann-Holter, 'Abreisendmachung', pp. 52–60.
81 *Neue Freie Presse*, 19 September 1917.
82 Julie Thorpe, 'Displacing empire: refugee welfare, national activism and state legitimacy in Austria-Hungary in the First World War', in Panikos Panayi and Pippa Virdee (eds), *Refugees and the End of Empire: Imperial Collapse and Forced Migration in the Twentieth Century* (Basingstoke: Palgrave, 2011), pp. 102–26 (here pp. 118–19); Mentzel, 'Kriegsflüchtlinge', pp. 453–4.
83 Compare the law of 5 December 1918, 'über das deutsch-österreichische Staatsbürgerrecht', http://alex.onb.ac.at/cgi-content/alex?aid=sgb&datum=1918&size=45&page=151 [accessed 1 August 2016] with the remarks of Hoffmann-Holter, 'Abreisendmachung', pp. 148–59, and Mentzel, 'Kriegsflüchtlinge', pp. 453–4.

7

Between refugees and the state: Hungarian Jewry and the wartime Jewish refugee crisis in Austria-Hungary[1]

Rebekah Klein-Pejšová

Introduction

Galician Jews crossed the border by the thousands into the Kingdom of Hungary when Russian troops advanced on the Eastern Front in September 1914. They fled from the Russian army, aware of the fate of Jews in Russia's western borderlands expelled *en masse* from their homes and sent deep into the interior of the empire by military commanders fearful of breaches in border security.[2] Their entry marked the beginning of a large-scale Jewish refugee crisis in Austria-Hungary, a significant part of the total population displacement caused by the First World War. By the time the Central Powers regained control over Galicia in June 1915, making repatriation possible, an estimated half a million Galician Jews had been dislocated.[3] In their movement toward the interior of the Monarchy, Jewish refugees passed in plain view of the local population, of government officials, of soldiers and other military personnel. Their long-term presence triggered an intense interest in the so-called 'Jewish Question' at all levels, not least among the Hungarian Jewish population itself. The wartime Jewish Question was in large part a contestation of Jewish loyalty to Hungary, calculated according to military sacrifice.

The presence of Jewish refugees throughout the war, in the countryside as well as in Budapest, reminded Hungary's population of the connection between the wartime refugees and the large-scale immigration into Hungary from Galicia that was the foundation of the contemporary Hungarian Jewish community.[4] Jews from Galicia migrated southward into Hungary in large numbers beginning in the early 1780s, shortly after Joseph II issued his Edicts of Toleration that extended to newly Habsburg-acquired Galicia from partitioned Poland. The Hungarian

Jewish population grew from about 83,000 in 1787 to about 130,000 in 1805, and continued to expand at a rate of 40 to 50 per cent every 20 years until 1880, largely due to immigration. In 1880, the Hungarian Jewish population stood at 624,700. It had reached 910,000 by 1910.[5] As József Patai, the well-known Hungarian Jewish writer, poet and editor of the Zionist monthly *Múlt és Jövő* (Past and Future) wrote towards the close of the war, 'When the Jew-haters speak or write about "the Galicians" in parliament or in the press, they hardly mean those couple of hundred Galician refugees who remain here today, but really the children and grandchildren of yesterday's Galicians, namely all of Hungarian Jewry, just as it is'.[6]

While Galician Jews experienced the war as both soldiers and refugees, their circumstances as refugees were more visible. Jewish refugees were a conspicuous feature of the landscape. Their lingering presence fuelled the resentment of the local population. It compounded existing anti-Jewish sentiment and wartime stereotypes of the Jews as profiteers, hawkers, smugglers and shirkers. Consumed by their own wartime distress, locals complained that the Jewish refugees were dirty and loud, that the refugee presence raised food prices and threatened their ability to provide for themselves. Jewish refugees loitered in large groups on the streets and in coffeehouses, locals said; they lived off aid, engaged in profiteering and dishonest business practices, and shirked military duty. Government officials, politicians, newspaper columnists and ordinary members of the public engaged in variations on these themes, arguing for refugee removal and repatriation. As anti-Jewish feeling proliferated throughout the war, the customary complaints about the refugees spread to the Jewish population as a whole.[7]

Studies of the wartime Jewish refugee crisis in Austria-Hungary have typically focused on refugee migration into major centres further westward, like the imperial capital Vienna, or even Bohemia's provincial capital Prague, and its relationship to the development of Jewish national politics and culture. Considerably less attention has been given to the question of Hungarian territory. Yet shifting our attention to wartime Hungary deepens our understanding of the connection between citizenship and resource distribution, of local Hungarian Jewish community strategies of intervention with the administration on behalf of the refugees and their implications, of the successes and limitations of aid from diaspora networks, and of the political, cultural and regional diversity of Hungarian Jewry before 1918. With its focus on interactions between the Jewish refugees, Hungarian Jews, and the Hungarian state administration, this chapter also highlights questions relevant to the evolution and contours of antisemitism in Hungary, and to the perceptions and self-understanding of the Jewish population within Hungarian society.

Arrival in Hungary

Hundreds of communications arrived at Budapest from the local administration in Bártfa (Bartfeld, Bardejov) from September to November 1914, detailing the continuous arrival of Galician Jewish refugees and their desperate condition, and anxious for orders on how to handle the influx.[8] Bártfa, close to the border with Austrian Galicia, was the point of entry into Hungary for Galician Jewish refugees. With just over 6,000 inhabitants, it was the first significant administrative centre across the Carpathian Mountains.[9] The town had a traditional Jewish population of nearly 1,500 which had settled there beginning in 1808, with a strong Hasidic constituency that tended to dominate communal affairs.[10] Many of the Jewish families in Bártfa had themselves previously emigrated from Galicia, and tended to maintain cross-border communal ties with Galician Jewish communities, as was usual for Jews of this north-western border region.[11]

On the move since September 1914 when they fled from invading Russian troops, Galician Jewish refugees began arriving rapidly and in great numbers in mid-November. In the space of 72 hours beginning on 12 November, more than 10,000 arrived on foot and by wagon, pulling their children along in carts. Upon their arrival, the Lord Lieutenant (*főispán*) of Sáros county, where Bártfa was located, noted that they were indeed in a state of great privation. Contagious diseases had broken out among them, including numerous cases of scarlet fever among the children.[12] The military commander assigned by Budapest to Bártfa immediately arranged for their transport to the interior of the Monarchy. Equipped with an official policy hewn out of the chaotic improvisations that characterised the initial refugee arrangements, he divided them into groups based on wealth: those with means to provide for themselves who would not require aid from the state, and those without means who would require aid. Those with financial means he sent on to Kassa (Kaschau, Košice) and Budapest in Hungary, Graz and Vienna in Austria. He then ordered those without means on to the newly constructed barracks at Ungarisch Hradisch (Uherské Hradiště), organised by the Israelitische Allianz zu Wien, in Moravia. Few of the refugees could make this trip by train, as the six trains assigned to Bártfa were reserved for the transport of wounded soldiers, munitions and supplies. Some of the remaining refugees left the town in wagons, but the majority set off on foot, carrying their belongings. They completely inundated the countryside.[13]

In organising the movement of Jewish refugees arriving in Hungary, the state was primarily concerned with citizenship, then wealth and health. Austro-Hungarian policy toward the Galician Jewish refugees on the territory of Hungary depended, above all, on their classification as citizens of Austria. As Austrian citizens, the refugees were entitled to receive state aid from the Austrian treasury.[14] Austrian citizens were, however, to receive this aid while on Austrian territory, with the exception of limited Austrian state aid to refugees sojourning in Budapest. This proviso required that Galician Jewish refugees without means leave Hungarian territory for Austria. In Austria, refugees were temporarily resettled in barracks or other accommodation in Moravia and Bohemia until they could be repatriated.

From October 1914, Hungary sent newly arriving refugees without means directly to Austria, as well as beginning to transport those sojourning in Budapest to Vienna. Once in Austria, incoming Jewish refugees were redirected to Moravia. They then passed through the refugee camp at Ungarisch Hradisch, which served as a way station for redirecting the refugees to tens of smaller camps and other means of accommodation in Moravia and Bohemia.[15] Refugees with means were sent on to the urban centres of the Monarchy. By the end of 1914, there were Galician Jewish refugees with means sojourning in nearly every city in Hungary where they were required to report regularly – and frequently – to the local police in order to confirm their financial solvency.[16] The state was also keenly interested in refugee health, especially as it pertained to the potential spread of illness from refugees to soldiers or to the general public. Refugees without means suffering from serious illness were often granted extended sojourn in Hungary during the winter of 1914–15, on the understanding that they relocate to Ungarisch Hradisch.[17] Local Jewish communities were required to confirm the departure of refugees whose sojourn had been extended for health reasons.[18]

Jewish refugee aid in the Hungarian provinces

The wartime Jewish refugee crisis was an urgent and self-defining issue for Hungarian Jewish communities. It was the question around which organised Jewish self-help efforts galvanised during the war and had a significant impact on the growth of feelings of Jewish solidarity, self-reliance and interdependence. At the same time, responses to the needs of the Jewish refugees from Galicia worked to describe a deepening division between the Jewish communities actively involved in refugee aid and the Hungarian Jewish leadership in Budapest. How Jewish communities handled the refugee crisis reveals the contours of their evolving relationship with the state, with each other, and with the Jewish world beyond their borders.

The extended winter sojourn on Hungarian territory, granted in exceptional cases to the sick and the old rather than forcing them to make the hazardous journey to Austria (Moravia and Bohemia), seemed to many Hungarian Jewish communities a course of action that should be applied to the Galician Jewish refugees more broadly: a population consisting primarily of women, children and the elderly whose husbands and sons were off fighting for the Monarchy. In their handling of the Jewish refugee crisis, provincial Hungarian Jewish communities sought to take the refugees out of the public eye as quickly as possible. It was in their own, as well as the best interest of the refugees to provide for them within the Jewish community. They began to provide for the refugees out of pocket. This strategy, however, was unsustainable. The communities would soon face financial devastation.[19] Provincial community leaders petitioned Budapest to divert the Austrian state aid the Galician Jewish refugees would receive in the refugee camps to them just where they were. Rabbi Koloman Wéber of the Orthodox Jewish community in Pőstyén (Piešťany) was the champion of this strategy. His successful intervention with the Austrian and Hungarian Ministries of the Interior on behalf of the Galician Jewish refugees in his community made him a celebrated and imitated refugee advocate.[20]

Budapest did not approve similar Jewish community petitions from Pozsony (Bratislava) and Stomfa (Štupava). The Lord Lieutenant for Nyitra county in the north-west had sent a report to the Hungarian Minister of the Interior in November urging him to prevent the continued entry of Galician Jewish refugees into Pőstyén, and send the ones there immediately to Ungarisch Hradisch. His concerns for the convalescence of military personnel trumped further humanitarian considerations. He emphasised the refugee threat of contagion, the effect of their competition for scarce provisions on costs, and their unwelcome occupation of otherwise intended accommodations:

> In Pőstyén, many hundreds of wounded soldiers and officers are under continuous hospitalisation, and the first order of duty of the authorities is

to prevent any danger which may befall the armed forces by way of possible introduction of contagious diseases through the refugees ... Refugee entry in boundless numbers is also alarming because they have already occupied the accommodations maintained for convalescing soldiers, they have extraordinarily raised the prices of foodstuffs, and their stay here for a longer period of time due to excessive influx could endanger providing for the inhabitants.[21]

Jewish refugee aid and conflict with Hungarian state policy

Rabbi Wéber's success on behalf of the refugees already provided for by his community in Pőstyén was exceptional. While other provincial Hungarian Jewish communities energetically intervened on behalf of the Galician Jewish refugees sojourning in their towns (namely Pozsony, Stomfa, Győr, Hajdúnanás, Vágujhely, Miskolc and Ónod), their requests to receive the same temporary Austrian aid available as in Budapest was rejected. Rabbi Snyders of Győr appealed directly to the Austrian Ministry of the Interior, as Rabbi Wéber of Pőstyén had done, but his petition was not approved.[22] Budapest's denial of these appeals underscored official state policy toward refugees without means. Only three categories of refugees would be permitted to remain in Hungary: the elderly and gravely ill could stay through the winter before relocation to Austria; those with independent means to support themselves as regularly verified by the local administration; and those who were fully supported by aid from local Jewish communities, money from relatives in America, or employment by Hungarian citizens in Hungarian firms.[23]

In contrast to Austria, where Jewish refugee relief could be framed as 'patriotic war work', and the Austrian administration imagined that providing refugee aid was a demonstration of the 'deep and intuitive understanding of the community of fate that binds together all of the empire's peoples', in Hungary refugee aid led to a conflict with state policy.[24] Where the goal of Jewish refugee policy was their speedy removal from Hungarian territory, providing and petitioning for their extended stay ran counter to that end. In their Austrian Jewish refugee aid work, provincial Hungarian Jewish communities found themselves in the position of placing their solidarity to their group above their loyalty to the state – in this instance alone – to undertake what they believed to be the right response to the crisis. For this reason, they continuously invoked the husbands and sons of the refugees who were fighting the enemy in the Carpathians as soldiers in the Austro-Hungarian army. Refugee advocates repeatedly emphasised that the refugees whom the local population saw in the streets and the train stations were the families of the soldiers. Why should they be denied aid from the state for which their husbands and sons were sacrificing themselves? The soldiers, however, were invisible, while the refugees were ever-present. Their perceived undesirable presence diluted the virtues of the blood spilled on the battlefield for Hungary by their kin.

Not all Jewish refugees on the territory of Hungary during the war were Austrian citizens, however. The Hungarian administration's policy toward refugees with Hungarian citizenship underscores the primacy of state belonging in connection with refugee aid. The Eastern Front cut across the Carpathian Mountains into north-eastern Hungary, displacing Hungarian citizens in Sáros, Zemplén, Ung, Bereg and Mármaros counties. Jews from Transylvania later fled to the Hungarian interior with the Romanian invasion of 1916. The evidence shows that monies from the Hungarian treasury were allocated to people in this category where they were. Hungarian state aid for Jewish refugees from Hungary was strikingly forthcoming when compared to the struggle to divert Austrian monies to Austrian Jewish refugees sojourning in Hungary during the winter of 1914–15.[25]

In April 1915, following exceptional winter circumstances, the Hungarian Minister of the Interior ordered the removal of all Austrian Jewish refugees without means from the territory of Hungary. No state aid would be available to those who remained in Hungary after 15 May in any district, including Budapest. They were to be sent to destinations in Bohemia and Moravia, as well as on to Tyrol and Steiermark if necessary, via the camp at Ungarisch Hradisch, which would serve as a transit hub and health inspection station for refugees entering western Austria.[26] The removal of the refugees would begin in the provinces and then continue in Budapest.[27] According to figures compiled by the Viennese Allianz at the end of 1914, there were approximately 30,000 Austrian Jewish refugees in Hungary, 20,000 of which were located in Budapest. The *Jüdische Zeitung*, a Jewish national paper published in Vienna, estimated 30,000 refugees in Budapest alone.[28] Given these approximations, it is likely that up to 50,000 refugees awaited transport to Austria in April 1915.

The Jewish press derided the accommodation which awaited the Austrian Jewish refugees in Austria as woefully inadequate. The press complained that the camps were dangerously overcrowded, dirty and cold, and that the social and religious needs of the refugees, especially regarding the provision of kosher food, were neglected. Other types of accommodation made available to the refugees in Austria ranged from acceptable to overcrowded and dirty, and included wet barns and school buildings. Where possible, refugees made their way to stay with friends or family in Vienna and Bohemia rather than remain in the facilities provided by the state. Jewish organisations repeatedly attempted to persuade the Austrian Minister of the Interior to improve the situation. Complaints about the conditions in the western Austrian refugee camps appeared in the press early in the war, in the autumn of 1914 and through the summer of 1915.[29]

Dr Bloch's *Österreichische Wochenschrift* presented the decision of the Hungarian Minister of the Interior to remove the refugees as an abrupt change in state policy. The paper claimed that it was a departure from the recent joint decision reached by the Austrian and Hungarian governments to allow Austrian Jewish refugees without means to remain in Budapest and receive state support there unless they were engaged in illegal business, had been arrested for a crime, were under the strong suspicion of the state, or had themselves volunteered to leave.[30] The change of course, the paper indignantly reported, was the result of the activity of the official Refugee Aid Committee in Budapest.

The Budapest-based *Allgemeine Jüdische Zeitung* indignantly declared that an official Refugee Aid Committee composed of five Orthodox and five Neolog Jews functioning under the Vice-Mayor's office of Budapest was responsible for advising the Ministry of the Interior to order the immediate departure of the refugees. This body, argued the paper, decided that only those refugees who had left Hungary for Austria by 15 May would be eligible to receive state aid.[31] As the *Allgemeine Jüdische Zeitung* bitterly observed:

> The 'help' that it [the aid committee] provides for the refugees mostly consists of distributing the aid that comes from the Austrian state to those poor refugees who, for a bowl of lentils, are willing to sell their birthright as a citizen of the other half of the monarchy driven to Hungary by its enemies, so that they may stay in this half of the monarchy. Yes, the worthy aid committee also zealously helps the local masses of refugees – against their own will and mostly to their greatest dismay – evacuate Budapest earlier and in greater numbers.[32]

In addition, the paper pointedly declared that sending the refugees to Bohemian villages where there was no local Jewish population, or to hastily constructed, notoriously inadequate barracks in Moravia, was a religious, moral and material catastrophe. Instead of 'Refugee Aid

Committee', it wryly suggested that the organisation's name be changed to the 'Anti-Refugee Committee' (*Flüchtlingsgegner Komitee*).[33]

The *Ungarländische Jüdische Zeitung*, in the same vein, accused the Hungarian Jewish leadership of treating their Galician brothers poorly. It called attention to the 'high, widely visible stage' upon which the Refugee Aid Committee had acted, and wondered if they were aware of the great responsibility with which they were confronted.[34] The paper emphasised that it was incumbent upon the Refugee Aid Committee to concentrate on the rights, honour and dignity of the Jewish refugees, even for egotistical reasons, as 'their honour is indeed our honour, their dignity is our dignity, and their rights are our rights'.[35]

Jews and Jewish communities in Hungary and Austria blamed the Hungarian Jewish leadership in Budapest for the removal of the Austrian Jewish refugees from Hungarian territory. Yet though the Refugee Aid Committee aided the action, it was not their invention, nor did it represent a change of course in the policy of the Hungarian Ministry of the Interior toward the Jewish refugees. The body's collaboration with the government, at the same time that provincial Jewish communities struggled out of pocket to provide for the refugees, earned it the disdain of Austro-Hungarian Jewish public opinion. The Refugee Aid Committee's fear of appearing less than committed to the overall Hungarian war effort, or less than loyal to Hungary, appeared to outweigh its moral imperative to the refugees.

The activity of the Refugee Aid Committee paralleled that of the leadership of the Budapest Jewish Community in the autumn of 1914, when it organised the transport of Jewish refugees from Galicia and the Bukovina from Budapest to Vienna. That enterprise, too, went hand-in-hand with the Hungarian state policy toward the refugees. The Pest Jewish community leadership drew up lists of over 2,000 refugees sojourning in Budapest, all of them medically screened on the Jewish Community's bill, and sent to Vienna via the transit camp at Ungarisch Hradisch in a sealed train, so that the local population would not see them.[36]

Petitions for refugee residency

The Hungarian Minister of the Interior ordered the repatriation of the more than 5,000 Galician Jewish refugees who remained on the territory of Hungary after the Hungarian administration's May efforts to remove them by 15 August 1915.[37] At that time, the Central Powers had nearly reconquered Galicia in its entirety.[38] The clearance was unsuccessful. The

Minister of the Interior set a new October deadline. Yet thousands of refugees remained in the city. Approximately 1,500 predominantly elderly and infirm Austrian Jewish refugees continued their sojourn in Budapest through the summer. The remainder included Galician rabbis granted leave not to be transferred to towns in Bohemia and Moravia where there was no Jewish community, and also children anticipating registration in local schools for the coming year.[39] More Jewish refugees, Hungarian and Austrian, arrived in Hungary shortly after the Romanian army invaded Transylvania. By the end of 1916, nearly 20,000 Jewish refugees still remained in Budapest and the territory of Hungary overall.[40]

The continuing refugee presence called for re-evaluation of residence permissibility. Widespread cases of refugee employment to ease the wartime labour shortage particularly heightened the Hungarian government's anxiety that large numbers of refugees would remain in the state indefinitely.[41] The Minister of Commerce addressed the issue in May 1915, essentially to reiterate earlier decisions that the Austrian Jewish refugees were to remain in Hungary solely on a temporary basis, since they did not come to the country with the intention to settle. All Austrian refugees were required to return to their homes as soon as the cause of their forced departure came to an end.[42]

The administration feared that large-scale refugee entry into the Hungarian workforce, especially in the industrial and commercial sectors, would have a disastrous impact on the well-being of the country after the war. Mass refugee employment in industry and commerce would inhibit Hungary's restoration to pre-war standards, argued the Minister of Commerce, because of their 'lower standard of work and lack of discipline'. The refugees stood on a 'lower cultural plane', he wrote, with a few 'inconsequential' exceptions, and their 'morally undisciplined' character and weak material status made them undesirable elements.[43] In addition, the refugees would take the jobs of demobilised soldiers, especially those who suffered injuries, such as the loss of limbs, which prevented them from returning to their pre-war occupations.

Yet even the Minister of Commerce saw no legal obstacle to the employment of small numbers of exceptional refugees, provided that they received permanent residency in Hungary. He advised that residency permits be granted only in rare cases.[44] Refugee right of residency applications were to be based on a standing 1903 law, which called for proof of personal identity and state citizenship, a statement of why residency in Hungary was necessary, documentation of moral record, and finally proof of ability to provide for oneself and one's family. The Minister of

Commerce emphasised the importance of the refugees' moral record in his communications.[45]

As news spread of the opportunity, hundreds of refugees in Budapest and the provinces sent in residency applications to the Ministry of the Interior.[46] Applications included information about the families' occupations, ages and places of origin; wartime accommodations of the refugee population in Hungary; and an explanation of the reasons for the need of right of residency in Hungary. Refugees described their situation before the war, their initial displacement, and their journeys. Since nearly all applications were submitted in Magyar (with a small number in German), a language that all but Hungarian Jewish refugees from the north-eastern counties and Transylvania were unlikely to know, it is likely that local Hungarian Jews, including relatives and friends who had earlier immigrated to Hungary, wrote the text for them. In some cases, local Jewish communities or firms in which refugees were employed submitted applications on behalf of the refugees.[47]

In the rare cases where the Minister of the Interior granted right of residency, accepted applications demonstrated useful employment in the war industry, no record of having collected state aid (for refugees sojourning in Budapest), and critically, good hygiene. Special permission for extended residency in Hungary, whether or not the applicant fulfilled these criteria, was often granted to rabbis and their families and in rare cases to individuals able to provide medical proof of suffering from a life-threatening illness. In cases where the state wished to verify applicant claims (especially medical), or undertake a first-hand examination of moral character, a police detective was dispatched to investigate.

Refugee hygiene was a central concern of the state. This concern went beyond the usual screenings for illness and disease which accompanied refugee movement and sojourn as a matter of course, to the examination of day-to-day personal hygiene. Personal hygiene was a leading factor in the Minister of the Interior's decisions to accept or reject the right of residency applications submitted by Austrian Jewish refugees. Rejected applications typically condemned the applicant for keeping the apartment 'so dirty that it [posed] a risk to public health'.[48] While public health provided the pretext, it was clear that the state regarded personal hygiene as evidence of good moral character. This included keeping a 'clean, well-aired apartment'.[49]

The police investigation of rabbis from Galicia who had been granted permission for an extended sojourn in Budapest based on religious considerations bears out this point. Not only did the rabbis and their families live in 'filthy apartments' and 'not one of them was fit to work', the resulting police report observed, but 'they [had become] so accustomed to the filth that they themselves [were] not aware of the lack of cleanliness'. The report recommended that the extended right of residency granted to these rabbis and their families be limited to the most narrow definition possible. The Galician rabbis received permission to remain in Budapest as they successfully argued that they could not fulfil their religious obligations in the small Bohemian and Moravian towns in which they were assigned to be resettled.[50]

Heinrich Klinger, owner of the well-known Linen and Jute Goods Factory in Pozsony, had remarkable success in securing residency for his Austrian Jewish refugee employees. Klinger applied at least three times on behalf of at least 61 people, including family members of employees.[51] Klinger first intervened with the Hungarian administration in November 1915 concerning a repatriation order that would affect 37 of his employees. He argued for their continued employment in his factory based on their importance to the war effort:

> I have employed a number of both male and female Galician refugees in my factory here for over a year, partially in tent-making and the rest in war materiel preparation. I employ these Galician refugees exclusively to fulfil military shipment orders. I can hardly replace their work because of the current labour shortage ... they are already well-experienced and the possible training of a new workforce would be quite time-consuming.

Klinger requested that his employees be granted permission to remain in Pozsony until at least June 1916, and that the border police be informed accordingly as a matter of urgency. The Minister of the Interior approved his request. His request was fulfilled.[52]

Klinger's subsequent applications were more intrepid. At the end of March 1916, Klinger urged the Hungarian administration not only to grant at least an additional three months of residency to 17 male and female Galician refugees he employed, but to also extend the residency of 6 of their family members employed in other area factories, as well as to another 18 family members (only 8 of them children) who did not work. He argued that the majority of his workforce was comprised of women, who would not remain in Pozsony if their children were repatriated.[53] If their children left, his workforce would leave, the Klinger factory would not be able to meet war materiel demands, and the war effort would consequently suffer.

Klinger also managed to hold on to three male employees who had been called to military service, in addition to five other Galician Jewish refugees who worked for him. He wrote to the Minister of the Interior in early October to request permission for these eight Galician Jewish refugees to remain employed in his factory in spite of the order and the imminent removal of Galician refugees from the city of Pozsony. In closing, Klinger expressed the hope that His Excellency would grant this petition as he had the others that came before. A handwritten note confirms that indeed Klinger's request was met.[54] There were no police investigations of Klinger's employees.

The case of Mózes Imber is a more typical example of a successful residency application without an influential sponsor like Heinrich Klinger. Mózes Imber fled to Budapest with his wife and daughter from Zalozce, Galicia in the first weeks after the outbreak of the war. At the time of his application in May 1916, Zalozce was still under Russian occupation. Imber noted that their home lay merely four kilometres from the Russian border. The family had already been residing for a year and a quarter in an apartment on Népszinház Street in Budapest's eighth district:

> Every single one of my personal belongings and possessions has been lost. We fled from our home, and our return there would mean an uncertain future, even if our region were already free. In Budapest I earn my bread with manual labour. As the ... attached identity papers prove, I am steadily employed as a skilled leather-worker at [one of the bigger] and well-funded firms ... there is a great shortage of labour in this profession and I am needed. The same papers contain the required declaration from the firm in question that [it] will not dismiss [me] from this service for the duration of the war ... [Please do not remove refugees from the country] who earn their bread with honest work and who will in no way become a burden to society.[55]

The Imber family was granted residency in Hungary, justified on the grounds that Imber was a highly skilled leather-worker at the Leather Manufacturing Centre of the Hungarian Crown Lands (*A Magyar Szent Korona Országainak Böripari Központja*), who had indeed owned his own leather shop in Zolozce, and who still could not return home because of the Russian occupation. Furthermore, the police detective found 'the greatest order and cleanliness' when he visited the Imber apartment. The Imber family also demonstrated their stability and self-sufficiency by having remained in their Népszinház Street apartment since their arrival in Budapest and, more significantly, by never collecting refugee aid monies.⁵⁶ In order to qualify as an exceptional case for residency, as Imber did, refugees had to prove their usefulness to the state, usually through employment in the war industry, in conjunction with a solid moral record, and be from a region that was still under Russian occupation. The police looked for the ability to support oneself through honest labour (so not collecting refugee aid 'like the rest of the *Galicianers*'), employer testimony, and, notably, cleanliness of person and accommodations.⁵⁷

Conversely, the factors constituting grounds for the rejection of right of residency applications were the widespread and predictable results of the condition of being a refugee: unemployment, poverty, dependence on aid, and poor hygiene. Poor hygiene was often a consequence of residence in inadequate accommodation and lack of access to proper hygienic facilities. The story of the unexceptional Jewish refugee is reflected in the rejected residency application. The application opened with a formulaic recitation of the events which led to the condition of being a refugee in Hungary. Beginning with the invasion of the Russian enemy, applicants recounted fleeing their homes with their families and losing all of their worldly possessions, and then finding temporary accommodations in Budapest or elsewhere in Hungary. They then described the work that they had been able to find, usually as tailors, shop assistants or barbers. Next, applicants usually discussed illnesses or other additional family hardships, and reasons why they were not able to return to their homes. Most applications concluded with a plea to the Minister of the Interior to be merciful and take pity on them, and to kindly grant them residency in Hungary.

Refugees whose residency applications were rejected left in a series of transports headed either for repatriation or temporary resettlement in Bohemia and Moravia. The few who remained found themselves in the company of the documented rabbis, the gravely ill, refugees with means, and those fully supported by local Hungarian Jewish communities as the war drew on and on. The Hungarian Minister of the Interior made another push for refugee repatriation in September 1917, stressing dire shortages of provisions and accommodation. According to a telegram sent to the Emperor-King from concerned Budapest Jews, Hungarian authorities '[rounded] up [the refugees] like dogs on the street' and sent them away.⁵⁸ In November, the administration announced that more than 9,000 of the estimated 25,000 refugees had been removed, and the other 16,000 soon would be. The Hungarian Jewish newspaper *Egyenlőség* noted the use of the term 'Galizianer' in a derogatory manner in the Hungarian House of Representatives during the discussion of this issue.⁵⁹ Despite the ongoing efforts of the Hungarian administration, several hundred Galician Jewish refugees still sojourned in Hungary at the end of the war.[60]

Conclusion

The newly pervasive and outspoken so-called Jewish Question emerged from the social crisis catalysed by the war. This 'Jewish Question' was quantified in blood: the Hungarian antisemitic press asked 'has the proportion of Jewish sacrifices come to their five per cent of the total population?'[61] Anticipating the accusation, the Budapest-based Hungarian Jewish newspaper *Egyenlőség* as early as December 1914 created a column dedicated to listing the names of fallen Jewish soldiers from the Kingdom of Hungary. In 1916, József Patai and his colleagues at *Múlt és Jövő* created the *Magyar Zsidó Hadi Archivum* [The Hungarian Jewish War Archive] in order to document the fallen Hungarian Jewish soldiers, 'our fallen heroes', with photographs, letters from the front, poems and other contributions. Fighting, suffering and especially dying for Hungary was the most compelling evidence of Jewish loyalty to Hungary and fitness for inclusion within the Magyar nation. Hungarian Jews sought to release themselves from popular charges of shirking and cowardice by presenting lists with the names of Jewish soldiers from the Kingdom of Hungary. The interwar publication, *Magyar Zsidó Lexikon* [The Hungarian Jewish Lexicon] spent three pages of its five-page entry about the war presenting statistics on fallen and wounded Jewish soldiers, and other proofs of Hungarian Jewish patriotism.[62]

Yet despite their efforts, it was not the story of the brave and loyal Hungarian Jewish soldier which would have the greatest influence on the Jews' position in post-war Hungary, but that of the foreign Jewish refugee. The collapse of Austria-Hungary and the subsequent peace settlement that reduced Hungarian territory by 70 per cent proved devastating for Hungary and Hungarian Jewry. Instead of the old multinational Kingdom in which Jews had contributed and thrived in a mutually beneficial relationship with the government, the defeated post-war state was virtually homogenous, and an impoverished pariah state subject to a series of desperate political upheavals, each intended to preserve the pre-war state's territory. Many Hungarians believed 'Jewish shirkers' and 'traitors' to be responsible for Hungary's humiliation. Hungary's new Right pointed to the Jews as a grave national security risk and social threat. 'Right-wing papers seized on [Galician Jewish refugees] as proof that an alien menace had come across the border and penetrated to the centre of Hungary', writes Paul Hanebrink about Hungarian antisemitism toward the end of the war.[63] By 1918, as József Patai shrewdly observed, talk of 'the Galicians' in parliament and the press referred to all of Hungarian Jewry. The refugee crisis had merged internal and external aspects of the 'Jewish Question' into a singular terrifying perception of an internal enemy.[64]

The war experience threatened to tear up Hungarian Jewry's emancipation contract, originally drafted by the great reformers of the mid-nineteenth century, who called for an end to Jewish immigration to Hungary and a dissolution of Orthodoxy.[65] Jews in the rump state sought to reaffirm their loyalty, patriotism and continued devotion to post-war Hungary and the Hungarian nation. They appealed to the international Jewish community on Hungary's behalf, and expressed their passion for the cause most profoundly by courting former Hungarian Jews in newly created or transformed neighbouring states. This was a problematic decision that had fateful consequences.[66] The war intensified the questioning of Jewish loyalty to the state rather than eradicating it. Subsequently, what it meant to be a Hungarian Jew was reconfigured – both within and beyond Hungary's Trianon borders – alongside the interwar Hungarian government's revisionist ambitions.

Notes

1 A portion of this chapter originally appeared in 'Beyond the "infamous concentration camps of the old monarchy"': Jewish refugee policy from wartime Austria-Hungary to interwar Czechoslovakia', *Austrian History Yearbook*, no. 45 (2014), 150–66. © Center for Austrian Studies, University of Minnesota 2014, reprinted with the permission of Cambridge University Press.
2 Peter Gatrell, *A Whole Empire Walking: Refugees in Russia During World War I* (Bloomington: Indiana University Press, 1999), pp. 16–17. Russian troops often mistook the Yiddish of widespread vernacular usage by this Jewish population for German, a perception that heighted their suspicion that Jews were spying for the enemy.
3 American Jewish Committee, *Jews in the Eastern War Zone* (New York, 1916), pp. 84–7.
4 Walter Pietsch, 'A zsidók bevándorlása Galiciából és a magyarországi zsidóság', *Valóság*, 31, no. 11 (1988), 46–69.
5 William O. McCagg, Jr., *History of Habsburg Jews, 1670–1918* (Bloomington: Indiana University Press, 1989), p. 125.
6 József Patai, 'Az Antiszitizmusz Magyarországon: a Galiciak és a Morál', *Mült és Jövő*, August 1918, 283–5.

7 David Rechter, *The Jews of Vienna and the First World War* (London: The Littman Library of Jewish Civilization, 2001), pp. 78, 92, 97.
8 The boxes containing these telegraph messages and copies of telephone conversation transcripts concerning the daily arrival and movement of the Galician Jewish refugees are located in Magyar Országos Levéltár (MOL), Belügyminiszterium fond K148, Elnöki Iratok 1915, box 493, file 37, inventory no. 55; and MOL, fond K148, EI 1915, box 493, file 37, inventory no. 80.
9 *Magyar Statisztikai Évkönyv*, IX (Budapest, 1902), 13. The population of Bártfá was 6,096 in 1900. Chart: 'A városok népességnek száma és szaporodása 1869–től 1900–ig.'
10 Maroš Borský, 'Jewish communities and their urban context: a case study of Košice, Prešov, and Bardejov', *Architektura a urbanizmus*, 37, nos. 3–4 (2004), 131–2.
11 Halász, Iván, 'A szlovák nemzeti politika és a zsidóság a dualismus idején', *Limes*, vol. 1 (Spring 1999), 44.
12 MOL, fond K148, EI 1915, box 493, file 37, inv. no. 55. The first telephone call by the Lord Lieutenant of Sáros County to the Ministry of the Interior in Budapest regarding this group of refugees took place on 14 November 1914 at 4:45am.
13 MOL, fond K148, EI 1915, box 493, file 37, inv. no. 55. Telephone call to Budapest on 16 November 1914 at 10:35am.
14 MOL, fond K148, EI 1917, box 600, file 37, inv. no. 22447.
15 MOL, fond K148, EI 1914, box 37, folders 8488 and 8663; MOL, fond K148, EI 1915, box 37, folder 80.
16 MOL, fond K148, EI 1915, box 493, folder 37, inv. no. 55 Report sent to the Ministry of the Interior in Vienna from Budapest 29 December 1914; MOL, fond K148, EI 1914, box 37, folder 8488. Letter sent from Galician Jewish refugees in Pozsony (Pressburg, later Bratislava) to the Minister of the Interior in Budapest, 10 November 1914.
17 MOL, fond K148, EI 1915, box 493, folder 37, inv. no. 55. Decision sent from Budapest to the mayor of Kassa on 22 February 1915.
18 MOL, fond K148, EI 1916, box 542, folder 37, inv. no. 457.
19 Slovenský národný archív, fond Ministerstvo s plnou mocou pre správu Slovenska, box 258, folder 885. Reports on consequences of the war by the Volksverband der Jüden für die Slovakei/Ľudový zväz židov pre Slovensko.
20 MOL, fond K148, EI 1915, box 494, folder 37. Rabbi Wéber's initial telegram to the Austrian Ministry of the Interior; MOL, fond K148, EI 1915, box 494, folder 37. Rabbi Wéber's petition for fund disbursement to the Hungarian Ministry of the Interior, 19 January 1915; MOL, fond K148, EI 1915, box 494, folder 37. Approval for disbursement from the Hungarian Ministry of the Interior, 'Pöstyén', *Ungarländische Jüdische Zeitung* (*UJZ*), 24 January 1915.

21 MOL, fond K148, EI 1915, box 37, inv. no. 80. Report of the Főispán of Nyitra County to the Hungarian Ministry of the Interior in Budapest, 30 November 1914.
22 MOL, fond K148, EI 1915, box 37, folder 55, inv. no. 586; MOL, fond K148, EI, 1915, box 37, folder, 55, inv. No. 590: Report of the decision not to allow disbursement of Austrian state aid to Győr.
23 Monies from relatives in America passed through the New York based Transatlantic Trust Company. The transfer of funds from America, issues of delivery and distribution were handled by the Finance Ministry. MOL, fond K148, EI 1916, box 541, folder 37. The factory of Heinrich Klinger in Pozsony was especially active in employing Galician Jewish refugees in its war industry production. Materials on refugee employment are located in MOL, fond K148, EI 1916, box 541, folder 37; MOL, fond K148, EI 1916, box 543, folder 37; and MOL, fond K148, EI 1916, box 544, folder 37.
24 Rechter, *The Jews of Vienna*, p. 75; Marsha Rozenblit, *Reconstructing a National Identity: the Jews of Habsburg Austria During World War One* (New York: Oxford University Press, 2001), p. 59.
25 'Report from the mayor of Nyiregyhaza to the Ministry of the Interior in Budapest, 20 June 1915', MOL, fond K148, EI 1915, box 504, folder 37; and 'Report from the mayor of Nyiregyhaza to the Ministry of the Interior in Budapest April 9, 1915', MOL, fond K148, EI 1915, box 503, folder 37. There were 645 Jews living in Zboró in 1900. JewishGen, Zborov, Slovakia. http://data.jewishgen.org/wconnect/wc.dll?jg~jgsys~community~-847442 [accessed August 31, 2015].
26 Materials documenting the resettlement of Austrian Jewish refugees from Budapest and the provinces are located in MOL, fond K148, EI 1915, box 502, folder 37 under the heading 'Kriegsflüchtlinge: Übersiedlung in ein anderes Kronland'.
27 'Die galizischen Flüchtlinge in Ungarn', Dr. Bloch's *Österreichische Wochenschrift* [ÖW], 16 April 1915, reprinted from the *Allgemeine Jüdische Zeitung* (*AJZ*) published in Budapest. Bloch notes that the article remained unaltered by the censor; 'Der Exodus der Galizianer', UJZ, 11 April 1915. Materials documenting the resettlement of Austrian Jewish refugees from Budapest and the provinces are located in MOL, fond K148, EI 1915, box 502, folder 37 under the heading 'Kriegsflüchtlinge: Übersiedlung in ein anderes Kronland'.
28 *Bericht der Israelitischen Allianz zu Wien* 42 (1914), 19–20, in Rechter, *The Jews of Vienna* 80; and 'Hilfsaktion der ungarischen Zionisten', *Jüdische Zeitung* (JZ), 1 January 1915.
29 Camp conditions are discussed by Rechter, *The Jews of Vienna*, p. 78; Rozenblit, *Reconstructing a National Identity*, p. 66; JZ: 'Die mährischen Flüchtlingslager', 30 October 1914, 'Die galizischen Flüchtlinge', 27 November 1914, 'Die Flüchtlingsforsorge des Zion: Zentralkomitees

Delegierte des Zionistischen Zentralkomitees in Gaya', 1 January 1915; ÖW: 'Ein neues Heim für die Flüchtlinge', 20 November 1914, 'Die Barckenlager in Nikolsburg', 4 December 1914, 'Aus jüdische Barackenlager von Bruck a. L.', 30 July 1915.

30 'Ausweisung der galizischen Kriegsflüchtlinge aus Budapest und den ungarischen Provinzstädten', ÖW, 7 May 1915. The ÖW reprinted the following dual governmental communiqué ('Vereinbarung der beiden Regierung über die Behandlung der galizischen Flüchtlinge in Ungarn') originally published in the *Neue Freie Presse* on 27 April 1915.

31 AJZ, 25 April 1915, in 'Ausweisung der galizischen Kriegsflüchtlinge aus Budapest und den ungarischen Provinzstädten', ÖW, 7 May 1915.

32 AJZ, 1 May 1915, reprinted in 'Ausweisung der galizischen Kriegsflüchtlinge aus Budapest und den ungarischen Provinzstädten', ÖW, 7 May 1915.

33 AJZ, 1 May 1915.

34 'Abscheid der Galizianer', UJZ, 11 April 1915.

35 'Abscheid der Galizianer'.

36 MOL, fond K148, EI 1915, box 37, folder 80 contains a thick folder of documents relating to this episode. The Pest Jewish Community composed the transport lists by family, including each individual's name, age, place of origin, and occupation where applicable.

37 Avigdor Löwenheim, 'The leadership of the Neolog Jewish congregation of Pest in the years 1914–19: its status and activity in the Jewish community', PhD dissertation, Hebrew University in Jerusalem, 1991, cited in Rechter, *The Jews of Vienna*, p. 81.

38 MOL, fond K148, EI 1915, box 504, folder 37, 19 July 1915. The order lists the localities to which the refugees were to return. Jewish refugees from the northern Hungarian regions which had made up part of the Eastern Front (in Ung, Bereg and Máramaros counties) had been required to return to their original residences in March. An exception was made for Sáros and Zemplén counties where heavy fighting continued. MOL, fond K148, EI 1915, box 502, folder 37.

39 MOL, fond K148, EI 1916, box 544, folder 37, Vienna, 1 August 1916.

40 *Bericht der Israelitischen Allianz zu Wien* 44 (1916), 10–12, 15, cited in Rechter, *The Jews of Vienna*, p. 81.

41 The labour shortage in Hungary became critical in 1916. Women, youth and prisoners of war were employed to compensate. Refugee employment appears to have been a compensatory measure as well. Deák (1971), p. 17.

42 MOL, fond K148, EI 1915, box 502, folder 37, report from the Minister of Commerce to the Minister of the Interior, Budapest, 28 May 1915.

43 MOL, fond K148, EI 1915, box 502, folder 37, report from the Minister of Commerce to the Minister of the Interior, Budapest, 28 May 1915.

44 MOL, fond K148, EI 1915, box 502, folder 37, report from the Minister of Commerce to the Minister of the Interior, Budapest, 28 May 1915.

Hungarian Jewry and the wartime crisis in Austria-Hungary

45 Refugees coming from the Austrian part of the Dual Habsburg Monarchy were also considered foreigners under Hungarian law. The residency law for foreigners on the territory of the Hungary: 1903, article five, paragraph three. MOL, fond K148, EI 1915, box 502, folder, 37.
46 The bulk of the applications are located in MOL, fond K148, EI 1916, box 543, folder 37 and MOL, fond K148, EI 1916, box 544, folder 37.
47 Examples include an application on behalf of ten women workers submitted by the social welfare division of the Budapest Jewish Community on 18 April 1916 (rejected) MOL, fond K148 EI 1916, box 543, folder 37, and on behalf of Jakob Chaim, submitted by his employer Dr. Bruckner és Pollitzer of the Nobel Dynamite Factory in Pozsony on 17 November 1916 (accepted) MOL, fond K148, EI 1917, box 599, folder 37.
48 From the police report regarding the application of Izrael Braunwasser and family who did needle-work for the firm of Strausz and Dénes in Budapest submitted 30 April 1916. MOL, fond K148, EI 1916, box 543, folder 37. The family of four lived and worked in a one-room apartment at 40 István Street.
49 From Márkus Láng's successful application for right of residency in Hungary. The police detective noted the cleanliness of the apartment's two rooms and kitchen in his report. MOL, fond K148, EI 1916, box 542, folder 37, Report submitted 30 April 1916.
50 Police report regarding the application of the rabbis from Galicia who sought the right of residency in Hungary submitted 20 April 1916. MOL, fond K148, EI 1916, box 543, folder 37. On cleanliness and morality, the importance and implications of the view of refugees as dirty, diseased, and a threat to public health see Paul Weindling, *Epidemics and Genocide in Eastern Europe, 1890–1945* (Oxford: Oxford University Press, 2000).
51 Heinrich Klinger was a well-known producer of linen and jute goods with factories throughout Austria-Hungary, including Vienna, Budapest, Brünn (Brno) and Pozsony.
52 MOL, fond K148, EI 1916, box 541, folder 37, submitted by Heinrich Klinger to the Hungarian Minister of the Interior in Budapest from Pozsony on 10 November 1915.
53 MOL, fond K148, EI 1916, box 543, folder 37, Heinrich Klinger to the Minister of the Interior in Budapest, 29 March 1916.
54 MOL, fond K148, EI 1916, box 544, folder 37, Heinrich Klinger to the Minister of the Interior in Budapest, 2 October 1916.
55 MOL, fond K148, EI 1916, box 543, folder 37, Mózes Imber to the Minister of the Interior in Budapest, 20 May 1916.
56 MOL, fond K148, EI 1916, box 543, folder 37, police report on the Imber application.
57 MOL, fond K148, EI 1916, box 543, folder 37, police report on Márkus Wolf Halberstamm, May 1, 1916.

58 'Die Ausweisung der Fremden aus Budapest', *ÖW*, October 12, 1917. Quoting *Egyenlőség*.
59 'Die Frage der galizischen Flüchtlinge im ungarischen Abgeordnetenhause', *ÖW*, November 16, 1917.
60 Slovenský národný archív, fond Ministerstvo s plnou mocou pre správu Slovenska, box 392, folder 609, Report summarising the care of war refugees, submitted to the Minister for the Administration of Slovakia on 11 March 1921.
61 Ferenc Fejtő, *Magyarság, Zsidóság* (Budapest: MTA Történettudományi Intézete, 2000), 168–9. In Hungarian the question read: 'Vajon a zsidó áldoztok aránya kiteszi-e az össznépességi 5%-ot?'
62 Péter Ujvári (ed.), *Magyar Zsidó Lexikon* (Budapest: A Magyar Zsidó Lexikon Kiadása, 1929), pp. 950–2.
63 Paul A. Hanebrink, *In Defense of Christian Hungary: Religion, Nationalism, and Antisemitism, 1890–1944* (Ithaca: Cornell University Press, 2006), p. 57.
64 Hanebrink, *In Defense of Christian Hungary*, p. 57.
65 McCagg, *History of Habsburg Jews*, pp. 133–4.
66 See 'Memorandum of the Jews of Hungary to the Jews throughout the World', the Central Hungarian Jewish Association (Magyar Zsidó Központi Szövetség), YIVO, RG348 Wolf-Mowshowitch collection, box 18, folder 160, and Rebekah Klein-Pejšová, *Mapping Jewish Loyalties in Interwar Slovakia* (Bloomington: Indiana University Press, 2015).

8

Beyond the borders: displaced persons in the Italian linguistic space during the First World War

Marco Mondini and Francesco Frizzera[1]

Introduction

Italy is still a marginal case in the international history of the First World War despite its peculiarities or perhaps because of its many contradictions.[2] The paradoxes enveloping the history of the 'Italian war' begin with the political and cultural background to the Kingdom of Italy's commitment and the oddness of its timing in entering the war. Alone among the main European powers, Italy at first declared its neutrality and waited nearly a year before joining in. When it did, this was hailed by the largely conservative and government-aligned press as the last campaign of the Risorgimento, an act that would finally enable all Italians (including the Italian-speaking communities still living in the southern provinces of Austria-Hungary) to participate as a single nation state. But among the politicians in power at the start of the war, Mazzini's romantic and democratic ideal of nationhood or Cavour's inspired political design counted for less than the desire to ensure that Italy gained control over the upper Adriatic and secured a place at the council table of the major European powers. Before fighting the country's former Allies, Prime Minister Antonio Salandra and his foreign minister Sidney Sonnino extracted a multiple promise, namely that Italy might annex all the frontier provinces partly or wholly occupied by Italian-speaking communities, those whom contemporary nationalist parlance referred to as the *irridenti*, 'those still to be redeemed'. In addition, they anticipated the acquisition of the territory of Bolzano, inhabited by 250,000 Austro-Germans, and sought the assurance of an eastern military frontier incorporating many areas where the majority language was actually Slavonic. Meanwhile, they abandoned the city of Fiume to its fate: although inhabited by a culturally and linguistically Italian population, nevertheless in the Allied plans of 1914 it was destined to be the port of a much-reduced yet still intact Habsburg Empire.[3]

War was to be the 'baptism of fire' for the Italian nation when the recently unified state (it was but fifty years old) would show the world it was worthy to sit alongside the great powers. As it was, the country entered the war at a time of profound social and political divisions, against the wishes of most of the population and without the government having a majority in parliament. The ideological rift between a minority of *interventisti* (who met a few weeks before conflict broke out in Europe, clamouring for war alongside the Entente) and a majority of *neutralisti* (who felt it more prudent to stay out of hostilities) soon erupted into violent and widespread street fighting. An unexpectedly violent confrontation erupted in many cities between enclaves of middle-class pro-war youths and their opponents until the Italian army opened fire against Austria-Hungary (not Germany) in May 1915. Then there was the royal army: according to the 'nation under arms' theorists and a broad band of right-wing journalists, it was supposed to be the most tangible demonstration of national unity, a compact, disciplined, egalitarian community of warrior citizens devoted to the monarch. In actual fact it summed up all the inequalities that still dogged liberal Italy. Not all young adult males took part in the so-called 'last campaign of the Risorgimento'. Sacrificing oneself for the fatherland depended on one's place in the social hierarchy: social privilege and helpful social contacts could secure exemption from the ordeal of battle.[4]

In its impact on civilians the Italian war was again rather different from that of other European powers engaged in the 1914–18 war. In the first place, the civilians who were exposed to the impact of total war – members of communities that were deported, evacuated or interned – were subjects of both warring sides. The war-zone *regnicoli* – that is, the inhabitants of the Kingdom (*Regno d'Italia*) in May 1915 – who had to abandon their homes because of forced evacuation, internment, voluntary flight from the perils of combat or during the occupation of their province by Austrian and German troops, numbered over 600,000 at one stage or other of the hostilities.[5] One must add to these the so-called 'Italians of Austria', that is Italian-speaking subjects of the Dual Monarchy living in the frontier provinces of Trentino, Trieste and the Litorale, perhaps as many as 900,000 people, according to the not always reliable censuses of the Habsburg officials, whose homeland suffered an unusual and undoubtedly painful process of twofold militarisation. On the one side, the 'Italians of Austria' (especially in the Trentino) were interned and deported en masse within the Habsburg empire; on the other, those living in the limited areas conquered by the Italian army's first offensives in 1915 were forcibly removed to places deep within the peninsula, likewise for reasons of political prudence. By 1918 there were nearly 90,000 *irredenti* in the Kingdom of Italy, whilst perhaps 120,000 'Italians of Austria' (more or less one third of the remaining civilian population) were wartime refugees, internees or evacuees in Austria, Bohemia or Moravia.

This dual upheaval of fugitives and evacuees, towards the south if under the Italian army and government, to the north if under the Austrians, meant that often the subjects of the Kingdom of Italy and the Austro-Hungarian Empire got lumped together both in practice and, at times, in bureaucratic formula under the same ethnic and cultural label of 'Italians'. The twofold 'diaspora' of frontier Italians is a prime example of how unreliable the traditional categories of political history may be in reconstructing the brutality of modern war towards civilians.[6] Rather than talking of refugees, evacuees and internees in Italy, it would be more appropriate to assess the impact of conflict on civilians in the 'Italian linguistic space'. Such a category would have the advantage of allowing us legitimately to analyse the effect of the war on all Italian-speaking communities, without the limitation imposed by political frontiers at the outbreak of war.[7] Besides, in the eyes of the Italian state, although bureaucratic distinctions were formally maintained until the annexation of the so-called 'new provinces' (Trentino, Venezia Giulia and Dalmazia) in 1919, civilians forcibly or voluntarily transferred to the Italian hinterland were de facto lumped together with the *regnicoli*.[8] One month after the outbreak of hostilities the Ministry of the Interior recommended that the prefects of the Kingdom should adopt a series of prudent health and police measures that made no distinction (for better, in terms of welfare; for worse, if one thinks of surveillance and repression) between Italian citizens and *irredenti*, although officially the Italian-speaking areas invaded (or 'liberated') by the royal army were administered as temporarily occupied foreign territory.[9] This picture was mirrored in reverse on the Habsburg side: belonging to an Italian minority was equated with treachery, and this gave rise to a policy of deliberate brutality against the refugees, who were often treated like a collective enemy within the nation. This chapter disentangles these ambiguities in the Italian case, summarising events and policies relating to refugees in the Kingdom of Italy from 1915 to 1918, and then tracing in more detail the fate of the

Italian community in Trentino that was crushed by the twofold militarisation of their own territory.

Refugees, fugitives, evacuees, internees: timeframe and categories of displaced persons in the Italian Great War

During the First World War in Italy the question of refugees was vexed and ambiguous, even from a semantic viewpoint. Italian lacks a useful portmanteau expression like 'displaced persons'. At the outbreak of war the term *profughi* was used to describe the half million or so Italian émigrés temporarily or permanently living in the war zone who were forcibly repatriated by summer 1914. Over 70,000 émigrés were sent back to the Kingdom of Italy from the Swiss Confederation or across it; some 200,000 returned from France (which at the time had an Italian immigrant population of nearly half a million); about the same number had to return from Germany and above all from the Habsburg Empire which traditionally absorbed a flourishing population of seasonal émigrés. (In only two months the province of Udine witnessed the repatriation of about 70,000 émigrés, which represented 10 per cent the overall population.) On top of these, between 1915 and 1918 some 300,000 adult males came back home voluntarily to fight.[10]

For the Kingdom of Italy this mass of *rimpatriati*, as they were soon styled, marked the first traumatic social and economic consequences of war in Europe in the form of a wave of unemployment caused by the sudden arrival of a mass of poor labouring men and women who required assistance. This led to the first local civil welfare facilities being set up, which would subsequently be extended.

Following 24 May 1915, the term refugee (*profughi*) stood for 'non-*regnicoli* shifted for military purposes out of territories occupied by Italian troops'. The term *fuorusciti* (expatriates) denoted '*regnicoli* and non-*regnicoli* living normally in *irredente* ('unliberated') lands (Trentino, Trieste and Dalmazia) who voluntarily sought refuge in Italy as of the outbreak of European war'.[11] A fourth bureaucratic category was the 'internees'. These were mainly 'Italians of Austria', though also a minority of subjects of the Kingdom of Italy, including members of suspect organisations like the socialist party or trade unionists tainted with neutral feelings, or anarchist groups, or priests accused of pro-Austrian sentiment or pacifism. The list included schoolmasters and private citizens guilty of voicing doubts over the legitimacy of going to war or else expressing 'scorn for the fatherland'. They were removed from the war zone and put under house arrest as 'suspects', potentially dangerous to military operations. Although estimates are still uncertain, the number of 'internees' from border areas probably lies between 3,000 and 5,000 individuals.[12]

The definitions of *rimpatriati, profughi, fuorusciti* and *internati* still fail to cover the full spectrum of displaced persons on the Italian-Austrian front. Curiously enough, at the outbreak of hostilities no formal label existed to denote subjects of the Kingdom of Italy forcibly evacuated or voluntarily fleeing from the declared war zone. From the first days of fighting, the war zone included an extensive portion of national territory, roughly all the north-east of the Kingdom from Lombardy to the Austrian frontier, as well as various coastal regions. It was run under well-nigh absolute military command conferred by exceptional wartime legislation. For purely military requirements, the army command could intern any suspect individual and clear – in part or entirely – any inhabited area falling within the 'operational zone' at the front.[13] Of the six million Italian subjects resident in the war zone, an uncertain number of people, probably several thousand, were evacuated in the first weeks, adding to the first flow of refugees who fled of their own accord. Whether or not they posed a threat to popular support for the war effort, news of this relatively small group of evacuees was withheld from the public. The existence of 'Italian refugees' was not officially acknowledged until December 1915 when Prime Minister Salandra was asked the question in parliament and gave the first official confirmation that there existed what one might be called 'internal refugees', that is, people not returning from abroad nor those belonging to the *irredente* provinces. Salandra confirmed that the government would now look after the 'refugees' whom he defined as follows:

> Refugees are persons who have had to be sent away en masse from municipalities in the operational zone since the fatal consequences of war would prevent them living there without grave danger to their lives. It was not possible to let the inhabitants of such municipalities … flee uncontrollably in a state of understandable panic at some immediate danger …They had to be required to decamp and be housed wherever possible in various provinces of the Kingdom.

From an Italian perspective, the war at this point was a gruelling offensive without major results on the Isonzo front or the relatively less bloody Val d'Adige offensive. Any real problem posed by Italian (that is, *regnicoli*) refugees could still be concealed, and their presence passed largely unnoticed. But a few months later the Habsburg counterattack in

May–June 1916 (the so-called *Strafexpedition*) caused the Trentino front to buckle: Austria overran the densely populated strip of territory within the old frontier between Altipiano di Asiago and Val Lagarina. The most visible consequence was the sudden flight or enforced evacuation of some 110,000 civilians. Over 75,000 of them came from the northern districts of Vicenza province alone. They poured towards the plain in disorder, some under their own steam amid the pandemonium of the retreat, whilst others were ordered to leave and were sent on their way southwards or in the direction of towns in the north-west.[14] The civilian exodus in spring 1916 was a point of no return in people's perception of the war (one might equally say, of Italian public opinion's perception of what war meant in general). It had highly significant administrative repercussions. The issue of refugees ceased to be a spatially limited problem of public order and became a permanent aspect of coping with the war. The government was obliged to provide fairly wide-reaching forms of welfare for the mass of people deprived of all resources for what might be an indefinite time. In this respect an important part was played by voluntary civic aid committees that formed spontaneously in the main cities along the peninsula, and that supplemented the meagre resources allotted by the state. Civil society in fact provided substantial aid to the 'fugitive communities', enabling them to survive and thrive.[15]

It is no surprise that only a few weeks after the *Strafexpedition* the Ministry of the Interior in July 1916 published a circular restating the official categories that denoted civilians forced by war to quit their homes. From that moment on, *profugo* would mean not just Austrian subjects cleared out of the Italian-occupied border zone for reasons of security, but also civilians of the Kingdom of Italy evacuated by order of the High Command or local army commanders on military grounds. It is still not clear whether this was a desire to safeguard that population from the danger of foreign invasion or an intention by government and supreme command acting in consort to adopt a 'scorched earth' policy in territory occupied by the Austrians, in order to deprive the latter of all possible resources.[16] What is clear is that a refugee policy was implemented – though not officially recognised immediately – to meet two objectives: one was to remove refugees from their homeland and split up the community into as many fragments as possible, such as single or small groups of family nuclei. The decision to direct the refugee flows as far as possible from the theatre of warfare was not just for logistic reasons – it was clearly easier to accommodate thousands of families in large towns of the industrial north than in a heavily militarised region which might be invaded or bombarded at any time – but was also for the sake of security. It was vital to prevent individuals and groups from returning spontaneously (a not altogether theoretical possibility, since even during the May 1916 evacuation several hundred refugees eluded military control), while the ability to discipline and control the numerous refugees grew in proportion to their being scattered in remote provinces from which it was hard for them to escape. Such criteria were not always followed to the letter in the first bedlam of civilian management, but there can be no doubt these security issues lay behind Italian refugee policy from that time on.[17]

Precautionary police surveillance of evacuees on behalf of the host provinces was also a way of repressing defeatism and war-weariness which became obsessive after the Caporetto disaster in October–November 1917. The Eastern Front collapsed, the front line on the river Piave and at Monte Grappa fell back as a broad area of the north-east provinces was lost to the enemy. The ensuing stampede or enforced evacuation into the Italian hinterland involved about half a million civilians: 250,000 people fled from zones occupied by the Austrians and Germans in Friuli and eastern Veneto, and about the same number fled from the front-line provinces of Vicenza, Verona, Padua and Treviso. This posed a colossal challenge to national civil welfare. It also tested and in many respects belied the high-flown rhetoric that spoke of distant regions rallying round to ensure that the nation stood firm and united at its hour of need.[18]

Domestic exile: friction between refugees and the local population

In March 1918 the Ministry of the Interior asked the prefects for information on how refugees were being treated in the far-flung provinces to which they had been sent. After laborious dismemberment of town and village communities, involving much negotiation between centre and periphery, half a million fugitives-evacuees-refugees had been distributed, sometimes by force, to virtually all 70 provinces of the Kingdom (see map 8.1).

Most prefects reported back to the Ministry that relations between refugees and the local population were generally good. The main complaints were about the weather and local customs being different, or about inadequate welcoming facilities; where there were no suitable public buildings, private ones were hired, though in many small villages even these were non-existent. Only in rare cases did prefects mention host communities'

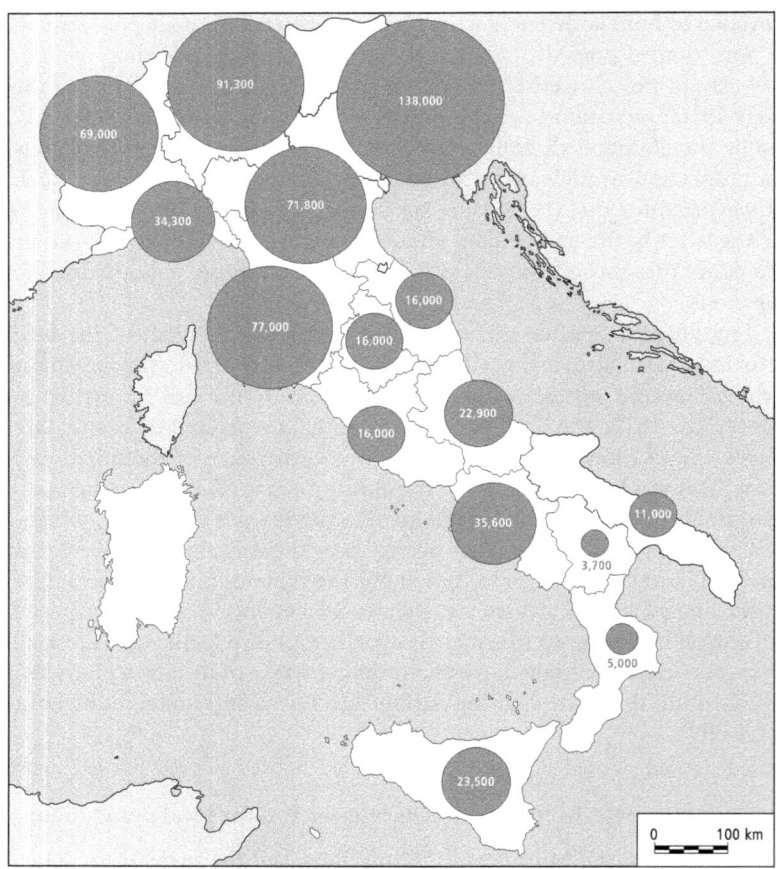

Map 8.1 Italy's refugees during the First World War.

disgruntlement at the arrival of fugitives in their tens, hundreds and even thousands (in the big cities) who would henceforth become scapegoats for all the vexations of war.[19] But a parallel source – letters from refugees to their exile administrations or the government – revealed clearly that the encounter between refugees and local populations bred more antagonism than solidarity, especially in the south of the peninsula. Social friction, in the first place, resulted from the fact that exiles received a regular, albeit slender, allowance from the state and certain welfare benefits. In a country groaning under wartime economic restrictions, they were seen as rivals for food, and potential competitors for local work. In Naples, Macerata and Umbria, refugees were publicly accused of causing a food shortage and soaring prices; words sometimes led to blows which the authorities had difficulty in calming.[20]

There was also cultural antagonism. Caporetto caused the first mass migration in the Italian peninsula and, standard Italian being in limited use, there were problems of communication especially among women and the older generation. Religious, family and even sexual customs bred friction, as did eating habits and ways of spending leisure time. Tension would often flare into open hostility: the Venetians and Friulani were accused of immorality and dissolute behaviour; unsurprisingly in the overwrought climate of nationalism, they were suspected of being pro-Austrian. An obsession arose over refugee spies leaking reserved information or sending signals to Austrian aeroplanes and ships. Reports of the 'enemy in our midst' piled up daily on the desks of prefects and government ministers. Discontent and marginalisation were staple fare in what would be recalled as a clash between different components of the nation. 'We've been suffering here for five months', wrote the family spokesmen of a farming enclave from Valsugana (above Vicenza) transferred to the province of Lecce. They begged their member of parliament to help them 'get away from these parts … better beneath the bombs than among these foreigners'.[21]

Trentino: Italian-speaking refugees across the borders

After the outbreak of the First World War, the southern border area of Trentino (at that time part of the Hapsburg Empire) became a battlefield. The Austrian army decided to evacuate the Italian-speaking population living near the front, displacing about 78,000 people to Bohemia, Moravia, Upper Austria and Lower Austria. Meanwhile, the Italian army occupied the southern districts of Trentino and resettled 27,000 Italian-speaking citizens of Austria–Hungary to the internal provinces of the Kingdom of Italy. Here they found another 7,000 Italian-speaking refugees who had fled from Trentino for political reasons before Italy entered the war. Overall, 110,000 people coming from Trentino – amounting to one-third of the total population of the region – were scattered in Austria-Hungary and in Italy. These people experienced the war differently: they met different populations, redrew the boundaries between 'us' and 'them', lived without civil rights in two different states, and were often treated as the 'enemy within'.

We can argue that the war experience of this population shows that nationalism is a 'cognitive phenomenon', only partially connected with the culture/politics dichotomy.[22] The rural population of Trentino in fact shared a multi-layered identity before the war.[23] They were aware of their Italian culture and language; at the same time they appeared loyal to the Habsburg Empire alongside or perhaps in spite of their nationality.[24] For these people the term 'homeland' described both their region and the Austrian state, depending on the circumstances. Only a small minority, composed of intellectuals belonging to the middle class, shared pro-Italian feelings in overtly political terms.[25] This pre-war context changed radically throughout the course of the war. The experience of refugeedom, both in Austria and in Italy, provoked a change in this identity, leading the refugees to focus on mutually exclusive aspects of their self-representation.

Although the civilian authorities of the region considered the Italian-speaking inhabitants of Trentino as loyal Austrian citizens, the same people were considered traitors by the Austrian military authorities.[26] Consequently, after the outbreak of the war, the upper class of the region were deported to the internment camp at Katzenau, which housed 2,105 people, and the indigent population was moved as far as possible from the southern front.[27] Furthermore, commissions were created to pick up from the refugees' trains those men able to work, in order to supplement the workforce.[28] As happened in eastern Galicia during the autumn of 1914, this evacuation allowed the military to seize the population's assets by simplifying the process of requisition.[29] The threat of the 'enemy within' informed the behaviour of the lower military authorities, who decided to displace as many people as possible from the border regions. The implementation out of the evacuation plan designed for the Italian-speaking population of Trentino demonstrates this point clearly: during spring 1915 the Austrian authorities planned the displacement of the civilians living along the front line in case of war. The government of Tyrol anticipated the evacuation of 30,000 Italian-speaking inhabitants from the region.[30] In fact, when the military gained power on 23 May 1915, about 75,000 Italian-speaking citizens of South Tyrol were quickly and compulsorily expelled from the 'war zone'.[31]

When it came to managing the Italian 'refugee crisis', the Austrian government decided to adopt the same plan designed for Ukrainians, Jews and Poles in autumn 1914. Even though that plan was more expensive than the simple displacement in rural areas, and the terrible hygienic conditions of the 'wood-cities' were well known, the Habsburg authorities decided to build *Flüchtlingslager* (refugee camps) in the German-speaking provinces, while the Czech countryside was chosen for the settlement in villages (see chapters 6 and 7).[32] This programme had two main goals: to avoid a clash between the refugees and the local civilian population, particularly the German-speaking population, and to control the refugees, since they were considered 'potential traitors' and a risk to local sanitary conditions.[33] All those unable to work, due to the great number of children, illness or age, and all persons showing dangerous behaviour – such as those making complaints or regarded as manifesting moral turpitude or health problems – were ordered to be sent to concentration camps, where they lived in alarmingly unhygienic conditions with a poor supply of food.[34] All others were taken to small villages where they constituted no more than two per cent of the local population.[35] They were tightly controlled and implicitly forced to work to survive, since the state subvention for the refugees was insufficient for their survival.[36] Moreover, those who refused a job offer could be sent to the refugee camps, where living conditions were even worse.[37]

Refugee camps represented the turning point of the whole displacement policy. Firstly, the choice to create camps for the indigent evacuees reveals how much the Austrian authorities feared the potential political untrustworthiness of the population living near the front who spoke the language of the enemy.[38] Secondly, the refugee camps could be used as a deterrent against the possible unruly behaviour of those displaced in villages and as a source of labour.[39] The refugees were taken to the most productive areas of the empire. Those who were able to work would be employed in farms or factories; those unable to work were locked inside the *Flüchtlingslager*, where factories and farms had been built to exploit the marginal labour of women, the elderly and children.[40] The camp system allowed the Austrian authorities to keep the suspect nationalities from the border regions under control and to exploit this workforce for the war effort. The refugee camps became a reservoir of labour where employers could find cheap workers for summer tasks or to contribute to public works.[41] In sum, they were managed as an 'enemy within'.[42]

At the same time, the state system of refugee welfare was designed not only to exploit the presence of the refugees in the most productive regions of the state, but also to improve their living conditions, often with the help of private welfare associations.[43] To be sure, however, the displaced population lived for years at a bare subsistence level. In the concentration camps, the mortality rate was up to 40 times higher than outside.[44] Inside the camps, the abuse of power was the norm, and the lack of food was an everyday experience.[45] Meanwhile, the refugees in the villages were confronted with a suspicious local population whose feelings were in some way justified by the presence of the soldiers and the police. Above all, living together was problematic because of national and social prejudices: the refugees' clothes were dirty, they were perceived as lazy – even though many were unable to work because of age or illness and they had to beg for food. They spoke the language of the enemy and came from a non-occupied region. Nevertheless, the government subsidised them, while the locals had been starving.[46] By these means, they were gradually perceived as unwanted guests and competitors in the labour market. This emerged clearly when the lack of food and goods became an everyday problem in the internal regions of the Habsburg Empire, particularly after the spring of 1917.

Diaries and letters of complaint vividly described refugees' conditions and how they were treated.[47] This experience transformed their collective identity and self-representation. They increasingly represented themselves as 'banished' persons rather than as 'refugees'. The diaries show that relations with the German-speaking population of Lower and Upper Austria deteriorated after a few months.[48] The same happened in Bohemia and Moravia once a lack of food and other basic subsistence items became evident.[49] Above all, refugees expressed a sense of connection with their own region, which assumed the character of 'homeland', whilst expressions of loyalty toward the Habsburg or to the Austrian state as 'homeland' gradually disappeared from diaries and memoirs (see Figure 8.1). The climax of this shift appeared in the accounts written during autumn 1918, when the new Austrian state (*Deutsch-österreich*) intentionally rejected non-German refugees and brought assistance to an end.[50] Meanwhile, the local population expelled the unwanted guests, often resorting to violence in villages (Bohemia and Moravia) and in refugee camps (Lower and Upper Austria) alike.[51]

In conclusion, the Italian army intervened after the Armistice beyond the Brenner Pass to protect the Italian-speaking refugees and to organise their repatriation, guaranteeing their safety and distributing food.[52] This marked the final step of the change in the self-representation of the refugees displaced in Austria.

The war experience of the refugees from Trentino who were displaced in Italy seems different for many reasons. According to propaganda, the Italian army fought to free their 'Italian brothers' who were living under the Habsburg yoke. The occupying army and the local population shared a common language and culture. The Italian public knew

Displaced persons in the Italian linguistic space

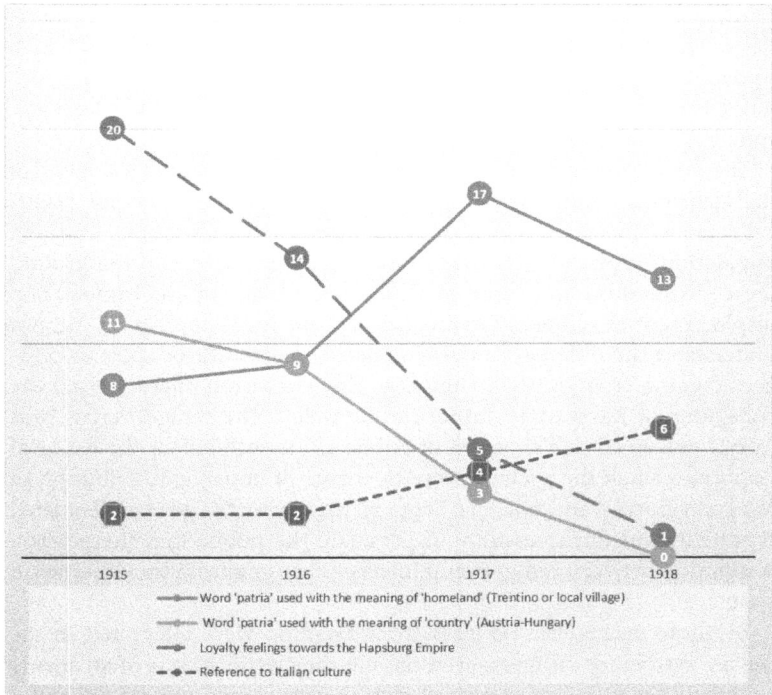

Figure 8.1 Semantic analysis of diaries written by Trentino refugees in Austria-Hungary.

the Trentino's population through the speeches of irredentists, who depicted the inhabitants of the region in reassuring terms: 'a feeling runs through towns and villages [of Trentino]: up there everyone is awaiting redemption … All of them have been looking at the motherland [i.e. the Italian Kingdom]'.[53]

Indeed, the reality on the ground struck the Italian army. After a few months, the Italian High Command expressed its opinion about the supposed loyalty of the population living in the occupied districts: 'the few people who shared pro-Italian feelings fled to Italy before the war or were interned by the Austrian authorities. The Austrian government left only priests and people loyal to the Habsburgs in the occupied area … They seem unenthusiastic about our occupation and ready to inflict damage on us at the right time'.[54] The occupation policy and the rationale for the evacuations reflected this observation.

After the change in the front line in spring 1916, the military authorities opted for the displacement of civilians living in the occupied area, some 27,000 people. They were scattered throughout all the Italian provinces, from the north-west as far as Sicily, with the exception of the war zone in the north-eastern corner of Italy.[55]

The government decided to manage the Italian-speaking citizens of the Habsburg Empire as refugees rather than enemy aliens for political reasons. The same is true of policy towards the Slovenian-speaking population displaced from the Isonzo valley. However, on the ground these distinctions were minimal. Since the place of internment and displacement of refugees often coincided, the local population did not understand the difference between enemy, enemy aliens, spies or refugees coming from Austria-Hungary. This confusion characterised the behaviour of lower state authorities as well.[56] The refugee 'crisis' was in fact perceived as a problem of public safety well before the battle of Caporetto when the prefects were in charge of housing, distribution of food and clothes, and financial support. Moreover, the government tried repeatedly but unsuccessfully to persuade the public that there was a distinction between refugees and internees coming from the occupation zone.

By these means, the refugees from Trentino were integrated in the welfare system for refugees, even though they were citizens of an enemy country. They were not incarcerated in refugee camps and did not suffer starvation, but their relations with the local population, the army and the lower state authorities were badly affected by prejudice and by a lack of rules.[57] It is therefore possible to speak of a lack of organisation that characterised the first contact between refugees and their new state.[58] Doubts about their loyalty led to misunderstandings and to their dispersion across the territory of the state.[59]

This situation worsened when refugees from Veneto and Friuli flooded the Italian Kingdom during the autumn of 1917. Now the difference between upper-class and ordinary refugees became clear. The Italians could count on a pressure group in the Italian parliament, whose deputies worked to establish genuine welfare provision. At the same time, those who fled from Veneto represented themselves as people who had chosen to free themselves from Austrian occupation and because of this choice had sacrificed all their property and assets.[60] The weak narrative of the irredentists living in Milan and Florence could not compete with this representation, because the husbands, sons and brothers of the Trentino refugees were fighting for the enemy. In the prevailing framework of social marginality, the result was that private associations and authorities helped the refugees coming from Trentino or the Isonzo valley only after the Italian citizens fled in autumn 1917.[61] Only the irredentists, co-ordinated by the *Commissione centrale di patronato tra fuoriusciti adriatici e trentini*, stressed the necessity to carry out surveys in all the displacement villages to control the effectiveness of the policy developed by the Ministry of the Interior with the aim of improving the refugees' living conditions and promoting patriotic feelings among Italians from across the border. This is true also for the Slovenian-speaking people displaced from the Isonzo valley.[62] As a consequence, those who showed pro-Italian feelings could count on economic benefits and better housing or workplaces, through the mediation of irredentists. All of the others, most of them women, the elderly and children, could rely only on their limited personal means. Moreover, the shadow of loyalty toward the Habsburg Empire meant the displacement in small places of southern Italy, losing every contact with the network of compatriots.[63]

Conclusion

To sum up, the refugees from Trentino were legally supported and subsidised as compatriots in Italy. In terms of everyday life, however, they did not integrate themselves into the host community, with the exception of those places – usually big cities – where irredentist groups were active. On the contrary, they demonstrated pro-Italian feelings only in order to gain concrete benefits, to avoid internment measures, and to gain the respect of the local population. Most of them kept a low profile rather than taking an explicit stance on loyalty issues. In practice, contact with the new state was negative, above all for those who experienced internment or other forms of ill-treatment.

The refugees displaced to the internal regions of Austria redrew their multi-layered identity, stressing their 'Italian-ness' and 'Trentin-ness', rather than 'Austrian-ness' or 'Tyrol-ness'. The refugees sent to the Italian Kingdom, despite the struggle of irredentists to emphasise the cultural brotherhood between hosts and guests, did not internalise pro-Italian political feelings. On the contrary, it was the obsession of the Italian authorities to find spies and to adopt internment measures, as well as the inefficiency of Italian welfare provision, that marked the experience of displacement and the first contact of displaced persons from Trentino with the Italian state.

Notes

1 This chapter is based on research conducted in the framework of the project 'The first world war 1914–1918. Trentino, Italy, Europe', Istituto Storico Italo Germanico – FBK and University of Trento http://isig.fbk.eu/projects/world-war-i-1914-1918-trentino-italy-europe [accessed 9 November 2016], funded for the years 2013–2015 by the Autonomous Province of Trento. The text was planned together, but Mondini was largely responsible for the first half and Frizzera for the second half.

2 On how the case of Italy was marginalised and how most Italian-speaking historians lagged behind in the latest European historical assessment of the Great War, see Oliver Janz, 'Zwischen Konsens und Dissens: Zur Historiographie des Ersten Weltkriegs in Italien', in A. Baurkämper and E. Julien (eds), *Durchhalten! Krieg und Gesellschaft im Vergleich 1914–1918* (Göttingen: Vandenhoeck & Ruprecht, 2010), pp. 195–216; M. Mondini, *L'historiographie italienne face à la Grande Guerre: saisons et ruptures*, in *Histoire@Politique*, 2014, 22, www.histoire-politique.fr [accessed 9 November 2016]. See also Jay Winter (ed.), *The Cambridge History of the First World War* (3 vols, Cambridge: Cambridge University Press, 2013–14), where the only article doing justice to the cultural, political and military peculiarities of the Italian situation is by N. Labanca, 'The Italian front', vol. I, pp. 266–96.

3 A. Varsori, *Radioso maggio: Come l'Italia entrò in guerra* (Bologna; Il Mulino, 2015).

4 On the bizarre timing and peculiarities of the Italian war, see M. Mondini, *La guerra italiana: Partire, raccontare, tornare 1914–1918* (Bologna: Il Mulino, 2014).

5 G. Pietra, *Gli esodi in Italia durante la guerra mondiale (1915–1918)* (Roma: Failli, 1938), pp. 15–21; Ministero per le Terre Liberate, *Censimento dei profughi di guerra* (Roma: Tipografia del Ministero dell'Interno, 1919), pp. 221–7. The figures are highly approximate. The Italian authorities were unable to find out exactly who was present in 1917, making allowance for the homecomings of 1915 and the mass departure of servicemen. See G. Mortara, *La salute pubblica in Italia durante e dopo la guerra* (Bari: Laterza, 1925), p. 70.

6 Peter Gatrell and Philippe Nivet, 'Refugees and exiles', in Jay Winter (ed.) *The Cambridge History of the First World War* (Cambridge: Cambridge University Press, 2014), vol. 3, pp. 186–216.

7 On the origin of the 'cultural space' category as a tool of analysis transcending the limited fields of national analysis, see A. Boschetti, *Pour un comparatiste réflexif*, in Boschetti (ed.), *L'espace culturel transnational* (Paris: Nouveau Monde, 2010), pp. 7–54.

8 This anomaly is normally overlooked by Italian historians specialising in the refugee phenomenon. See the two simplified frameworks suggested

Displaced persons in the Italian linguistic space

by D. Ceschin, *L'esilio in Italia: i profughi di guerra*, in M. Isnenghi and D. Ceschin (eds), *Gli italiani in guerra*, III-1, *La Grande Guerra: dall'intervento alla vittoria mutilata* (Turin: UTET, 2008), pp. 260–74, and D. Ceschin, *Italiani rifugiati*, in N. Labanca (ed.), *Dizionario storico della prima guerra mondiale* (Rome-Bari: Laterza, 2014), pp. 311–23.

9 Archivio Centrale dello Stato (ACS), Presidenza del Consiglio dei Ministri (PCM), busta (b.) 72 bis, Ministero dell'Interno – Direzione generale di sanità pubblica, *Misure per i profughi di guerra* (24 June 1915). For the legal status of territories occupied in 1915, see the findings of a series of Armed Command meetings in July 1915 and again in March 1916, and the reports kept at ACS, Ministero della Guerra, Comando Supremo (CS), b. 204, and the copy of the Supreme Command's decree on 2 July 1915, *Disposizioni generali per le terre occupate*.

10 Ministero Agricoltura, *Dati statistici sui rimpatriati per cause di guerra*, Rome 1915; F. Calimani, *I profughi di guerra italiani rimpatriati attraverso la Svizzera* (Rome: Cartiere Centrali, 1915).

11 ACS, Presidenza Consiglio dei Ministri (PCM), Alto Commissariato Profughi di Guerra, b. 18, from the Ministero dell'Interno to Prefetti del Regno, 17/09/1915.

12 G. Procacci, *L'internamento dei civili in Italia durante il conflitto*, in Procacci, ed, *Warfare – Welfare* (Rome: Carocci, 2013), pp. 97–156. For a list of the internee categories and a few estimates of the numbers, see ACS, Ministero dell'Interno, Direzione Generale di pubblica sicurezza, Divisione Polizia Giudiziaria e polizia amministrativa e sociale, Profughi e internati di guerra (1915–20), bb. 1235–6 (Internees in the mainland provinces), and 1312–17 (Internees in Sardinia).

13 N. Labanca, *Zona di guerra*, in M. Isnenghi and D. Ceschin (eds), *Gli italiani in guerra*, III-2, *La Grande Guerra: dall'intervento alla vittoria mutilata* (Turin: UTET, 2008), pp. 606–20.

14 N. Labanca, *La popolazione dell'alto vicentino di fronte alla Strafexpedition*, in V. Corà and P. Pozzato (eds), *1916: la Strafexpedition* (Udine: Gaspari, 2003), pp. 248–80.

15 Mondini, *La guerra italiana*, pp. 95–106.

16 ACS, Ministero Interno, Direzione Generale di Pubblica Sicurezza, Divisione Polizia Giudiziaria, Profughi e Internati di guerra, b. 27, f. 1084, from the Ministro Interno to the Prefetti del Regno, *Profughi*, 27/07/1916.

17 In 1916, 110,000 *regnicoli* and *non-regnicoli* refugees were distributed between 25 provinces, which is more or less one third of the whole country, including the Po Valley and Sicily. See ACS, Ministero Interno, Direzione Generale di Pubblica Sicurezza, Divisione Polizia Giudiziaria, Refugees and war internees, b. 1241, refugee division per province.

18 D. Ceschin, *Gli esuli di Caporetto: i profughi in Italia durante la guerra* (Rome-Bari: Laterza, 2006).

19 ACS, Ministero Interno, Direzione Generale di Pubblica Sicurezza, Divisione Polizia giudiziaria, Refugees and war internees (1915-20), b. 757, 1/03/1918, from the Ministro Interno to the Prefetti del Regno.
20 Ceschin, *Gli esuli di Caporetto*, p. 195.
21 Municipal Archive at Bassano del Grappa, XII, 1918, b. 20-1, letter from Giovanni Cortese and others, 30 April 1918.
22 U. Özkirimli, *Contemporary Debates on Nationalism: a Critical Engagement* (Basingstoke: Palgrave, 2005), p. 163
23 L. Cole (ed.), *Different Paths to the Nation: Regional and National Identities in Central Europe and Italy, 1830-1870* (Basingstoke: Palgrave, 2007), pp. 1-15; P. Thaler, 'Una nazione non è fatta solo di nazionalisti', *Quaderni storici*, 128, no. 2 (2008), 515-25 (here p. 523); G. Stourzh, 'The ethnicizing of politics and "national indifference" in late imperial Austria', in G. Stourzh, *Der Umfang der österreichischen Geschichte: ausgewählte Studien 1990-2010* (Vienna: Bohlau, 2011), pp. 307-9.
24 D. Leoni and C. Zadra, 'Classi popolari e questione nazionale al tempo della prima guerra mondiale: spunti di ricerca nell'area trentina', *Materiali di lavoro*, 1, no. 1 (1983), 5-26; O. Überegger, *L'altra guerra: la giurisdizione militare in Tirolo durante la prima guerra mondiale* (Trento: Società di Studi Trentini di Scienze Storiche, 2004), p. 428. See also Pieter M. Judson, *Guardians of the Nation: Activists on the Language Frontiers of Imperial Austria* (Cambridge, MA: Harvard University Press, 2006); Tara Zahra, 'Imagined non-communities: national indifference as a category of analysis', *Slavic Review*, 69, no. 1 (2010), 93-119.
25 E. Tonezzer, *Il corpo, il confine, la patria: associazionismo sportivo in Trentino (1870-1914)* (Bologna: Il Mulino, 2011), pp. 66-7.
26 G. Pircher, *Militari, amministrazione e politica in Tirolo durante la prima guerra mondiale* (Trento: Società di Studi Trentini di Scienze Storiche, 2005), p. 45; O. Überegger, *Heimatfronten: Dokumente zur Erfahrungsgeschichte der Tiroler Kriegsgesellschaft im ersten Weltkrieg* (Innsbruck: Universitätsverlag Wagner, 2006), pp. 908-19.
27 C. Ambrosi, *Vite internate: Katzenau 1915-1917* (Trento: Società di Studi trentini di Scienze storiche, 2008).
28 TLA, Statth. Präs, 1916, XII, 76e, Räumung von Südtirol, Zl. 2459/86, Bezirkshauptmann Borgo an Statt. Tirol, Evakuierung: Auswahl von Arbeitern, 03/06/1915. OESTA, KA, KM, Abt. 10, Zl. 8223, Arbeiterabteilungen aus evakuierter Bevölkerung Galiziens, 22/09/1914.
29 OESTA, AVA, MdI, Präs, sign. 19/3, Zl. 11199, 31/05/1915, Evakuierung südlicher Grenzgebiete.
30 TLA, Statth.-Präs., 1915, 1193 - XII 76 e, Franz Rohr an Mil. Kdo Innsbruck, 7/4/1915; OESTA, AVA, MdI, Präs, sign. 19/3, 1915, Zl. 7975, 19/04/1915, Evakuierung von Pola, Triest und Südtirol.
31 D. Leoni, C. Zadra, *La città di legno: profughi trentini in Austria. (1915-1918)*

(Trento: Temi, 1981), p. 19; OESTA, AVA, MdI, Präs, sign. 19/3, 1915, Zl. 10888/1915, 24/05/1915, Statth. Innsbruck an Min. des Innern.
32 OESTA, AVA, Präs, Sign. 19/3, Zl. 16.053, 11/11/1914; Walther Mentzel, 'Kriegsflüchtlinge in Cisleithanien, 1914–1918', in Gernot Heiss and Oliver Rathkolb (eds), *Asylland wider Willen: Flüchtlinge in Österreich im europäischen Kontext seit 1914* (Vienna: Boltzmann Institut, 1996), pp. 17–44 (here p. 22).
33 Haus der Abgeordneten, *Stenographische Protokolle*, XXIX Session am 10. Oktober 1917, Halban's speech.
34 H. Kuprian, 'Frondienst redivivus im XX. Jahrhundert!' Arbeitszwang am Beispiel von Flucht, Vertreibung und Internierung in Österreich während des Ersten Weltkrieges', *Geschichte und Region-Storia e Regione*, no. 12 (2013), 15–38 (here p. 34).
35 Kaiserliche Verordnung vom 11/08/1914, RGBl. 1914 Nr. 213, betreffend den Schutz der zu Zwecken der Kriegsführung aus ihrem Aufenthaltsorte zwangsweise entfernten Zivilpersonen, para. 6.
36 OESTA, AVA, MdI, Präs.,sign. 19/3, Zl. 10256, 20/05/1915, Staats- und Sicherheitspolizeiliche Sondernmaßnahmen wegen der galizischen Flüchtlinge.
37 OESTA, AVA, MdI, Allg. Sign. 19, Zl. 5754/15, 16/02/1915, Erlass des MdI.
38 NÖLA, Sign. P, XII a, Zl. 3004/1915, Italienische Flüchtlinge aus Südtirol, Görz und Gradisca; Unterbringung.
39 OESTA, KA, MK, Zl. 7429, 13/12/1917, Hintanhaltung von Zeitungsangriffen gegen die Flüchtlingfürsorge.
40 OESTA, AVA, MdI, Allg., sign. 19, Zl. 6268/18, 28/01/1918, Tätigkeitsbericht der Niederösterreichischen Statthalterei; Walther Mentzel, 'Kriegsflüchtlinge in Cisleithanien im Ersten Weltkrieg', PhD dissertation, University of Vienna, 1997, pp. 326–33.
41 F. von Wiser, 'Staatliche Kulturarbeit für Flüchtlinge', *Österreichische Rundschau*, 45 (1915), n. 5, pp. 203–11.
42 Matthew Stibbe, 'Civilian internment and civilian internees in Europe 1914–1920', *Immigrants and Minorities*, 26, nos. 1–2 (2008), 49–81; Stibbe, 'The internment of civilians during the First World War and the response of the International Committee of the Red Cross', *Journal of Contemporary History*, 41, no. 1 (2006), 5–19; Julie Thorpe, 'Displacing empire: refugee welfare, national activism and state legitimacy in Austria-Hungary in the First World War', in Panikos Panayi and Pippa Virdee (eds), *Refugees and the End of Empire: Imperial Collapse and Forced Migration in the Twentieth Century* (Basingstoke: Palgrave Macmillan, 2011), pp. 102–26.
43 OESTA, AVA, MdI, Allg., Sign. 19, Zl. 6900, Flüchtlingsfürsorge, Evidenz der lokalen Hilfskomitees, 22/02/1915; B. Hoffmann-Holter, *'Abreisendmachung': Jüdische Kriegsflüchtlinge in Wien 1914 bis 1923* (Vienna: Bohlau, 1995), p. 49. W. Winkler, *Die Einkommenverschiebungen in Österreich während des Weltkrieges* (Wien, 1930), p. 273.

44 OESTA, AVA, MdI, All. 19, Zl. 25526/17, 29/05/1917, Sanitäre Flüchtlingsfürsorge. Barackenlager, Morbiditäts- und Mortalitätsstatistik.
45 OESTA, BKA, KFL, K. 77, ZL. 5429, Lista delle punizioni inflitte ai profughi di Braunau; OESTA, AVA, MdI, All. 19, Zl. 12027/1916, I.R. Campo di Concentramento di Braunau am Inn, Regolamento Interno delle baracche.
46 NOLA, Präs., SIGN. P, XIIa, ZL. 4050, 09/08/1915, BH Pöggstall an Statth. Präs, Betreff: Flüchtlinge, Unterbringung, z. Zl. 4049/6 P v. 26. Juli 1915.
47 AAVV, *Scritture di guerra*, 4, Trento-Rovereto, 1996, p. 117.
48 NOLA, Präs., SIGN. P, XIIa, ZL. 4050, 09/08/1915, BH Pöggstall an Statth. Präs, Betreff: Flüchtlinge, Unterbringung, z. Zl. 4049/6 P v. 26/7/1915
49 ÖESTA, AVA, Min. des Innern, All. 19, Nr. 33133/18, 31/05/1918, Statth. Innsbruck an Statth. Brunn, Betreff: Flüchtlinge aus dem Süden; Rückkehr in die Heimat. ÖESTA, AVA, Min des Innern, All. 19, Nr. 46811, 22/07/1918, Flüchtlingsfürsorge; Anfrage der Abgeordneten Mon. Delugan und Genossen betreffend Überstände bei der Repartierung der Flüchtlinge.
50 ACS, CS, SGAC, b. 789, Telegramma Nr. 4999-79-30, 04/12/1918, Commissione militare Innsbruck a SGAC.
51 ACS, CS, SGAC, b. 789, Telegramma Nr. 3861-92-26, 20/11/1918, Pecori Giraldi a SGAC.
52 F. Frizzera, 'Il rimpatrio dei profughi trentini dalle regioni interne dell'Austria-Ungheria: un processo pluriennale, specchio delle difficoltà di un Impero', *Studi trentini di scienze storiche*, 94, no. 2 (2015), 413–49.
53 A. Miorelli, 'Trentini internati in Italia (1915–20)', *Annali Museo Storico Italiano della Guerra*, nos. 17–22 (2009–14), 203–55 (here p. 206).
54 ACS, CS, b. 233, 05/02/1916, Comando V Corpo Armata a I Armata, *Internamento di persone sospette dai territori occupati*.
55 Manuela Broz, *Profughi trentini in Italia durante la Prima guerra mondiale, 1915–1918* (Verona: Tesi di laurea, 1990).
56 ACS, CS, b. 222, Sgomberi I Armata, Nr. 4850, 24/01/1916, Telegramma Comm. Civile Borgo Barbieri a SGAC.
57 Ceschin, *Gli esuli di Caporetto*, p. 276.
58 Broz, *Profughi trentini in Italia*, p. 107.
59 O. Brentari, 'Relazione della Lega Nazionale Italiana sulle condizioni materiali e morali dei profughi', *Italia Bella*, 4 giugno 1916, 9, no. 1, 7–10.
60 Ceschin, *Gli esuli di Caporetto*, pp. 47–52.
61 Broz, *Profughi trentini in Italia*, p. 181.
62 B. Coceani, *L'opera della Commissione di patronato tra i fuoriusciti adriatici e trentini durante la grande guerra* (Trieste: EL, 1938).
63 ACS, PCM, Guerra Europea, b. 129, 09/02/1917, Min. dell'Interno a Paolo Boselli.

9

Belgian refugees during the First World War (France, Britain, Netherlands)

Michaël Amara

Introduction: the exodus

The German invasion of Belgium in the First World War, from August to October 1914, led to the flight of more or less 1.5 million Belgian civilians. The vast majority of them sought asylum abroad, in the Netherlands, France and Great Britain. The magnitude of this exodus gave birth to a huge diaspora unique in the history of Belgium. Hundreds of thousands of men, women and children of all ages and social classes herded into refugee camps, lived off charity, or worked in war factories; their experience was very different to the Belgians who lived under the German occupation.

During the first weeks of the war, Belgium was the scene of violent fighting. The constant inroads made by the French and British armies, the retreat of the Belgian army and the rapid advance of the Germans troops brought the war to even the most remote villages. In August 1914, battles that took place around Charleroi or Mons were particularly violent. Liège suffered the first aerial bombing in history. The desire to find shelter and the fear of being trapped by bombing or shelling were often enough to encourage the first departures. At the outset, the regions directly affected by the war were the first to be faced with exodus. However, this fact alone could not explain the scale of the population movements that affected the country. The fear generated by the behaviour of the German soldiers pushed many Belgians into fleeing. It was clear that their civilian status offered no protection at all. Anyone could be subject to German atrocities. Just the presence of the enemy posed a threat.

From the first days of the war, Germans committed war crimes against civilian populations. Summary executions, the taking of hostages, the use of human shields, sacking of whole towns and villages, nothing was spared. Under the pretext of curbing the activities of alleged snipers, the German army launched a deliberate policy of terror and intimidation. On 8 August 1914, only four days after the start of the invasion, close to 850 civilians had already been killed by the Germans and over 1,300 buildings had been set on fire.[1] In this situation, flight seemed to hold out the only hope of safety for the populations of many cities or villages. An incredible panic rapidly infected the whole country and spread more quickly as the refugees recounted their experiences in horrifying detail and conveyed the terror in advance of the front line. Less than one month after the beginning of the war, the mere announcement of the arrival of the Germans was enough to drive men, women and children from their homes. Thousands of Belgians, mostly from the Liège area, had sought refuge in the Dutch Limburg and in the south, the retreat of the Allied troops during the Battle of the Frontiers had been followed by a mass flight of civilians to France. At the same time, refugees had begun to congregate in Flanders.

At the beginning of October 1914, the fall of Antwerp marked the start of one of the largest population movements Belgium has ever seen. From the end of August, the fortified city of Antwerp had seemed like a safe haven for thousands of refugees. The city had seen thousands of villagers pour in from the whole surrounding area. This arrival of a massive quantity of non-combatants in this strategic place created the risk of irretrievable chaos. To cope with this situation, the Belgian authorities organised the evacuation of the refugees. With the agreement of the British government, a special route linking Antwerp and Tilbury was established. During September 1914, some 10,000 Belgians were evacuated to Great Britain. Others were sent to Ghent and towns close to the Dutch border.[2] It was at this moment that the Germans started the attack on the fortified camp. The shelling was extraordinarily violent. By 2 October the Belgian army was forced to begin its withdrawal. The fate of Antwerp was sealed. By announcing the imminent bombardment of the city, the Belgian military authorities gave the signal for an amazing exodus. Some left in the direction of the Belgian coast. Others went to the Dutch border. Tens of thousands of people packed together in a huge crush on the quays of the port in search of any craft that might take them north. At the same time, an immense procession of refugees filled the roads leading to the Netherlands. On 7 October alone, 30,000 refugees entered the Dutch town of Roosendaal. On 13 October, 23,000 refugees lived in Rotterdam. When the bombardment stopped, Antwerp was empty. In the space of just a few days, hundreds of thousands of Belgians had sought refuge in the Netherlands.[3]

However, the fall of Antwerp did not signify the end of the exodus. The progress of the German Army through east and west Flanders – two densely populated provinces, already overcrowded by refugees – provoked massive displacements of populations. Among the refugees massed on the coast, the panic reached its height in the final hours before the arrival of the Germans, when the Belgian government's departure to Le Havre was known. Thousands of terrified people rushed to the ports in search of a boat that could take them across the Channel. In a few days, hundreds of boats full of refugees reached the English coast. At least 26,000 refugees arrived in Folkestone during the days following the fall of Ostend.[4] Those who did not manage to find a boat walked along the coast towards Zeeland or France, where they arrived en masse in Calais and Dunkirk. French authorities sought to disperse them in order to avoid overcrowding areas near the front. From the north, many were transported by train to Normandy. The rest were taken by boat to La Rochelle, from where they were transported to the various departements in southwest and central France.

With the end of the war of movement, in mid-October 1914, the mass departures of Belgians abroad ended. According to estimates, the number of Belgian refugees in the Netherlands reached close to one million in the first few days of October 1914, but their number subsequently decreased rapidly, falling to about 125,000 by the end of 1914. By 1916 the number of Belgian refugees in the Netherlands had stabilised at around 100,000. Another 200,000 Belgian refugees reached the coast of Britain, but as a result of departures for France, their number gradually declined, and remained stable at around 150,000. Unlike what happened in Britain or in the Netherlands, the number of Belgians taking refuge in France increased throughout the conflict to reach 325,000 shortly before the Armistice. Most of this increase resulted from the evacuation of the population located around the front line, namely Flemish civilians and displaced people, who had sought shelter in the small corner of unoccupied Belgium. Throughout the war, under the pressure of the Belgian and Allied armies, thousands of Belgians were evacuated from the combat zones to France. Among them were more than 12,000 were children who were herded together in school colonies situated in the Paris region or in Normandy. At the end of 1914, excluding the tens of thousands of Belgian soldiers imprisoned in Germany, interned in the Netherlands or based in France, Belgian civilians were spread between Glasgow and Marseille or Amsterdam and Bordeaux. It is difficult to produce precise statistics, but the total number of Belgian refugees who settled abroad during the First World War may reasonably be put at around 600,000 or some 8 per cent of the Belgian population at that time.[5]

Humanitarian action and solidarity

In each of the host countries, the arrival of Belgian refugees led to unprecedented humanitarian action. All these people had to be fed and accommodated. It is impossible to account for the scale of these efforts without understanding the particular significance of the invasion of Belgium in the public opinion of these countries. For populations still relatively spared by the conflict, the arrival of the refugees was often their first direct contact with the war. And it was a shock to them. The sight of these civilians, clothed in rags and dispossessed of their goods provoked pity, fear and indignation all at once. During the first few months of the war, the experience of the Belgian refugees had a vivid impact on the image of the conflict. They symbolised a new kind of war, targeting civilians as well as soldiers. This was reinforced by the fact that among the arguments used by the Allies to justify going to war, the violation of Belgian neutrality and the image of the Germans attacking innocent civilians played a central role. Images of the exodus and tales of the flight of the refugees purchased by German troops were widely popularised by Allied propaganda. Charity sales, fundraisers or events organised for the refugees were intended to help them but also offered the opportunities for drawing attention to the cruelty of the Germans, an enemy that had to be destroyed for the good of civilisation. In France and Great Britain, the efforts to help refugees contributed to the mobilisation of the home front.

The concern for the Belgian refugees was increased further by the fact that they were seen not only as the innocent victims of German brutality but also as the embodiment of the heroes who had dared to face up to them. What better way to pay tribute to the heroism of 'Poor Little Belgium' than to extend a warm welcome to its children? Helping became a moral as well as a patriotic duty. For numerous volunteers (among them were many women who could not serve under the flag), doing their bit to help the refugees seemed like a way of participating in the war effort. Everyone wanted to do something to help 'their own' Belgian refugees, showing them off as a sign of patriotism. Everywhere, spontaneously, on the initiative of local worthies, churches or civic authorities, relief committees were set up to aid the Belgians. In Britain alone, at the end of 1914, there were some 2,000 relief committees scattered all over the country. Some of these associations took charge of all the refugees' needs while others specialised in specific areas: forming reception committees in railway stations and ports; serving meals; distributing clothes; giving help with finding accommodation and jobs.[6]

In Britain, the main refugee relief organisation was set up in the first days of the war at the instigation of charitable figures in London high society. Within a few days, thousands of offers of shelter poured into the offices of the new War Refugees Committee (WRC). At the beginning of August 1914, there were so many volunteers that they outnumbered the refugees. At the height of the exodus, the committee placed tens of thousands of refugees with British families or in hostels run by hundreds of small organisations. In the Netherlands, refugee relief committees sprang up all over the country from August onwards to collect money and food. The Netherlands Committee for the Support of Belgian and Other Victims in Amsterdam soon became the largest organisation and tried to co-ordinate the activities of the different bodies. Under its auspices, entire trainloads of food and clothing were dispatched to southern Holland. In France also, numerous committees set up clothing distribution centres or refectories and provided valuable help with finding accommodation. From the outset however, French authorities were more directly involved in assisting the refugees. The country had to help its own displaced people and French government intervention in social policy was traditionally more developed. In December 1914, the French government created an allowance for all destitute refugees. Remarkably, no distinction between French and Belgian citizens was made.

This financial help was maintained throughout the war and enabled the poorest refugees to avoid destitution.[7] In Great Britain, only towards the end of 1914, as people's generosity began to wane, did the British government feel obliged to play a greater part in meeting the costs of helping the refugees. As early as 1915, the state had not only to sustain but also to substitute for private philanthropy in cases where charitable energy was not sufficient. The bulk of the WRC's income came from the state but this involvement remained secret. The authorities did not want to discourage charitable donations and hoped that the committee's private efforts would pre-empt allegations that the state was supporting refugees ahead of its own citizens. However refugee relief was clearly part of the new state interventions in the social field.

In both Great Britain and the Netherlands, social status largely determined the nature of refugee relief. Refugees of a better class received preferential treatment from the WRC. These differences were visible in the arrangements made at Alexandra Palace, the place through which the refugees arriving in London transited. The poorest refugees were herded straight away into vast dormitories whereas the upper-class refugees were given tiny furnished rooms on the first floor.[8] The Netherlands also made distinction of this kind one of the guiding principles of its policy. The Dutch government distinguished between upper-class, middle-class and working-class refugees. Those who fell into the second and third categories were liable to be sent to refugee camps, whereas the Dutch authorities paid a special allowance to members of the upper class who had run out of funds, in order to prevent them from having to live in camps. In 1915, the Dutch authorities created a special status for the refugees from the upper class who had run out of funds. The government paid them a special allowance to prevent them from having to live in camps.[9] The sole aim of this was to avoid the unpleasant consequences that could result from contact between rich and poor, to preserve the Belgian social order, which was considered by some to be an essential guarantee for the successful recovery of Belgium after the war. The relief effort for the refugees showed remarkable solidarity but demonstrated also all the characteristics of charity at that time.

In Great Britain and France, private and official aid helped to cope with the influx of Belgians. In the Netherlands, the number of refugees threatened the entire stability of the country. In September 1914, the Queen of the Netherlands had announced in her speech from the throne that her nation was ready to offer hospitality to 'all the victims of the war'. It was a means to assert the neutrality of the country, to appear as a haven of peace in the turmoil of war. But the scale of the exodus and the unexpected prolongation of the war compelled the Dutch government to adapt this promise. Meeting the needs of nearly one million refugees in a country with 6.3 million people ran the risk of plunging Holland into chaos.

So far as the Netherlands was concerned, it was not possible to expel the Belgian refugees by force. From mid-October 1914, the Dutch government sought the aid of the municipal authorities of Antwerp to persuade the refugees to return home. Reassured by German promises, hundreds of thousands of refugees returned to Belgium. Those who insisted on remaining in Holland nevertheless became too heavy a burden for the country. Camps set up in different parts of the country soon after the arrival of the first refugees proved to be ill-suited to provide longer-term accommodation. As winter approached, life in some of these camps became especially hard. With the autumn rains, the

Hontenisse camp quickly became a pool of mud, and the situation was not helped by the onset of the harsh winter of 1914. Every day, refugees trooped out of their tents to huddle together in communal rooms in search of a little warmth. Then, to crown it all, the first case of typhoid fever was reported in November, and a large part of the camp had to be quarantined. Some newspapers and a part of the Dutch public opinion began to denounce the living conditions in those camps.[10]

The first improvised measures had to be replaced by the development of a coherent policy, as the efforts of private charity gradually declined and there was increasing pressure from the army for southern Holland to be cleared of its refugees. In November 1914, the Prime Minister informed the local authorities of his plan to assemble all the indigent refugees in 'Belgian villages' specially built to host them. In theory, no refugees would be forced into camps against their will. In fact, they had no choice. On 27 November 1914, the refugees assembled on the quays of Amsterdam began to be evacuated to a camp situated in Nunspeet. In Zeeland, under pressure from the military authorities and in spite of the opposition of some relief committees, the poorest refugees were evacuated during April and May 1915. These measures were justified by humanitarian reasons. But in fact, they were part of a policy called 'sweet pressure' aimed at discouraging the Belgian refugees unable to provide for their needs from staying in the Netherlands. And this initiative paid great dividends. Tens of thousands of refugees preferred to go home or to leave for France or England than be forced to live in camps.

Finally, the Dutch government set up four large camps euphemistically referred as 'heavens' or 'Belgian villages', in order to avoid the negative association with erstwhile 'concentration camps' from the South African War. They were designed to house up to 20,000 refugees and three of them (Nunspeet, Uden and Gouda) remained in operation until the end of the war. These camps were very different from the first ones set up in the south. They were built to last and designed as genuine villages organised around vast dormitories and refectories, each with their own schools, clinics, post offices and churches. Despite the best efforts of the Dutch authorities, from the start, these camps had a very bad reputation. For many refugees, the hardest thing to bear was the restriction on freedom of movement. In December 1914, the Prime Minister had declared that 'the government would like to consider the refugees as their guests, and while sheltered in Belgian villages they must be allowed as much freedom of movement as possible'. However, in the first few months of the war, these instructions were interpreted restrictively and exit permits were often issued only very sparingly.[11] Afraid of being treated as prisoners, many Belgians left the Netherlands. However, from 1915, those camps gradually formed real little Belgian villages in the Netherlands, enabling the poorest refugees to live in decent conditions throughout the war.

In France and Great Britain the initial support gradually dwindled. As the host countries began to suffer their own privations, and were mourning the loss of their own loved ones, the refugees were relegated to the status of just one group of victims among many others – orphans, widows, disabled veterans. People became more and more indifferent to their suffering. Now that every family confronted the war, refugees found themselves accused of excessive comfort, opportunism or idleness. In England, Christmas 1914 saw thousands of refugees pouring back into London, returned by individuals or local committees who had run of money. In France, the allowance they received sometimes provoked bitterness or jealousy. This allowance was seen as particularly unfair because it was believed to discourage some of the refugees from working. Local populations demanded from them a total participation in the war effort. From 1915, the prolongation of the war and the dwindling of the charity effort forced many refugees to support themselves by finding work.

A useful workforce

In the Netherlands, apart from certain industrial centres around Rotterdam or in Limburg, unemployment was high among Belgian refugees. The trade unions, as well as many municipal authorities created a series of obstacles to their employment, to prevent them from competing with Dutch workers. Many Belgians owed their jobs to the sewing and dressmaking shops that were set up by charities. Rockefeller Foundation sewing shops were opened in some thirty towns and funded from June 1915 by the Dutch government. By offering paid employment to over 5,000 Belgian workers, they became the major employer of Belgian labour in Holland.[12]

In Great Britain, as in France, the requirements of the war industry rapidly assumed great importance. In the context of the shortage of manpower provoked by the departure of men for the front, the Belgian refugees appeared to be a particularly useful source of substitute manpower. In Great Britain, at the outset, the government discouraged giving the refugees work, out of conviction that the war was going to lead to a massive rise in unemployment. The authorities promoted the creation of small basketwork or carpentry workshops as a way to occupy the

Belgians. However, the situation changed completely when shortage of manpower began to be felt. From the end of 1914, the Belgians entered the British war industry in force. The importance attached to this source of manpower is indicated by the fact that the British government put major resources into transferring qualified workers and their families who were refugees in the Netherlands to Britain. At the beginning of 1916, the Commission for the Transportation of Belgian Refugees, run by the Board of Trade and located in Rotterdam had supervised the transfer of some 30,000 Belgian refugees across the Channel. Some 5,800 Belgians were hired by Vickers Ltd. at Barrow-in-Furness and over 1,300 by Armstrong Whitworth Co. in Glasgow and Newcastle-upon-Tyne. Belgians were present in hundreds of factories. In 1918, with about 30,000 Belgians employed in ammunitions factories (including more than 7,000 women) refugees represented one of the largest groups of foreign workers in British industry.

This massive influx of foreign manpower inevitably caused some problems. This was particularly true in England. Ignoring the language or the rules in the local industry, the Belgians often had great difficulty integrating into local firms. British trade unions accused Belgian workers of working too energetically and complying only half-heartedly with existing collective agreements, thereby jeopardising the hard won social gains of British labour. To minimise these tensions, the refugees were often grouped together in all-Belgian teams, and British and Belgian governments encouraged the organisation of factories using exclusively Belgian refugees. The two main factories – the Pelabon Works at Richmond-upon-Thames and the Kryn and Lahy factories in Letchworth – had over 3,000 workers by the middle of 1917. In Richmond, the factory attracted around it a population of Belgian 6,000 refugees and subsidised the creation of primary schools or a clinic. A third large Belgian industrial centre was created in 1916 at Birtley. The National Projectile Factory was the result of a collaborative venture between the two countries. While the British government agreed to pay for the construction of the factory and to supply power and raw materials, the Belgian government provided the manpower.

The factory became one of the most productive in Britain. Most of the Birtley workers were discharged soldiers but in order to provide their families with accommodation, the authorities created an entire new Belgian village with as many as 7,000 inhabitants, which was named Elisabethville. There were hostels for single men and cottages for the families. The gated complex was completely self-contained with shops, schools, theatres, a church and a cemetery.[13]

In France, the Belgian refugees were put to work in a total of more than 1,600 companies. On the outskirts of Paris, at Billancourt, in 1917, some 700 Belgian workers were employed by Renault.[14] Dispersed all over the country at the time of the exodus, thousands of workers left the places they had originally been assigned to in 1915. Dockers went to settle in Rouen or Le Havre; large numbers of metal workers, weavers and spinners settled in the Paris area; 5,000 Belgian women found jobs in the war industry. Agricultural workers who had been evacuated to areas where work was scarce gradually emigrated towards the north areas of large-scale farming where agricultural methods were similar to those used in Belgium and where the scarcity of manpower offered the hope of high wages. In some of these areas, Belgian farm workers were well known and highly prized because local farmers had long used Flemish labour for seasonal tasks. The absorption of the Belgians into the workforce caused fewer problems in France than in Britain. More dispersed across the country, they were less visible but also a familiar sight in places of work. Many refugees earned good wages, and often sent a part of them to their families who had stayed behind in occupied Belgium.

From solidarity to confrontation

In spite of their determination to participate in the war effort, Belgians did not escape criticism. In fact, the question of military service crystallised a large part of the resentment of the local communities against the refugees. In Belgium, generalised military service was only introduced in 1913. When the war broke out in 1914, the Belgian army mobilised only the professional soldiers and the men who had done their military service. The concept of the 'nation in arms' was foreign to the great majority of Belgians. In 1914, thousands of Belgian men of fighting age were legally never called up for service and lived freely behind the front. In this context, many Belgians were rapidly seen as cowards. The disappointment of the host communities was all the more acute because they had initially been perceived as heroes. In 1915, the Belgian government's decision to mobilise all unmarried men between the ages of 18 and 30 was welcomed but when in 1916 Great Britain found itself obliged to mobilise all men between 18 and 41, the Belgian laws soon seemed unfair, at a time when British youth was paying a heavy toll in the trenches of Flanders. In France too, for the wives or mothers of soldiers who had gone to the front, the sight of these young Belgians strolling freely about the streets became intolerable.

Belgian refugees (France, Britain, Netherlands)

In spring 1916, some British newspapers attacked the privileges enjoyed by the Belgians. A slogan began to spread: 'Fight or go!' It was no coincidence that anti-Belgian riots broke out in Fulham and Richmond in May 1916 a few weeks after the Military Service Act came into force. In May 1916, the Metropolitan Police explained this by 'the fact that Belgians and other subjects of Allied nations, who are of military age, are thought to be taking up occupations recently vacated by Englishmen who, under the Military Service Act, are now compulsorily called to the colours'.[15] Belgians were accused of taking advantage of the situation to buy empty corner shops or to seduce soldiers' wives. To calm the situation, the Belgian government in exile was forced to pass a legislative order on 21 July 1916 calling up Belgians from 18 to 40 years of age in order to bring Belgian legislation into line with that in force on the other side of the Channel. This new law improved the situation but many refugees continued to be called cowards or profiteers. For them, it was particularly unfair that thousands of Belgian men in exile were called to arms while their brothers stayed in occupied Belgium and escaped mobilisation. Many felt that they alone paid the 'blood tax'.[16]

In Great Britain and to a lesser extent in France, the search for jobs forced many refugees to settle in heavily populated working-class areas. They often formed little colonies there which illustrated the limited integration of the Belgians into the host societies and the way these communities clung to their own identity. Where it was possible, the refugees re-created a social and recreational structure through hundreds of theatre groups, choirs and sports clubs. Many of these clubs or committees were agitated by tensions between Catholic and laics or Flemish- and French-speakers. In Nantes, Lyon and Glasgow, Belgian communities in exile exported the traditional political and linguistic cleavages of Belgium but paradoxically, these divisions were a constitutive element of their national identity. The refugees met in Belgian bistros and read their own press. They also created a network of small business and Belgian shops: bakers, butchers or grocers who could offer them the specialties they were accustomed to. In England, horsemeat was considered unsuitable for human consumption and the idea of eating horse often aroused distaste among British people. Nevertheless, Belgian horse butchers' shops opened all over the country. By maintaining national customs, these communities kept the memory of their homeland alive. Only a few planned to settle definitively in the host countries. The exile could not be other than temporary. A good patriot could not consider staying abroad. That meant accepting the occupation of Belgium as a fait accompli. In these conditions, there was no reason to make efforts to integrate into the host societies. Given the context of war, it is difficult to use some of the traditional indicators of immigrant integration but it is important to note that only 281 Belgian women married a British citizen and that fewer than 40 Belgians obtained British citizenship during the war.[17]

However, the Belgian government in exile was anxious to prevent the refugee populations from permanently settling in their host countries. In 1915, the Belgian authorities in England published a handbook of suggestions and advice to the refugees. In these instructions, a question was asked: 'Where shall the refugees fix their hopes?' The answer was clear:

> Hospitality may cheer and comfort the Belgian refugee; it can never make him forget the grief of exile, nor distract him from his burning desire to return to his own country, and that country will stand in need of her children, and of their united efforts to restore her beauty, her fertility, and her riches. The time of refuge in Great Britain must prepare the Belgians for the heavy task which awaits them on their return. No one should think of avoiding this task, or should dream of settling abroad, unless for exceptional and various reasons'.[18]

In this context, the Belgian government attached great importance to preserving and promoting national pride among the refugees. Throughout the entire war, ministers and members of parliament in exile travelled the length and breadth of the host countries to visit the various Belgian communities and keep up the refugees' morale. Everywhere, the birthdays of the King or Queen, the National Day and the King's Day provided a chance for festivities intended to boost the patriotism of the Belgians and to keep alive their hope for an imminent return.

In the task of developing patriotism and national pride, the government in Le Havre was able to count on the support of the Belgian clergy in exile. At the end of 1916, there were some 200 Belgian priests in Britain.[19] In France and in the Netherlands, priests were present wherever Belgian communities existed. Most of them lived as true missionaries, regularly visiting families who were dispersed all over the country. With the support of the local Catholic hierarchies, they celebrated masses and gave all the sacraments. For many of the refugees, their priests often became their only support, a valued counsellor who did his best to smooth out problems with the host families or local committees. While they tried to maintain a sense of national feeling and loyalty to the King, all of them sought to preserve the Catholic faith in communities who had been made vulnerable by exile.

Belgian refugees (France, Britain, Netherlands)

In their fight against what Belgian authorities have described as the 'denationalisation' of the exiled people, the Belgian schools were an extremely important weapon. After a few months of lessons in French, British or Dutch schools, some feared that a part of the young Belgians would be deprived of the knowledge needed to become integrated when they rejoined the Belgian school system. This fear increased in 1915, when it was found that children of refugees were starting to have difficulties with their own language. This assimilation of children into the host communities was seen as a serious danger and convinced Belgian authorities to create a network of Belgian schools in each of the host countries. The total number of refugee children being taught in such schools was estimated at 26,000 in 1917.[20] In these schools, teachers were recruited almost exclusively from the ranks of refugees. The teaching was based on textbooks used in Belgium and the emphasis was on studying Belgian history and learning to recite patriotic poems and songs. It was impossible to create a Belgian school in each and every village that housed Belgian families, and many children had no choice but to attend the schools of the host countries, but the establishment of this Belgian education system in exile nevertheless represented a real effort and was a sign of a strong desire to combat the assimilation of the refugees into the societies that offered them shelter.

As the war progressed and the frustrations and anxieties of the home front intensified, anti-Belgian sentiments grew in each country. The refugees were sometimes accused of stealing the jobs of workers sent to the front, of being not grateful enough or of contributing to the rise in prices and rents by crowding together in working-class suburbs. In the Netherlands, in 1917, they were sometimes accused of contributing to food shortages. Some experienced xenophobic reactions traditionally caused by the massive influx of foreigners. People grew weary of the little cultural differences that had been amusing at the start of the war, but that now seemed irritating. It is important not to generalise about these xenophobic reactions, but there is no denying that the refugees had to face up to them in all the host countries. Some of the accusations levelled at the Belgians revealed different standards of behaviour, as when they were criticised for being too noisy in public places, for their fondness of beer, or for some of their eating habits. But other charges made against them seem to have originated in pure xenophobia. Familiar accusations such as excessive taste for alcohol, lax morals, dirtiness or laziness, seem to have been the old clichés attached to unwelcome foreigners. Some minor incidents were enough to lead to systematic generalisations and condemnations. In 1917, five refugees from Elisabethville were arrested with prostitutes in Durham. Immediately rumours about the immorality of the Belgians began spreading all over the area. In fact, Belgian offenders were rare.

In France, we find some traces of violent tensions between French and Belgians in Normandy, in 1917. In Le Havre, refugees were insulted and some came to blows. But these incidents were rare. Workers from Africa or Asia were victims of much more violent riots. In Great Britain, Belgians were not totally protected from the rising anti-alienism. They sometimes became scapegoats for the problems created by the war. In 1918, a trade union in Newcastle demanded the departure of all Belgian workers to the front.[21] Belgians faced problems of being defined as aliens. The Aliens Restriction Act (1914) made a distinction between alien friends and enemy aliens but the regulations imposed by the law (restrictions on their freedom of movement, registration provisions, etc.) affected their daily lives and were considered unfair and stigmatising. Some suffered from being confused with enemies. In Scotland, suspected refugees were regularly arrested by policemen who thought they were speaking German. Flemish-speaking refugees, who might be mistaken for Germans, were particularly vulnerable.[22] Nevertheless, despite the tensions that occurred, particularly in parts of London, it is important to note that the resentment against refugees was generally occasional and minor. This favourable treatment was no doubt based on the assumption that they would leave the country as soon as the war ceased. This indeed happened.

Returning home

The end of the war gave rise to great expectations among refugees. The vast majority were impatient to return to their families after years of absence. In February 1919, special trains were routed to the various Dutch camps to begin the repatriation of their inmates. By July 1919, a large majority of the refugees in the Netherlands had returned home. The British authorities, deeply concerned with the impending economic crisis, immediately took measures for the quick repatriation of the refugees. The announcement made by the British government a few days after the end of the war was clear: 'From the British point of view it is desirable that the whole of the working-class refugees, and all the others who are not able to support themselves, should be repatriated as early as possible. Unless this is done, labour difficulties are likely to arise'.[23] It was not proposed to compel any refugees to return against their will, but those who didn't return would not receive any future assistance. They were no longer really welcome. An enormous effort was made to repatriate the refugees as quickly as possible. Between December 1918 and May 1919, the British authorities paid for the return of over 65,000 Belgians, in addition to which there were those who returned under their own steam. By mid-1919, almost all Belgians had left the country. In December 1919, representations were made to the Home Secretary to work actively for the return of the last refugees. But, by this time, the presence of the Belgians was already just a memory. In the Netherlands and Great Britain, the few refugees who settled permanently after the war were exceptional cases. In 1911, some 4,800 Belgians lived in Britain; 9,800 were recorded in the 1921 census. Fewer than 5,000 refugees settled definitively across the Channel after the war.[24]

The situation was different in France. The country had been bled dry demographically by four years of war and didn't apply the same pressure to repatriate the Belgian refugees. The Belgian population in France rose from 287,000 in 1911 to 349,000 in 1921. It is difficult to determine how much of this increase was due to the refugees, although it is certain that the settlement of former refugees played a significant part. The fertility and cheapness of land were an attraction, and several thousand former refugees settled permanently in France. These Flemish farmers were joined by other members of their family and gradually integrated into French society. It was particularly the case in Normandy.

Just after the war, the British and Dutch parliaments adopted laws intended to limit the influx of foreign refugees. The new Dutch Law on foreigners came into force in 1918. These new regulations reinforced the control of refugees arriving on Dutch soil. All foreigners were now obliged to inform the police authorities within 24 hours of their arrival. The authorities were given the power to send them to reception centres and those who refused to accept these requirements were liable to fines or prison sentence. The major provisions of the laws voted in London and The Hague remained in force until after the Second World War and marked the start of restrictive measures concerning refugee asylum. In the Netherlands, as in Britain, the reception of the Belgian refugees was thus only an episode opened by the war and then closed.

For many refugees, the end of the war did not mean the end of their troubles. The situation was the most difficult for those refugees from the regions devastated by the war. The countryside in a strip of territory from 10 to 20 km wide and 60 km long had become a vast desert. At the beginning of 1919, 70 per cent of the population of the devastated areas had not yet returned. Most of them tried to go back to their original houses after the winter of 1918–19. Sometimes living in trenches or blockhouses, they collected debris and made use of the stocks left behind the armies in order to build temporary shelter. For months, hundreds of families continued to live in appalling conditions, so that the trauma of war and exile was prolonged. A few villages of barrack huts continued to exist until the mid-1920s.

For the others, return was often a great disillusionment. They came back in indifference or even hostility. Some were treated as cowards and had to face the animosity of Belgians who had stayed behind. The fact that they had fled, that they had escaped four years of occupation and deprivation was held against them. They were considered by many as privileged people or as deserters who had failed to demonstrate sufficient courage in the face of the enemy. Their contribution to the war effort was judged marginal at best. This was evident in the commemorations organised after the war. In post-war Belgium, the entire memorial space was occupied by Belgian soldiers, civilians massacred in 1914, and patriots shot dead by the Germans.[25] There was no place for the refugees in the memory of the war. For the majority of Belgians, the years of the occupation were remembered as a time of hunger and oppression. The experience of the refugees was very different and quickly lapsed into obscurity. The former refugees themselves made no effort to keep this memory alive. Belgians who had been refugees erected no monuments, created no associations and kept their experience under silence. This silence was perhaps the price to pay to reintegrate themselves into their communities.

Conclusion

The unexpected length of the war, cultural differences that were sometimes too wide, and reactions that could border on the xenophobic sometimes soured relations between Belgian refugees and local communities. The fact remains, however, that most of the exiles received a warm welcome and that, even if they became a weight on the various host countries, all energies were gathered to cater for their needs, at both popular and official levels. Far from being just a burden, they made a significant economic contribution in Britain and France to sectors whose workforce had been depleted by mobilisation. Their participation in the strengthening of the Belgian army was very important. After the war, Belgian refugees' experience was nevertheless totally forgotten. Some monuments were erected in Le Havre, London and Amesfoort to celebrate the hospitality given to them but they failed to keep alive the memory of the exiles. Sometimes, bonds between former refugees and their hosts outlasted the war but it was quite rare. The exodus of May 1940 in particular and the Second World War in general totally overshadowed the First World War in Belgian memories. Today, owing to the end of the amnesia regarding the years 1914–18, Belgians can finally find their place in the history of Europe's refugees.

Notes

1 John Horne and Alan Kramer, *German Atrocities, 1914: a History of Denial* (New Haven-London: Yale University Press, 2001), p. 13.
2 *Comité officiel belge de Secours aux Réfugiés. Rapport sur son action et son œuvre à Anvers (28 août au 5 octobre 1914) et à Ostende (6 au 12 octobre 1914)* (Le Havre: Imprimerie du journal Le Havre, 1915), p. 45.
3 Evelyn de Roodt, *Oorlogsgasten: Vluchtelingen en krijgsgevangen in Nederland tijdens de Eerste Wereldoorlog* (Zaltbommel: Europese Bibliotheek, 2000), p. 153; Maartje M. Abbenhuis, *The Art of Staying Neutral: the Netherlands in the First World War, 1914–1918* (Amsterdam University Press, 2006); Susanne Wolf, *Guarded Neutrality: Diplomacy and Internment in the Netherlands During the First World War* (Leiden: Brill, 2013).
4 *Report on the Work Undertaken by the British Government in the Reception and Care of the Belgian Refugees* (London: HMSO, 1920), p. 6.
5 Michaël Amara, *Des Belges à l'épreuve de l'Exil: les réfugiés de la Première Guerre mondiale (France, Grande-Bretagne, Pays-Bas)* (Bruxelles: Editions de l'Université de Bruxelles, 2008).
6 *Report of the War Refugees Committee, August 1916* (London: Crowther & Goodman Ltd., 1916), p. 56.
7 Philippe Nivet, *Les Réfugiés français de la Grande Guerre, 1914–1920: les 'Boches du Nord'* (Paris: Economica, 2004), pp. 115–20.
8 Peter Cahalan, *Belgian Refugee Relief in England During the Great War* (New York: Garland, 1982), pp. 161–2. New work on Belgian refugee relief efforts in Britain includes Rebecca Gill, "Brave little Belgium" arrives in Huddersfield … voluntary action, local politics and the history of international relief work', *Immigrants and Minorities*, 34, no. 2 (2016), 132–50, and Jacqueline Wilkinson, 'Administering relief: Glasgow Corporation's support for Scotland's c. 20,000 Belgian refugees', *Immigrants and Minorities*, 34, no. 2 (2016), 171–91.
9 Amara, *Des Belges à l'épreuve de l'Exil*, pp. 246–7.
10 de Roodt, *Oorlogsgasten*, pp. 159–61.

11 Amara, *Des Belges à l'épreuve de l'Exil*, pp. 244–6.
12 *Verslag van de werkzaamheden der Centrale Commissie tot behartiging van de belangen der naar Nederland uitgeweken vluchtelingen. 1914–1919* (Den Haag, 1920), pp. 79–93.
13 Amara, *Des Belges à l'épreuve de l'Exil*, pp. 199–203. See also Daniel Laqua, 'Belgian exiles, the British and the Great War: the Birtley Belgians of Elisabethville', *Immigrants and Minorities*, 34, no. 2 (2016), 113–31; Christophe Declercq and Helen Baker, 'The Pelabon Munitions works and the Belgian village on the Thames: community and forgetfulness in outer-metropolitan suburbs', *Immigrants and Minorities*, 34, no. 2 (2016), 151–70.
14 National Archives of Belgium, Brussels, I 565, Office national du Travail, 50, Département de la Seine. Enquête au sujet de la main-d'œuvre belge faite du 9 mai 1916 au 1er mars 1917.
15 National Archives of Belgium, Archives of the Belgian Relief Fund, 17, Letter from the Commissioner of the Police of the Metropolis S.W. to the Belgian consul in London, 29 May 1916.
16 Amara, *Des Belges à l'épreuve de l'Exil*, pp. 285–314.
17 *Report on the Work Undertaken*, pp. 82–4.
18 *Aux réfugiés belges! Conseils et renseignements* (London: Comité officiel belge pour l'Angleterre, 1915), p. 6.
19 *Comité officiel belge pour l'Angleterre. Rapport adressé à Monsieur le Ministre de l'Intérieur, 31 août 1917* (Bruxelles-Londres: Adhémar Dumoulin, 1918), p. 65.
20 Fernand Van Langenhove, *L'action du gouvernement belge en matière économique pendant la guerre* (Paris and New Haven: Presses universitaires de France and Yale University Press, 1927), p. 35.
21 Amara, *Des Belges à l'épreuve de l'Exil*, p. 361.
22 Tony Kushner and Katharine Knox, *Refugees in an Age of Genocide: Global, National and Local Perspectives During the Twentieth Century* (London: Cass, 1999), p. 61; Tony Kushner, 'Local heroes: Belgian refugees in Britain during the First World War', *Immigrants and Minorities*, 18, no. 1 (1999), 1–28.
23 *Report on the Work Undertaken*, pp. 37–8.
24 Colin Holmes, *John Bull's Island: Immigration and British Society, 1871–1971* (Basingstoke: Macmillan, 1988), p. 101.
25 Laurence van Ypersele, 'Sortir de la Grande Guerre: la Belgique', in Stéphane Audoin-Rouzeau and Christophe Prochasson (eds), *Sortir de la Grande Guerre: le monde et l'après-1918* (Paris: Tallandier, 2008), pp. 213–36.

10

Citizenship on the move: refugee communities and the state in France, 1914–18

Alex Dowdall

Introduction

The outbreak of war in 1914 generated large-scale population displacement in France, as in other belligerent states. In the combat zones of the north and east, few civilians could avoid the conflict's direct impact. The movements of armies, German atrocities, bombardments of towns by both sides, and the fears that these events engendered, prompted large numbers to flee. In mid-October 1914, the parish priest of Noeux-les-Mines, a town that would soon be enveloped by the evolving trench system, described the passage of these refugees:

> Everyone agrees how sad it is, this continuous exodus of thousands of people leaving their invaded regions and parading their misery along all the roads. It is pitiful to see these processions of families – mainly women and children because most of the men have gone to war – fleeing the enemy, wandering from village to village, unable to find sustenance, sometimes even leaving one of theirs dead from hunger or cold behind a haystack or a hedgerow. What a sad thing war is![1]

Over the course of the war, many more joined these initial groups in parading their misery along France's roads. As the testimony of the parish priest of Noeux-les-Mines illustrates, their displacement embodied the dissolution of the boundaries between front and home front, and between combatant and non-combatant that was characteristic of the totalising logic underpinning this conflict. The state's responses to these refugees, as well as refugees' attitudes towards the state, are key to understanding how France engaged in such a conflict.

Compared to the multinational empires of central and eastern Europe,

French society ultimately proved resilient in the face of over four years of industrialised war. The initial mobilisation of 1914–15 was a success, and although social pressures erupted in 1917 in the form of strikes in factories and mutinies in the army, these were overcome through a state-led remobilisation campaign which shored up morale until November 1918.[2] These wartime processes of social and cultural mobilisation were shaped by models of republican citizenship which emphasised the reciprocal rights and obligations of state and citizen.[3] This chapter considers how such models of citizenship shaped France's refugee population.

Existing historiography suggests that citizenship may not have been a determining category for French refugees who, it is argued, were alienated by the state. Historians have claimed that early in the war refugees were warmly welcomed in the French interior as a physical manifestation of German barbarism. The sense of national solidarity that they initially provoked helped solidify the 'war cultures' emerging in late 1914, and was integral to the mobilisation of French people behind the war effort. But as the war progressed and suffering spread across society, in the form of material hardship and personal losses, these warm welcomes began to wane. Refugees could no longer live up to the stylised image of the 'heroic victim' presented of them early in the war. Resentment focused on supposedly undeserving and workshy refugees, whose welfare entitlements were a drain on the economy.[4] In certain cases refugees, particularly those repatriated from German-occupied France, were denounced as 'Boches du Nord' – suspect elements having been in intimate contact with the enemy.[5] In his comprehensive study, Philippe Nivet concludes that as a result of these attitudes, 'refugees remained on the margins of French society', and that 'the often negative reactions – both of host populations towards refugees, and of refugees themselves towards their compatriots from other regions – contradict the idea that the Great War was a determining moment for the unification of the nation'.[6]

This historiography is, however, problematic, given its almost exclusive concern with the attitudes of the state and host communities towards refugees. It devotes little attention to the actions, expectations and experiences of refugees themselves. This is despite the fact that French refugees were highly organised and vocal. This chapter attempts to redress this imbalance by considering refugees as active citizens capable of engaging with the wartime state in ways similar to other sections of the population. Its focus is therefore specifically on French refugees who, although displaced, remained within their country of citizenship throughout the

Refugee communities and the state in France

war. Belgian and Serbian refugees in France fall outside the scope of this chapter.[7] It explores the internal dynamics of refugee groups, and in particular how geographic patterns of displacement facilitated the preservation of local communities and identities in exile. It then considers how membership of these local communities helped refugees manage the terms of their displacement as citizens of the French Republic. By examining French refugees in this way – as citizens rather than victims – we can see that they were much more than the objects around which host communities mobilised, or a problem for the state to solve. Rather, refugees were intimately involved in the negotiations between state and citizen that characterised the processes of social and cultural mobilisation of wartime France.

The geography of displacement

Mass population displacement was one of France's most significant wartime demographic events. By January 1915, when the Western Front had stabilised, 560,000 refugees – 450,000 French and 110,000 Allied, mainly Belgians – had fled their homes for the French interior.[8] During the period of static warfare the number continued to grow, albeit more slowly and consistently. To begin with, authorities on the Allied side rarely forced the evacuation of those who had remained near the front, but nonetheless civilians gradually fled difficult conditions.[9] At the same time, a distinct category of war refugees was created in the German-occupied zones – the *rapatriés*. These people were predominantly elderly, sick and children, and the German Army returned them to unoccupied France via Switzerland to place a burden on the French war effort. Their exact number is unclear, but by April 1916 almost one hundred thousand had passed through Switzerland.[10] By February 1918, the number of refugees in France had risen to 1.3 million, just over one million of whom were French. Early 1918 then saw a fresh round of displacement, as Allied commanders began evacuating front-line regions, and the German spring offensive broke the deadlock on the Western Front. As many refugees left their homes during the last six months of war as during the invasion of 1914. In September 1918, the total number of refugees in France reached a high of 1.85 million – 1.56 million French, and 290,000 Allied.[11]

For many French refugees, displacement was not necessarily isolating, as groups from the same location often remained together. In fact, many only moved a short distance from their homes, and remained in familiar environments where they drew on existing social and family networks.

According to the prefect of the Pas-de-Calais, most refugees from his department wished to remain 'in the midst of populations that have the same customs and morals as themselves'.[12] By September 1918, 23 per cent of all refugees were living in eight of the ten front-line, invaded departments.[13]

However, even among the three-quarters of refugees who did not remain at the front, and instead travelled into the French interior, settlement patterns ensured that those from the same communities remained together. On the few occasions prior to 1918 that Allied authorities organised civilian evacuations from the front they sent evacuees in groups to locations in the interior. Thus, in late 1914, 400 elderly people in municipal care were evacuated from Arras to Neuville-sous-Montreuil.[14] In early 1918, when Allied authorities began to undertake mass evacuations, they again sent people in groups to the interior. In February 1918, for instance, almost 35,000 civilians were evacuated from Nancy in groups of between 800 and 1000.[15] Many left for the Yonne and the Loir-et-Cher, 1,200 sheltered in a disused artillery barracks in Caen, and the town's children were placed in school camps in the Ille-et-Vilaine and the Calvados.[16]

Most departures from the front were, however, less orderly. The German invasion of 1914 generated chaotic conditions, while departures in the middle years of the war were haphazard. Nonetheless, as refugees from the same communities sought each other out, groups coalesced in the interior. This is clearly demonstrated by statistics compiled by the Ministry of the Interior in September 1918, and plotted on a series of maps (see Map 10.1). Refugees were not spread evenly across the country. Although small-to-medium-sized groups from the Nord and the Pas-de-Calais were located throughout France, the largest groups congregated in Paris and the departments to the south and west of their homes, along the Channel coast. This trend was even more marked among refugees from the Marne and the Meurthe-et-Moselle, most of whom were located in Paris and the departments immediately south of their homes.

Furthermore, it is clear that within departments, even those hosting relatively low numbers of refugees, important groups settled together in urban centres. In April 1916, France's prefects reported on the location of refugees from the Marne and its largest town, Reims. They noted that, for instance, out of 320 refugees from the Marne in the Maine-et-Loire, 151 were in Angers; out of 262 *marnais* in the Bouches-du-Rhône, 206 inhabited Marseilles, and 251 out of 363 in the Alpes-Maritimes were in Nice.[17] Refugees from elsewhere seem to have followed suit, as far as can be told from scattered evidence. Refugee coalminers from the Pas-de-Calais

Refugee communities and the state in France

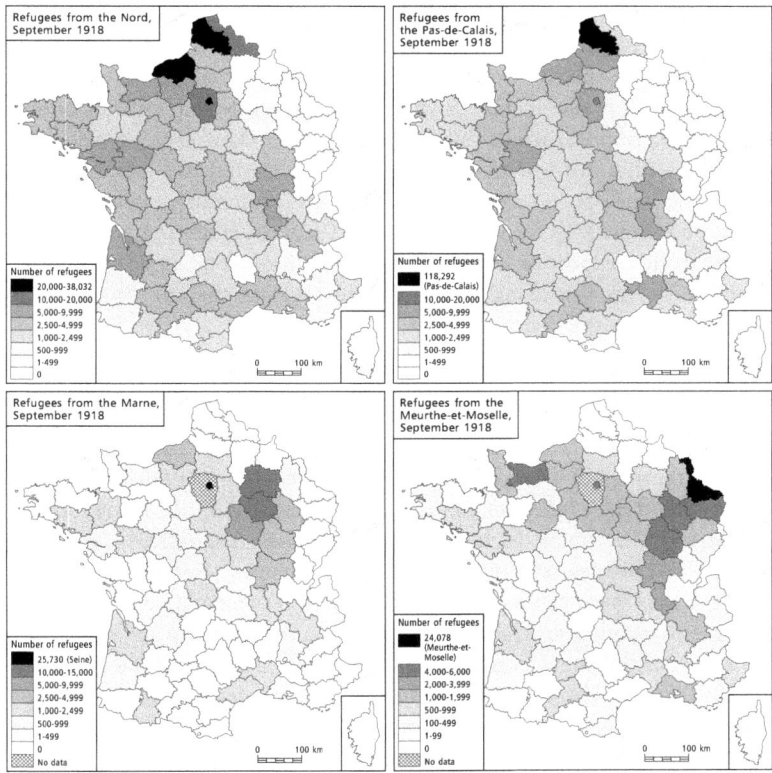

Map 10.1 Location of refugees from four departments in France, September 1918.

moved together to work in central and southern mining towns such as Montceau-les-Mines, which hosted 1,351 miners from the German-occupied regions in December 1915.[18] In Paris, too, refugees from particular locations grouped together, often around the railway stations that were their gateways into the city – the *Gare du Nord* for refugees from the Nord, and the *Gare de l'Est* for those from the Marne.[19]

This collective geography of displacement, which saw refugees from the same locations cohabiting in a restricted number of towns within a restricted number of departments, meant that refugees lived, acted and thought about their conditions alongside others from their home communities. Admittedly, not all refugees settled together in large urban centres. Many ended up in rural locations and for some, particularly urban-dwellers, this could be frustrating. But even in these places groups were large, particularly relative to the small size of their host communities.[20] There were few instances where refugees ended up entirely alone. The broader importance of this fact emerged in Dampierre, a village in the Aube with a pre-war population of 467. It hosted five families from the Marne who, once settled, established a representative committee.[21] For these refugees, as for refugees across France, cohabiting with others from their home locality facilitated the formation of collective bonds and solidarities. This would be one of the key factors shaping the internal dynamics of refugee communities.

Dispersed communities

Refugees in towns and villages across France did the same as the five Marnais families in Dampierre and established representative committees to defend their interests. Refugees from Reims and the Marne formed associations in towns including Lyons, Dijon, Toulouse, Marseilles, Vichy, Nice, Bordeaux, Saint-Etienne and Orléans.[22] Refugees from the Pas-de-Calais were just as active and formed representative committees in Amiens, Boulogne, Calais, Saint-Omer and Saint Pol, to name but a few.[23] Many of these committees were small, and represented from a handful to several hundred individuals. But they increased their effectiveness by affiliating with national, state-funded committees operating out of Paris. Ten such committees, one for each invaded department, existed.

The impetus for forming these committees may have resulted partly from indifference and hostility expressed by host communities, as refugees failed to integrate and were obliged to turn to each other for mutual support.[24] But the importance of the committees' focus on refugees' home regions should not be overlooked. Groups of refugees established representative committees based on their regions of origin rather than their regions of displacement. This is an important distinction, as it meant that when refugees responded to displacement they did so primarily as members of the local communities they had left behind. They worked together because they were refugees *from* the Marne rather than because they were refugees *in* the Aube.

This focus meant that the representative committees worked to promote sociability and maintain local identities among refugees in exile. Their activities in this arena were wide-ranging. In Paris, the national organisations were social hubs and organised regular events. These were often large affairs, such as in early January 1915 when a meeting of the Marne committee, addressed by local senator Léon Bourgeois, was attended by over 2,000.[25] The Pas-de-Calais committee organised a series of conferences on reconstruction in 1917 that attracted almost 5,000 people.[26] A stream of lower-key events complemented these large meetings, from children's parties, to cinema screenings, guided museum visits, lectures examining local history, art and architecture, and monthly social evenings.[27] Most committees also had offices with regular hours where refugees could meet, talk, exchange information and read newspapers. Outside of Paris, the provincial committees were also highly active. The Marne refugee committee in Dijon was typical. In addition to regular committee meetings, it organised a lecture on Reims cathedral in March 1916, a party in October 1916, a gala evening in February 1917, and another lecture in June 1918.[28] Taken together, these activities reveal the continued strength of refugees' community ties.

Through their committees, refugees from the same region remained in close personal contact while in exile. But the committees were not alone in working to link refugees to their home communities. Local authorities remaining at the front had an important role to play, and felt particularly responsible for 'their' refugees. Émile Basly, mayor of Lens in the occupied Pas-de-Calais, asserted that after the German army evacuated his town to Belgium in spring 1917, he went to great efforts to reconstitute the community, including establishing a hospital and town hall in their host locality. As far as he was concerned, his duties as mayor did not end with evacuation as, while displaced, the community remained 'obsessed' with their abandoned home.[29] Authorities on the Allied side shared similar concerns, such as the town council of Nancy, which assured evacuees in February–March 1918 that it would 'follow them morally' to their new setting, and continue 'to administer them beyond the town'.[30] The local prefect gave practical application to these sentiments when he intervened in June 1918 to improve the conditions of '*our* little refugees' who were housed in sub-standard schoolrooms near Cherbourg.[31]

The activities of the representative committees thus created social bonds between refugees from the same locations, while authorities at the front felt they remained morally linked to their scattered communities. But added to this, strong imagined connections were fostered among refugees through the press, particularly by ten dedicated refugee newspapers, one for each invaded department, that were affiliated to the national representative committees. These also sought to preserve a sense of local identity among refugees. According to the opening editorial of one paper:

> It is created for [refugees from the Marne], – in order to give them, if possible, the information for which they are so eager during their involuntary and momentary exile; to defend their interests; ...[it] will be the connection between all refugees from Reims and the Marne, not only in Paris, but in all regions of France.[32]

A further aim of the refugee press was to bridge the divide between those who left, and the not unsubstantial numbers of civilians who remained in their homes under fire. The *Lion d'Arras*, a 'siege journal' founded in Arras in January 1916 and distributed both at the front and among refugees, stated in its opening editorial that it aimed to forge connections between *arrageois* in the French interior and those at the front as a means of keeping the community alive:

> The *Lion d'Arras* will be the bond between Arras of yesterday and Arras of tomorrow, between Arras at the front and Arras that is dispersed. If our work interests you, if you understand the need to maintain the soul of Arras intact and unified, then circulate this news-sheet.[33]

In practical terms, refugee newspapers tried to foster common feeling between those who had remained at the front and those temporarily dispersed by creating a reliable flow of information between both groups. Refugees were avid consumers of news about their homes. Exchanging information was a key aspect of the events described above, while refugees in different parts of France and those at the front wrote to each other, exchanging news and ensuring that contacts were personal as much as imagined.[34] Information from the front was precious and the medium through which refugees remained invested in their homes.

Refugee newspapers catered to this need for information. In the early months of war, they devoted considerable space to publishing the addresses of refugees in the interior so that relatives could locate them, as well as lists of soldiers and civilians from the front regions killed and wounded.[35] As the war continued, they consistently reported on life under fire at the front, from blackouts, to 14 July celebrations, the continued operation of municipal services, the work of postmen and firemen, as well as crimes, accidents, deaths and small news items.[36]

But above all, editors of the refugee press felt that in order for refugees to remain part of the communities of the front they needed to receive accurate reporting of the destruction caused to their home towns by German artillery. According to the *Lion d'Arras*, only it could provide refugees from Arras with such reporting, shorn of the sensationalism that surrounded reports of urban destruction in the national press. It undertook to narrate 'everyday life at the front ... the daily details of our wartime events, which all seem the same to the foreigner who does not know names or streets, but which will speak to the heart of those from Arras'. As a result, it hoped that all those from Arras 'dispersed to all corners of the land', would remain 'attached to the martyred town'.[37]

Although reporting was hampered by censorship, the refugee press nonetheless provided regular descriptions of the effects of bombardments, allowing refugees to engage imaginatively and emotionally with the gradual destruction of their homes. The *Bulletin de Meurthe-et-Moselle*, for instance, published a photograph of war ruins each week, accompanied by the caption 'never forget!' The *Bulletin des Réfugiés du Pas-de-Calais* described the ruins of Arras in highly emotive language. In one article, the author expressed his continued attachment to his home town, despite the German shelling that had transformed it into a 'formless chaos ... which brings tears to the eyes'. He claimed to still recognise it as the 'cradle of my distant childhood ... Arras, infinitely dear *petite patrie*, I salute you!'[38]

The press, along with representative organisations and local authorities at the front, consistently reminded refugees that they were members of broader communities, founded on their besieged home towns, and including those remaining at the front and those dispersed throughout France. When refugees viewed the war and their position in it, their field of vision was not confined to their locations of refuge. The *Lion d'Arras* claimed this explicitly in May 1916, when it wrote that post-war reconstruction would be completed quickly and efficiently as refugees from the town 'love their Arras ... in order to be sure you only have to have felt the heartbeat of our refugee meetings in Paris which only hope for the return to the martyred town ... They have a single soul extended towards the distressed city'.[39] While all may not have expressed themselves in such poetic terms, refugees did remain socially, emotionally and imaginatively engaged with their home communities while displaced. They did not face exile alone and isolated, but as members of clearly defined and well-organised local communities. This would shape their interactions with the wartime state.

Refugees, welfare and the state

Organised into networks based on their home communities, French refugees nonetheless experienced displacement as citizens of the French state. In this regard, they were party to the renegotiations of the reciprocal obligations of state and citizen that occurred in wartime France. The unprecedented industrial mobilisation, combined with extreme pressures placed on material conditions of life by shortages and price inflation, redefined the relationship between the French state and its citizens in multifarious ways. State intervention in the economy expanded greatly, as did its role in distributing welfare, leading to what Patrick Fridenson has described as a transformation of 'the power of the state and perceptions of its appropriate role in French society'.[40] In order to tackle wartime pressure on incomes the state negotiated wage agreements between employers and unions in war industries, and introduced or expanded social transfer payments, most notably the separation allowance for soldiers' dependents.[41] The effectiveness of such measures varied and, with some exceptions, incomes lagged behind inflation.[42] Nevertheless, state involvement in wage setting and the expansion of social transfer payments were significant developments. Alongside the evolution of military disability pensions from a form of charity into a soldier's right, they pointed towards the later creation of the French welfare state.[43] Interactions between the French state and refugees must be understood within the context of this broader shift in the underlying principle of wartime social policy from privileges to rights.

Refugees, like all citizens, had obligations towards the state. They were expected to contribute to the wartime economy, and some played key roles, such as refugee coal-miners from the Pas-de-Calais working in southern mining towns. Others went into burgeoning war industries as unskilled labourers, while the government established a series of national and regional labour bureaus to aid those struggling to find work. By January 1916 only approximately 25,000 heads of family, representing a total of some 60,000 refugees, were unemployed.[44]

But despite the successful integration of most refugees into the wartime economy, material hardship remained a fact of life for most, as they were forced to leave behind houses, jobs and fixed incomes. Many had only the possessions they could carry by hand and even those who eventually found employment struggled to get by. As a result, the state had a particular duty of care towards them. Initially, however, refugees were dependent on private charity or the improvised actions of local authorities. In late 1914, charities and local officials hastily organised soup kitchens in transit centres through which refugees passed. In Dunkerque, for instance, the town council distributed 25,000 free meals by early October 1914, while in Parisian train-stations refugees were welcomed with spontaneous charity.[45] In the *Gare de l'Est*, members of the public gave refugees 'food and quantities of clothing, because they appear deprived of almost everything'.[46]

Charitable endeavours, often under the patronage of local notables and elites within host communities, remained an important form of refugee aid throughout the war.[47] They were, however, far from adequate, and the government soon took co-ordinated action. The cornerstone of the national welfare system organised for refugees was the 'allocation' – a daily sum distributed on a means-tested basis. This was originally issued by local authorities alongside free meals and housing, and the amount varied from location to location.[48] The allocation was standardised nationally in December 1914, when the government directed municipal authorities to distribute 1fr25 per adult per day, plus 0.50fr per dependent child, to all refugees, French and Allied alike, on a means-tested basis. Unlike unemployment benefits, this figure was fixed at the same rate as the military separation allowance, thus implying that refugees were also suffering for the nation.[49] The government introduced further measures throughout the war, including free housing, rent supplements, and medical assistance for those in greatest need.[50]

The elaboration of the system of state aid culminated in February 1918, when the Minister of the Interior brought instructions before parliament instituting a 'refugee regime'. Better known as the 'Refugees' Charter', this widely publicised document did not introduce new measures, but codified benefits already in existence. It clarified which groups qualified for refugee aid, setting out three categories – those from the German-occupied zones who left in 1914 or were repatriated; those evacuated from the front by the French army; and those who left bombarded locations on the Allied side of the lines of their own volition. It also regularised the refugee allocation, laid down revised income levels for the means-test, and summarised the ancillary benefits available. By publicising these measures, the government sought to make refugees aware of their entitlements, and ensure greater fairness in the administration of aid by local authorities.[51]

But perhaps the Charter's most important feature was its preamble, which summarised the principles which had come to underlie refugee welfare by 1918. The nation had, it claimed, contracted a 'genuine debt… towards a category of citizens who have had to bear the heaviest part of the miseries provoked by the war and the sacrifices demanded by the national defence'. It asserted that as a result refugee aid 'does not constitute a favour that can be accorded or refused to those affected in an arbitrary manner, but a genuine right'. The Minister instructed civil servants and the public to act according to this 'essential notion' and to show 'real sympathy and active devotion' in their dealings with refugees, 'who have suffered more than others'. They were 'victims of the war', and providing them with aid was a 'patriotic duty' and a 'work of national solidarity'. The Charter thus melded the image, current throughout France since the invasion, of refugees as the war's quintessential victims in need of aid with the notion that this aid was theirs by right. Although the Charter displayed a degree of state paternalism, and allowed allocations to be withdrawn from those refusing work or displaying 'bad conduct', its assertion that refugee aid was accorded by right as a component of French citizenship was unambiguous.[52]

Yet, while a language of social rights structured the system of state refugee aid, this does not necessarily mean that all refugees were satisfied with their benefits or the manner in which they were administered. Notable gaps remained in the welfare system throughout the war, and the refugee press regularly exposed the poor living conditions that many faced. Reports focused on the insufficiency of the allocation, overcharging by unscrupulous shopkeepers, poor housing, high rents, evictions, as well as the hostility and indifference of local officials who were reluctant to grant refugees their full entitlements.[53] In the face of such conditions, refugees were not content to passively accept whatever benefits were granted to them. Like the state, they viewed displacement through the lens of democratic citizenship, and they campaigned to secure their rights and improve their conditions.

Refugees' locally organised representative committees played an important role here. The ten national committees were organised by parliamentarians and other notables from the front-line regions, and they played an important role lobbying government in favour of improved conditions for refugees.[54] In order to do so successfully, they combined to form the *union des comités centraux de réfugiés*. This pressure group worked closely with the influential *groupe parlementaire des régions envahies*, a parliamentary group of deputies and senators from the front-line regions, including such high-profile names as Léon Bourgeois and Émile Basly. Although the *groupe parlementaire* had a broad constituency and represented all those from the front-line regions – including those remaining under fire and those in the army – defending refugees' interests was at the heart of its mission. Both the *union des comités* and the *groupe parliamentaire* ensured that refugee welfare remained an issue of national importance through parliamentary speeches, debates and public meetings. They advised the government on issues concerning refugees, and although their demands were not always met, they ensured that refugees remained involved in the political process and had a strong voice inside and outside the French parliament.

But refugees were not wholly dependent on elected representatives and extra-parliamentary pressure groups to speak on their behalf. When they were confronted with difficult material conditions, individuals and groups across France spoke for themselves. Refugees were inveterate letter-writers and petitioned state authorities directly or demanded that their representative committees intercede on their behalf. In their letters to authorities, French refugees such as Raoul Cassin, an inhabitant of Reims displaced to Paris, invoked the obligations that the state had towards its citizens. Cassin wrote to the national committee for the Marne demanding that an inquiry be opened when the mayor of the eighteenth *arrondissement* 'arbitrarily' withdrew his allocation which, he asserted, was his 'right'.[55] Others were more forthright in their demands and appropriated the category of victimhood. One group in the Pas-de-Calais wrote to the local prefect describing themselves as 'martyrs'. They demanded he take measures to improve the lot of refugees, such as introducing price limits on essential products. But they also expressed their indignation that while they and the soldiers were suffering, others were acting 'vulgarly'. They suggested that the prefect could begin by punishing bars which allowed 'rowdy' and 'shrill' piano music.[56] Such demands reveal the privileged position that French refugees granted themselves within the moral hierarchy of wartime suffering. They, like the soldiers, were a category of citizens suffering for the nation, and they felt it was only right for the rest of the population and the state to recognise this fact.

Displacement did not, therefore, mean disengagement. Refugees, both individually and collectively through their representative committees, demanded their rights as citizens suffering for the nation. They appropriated the category of victimhood, and used it to pressure state authorities to improve welfare provisions. Refugees were not passive victims of material hardship, but assumed an active role in managing their conditions. This fact found its clearest expression in the forms of mutual assistance that refugees provided to each other. Indeed, the limitations of state and charitable aid were such that a primary objective of the national refugee committees was to provide material assistance to their respective constituencies. The committees distributed food and clothing to those arriving from the front, and operated soup kitchens, jobs bureaus, charitable workshops and free medical services.[57] They also provided emergency financial support to refugees facing particularly difficult situations. They distributed significant amounts of aid. As early as April 1915, the national committee for the Marne had provided new sets of clothing to 4,131 families, cash grants to 1,417 families, and had covered the costs of 3,348 medical consultations.[58] By August 1919 the Pas-de-Calais committee had distributed over 2.8 million francs in aid, while the Marne committee had distributed over 3.4 million.[59] When it came to refugees' welfare, the national committees played a key role in supplementing state aid.

Crucially, and in line with the forms of local identity discussed above, these distributions were made on the basis of region of origin, with each national committee only providing aid to refugees from its department. Individual refugees were highly aware of this and, alongside the demands they placed on state authorities, they also wrote to their representative committees seeking help. Only the records of the representative committee for the Marne have survived, but they provide further evidence of the extent to which individual refugees worked to improve their conditions. Over the course of the war the committee received approximately 45,000 requests from refugees, which it either dealt with itself by distributing aid from its funds, or forwarded to relevant local or state authorities.[60] We can assume that refugees petitioned the nine other committees just as intensely.

In these letters they foregrounded their specifically local, rather than national identities as a means of legitimising claims for mutual assistance. Many of those from the bombarded town of Reims, for instance, claimed that although they had left, they were still members of the assaulted community, and that this validated their claim for support. Some emphasised their local wartime experiences, including the suffering they had undergone during the invasion and the time they spent under fire before fleeing. In March 1916, for instance, one man asked for help as he was struggling to support his large family. When making his claim, he felt his biography and his credentials as a *rémois* were as relevant as his finances. He informed the committee that he had remained after the first bombardment of the town on 4 September 1914, living in a champagne company's cellars, where his wife gave birth to their eighth child, before reluctantly leaving in 1915.[61] Others reasserted their emotional attachments to their bombarded home, and described their frustrations at being separated from it. One woman in Vierzon with three young children asked for aid as she was sick and could not work. She asserted that as a refugee she had 'suffered more than under the shells' and that she 'really regretted having left [Reims], but my house was destroyed'.[62] Another woman in Fissy appealed to the Marne committee after the mayor of her host village stopped her allocation. She stated that she would have gone to the prefecture in Bourges, but she knew she would not receive a positive response. She told the Marne committee that she was appealing to it 'because during these hard times I have come to miss Reims despite its bombardments'.[63]

The aid distributed by the committees was not charity. Rather, it was a form of mutual assistance granted on the basis of local identity and solidarity. At first glance, this may seem to undermine the importance of French refugees' citizenship. It could be argued that local solidarity of this nature amounted to an attempt by refugees to bypass the state because of its failures to adequately organise aid, and thus undermined their attachment to the wartime national community. Such an interpretation, however, belies the central role that local identities and solidarities played within concepts of citizenship in early twentieth-century France.

Traditionally, the French Third Republic has been viewed as a centralising, Jacobin state, as characterised by Eugen Weber in his influential argument that after 1870 urban France 'colonised' the provinces using institutions such as the army and the primary school, and transformed 'peasants into Frenchmen'.[64] This picture has, however, been revised in recent years, and historians have shown that in late nineteenth- and early twentieth-century France, as across Europe, local politics and identities remained strong in the face of the consolidation of the nation state.[65] Such local particularism did not threaten the French state, which coexisted relatively harmoniously even with well-established, linguistically based regional identities such as Basque and Breton.[66] Indeed, a local sense of place was actively inculcated among citizens of the Third Republic. Significant powers over policing, education and budgets were devolved to local government in an effort to 'republicanise' communes, to foster participatory democracy on a local level and, as Jean-Marie Mayeur has argued, to transform the town-hall into 'a centre of political education' that contained 'the reality of local political life'.[67] French people learned to identify with their locality, or their *petite patrie*, as the tangible, everyday manifestation of the broader national community of which they were also a part. Each *petite patrie* was a building-block of a greater national whole, and France was represented as a diverse, yet unified nation. Stéphane Gerson has described how, in this way, the *petite patrie* became 'a keystone of civil participation and national identification'.[68]

These local iterations of citizenship gained particular importance in wartime, when continued support for the national war effort was generated, or eroded, on a local level. The German invasion provided an initial and urgent impetus for this. As John Horne has shown, it was represented in part as a violation of space and as a series of attacks on individual, local communities and identities and, through them, the nation itself.[69] As the conflict continued, local elites in communities across France helped articulate the symbols, languages and discourses that structured local engagement with the national and international war efforts.[70] For soldiers and civilians alike, the defence of their family homes and home communities were strong motivations for their continued support for the war.[71] This was nowhere more the case than amongst refugees.

French society's resilience over the course of almost four and a half years of brutal conflict depended in large part on the continued successful mobilisation of such local identities. We can see, therefore, that when refugees expressed local solidarity, they were drawing on forms of identity that supported – indeed, were central to – France's national mobilisation. Like many other French people, their engagement with the national war effort was mediated through their membership of their local community. In this respect, as in others, French refugees responded to war and displacement as active citizens rather than passive victims.

Conclusion

What is perhaps most distinctive about displacement in First World War France is not the hostility that certain host communities elicited towards refugees, but the relationships that refugees developed with each other and the state. During displacement, they were able to maintain and draw upon forms of local community identity and solidarity that supported, rather than undermined, the national war effort. This allowed them to continue to act and think as citizens, and to demand that the state treat them as such. Refugees' wartime experiences were not defined by victimhood and disempowerment, but by active citizenship and membership of tight-knit, local communities. The large refugee population did not, therefore, seriously threaten the social stability of wartime France. It is notable, for instance, that when France faced civil and military morale crises from mid-1917, with strikes in factories and mutinies in the army, there is no evidence that the situation was exacerbated by complaints or agitation among the country's more than a million well-organised refugees.

The relative quiescence of France's refugee population is all the more striking when viewed in a broader, international framework. In the context of state collapse refugees could act as a significant destabilising force. Peter Gatrell has shown, for instance, that in imperial Russia massive population displacement undermined 'established notions of social status and social control ... [and] challenged established political, social and cultural practices', thereby contributing to the processes of social disruption prior to the revolution.[72] Despite the fact that the French and Russian refugee populations were of similar magnitude, with roughly five per cent of the total population displaced, nothing similar happened in France.[73] Identifying the forms of citizenship and, especially, the local identities that French refugees used to cope with displacement may help us to understand why this was so.

Whether these local identities survived the First World War intact remains an open question. If a local sense of place nourished French refugees during the war, did this also motivate them to return home and reconstruct their shattered lives and communities after November 1918? Or did significant numbers choose instead to remain in their wartime host communities and create new lives for themselves? Given the current state of research, it is impossible to give a definitive answer.[74] What is clear, however, is that in the summer of 1940 France would ultimately succumb to the interlinked processes of population displacement and state collapse. The civilian population of northern France again took to the roads in the face of German invasion, this time in even greater numbers. As Nicole Dombrowski Risser has demonstrated, in the face of displacement this new generation of refugees also resorted to a language of rights, citizenship and entitlements, and demanded that the state protect them. The state's abject failure to do so compounded the military defeat.[75] Even if the Third Republic proved resilient in the face of war and population displacement between 1914 and 1918, the events of the summer of 1940 show that it was not fully immune.

Notes

1 Archives diocésaines d'Arras, Arras, 4 Z 84/3 A, Registre de Paroisse: Noeux-les-Mines, 14 October 1914.
2 John Horne, 'Remobilizing for "total war": France and Britain, 1917–1918', in J. Horne (ed.), *State, Society and Mobilization in Europe During the First World War* (Cambridge: Cambridge University Press, 1997), pp. 195–211.

3 John Horne, "'L'Impôt du sang": republican rhetoric and industrial warfare in France, 1914–1918', *Social History*, 14, no. 2 (1989), 201–23.
4 Philippe Nivet, *Les Réfugiés français de la Grande Guerre: les 'Boches du Nord'* (Paris: Economica, 2004), especially pp. 293–329; Pierre Purseigle, *Mobilisation, sacrifice et citoyenneté, Angleterre-France 1900–1918* (Paris: Les Belles Lettres, 2013), pp. 288–300; Michaël Amara, *Des Belges à l'épreuve de l'exil: les réfugiés de la Première Guerre Mondiale, France, Grande-Bretagne, Pays-Bas* (Bruxelles: Editions de l'université de Bruxelles, 2008), pp. 55–6, 68–70.
5 Nivet, *Réfugiés français*, pp. 377–82.
6 Nivet, *Réfugiés français* pp. 556–8.
7 For brief discussions of Belgian and Serbian refugees in France, see the chapters by Michaël Amara and Danilo Šarenac.
8 Michel Huber, *La Population de la France pendant la guerre* (Paris: Presses universitaires de France, 1931), p. 173.
9 Alex Dowdall, 'Civilians in the combat zone: Allied and German evacuation policies at the Western Front, 1914–1918', *First World War Studies*, 6, no. 3 (2015), 239–55.
10 N. Roger, *The Victims' Return, with an Historical Note by Eugène Pittard* (London: Constable, 1917), p. 134. Michel Huber calculates that 500,000 were repatriated between October 1914 and January 1919, but does not specify how many returned after the November 1918 Armistice. Huber, *Population de la France*, p. 189.
11 Huber, *Population de la France*, p. 173.
12 Archives départementales du Pas-de-Calais, Arras (ADPdC), M 1727, 'Le Pas-de-Calais pendant la guerre – Service des Réfugiés'.
13 Huber, *Population de la France*, pp. 182–4. As regards the two other invaded departments, figures do not exist for the Aisne, while the Ardennes was wholly occupied by the German Army.
14 ADPdC, 11 R 1135, report to prefect (Pas-de-Calais), 4 February 1915.
15 Service historique de la défense, Vincennes (SHD), 16 N 1661, prefect (Meurthe-et-Moselle) to Commander French Eighth Army, 26 February 1918; Ville de Nancy, *Rapport Relatif aux évacuations présenté par M. G. Simon, Maire de Nancy* (Nancy: Imprimerie Nancéienne, 1918), pp. 5–15.
16 SHD, 5 N 84, Ministry of the Interior to prefect (Meurthe-et-Moselle), 2 February 1918; SHD, 5 N 161, Ministry of War to prefect (Meurthe-et-Moselle), 8 February 1918; Archives municipales de Nancy (AMN), 4 H 282, 'Colonies Scolaires de la Ville de Nancy'.
17 Archives départementales de la Marne, Reims (ADM), 10 R 509, Maine-et-Loire, 10 R 506, Bouches-du-Rhône, 10 R 505, Alpes-Maritimes.
18 *Bulletin des Réfugiés du Pas-de-Calais*. Figure compiled from editions of 28 July, 4, 7, 11, 21 August, 1 September and 4 December 1915.
19 *Bulletin des Réfugiés du Pas-de-Calais*, 19 June 1915.

20 Nivet, *Réfugiés français*, pp. 106–7.
21 ADM, 10 R 505, Aube, Refugees in Dampierre to *Amicale de la Marne*, 7 January 1916.
22 J. Matot, *Reims et la Marne: almanach de la guerre* (Reims: Matot, 1916), pp. 579–86.
23 ADPdC, M 1727, 'Le Pas-de-Calais pendant la guerre – Service des Réfugiés'.
24 Amara, *Belges à l'épreuve*, pp. 322–6.
25 *Reims à Paris*, 9 January 1915.
26 *Bulletin des Réfugiés du Pas-de-Calais*, 6 and 13 December 1917.
27 See for instance *Reims à Paris*, 23 December 1914, 3 March 1915, 1 May 1915, 3 November 1917.
28 *Reims à Paris*, 4 March, 15 November 1916, 17 February 1917, 15 June 1918.
29 É. Basly, *Le Martyre de Lens, trois années de captivité* (Paris: Plon, 1918), pp. 260–3.
30 Ville de Nancy, *Rapport Relatif aux évacuations*, pp. 6–7.
31 Archives départementales de la Meurthe-et-Moselle, Nancy (ADMM), 8 R 217, prefect (Meurthe-et-Moselle) to the school director (Querqueville), 23 June 1918, emphasis in the original.
32 *Reims à Paris*, 23 December 1914.
33 *Lion d'Arras*, 1 January 1916.
34 For a representative example of such letters see ADPdC, 1 J 2008, which contains correspondence between the Leroux family of Arras and their friends displaced to Berck-Plage and Calais.
35 *Reims à Paris*, 21 April 1915.
36 See for instance *Petit Rémois*, 15 December 1915; *Reims à Paris*, 21 July 1915; *Bulletin des Réfugiés du Pas-de-Calais*, 30 June, 24 July, 17 November 1915.
37 *Lion d'Arras*, 1 January 1916.
38 *Bulletin des Réfugiés du Pas-de-Calais*, 7 July 1915.
39 *Lion d'Arras*, 5 May 1916.
40 Patrick Fridenson, 'The impact of the First World War on French workers', in Richard Wall and Jay Winter (eds), *The Upheaval of War: Family, Work and Welfare in Europe, 1914–1918* (Cambridge: Cambridge University Press, 1988), pp. 235–48 (here p. 236). See also F. Bock, 'L'Exubérance de l'état en France de 1914 à 1918', *Vingtième siècle: revue d'histoire*, no. 3 (1984), 41–51.
41 Susan Pedersen, *Family, Dependence and the Origins of the Welfare State: Britain and France, 1914–1945* (Cambridge: Cambridge University Press 1993), pp. 79–134; Thierry Bonzon, 'Transfer payments and social policy', in Jay Winter and Jean-Louis Robert (eds), *Capital Cities at War: Paris, London, Berlin, 1914–1918*, Vol. 1 (Cambridge: Cambridge University Press, 1997), pp. 286–302.
42 Fridenson, 'Impact of the First World War', p. 240.

43 Bonzon, 'Transfer payments', pp. 299–302; T.B. Smith, *Creating the Welfare State in France, 1880–1940* (London: McGill-Queen's University Press, 2003), pp. 13–91.
44 A. Fontaine, *L'Industrie française pendant la guerre* (Paris: Presses Universitaires de France, 1925), pp. 64–7.
45 A. Chatelle, *Dunkerque pendant la Guerre, 1914–1918* (Paris: Picart, 1925), pp. 18–19.
46 *Petit Parisien*, 29 August 1914.
47 Purseigle, *Mobilisation, sacrifice et citoyenneté*, pp. 286–91; Nivet, *Réfugiés français*, pp. 137–66.
48 Nivet, *Réfugiés français*, pp. 115–17.
49 Archives nationales, Paris (AN), F/23/3, Ministry of the Interior to mayors of France, 'Allocation et régime général', 1 December 1914. The allocation was raised to 1fr50 per day, plus 1fr per dependent, in August 1917. See *Journal Officiel de la République Française* (JO), 17 February 1918, 'Instructions portant fixation du régime des réfugiés'.
50 AN, F/23/3, Ministry of the Interior to prefects, 'Secours sur fonds de concours', 13 March 1915.
51 JO, 17 February 1918, 'régime des réfugiés'.
52 JO, 17 February 1918, 'régime des réfugiés'. See article 20 for the withdrawal of aid as a result of 'bad conduct'.
53 *Reims a Paris*, 28 June 1916 and 17 February 1917; *Bulletin des Réfugiés du Pas-de-Calais*, 28 July 1915, 16 July 1916, and 20 September 1916.
54 Nivet, *Réfugiés français*, pp. 153–66.
55 ADM, 10 R 100, letter from Raoul Cassin to *Amicale de la Marne*, 22 June 1915.
56 ADPdC, 120 R 10, letter from 'un groupe de martyres' to prefect (Pas-de-Calais), 7 May 1916.
57 *Reims à Paris*, 23 December 1914, 18 November 1916, 14 April 1917, and 6 February 1918; *Bulletin de Meurthe-et-Moselle*, 1 December 1914.
58 *Reims à Paris*, 12 June 1915.
59 Nivet, *Réfugiés français*, p. 162.
60 Letters sent to the committee by refugees, as well as responses, are contained in 173 folders between ADM, 10 R 92–256 and 10 R 505–13. Each folder sampled contains approximately 250 letters, suggesting a total of approximately 45,000.
61 ADM, 10 R 168, letter from M. Egée to *Amicale de la Marne*, 6 March 1916.
62 ADM, 10 R 508, letter from Mme. Membré to *Amicale de la Marne*, 22 March 1917.
63 ADM, 10 R 508, illegibly signed letter to *Amicale de la Marne*, 21 December 1916.
64 Eugen Weber, *Peasants into Frenchmen: the Modernization of Rural France, 1870–1914* (Stanford: Stanford University Press, 1976), p. 486.

65 Stéphane Gerson, *The Pride of Place: Local Memories and Political Culture in Nineteenth-Century France* (London: Cornell University Press, 2003); C. Applegate, 'A Europe of regions: reflections on the historiography of sub-national places in modern times', *American Historical Review*, 104, no. 4 (1999), 1157–82.
66 Maurice Agulhon, 'Le Centre et la périphérie', in Pierre Nora (ed.), *Les Lieux de mémoire*, vol. 2 (Gallimard: Quarto, 1997), pp. 2889–98.
67 J-M. Mayeur, *La Vie politique sous la Troisième République, 1870–1940* (Paris: Éditions du seuil, 1984), p. 81.
68 Stéphane Gerson, 'The local', in E. Berenson, V. Duclert and C. Prochasson (eds), *The French Republic: History, Values, Debates* (Ithaca, NY: Cornell University Press, 2011), pp. 213–20.
69 John Horne, 'Corps, lieux et nation: la France et l'invasion de 1914', *Annales. Histoire, sciences sociales*, 55, no. 1 (2000), 73–109 (here, p. 74).
70 Purseigle, *Mobilisation, sacrifice et citoyenneté*.
71 Jay Winter, 'Paris, London, Berlin 1914–1919: capital cities at war', in Winter and Robert (eds), *Capital Cities at War*, p. 6.
72 Peter Gatrell, *A Whole Empire Walking: Refugees in Russia During World War 1* (Bloomington: Indiana University Press, 1999), p. 4. For similar arguments in respect of refugees in the Austro-Hungarian Empire see Alexander Watson, *Ring of Steel: Germany and Austria-Hungary at War* (London: Allen Lane, 2014), pp. 198–206.
73 In France, there were 1.85 million refugees, of whom 1.5 million were French, in a pre-war population of 39.6 million. In Russia 6 million of approximately 120 million people were displaced. On the size of Russia's refugee population see Gatrell, *Whole Empire Walking*, p. 3.
74 The literature on post-war reconstruction is under-developed. The main work is Hugh Clout, *After the Ruins: Restoring the Countryside of Northern France after the Great War* (Exeter: University of Exeter Press 1996).
75 N. Dombrowski Risser, *France under Fire: German Invasion, Civilian Flight, and Family Survival During World War II* (Cambridge: Cambridge University Press, 2012).

11

Golgotha: the retreat of the Serbian army and civilians in 1915–16

Danilo Šarenac

Introduction

A passage in the novel *The Sixth Day* (*Dan šesti*), written by avant-garde Serbian author Rastko Petrović in 1935, portrays a grey wolf running through the woods in the south of the country. The wolf suddenly stops in his tracks, amazed at the sight of distant columns of men stretching as far as the eye can see. He rarely comes across human beings, so the wolf ponders what could have brought about this strange vision. The author solves the puzzle in the scene by revealing that this episode took place during the great retreat of the Serbian army and Serb civilians in the autumn of 1915. Petrović dedicated his novel to the events of the winter of 1915–16, in which he had participated as a 17-year-old schoolboy.[1] In Serbian popular narrative these dramatic developments marked the defining moment of the Great War: 'Golgotha'.

The conflict in the Balkans is seen as critical to understanding the origins of the First World War, but it typically disappears from view once attention shifts to the colossal battles on the Western and Eastern Fronts. Nevertheless, the Great War, together with the two Balkan Wars in 1912–13, completely transformed the region, reshaping its frontiers and its political and ethnic composition. The consequences continue to reverberate. Nevertheless, many of the most important aspects of the First World War in the Balkans are under-researched. The great retreat of Serbian officials, soldiers and civilians across Albania in 1915–16 is one such episode. Although its outline may be familiar, 'Golgotha' remains poorly understood in Serbia.

Golgotha (often referred to as the 'Albanian Golgotha') began on 25 November 1915 when the Serbian High Command ordered the army

Golgotha: the Serbian army and civilians

to cross the border and retreat towards the Adriatic. However, this was not the first such displacement to affect the Serbian population. Two major incursions by Habsburg forces in 1914 had already prompted the flight of civilians. Long columns of wagons, slowly moving over the rain-drenched roads, became one of the most recognisable images of the first year of the war. In addition, thousands of Serbs crossed from Serbia into Habsburg territory. Yet these upheavals encompassed only part of the country compared to 'Golgotha'. By February 1916 most troops and civilians had been evacuated, although the retreat only came to an end at the beginning of April when the final group of soldiers embarked on Entente ships. In 1916, the Serbian army regrouped and reassembled on the Salonika front. Meanwhile refugees had been dispersed all over Europe and northern Africa.

Map 11.1 Serbia during the First World War.

The presence of soldiers and civilians, including people of different social backgrounds, gave the retreat a 'national' character. Members of the royal family, parliamentary deputies, government ministers and civil servants retreated together with Serbian Orthodox clergy, peasants and the Belgrade poor. Influential artists, scientists and other professionals joined the throng. Many of the soldiers had served in the Serbian armed forces since 1912, but alongside these battle-hardened men were more vulnerable groups such as conscripts who had only recently been drafted into the army. Several thousand schoolboys aged between 15 and 17 were evacuated along with the adults. Around 40,000 Habsburg prisoners of war were also taken on the journey south. Priceless historical objects were transported, such as medieval manuscripts, books and relics, along with deposits belonging to the National Bank and documents from the National Archive. This contributed to a widespread feeling that the entire country was on the move.

Those who took part in the retreat likened it to a 'Greek tragedy', to Xenophon's 'Anabasis', and to Napoleon's retreat from Moscow, but they also used more direct terms such as 'catastrophe', 'people's misfortune' or simply 'the retreat'.[2] No-one described it as a victory, although in terms of military strategy the retreat enabled Serbia to remain in the war, to preserve the bulk of its troops and ultimately to avoid complete capitulation. The long-term effects were felt throughout the interwar years and beyond. Heartrending stories of the retreat formed a fundamental component of Serbia's popular remembrance culture as well as Serb national identity.

'Golgotha' vividly illustrates how the relationship between state and society was transformed due to the Great War. It marked the moment when citizens expected something from the state in exchange for their sacrifices. In addition, the great retreat not only challenged popular confidence in the state but also led contemporaries to question their entire worldview.[3]

Doomsday

The combined attack on Serbia by German and Austro-Hungarian forces began on 5 October 1915. Three days later Bulgaria attacked as well. Two months of fighting and withdrawal ensued. The government and High Command attempted to gain as much time as possible in order to link up with the Allied troops, hoping that they would reach the southern town of Niš before the Bulgarians. However, the Entente forces were too few in number to penetrate the Bulgarian lines. Milan Stojadinović

(1888–1961), an employee of the Serbian Finance Ministry, recorded the disappointment of people in Niš when they heard that help was not at hand. For days the town's muddy streets were filled with flags originally put up to greet the Allies but that had since been torn down by the strong winds.[4] By mid-October the key railway junctions in Macedonia (at Kumanovo and Skopje) had fallen into the hands of the Bulgarian army. Thus, the Serbian Kingdom became separated from its main supply port in Salonika as well as from the Allied troops.

The government urged the civilian population to stay in their homes, with two exceptions. Military conscripts were permitted to join the retreat lest the enemy intern them. For similar reasons, the government also ordered the evacuation of boys in the 11–15 age group: in eastern Serbia teachers took entire classes with them fearing that Bulgarian troops and irregulars would treat them as future combatants. One such evacuee was Rastko Petrović.[5] Many civilians disregarded the instruction and joined the retreat, fearing a repetition of the violence against civilians that took place in August 1914 during the first Austro-Hungarian incursion.[6] Retreating senior officers were often accompanied by family members who sat in trucks and cars together with their luxurious furniture and other belongings. Conscious that this created a poor impression, given that rank and file troops had left their families to the mercy of the enemy, the Serbian government attempted to put a stop to this practice, but with limited success.[7]

According to resident relief workers Claude and Alice Askew, working for the British Field Hospital attached to the Second Serbian Army, people in Niš had the look of hunted prey. Streets were jammed with people desperate to find out the latest news. The government printed leaflets stating that residents should remain calm, but the town fell into Bulgarian hands just few days later.[8] Many of its inhabitants ignored this injunction along with refugees arriving from other parts of central Serbia moved to Kraljevo, some 150km to the west. In the words of the French envoy in Serbia, Auguste Boppe, 'everything pointed to a retreat'. Boppe was astonished to see people from different backgrounds milling about together. Serbian Roma refugees mixed with the Russian sailors who had arrived in Kraljevo as part of the military mission to support Belgrade defences in 1914. Kraljevo changed overnight as the streets became filled with wounded combatants, unarmed soldiers and refugees.[9]

Once the retreat gathered pace, columns of people approached the so-called 'new territories', lands that Serbia had acquired during the Balkan Wars. Here the loyalty of the local population to the Serbian state was

Figure 11.1 Military and civilian wagons in Prokuplje, photograph by Samson Tchernoff.

highly questionable. The consequences of the fighting in 1912–13 were palpable, when fierce clashes took place between the Serbian army and the Ottoman auxiliary troops composed mostly of local Albanians. This violence contributed to growing inter-ethnic tensions. Furthermore, in September and October 1913 large-scale fighting erupted at the Serb-Albanian demarcation line when armed groups from Albania attacked the Serbs, in some cases with the assistance of the local Albanian population. Serbian troops succeeded in re-establishing control by means of harsh repression.[10] It is hardly surprising that two years later fears resurfaced that Serbian authority over Kosovo and Macedonia would again be challenged.

Kosovo

In early November 1915, around 300,000 Serbian soldiers and between 50,000 and 60,000 refugees gathered in Kosovo. This region had huge symbolic significance for Serb national identity, since it was here in 1389 that medieval Serbia crumbled after suffering defeat from the Ottomans on the Kosovo plains. Numerous historical sites known to refugees from folk tales and songs prompted reflection not only about the present crisis but about the entire history of Serbia.[11] Memories of their enduring presence in the Balkans prompted the thought among some Serbs that the present crisis would be overcome. But for others the dramatic collapse of government authority also evoked the moment in 1813 when the Serb revolt against Ottoman rule was crushed. The situation in 1915 seemed even worse and badly eroded the feelings of national pride that had been aroused during the war of 1912.

Golgotha: the Serbian army and civilians

These dramatic events provided rich material for those interested in observing social behaviour. Milenko Simonović, professor of literature wrote in his diary that each day in the life of a refugee guaranteed an abundance of extraordinary impressions across a broad emotional spectrum.[12] A German Slavist scholar, professor Gerhard Gesemann, who retreated along with Serb refugees invoked Gustav Le Bon's work on *Crowd Psychology* to make sense of the scenes he witnessed as people engaged in unusual and 'spontaneous' behaviour under the pressure of the retreat.[13] The director of the Belgrade National Theatre described how refugees lost all inhibition.[14] The Serb soldier Moša Mevorah, attached as a clerk to the Leskovac reserve hospital, described the daily use of corporal punishment on civilian refugees in Priština who were found guilty of petty crimes: 'hearing these men scream because of the pain they suffered was terrible to hear and to watch. And the women looked on. Oh, my God, how one's nerves have been shattered'.[15]

By the end of November, Serbian attempts to link up with the Entente forces had come to naught. The remnants of the Serbian army, now around 220,000 men, were trapped in the south-east of the country together with 80,000 refugees. One group was stationed near the town of Peć, close to the border with Montenegro, while a smaller group gravitated towards the town of Prizren near the Albanian mountains. They faced a stark choice, either to capitulate or to continue the retreat through Montenegro and Albania in the hope of joining the Allies on the Adriatic coast. On 25 November the Serbian High Command issued an order for the army to cross the Montenegrin and Albanian mountain chains, instructing each group to jettison unnecessary vehicles and equipment to facilitate movement across the narrow mountain passes. Although this decision was rapidly reversed with the aim of restoring the army's fighting capacity and in order to mount a counter-offensive, hopes of an offensive faded as reports came in that the Serbian lines had collapsed in the face of a fresh Bulgarian onslaught.

As a result, thousands of trucks, cars, wagons and artillery pieces were dismantled and buried or thrown into the ravines, or else sold to the local population for virtually nothing.[16] The morale of soldiers plummeted, since artillery pieces had acquired a cult status in the army as having been crucial for Serbian victories in 1912 and 1914. Historical and administrative records were also lost: although some documents were buried in the gardens of local trustworthy Serbs, King Peter I Karadjordjević (1844–1921) wrote in his diary that soldiers could only keep themselves warm by throwing precious government documents on to bonfires.[17] The Serb soldier Jelisije Andrić described his arrival in Peć at the end of November: 'we saw Albanians with white hats, barefoot, carrying things bought from the soldiers. They grabbed me in the middle of the road and asked how much I wanted for my cloak and blanket? Did it all have to be like this? Is this how things collapse? I remembered Tolstoy, his genius ... He should have seen this and then he might have written a new *War and Peace*.[18]

The knowledge that the army deliberately deprived itself of its most powerful weapons implied that their return to Serbia would not happen any time soon. For men in uniform who relied upon only limited information from the outside world this was too much to bear. They began to question the authority of the state. There were reports of mass desertion, on the grounds that the oath of loyalty did not extend beyond the state's borders.[19]

The exodus towards the Albanian frontier resumed. Serb military commanders attempted to maintain order, but their priority was the structure of the army rather than civilians. The Serbian High Command repeatedly instructed troops not to pillage Albanian property lest this instigate a revolt by Albanians. Nevertheless, minor skirmishes between Serb troops and armed Albanians erupted at various places, as in the village of Istok.[20] In general, neither the army leadership nor the government issued any guidance to civilians regarding their route or provisions.

Historical examples were invoked to debate the merit of flight or fight, such as a reference to the fact that after crushing the Serbian uprising in 1813, Duke Miloš Obrenović, one of the local rebel leaders, decided to remain behind in order to appease the returning Ottoman authorities and save the Serb population. According to this interpretation, those who fled were simply traitors.[21] But other observers dismissed this argument as Habsburg propaganda. Perhaps refugees made a calculated decision to leave Serbia. Mile Budak, an Austro-Hungarian prisoner of war wondered why refugees fled given that Habsburg or German troops were unlikely (as he put it) to treat civilians badly.[22] Observing the scene in Kosovska Mitrovica, Professor Gezemann wondered why urban residents, mostly civil servants and their families, decide to leave. He too decided that they were afraid of enemy occupation and believed that it was better for civilians to avoid the risk. Most refugees hoped for a change of military fortune, but until this happened they wanted to avoid any contact with the enemy.[23]

Leaving Prizren and Peć and approaching the country's border had a significant psychological impact on refugees. Serbian writer Branislav Nušić wrote that it was one thing to hide from the enemy, but that continuing the journey meant completely severing one's links with Serbia. After quitting Prizren, he wrote, 'no-one could really say where to go, and especially by what means'.[24] Tensions ran high: soldiers complained that they had to protect the rear of the columns where refugees were to be found. One soldier bemoaned the fact that civilians 'will end up in Italy, while the army will be left to rot in Albania'.[25] Those who decided to cross the mountains wanted to set off immediately before snow blocked the passes. When some refugees saw the mountains up close, they hesitated and turned back, colliding with those who resolved to make the journey at all costs. Food was already scarce in the area and rivers were polluted by excrement. The danger of disease grew by the day because no one tried to control the movement of this mass of people. Refugees were mixed together not only with men in uniform but also with prisoners of war. On the mountain passes the prisoners of war were forced to beg for food and to cut meat from dead horses, although others enjoyed better conditions, having been put to work on road repairs.[26]

Retreat via Montenegro

Two thirds of the retreating soldiers and civilians passed through Montenegro on their way to the Albanian coast. The columns crossed over mountains as high as 2000m (Žljeb and Čakor). As the slopes became steeper the exhausted animals began to collapse. One soldier described the scene on Čakor: 'this is the first time I have witnessed anything like this. Terrible! A bit further on, a horse was in agony, he stiffens, and falls down, exhausted ... A wagon passes over his body and he sinks further into the mud ... With a final effort he raises his head and tries to stand up. But it is all in vain. His eyes are terrible to behold!'[27]

Figure 11.2 The Serbian army in Rugova gorge, Peć, photograph by Samson Tchernoff.

The two Kingdoms of Serbia and Montenegro were Allies, but tensions existed among the two ruling dynasties. Montenegrin authorities welcomed the troops and helped organise food distribution for refugees. However, the local population was itself already exhausted by the war. As a teenager Milovan Djilas, one of the future leaders of Tito's partisans, witnessed enfeebled Serbian soldiers knocking at his house to ask for bread. Djilas recalled that his family did almost nothing to help them, although it had some food hidden away. He remembered that the Serbian soldiers 'passed through Montenegro as if through a foreign, wild and heartless country'.[28]

Eventually, about 90,000 people, mostly soldiers, along with women and children, reached Podgorica. Starvation was widespread, because many men had eaten their rations and found nothing to buy. Entire units contemplated desertion after failing to receive rations for days on end. Everyone wanted to get to Albania as soon as possible by getting on boats across Lake Shkodra, the only obstacle on their way to Shkoder (Scutari), just 20km from the Adriatic.

In Albania

The troops and civilians who moved through Albania encountered far more serious problems. The fearsome mountain peaks evoked not only natural beauty, but also brutality and even the end of civilisation. As Rastko Petrović wrote in 1924, 'All social laws were invalid here, you could kill a man and you would never answer for it, you could die and no one would care'.[29] Clashes with local Albanian tribes in the north also became part of the Golgotha narrative. Almost all military and civilian columns passing through Albania participated in skirmishes of varying intensity and suffered casualties accordingly.

Independent Albania was only two years old and since its separation from the Ottoman Empire it was in a state of constant internal fighting. Some Serbian units had been present in Albania since June 1915. They occupied Tirana and Elbasan, partly to stop the incursion of armed groups from Albania into Serbia, but also to get closer to the Albanian coastline, a long desired territorial ambition of Serbia.[30] Moreover, Serbia supported one of the Albanian leaders, Esad Pasha, but his authority did not stretch over the dangerous mountain passes at the northern-most part of Albania, and thus Serb influence in Albania guaranteed only limited support during the retreat.

Several places in Albania occupied an iconic status in Serbian national tradition, such as the Vezir bridge over the White Drin, which was completely covered with ice. Countless men and animals fell into the cold water: Moša Mevorah wrote in his journal that 'Some came out of the water, but some never did'.[31] Members of the Serbian political and military elite used this road because it was the shortest, but also because they wanted to avoid Montenegro for political reasons.

The shortest distance from the frontier to Shkoder was 115km, a journey that took only a few days in fine weather but that now lasted up to a fortnight due to the bitterly cold weather and the length of the refugee columns. Privileged elites fared better because they could rely on horses and on better protection, as well as travelling in relative comfort. Prince Regent Alexander Karadjordjević travelled on horseback followed with a handful of guards. His journey took just two days, and government officials made the trip in four days. These facts appear to have made a positive impression on soldiers because they felt that he shared their suffering.

Prolonged retreat

The first party of Serbian soldiers and refugees who reached the Adriatic were astonished to see that no preparations had apparently been made for their arrival. This was not entirely true. Refugees arriving in San Giovanni di Medua (Shëngjin) could see the wrecks of several ships belonging to the Italian merchant marine that had been sunk by mines before they had been able to unload supplies of food for the Serbians. Apart from the psychological distress this caused, the immediate issue was how to stave off hunger.

The Albanian town of Shkoder became the first meeting point for the exiles and the centre of the rump Serbian state. On 6 December the High Command arrived and resumed its functions, and the government held meetings to deal with the emergency. A special 'cabinet for nutrition' was formed to purchase provisions and distribute food. Military bakeries were also re-established but were unable to meet demand for bread. As before, regular reports surfaced about exhausted soldiers dying on the streets.[32]

By the second half of December 1915 the remnants of the Serbian army, together with refugees, gathered at two points on the coast. Those arriving from Montenegro stopped in Shkoder or nearby. Those who came down from the mountains collected further south, near the towns of Durres (Durazzo) and Kavaja. Some units were also located further north, close to Tirana and Elbasan. No one had a clear idea how many people survived the long march. Gesemann wrote about the grim outlook of those men who trekked over the Albanian mountains compared to the 'Montenegrins' who suffered less.[33]

To the astonishment of the Serbian authorities by the very end of the year around 140,000 soldiers had reached the Adriatic coast, including 89,000 in Shkoder alone. Along the coast Serb officers tried again to set up regimental structures and to assemble soldiers in army camps.[34] Civilians gathered on the shore hoping to be evacuated by the ships. In the meantime, as their diaries indicates, they relied on their family ties and friendship networks.[35]

Serb authorities suspected that the Italian side was not fully committed to saving Serbs, since the two Kingdoms were rivals over Albania, but also in Dalmatia due to the 'Yugoslav programme' of the Serbian government. The Serb envoy in Rome accused the Italian authorities of providing the Entente with false data about the number of refugees at the coast.[36] In order to get a clearer picture the French sent a special mission to Albania. On 22 December they disembarked in Valona. In the same week the French government approved the suggestion by General Joseph Joffre to transport the Serbian army to the island of Corfu, and to evacuate civilians to France or its colonies. One member of the French mission wrote: 'We can say without any exaggeration that the Serbian army is in a state of total disarray. In Shkoder individual soldiers wander the streets, and return to their units only during mealtimes. Order and discipline in a strict military sense no longer exist'.[37]

The groups of tents packed with people now became the hallmarks of the Medua coast. For nearly three weeks, up to 3,000 refugees lived there. Several deaths were reported each day in the makeshift camp. Serbian colonel Milan Nedić distinguished four groups of soldiers and refugees. The first group consisted of ill or wounded soldiers. The second group was made up of soldiers who wished to desert and who profited from the chaos in the embarkation zone. Foreigners made up a special category consisting of diplomats, doctors, nurses, plus a dozen or so Allied soldiers. The civilians were the fourth and most numerous group, many of them from Serbia, but others from Bosnia and Herzegovina, Vojvodina and Montenegro.

At times the crowds of civilians resembled a 'mob' as they overwhelmed the boarding area in Medua and disrupted the unloading of food.[38] British Admiral Ernest Troubridge (1862–1926) tried to introduce a degree of order into the situation in Medua, which he turned into an improvised port. At first, civilians were evacuated by the Italian transport ships once they finished unloading supplies. However, as the government left for Brindisi on 14 January 1916 leaving many people behind in Albania, it appeared that the government had neglected its duties towards Serb citizens. It was not only the civil authorities that lost credibility. One of the consequences of the military collapse in autumn of 1915 and the march through Albania was that the Serbian army and its leadership forfeited the prestige it held since 1912.[39]

Serb diplomat Slavko Grujić was one of the closest collaborators of Nikola Pašić. At the beginning of January 1916 he was sent to Brindisi as the Serbian 'delegate for refugees'. His report to the Serbian Prime Minister offered a vivid account of the difficulties that civilians encountered. On arriving in Brindisi, Grujić met with the commanders of the Italian navy to persuade them to send ships to Medua forthwith. He had only limited success. Grujić worked with the Serbian Relief Fund led by Robert Carr Bosanquet (1871–1935) in order to ensure that the boats were used to capacity. In Brindisi they hastily loaded as much food and clothes as they could from the supplies collected by members of the Serbian Relief Fund. Chaotic scenes ensued when the boat reached Medua on 19 January 1916. A group of 1,300 refugees had travelled on foot to Durres, but around 2,000 still awaited the boats. In Medua, panic set in because Habsburg troops were only 30km away.[40]

Grujić also listed the categories and numbers of refugees, providing valuable details and statistical data for the people who participated in Golgotha. In Medua we learn that there were 90 public servants, among whom was special officer Avram Lević, responsible for the safety of the Serbian treasury. There were 180 parliamentary deputies with family members. Some 600 pupils 15 years of age and over made up a separate category together with their teachers. The British mission comprised 150 men, women and children. Between Lezha and Medua Lević counted an additional 2,000 refugees of various backgrounds. There were 3,620 civilians in total. Grujić was allowed to take 500 on one boat and 700 on another. At first he won over the Italian officers and captains, asking them for as many people as possible to be embarked, neglecting the orders from their superiors in Brindisi. He also used the Serbian policemen who were among the refugees to create order while boarding was taking place. Namely, the refugees avoided going below deck, but the Serbian police forced them to do so in order to make more room for the newcomers. Over 700 men, women and children got into the first boat. Nevertheless, three sailboats packed with 150 civilians in each vessel also wanted to board. Grujić begged and argued with the Italian captain of the large

Citta di Bari, promising him highest Serbian decorations. 'He defended his views, angry at times, he claimed that neither he nor any of his crew has had any sleep during three consecutive nights, that he had his orders, he even raised his fist towards me', noted Grujić. Ultimately, the captain, backed down. 'He raised his hand, and he said that I can load as many as I want to, even if the boat will sink. We embarked an additional 800'. Eventually the two boats brought 2,000 people to Brindisi, including all senior pupils. Even when the refugees managed to get on to the boat the dangers were far from over. Artillery batteries fired several times during the trip when enemy planes flew overhead. On one occasion planes dropped four bombs just next to the *Citta di Bari*, although the ship's noise meant that neither passengers nor the crew were initially aware of the attack. Then panic set in. Lifeboats were prepared but, as Grujić wrote: 'In the first boat, to our disgrace, one Serbian officer jumped in ahead of everyone else'. Italian sailors took him off the lifeboat at the point of their bayonets. The next day close on 700 schoolchildren aged 15 reached Marseille. In total. more than 5,000 Serbian refugees were evacuated from Medua in the second half of January 1916.[41]

By late January Durres had become the focal point for the evacuation, because Habsburg forces were fast approaching Medua. The problem in Durres was that all available vessels were already in use to transport troops to Africa and Corfu. Prisoners of war were also being evacuated from Durres. In the end, the remaining Serbian troops had to march further south towards Valona, the only port in Albania suitable for larger ships to dock and take on thousands of soldiers without delay. Grujić underlined the significance of the aid provided by various philanthropic societies which had assisted Serbia since 1914. The great retreat prompted a huge effort in the UK and the USA, both through donations and by means of diplomatic channels, in order to speed up the rescue operation. Two names were regularly mentioned: Emily Simmonds (1888–1966) and Flora Sandes (1876–1956), who worked as a nurse in Serbia and participated in the retreat when she was following a Serbian regiment as an honorary corporal. The American Red Cross rented boats in order to transport food and supplies to Brindisi. Grujić also drew Pašić's attention to the fact that the number of civilians evacuated from Durres must have been higher than reported, because many were 'smuggled together with the officers and High Command'.[42]

Most Serbian refugees initially disembarked in Italy. Diplomat Slavko Grujić described the arrival of one refugee group to Brindisi. The Italian authorities had not made any preparation for their arrival: 'they did not expect so many people, and simply lost their head' wrote Grujić. Fearing epidemics, the local doctor wanted to inspect every single one of the 1,700 passengers. After an hour the doctor simply abandoned his attempts and allowed them all to disembark. No local officials were present at the site. Rich refugees were permitted to continue their journey wherever they wished, so long as they left Brindisi. Others were sent to the camp originally set up for prisoners of war and found themselves surrounded by barbed wire and armed guards. Richer ones again enjoyed special treatment, being allowed to go into Brindisi and buy food and clothing. Other refugees relied upon the Serbian Relief Fund and the local British Military Mission for deliveries of food. However, the general impression was that refugees were not welcome in Italy, and they were quickly moved on to France.[43]

The state in exile

The island of Corfu was the political and military focal point of Serbia in exile, but Serbian civilians were to be found grouped in North Africa, France and elsewhere in Europe. How the state would continue to function in exile posed a formidable challenge. Soon after it began work, the government in exile attempted to ascertain the whereabouts of its displaced citizens. One aim was to help their recuperation, the other to control their movement and behaviour. Moreover, Serbian authorities sought to include refugees in the war effort. Ultimately, bureaucratic contacts between the government and the citizens became a means of maintaining the state's sovereignty when it had lost control over national territory.

Serbian refugees and soldiers interpreted their displacement as a terrible yet also enlightening experience. Many of them had never travelled further then the neighbouring villages and now found themselves on huge boats heading across the Mediterranean Sea. They set eyes on palm, lemon and orange trees for the first time and noted in their diaries the intriguing folk costumes and customs of the local population they encountered abroad. Furthermore, some of them took the opportunity to expand their business horizons. Serbian entrepreneur Mališa Atanacković was a case in point. After visiting factories in France and Great Britain, Atanacković carefully noted the admirable work practices he hoped to introduce in his own business when he resumed his activities in Serbia.[44]

Italy served mainly as a transit point, but the situation in France was completely different, because refugees could count on substantial help from the government. In March 1915 France had celebrated 'Serbian Day', dedicated to Serb history and culture, and several Franco-Serbian societies were established, including one humanitarian organisation led by the wives of French and Serbian diplomats. One important initiative followed from the decision of the French parliament in November 1915 to approve the admission to French schools of Serb children who lost their fathers in the war. The resumption of their education enabled 4,000 children to enrol in French schools and colleges between 1916 and 1918 under the guidance of a Franco-Serbian committee of university professors.[45]

In the UK too, existing philanthropic and humanitarian societies welcomed Serbian refugees. Under the auspices of the Serbian Relief Fund, headed by Sir Arthur Evans and Robert William Seton-Watson, some 450 children attended various schools all over the UK. Some 25 children attended George Heriot's School Edinburgh, and a further 100 were divided between Oxford and Cambridge. As in France, English-language courses were given priority.[46]

However, the decision of the Serbian government to allow the youth to enrol in schools and universities came only after a bitter debate between the Minister of Education and Minister of War. From the latter's perspective, Serbia had been almost completely deprived of new recruits, who were needed as junior officers, and he got his way when some students were sent to the Salonika front. However, Minister of Education Ljuba Davidović insisted that the future demand of the Serbian state for the educated people should have the priority over the immediate needs of the front. Davidović's argument carried the day, having resonated very strongly, bearing in mind that numerous Serbian students had been killed or wounded in the first months of the war. In order to appease the army a special student battalion was formed in the Alpine village of Jausiers, but it was mostly for training purposes and few of the students ended up in Salonika.[47]

Other refugees too were carefully scrutinised in relation to their suitability for military duties. Several thousand refugees managed to get to Corfu together with the evacuated troops. Civilians were forbidden to stay on the island (it was declared a military zone) and were quickly shipped to various refugee colonies, but only after completing a medical inspection and answering questions about their personal status, in order to detect people who had evaded their military duty under the pretext of being unfit.[48]

Golgotha: the Serbian army and civilians

Figure 11.3 Serbian pupils in London, Saint Sava's Day 1918, photograph by Samson Tchernoff.

In France, refugees were scattered around the country. Richer refugees did not depend on help from the French or Serbian government. Many well-off families chose to move to London. Others could only get by with the help of charitable organisations and by finding low-paid jobs in order to support their families. Women often worked in French laundry shops or in textile production facilities, and many men worked on local farms. The workforce from the Serbian Military Technical Factory retreated to Corfu from where, at the request of the French government, they were sent to France in order to replace French workers who had been mobilised. Other workers were also in great demand.[49] A group of 29 young men and boys worked in a mine in Algeria where they were relatively well paid. When conditions deteriorated they looked for work elsewhere, but the French administration prevented them from leaving strategically important employment.[50]

Many refugees opposed being sent to Africa in the first place, but their complaints fell on deaf ears. Dozens of small Serbian colonies grew up in North Africa. In addition to civilians, around 60,000 Serbian soldiers stayed to convalesce in Algeria and Tunisia. Negative views of Africa changed once refugees approached the shores; they found a warm welcome from the local population led by the commander of the French army in Tunisia,

Admiral Émile Guépratte. Thanks to his interest in the fate of the refugees, the admiral was nicknamed 'the mother of the Serbs'. One of the central streets in Belgrade still bears his name. Serbian invalids, whether military or civilian, found training opportunities in local workshops where they mastered various crafts and managed to boost their income.[51]

As soon as the large refugee groups arrived in France it became obvious that the members of the Serbian diplomatic network could not manage to assist everyone. Consequently, the Serbian government decided that all work relating to refugees should be centralised in the Ministry of the Interior. Moreover, in order to co-ordinate the activities among the numerous colonies and the Corfu government, a special government commissar was appointed in Paris together with four subordinates, all refugees, one in Ajaccio, another in Algeria, and the others in Marseille and Nice. Each refugee colony communicated directly with the commissars. The Serbian Ministry of the Interior issued refugees with papers and also intervened to solve disputes between refugees.[52] On numerous occasions the appointed commissars and other officials complained about the deviant behaviour of the refugees, which included fights, harsh comments at the expense of the Corfu government, and even visits to the Austro-Hungarian consulates in order to provide intelligence information. The commissars often complained that they lacked any means of coercion, because the incidents took place on foreign soil. Cases of problematic behaviour were also reported among the students who at times neglected their university obligations or embraced socialist ideas. They were threatened with being sent to the Jausiers military camp.[53] The government attempted to keep its citizens informed about the war and its efforts to counter the propaganda of the Central Powers, but although more than 5,000 Serbian citizens lived in Greece, most of them refused to report to consular officials lest they be conscripted. A special Serbian refugee camp was organised in Salonika, run by the representatives of the Serbian government. Several Serbian schools were also organised in various Greek towns. However, the majority of refugees decided to live on their own in Salonika where they found jobs and accommodation.[54]

If their arrival in remote places presented an adventure, albeit a dangerous one, the disembarkation in Corsica, Marseille or Tunisia marked an immense cultural shock for the refugees. Cultural interaction sometimes revealed a degree of mutual ignorance. One Serb recalled how the local Corsicans asked the refugees if they were Christians.[55] British volunteer nurses at Corsica had trouble learning the Serbian language.[56] But proof of the good reception given to Serbs in Corsica was to be found in the local newspaper where one section was left to the refugees so that they could publish text in Serbian and in Cyrillic script.[57] As mentioned earlier, many refugees gained an education as well as various skills. This manifested itself in various ways: for example, Serbian pupils from George Heriot's School became pioneers of rugby in the new Kingdom of Serbs, Croats and Slovenes after 1919.[58]

The presence of Serbian refugees in the Entente countries had political implications. Serbia's uncompromising and prolonged resistance was endlessly praised in the media as a moral and courageous act. Photographic exhibitions informed the Allied public about events in Serbia and the great retreat. The photographer Samson Tchernoff, who followed the Serbian army across Albania, was sent to London by Nikola Pašić to arrange an exhibition of his war photographs under the title 'The Serbs in December 1915'. Russian Grand Duke Mikhail Romanov opened the exhibition at the Royal Institution on 5 June 1916, with Pašić himself in attendance. The exhibition transferred to New York in March 1918. Another photographer, Rista Marjanović, exhibited his photos of the retreat at the Inter-Allied Exhibition of War Photographs held at the Louvre in 1916.[59]

The 'Kosovo Day' campaign held in the UK in June 1916 presented a striking illustration of pro-Serb sentiment. The initiative came from members of the Serbian Relief Fund and those who worked with the numerous medical missions hitherto active in Serbia, notably Dr Elsie Inglis from the Scottish Women's Hospitals. Typical of the publicity given to this campaign was Bernard Partridge's poster of 'Heroic Serbia', which first appeared in *Punch* magazine. On 28 June, St. Vitus Day, 22 MPs tabled a motion in the House of Commons expressing Britain's gratitude for 'Serbia's heroism and long-lasting resistance'.[60]

For its part, the Serbian intellectual elite used every opportunity to promote its Yugoslav programme. At this time the great powers were still doubtful about the South Slav project, so any opportunity to influence public opinion in the Entente countries and explain the motivation behind the unification project was not to be missed. Numerous lectures and various publications made the case. Serb intellectuals linked the history of Serbia to that of its Allies in order to suggest that the wartime alliance was a 'natural' consequence of deep-seated relations.[61]

Danilo Šarenac

Figure 11.4 Kosovo Day poster by Bernard Partridge.

Conclusion

In 1921 King Alexander I Karadjordjević established the Albanian Commemorative Medal, which was to be awarded to all military personnel who participated in the retreat. Its main political purpose was to acknowledge their loyalty to the fatherland at a critical moment. This medal remains to this day a cherished family object in many Serbian families. Undoubtedly, Golgotha has been seen as one of the most significant events in Serbian national history. It enabled the Serbian army to regroup in Salonika and ultimately to contribute to the country's liberation, thereby realising the South Slav reunification.

Due to its powerful symbolism, 'Golgotha' reappeared in subsequent periods of national history, especially at times of crisis. In the late 1930s, for example, its memory was regularly invoked. In 1938 a 'Society of the Albanian Commemorative Medal' was founded by veterans who were disappointed at how successive governments had failed to preserve memory of the 'days of Golgotha'. The society provided an opportunity for Serb veterans to demonstrate that even great perils could be surmounted; in their view, Golgotha testified to the inherent strength and endurance of the Serbian national character.

However, interpretations of Golgotha diverged from the outset. Two military investigations were established during the war in order to determine who was responsible for the failure to deliver food to Serbian recruits during retreat. After the war the National Assembly launched a fresh investigation, but it too was inconclusive. The official master narrative was rather a discrete one signalling that any deeper study of the retreat might lead to unpleasant questions about military unpreparedness in early 1915: better, it seemed, to avoid addressing the fact that although the army achieved its main strategic objective the entire state structure came very close to collapse.

For many participants of Golgotha the first association of the retreat was not the notion of loyalty, but the numerous ugly scenes they witnessed along the way. Moreover, although estimates of the number of victims varied considerably, no-one could doubt the enormous price paid in human lives.[62] Some leaders saw the retreat as a unique example of national suffering that they hoped would never be repeated. General Dragoljub Mihailović, leader of the royalist resistance movement in Yugoslavia during the Second World War spoke to a British officer in 1942 about Golgotha. Mihailović described how he continued to be haunted by the suffering of the young Serbian recruits. He used this argument to justify his passive behaviour in the Second World War, which was designed to avoid mass German reprisals.[63]

It is more difficult to say how ordinary people made sense of the great Golgotha. Perhaps the numerous incidents involving Serbian refugees in France had something to do with the crisis of authority that resulted from the traumatic events. For their part, veterans often revealed a general ambivalence towards the national cause. Certainly they expressed a great sense of fatigue brought about by seven years of almost constant fighting between 1912 and 1918 in which Golgotha played a crucial role. One undoubtedly positive consequence was that many Serbs spent a lot of time abroad learning new skills. The new Serbian elite had been educated in France and warm relations with this country and all other host-countries remained one of the features of the Yugoslav interwar politics. As Nikola Pašić put it as the war ended, 'This contact with other people and their traditions must have a long term impact on the character of the new Serbia, one that will be born out of the rubble of the old Serbia. It will triumph over the chaos provoked by the seven years of fighting.'[64]

Notes

1 Rastko Petrović, *Dan Šesti* [The Sixth Day] (Belgrade: Nolit, 1961), pp. 60–4.
2 Petar Pešić, *Solunski front: vojno-politička akcija* [Salonika Front: Military-Political Action] (Belgrade: S.B. Cvijanović, 1921), p. 1; Jovan Hadži-Vasiljević, *Kroz Albaniju 1915 godine s Moravskom divizijom II poziva* [Through Albania in 1915 with the Moravska Division of the Second Levy] (Belgrade: Sveti Sava, 1929), p. 7.
3 The signs of this process were already visible in December of 1914 when the Serbian National Assembly passed a special law to assist those 'who were made misfortunate by the war'. *Zakon o pomoći nevoljnima u ratu i Pravilnik za izvršenje ovog zakona* [Law for Assisting the Misfortunate Ones in Times of War and Guidelines for its Application] (Niš: Državna Štamparija Kraljevine Srbije, 1915).
4 Milan M. Stojadinović, *Ni rat ni pakt: Jugoslavija između dva rata* [Yugoslavia Between the Two Wars] (Buenos Aires: El Economista, 1963), pp. 84–5.
5 Francesca M. Wilson, *In the Margins of Chaos: Recollections of the Relief Work in and Between Three Wars* (London: John Murray, 1944), p. 24.
6 Rudolf Archibald Reiss, *Comment les Austro-Hongrois ont fait la Guerre en Serbie: Observation direct d'un neutre* (Paris: A. Colin, 1915).
7 *Zapisnici sednica Ministarskog saveta Srbije: 1915–1918* [Proceedings of the Serbian Cabinet: 1915–18], eds Dragoslav Janković and Bogumil Hrabak (Belgrade: Serbian Archive, 1976), p. 224.

8 Alice and Claude Askew, *Opustošena zemlja: Srbija kako smo je mi videli* (Novi Sad: Platoneum, 2012), p. 118, originally published as *The Stricken Land: Serbia as We Saw It* (London: Eveleigh Nash, 1916). The Askews were also special correspondents for the *Daily Express*. They dedicated their work to 'the memory of the soldiers who perished in Serbia during the Great Retreat'.
9 Auguste Boppe, *Sa srpskom vladom od Niša do Krfa* [With the Serbian Government from Niš to Corfu] (Geneva: Ujedinjenje, 1918), pp. 12, 17.
10 'Bez milosti' [No mercy], *Politika*, 12 September 1913, p. 1; Igor Despot, *The Balkan Wars in the Eyes of the Warring Parties: Perceptions and Interpretations* (Bloomington: iUniverse, 2012), pp. 164–5.
11 Milan Nedić, *Srpska vojska na Albanskoj Golgoti* [The Serbian Army at the Albanian Golgotha] (Belgrade: Mninistarstvo Vojske i Mornarice, 1937), p. 1.
12 Milenko Simonović, *Tragedija srpskog naroda: dnevnik jednog dobrovoljca* [The Tragedy of the Serbian People: Journal of a Volunteer] (Novi Sad: Dnevnik, 2010), p. 29.
13 Gerhard Gesemann, *Sa srpskom vojskom kroz Albaniju 1915–16* [With the Serbian Army through Albania in 1915–16] (Belgrade: SKZ, 1984), p. 54.
14 Gesemann, *Sa srpskom*, p. 36.
15 Danilo Šarenac, 'Dnevnik sa puta evakuacije od 23. Octobra 1916 činovnika Moše Mevoraha' [Journal of the evacaution route taken by Moša Mevorah, beginning on 23 October 1916], *Zbornik Jevrejskog istorijskog muzeja*, 10, Belgrade, 2015, p. 127.
16 *Veliki rat Srbije*, pp. 75–89.
17 Petar I Karadjordjević, *Ratni dnevnik 1915–16* [War Diary 1915–16], ed. Dragoljub R. Živojinović (Topola: Zadužbina kralja Petra I, 1984), p. 167.
18 Jelisije Andrić, 'Pesnik na bojištu' [Poet on the battlefield], in *Kad su vojske prolazile* [When the Armies were Moving], ed. Dušan Paunić (Smederevska Palanka: Biblioteka 'Milutin Srećković', 2014), pp. 109–10.
19 Mileta M. Prodanović, *Ratni dnevnik 1914–18* [War Diary 1914–18] (Gornji Milanovac: Dečje novine, 1994), pp. 110–11.
20 *Veliki rat Srbije za oslobodjenje Srbije i ujedinjenje Srba, Hrvata i Slovenaca* [Serbia's Great War for Liberation and Unification of the Serbs, Croats and Slovenes], vol. 13 (Belgrade: Glavni djeneralštab, 1927), p. 19.
21 Panta M. Draškić, *Moji memoari* [My Memoirs], ed. Dušan Bataković (Belgrade: SKZ, 1990), p. 95.
22 Mile Budak, 'Ratno roblje' [War Slavery] in *Pripovijetke: Ratno roblje* [Short Stories: War Slavery], ed. Dubravko Jelčić (Zagreb: Matica Hrvatska, 1995), p. 219.
23 Gesemann, *Sa srpskom*, p. 54.
24 Branislav Nusić, *Devetstopetnaesta: Tragedija jednog naroda* [1915: Tragedy of a People] (Belgrade: Utopija, 2010), p. 295.

25 Gesemann, *Sa srpskom*, p. 72.
26 Petrović, *Dan Šesti*, p. 121.
27 Andrić, 'Pesnik na bojištu', p. 110.
28 Milovan Djilas, *Besudna zemlja* [Land without Justice] (Belgrade: Narodna knjiga, 2005), p. 75.
29 Milan Dedinac, 'Pogovor' [Afterword], in Petrović, *Dan Šesti*, p. 620.
30 Andrej Mitrović, *Serbia's Great War, 1914–1918* (London: Hurst, 2007), pp. 189–94.
31 Šarenac, 'Dnevnik sa puta evakuacije', p. 131.
32 Nedić, *Srpska vojska*, p. 156.
33 Gesemann, *Sa srpskom*, p. 147.
34 Nedić, *Srpska vojska*, p. 163.
35 Dragoslav V. Nenadić, 'Ispred neprijatelja' [In front of the enemy], in Milorad V. Petrović (ed.) *Trnovit put Srbije: 1914–1918* [The Thorny Road of Serbia: 1914–1918] (Belgrade: Bigz, 1974), pp. 67–73.
36 Nedić, *Srpska vojska*, p. 156.
37 Nedić, *Srpska vojska*, p. 175.
38 Nedić, *Srpska vojska*, pp. 195–6, 232.
39 David MacKenzie, *Apis: The Congenial Conspirator: the Life of Colonel Dragutin T. Dimitrijevic* (New York: East European Monographs, 1989).
40 Archives of Serbia, Ministarstvo inostranih dela, PO/492, pp. 3–7, Slavko Grujić, 'Report of the delegate for refugees in Brindisi, 15–28 January 1916'.
41 Grujić, 'Report'.
42 Grujić, 'Report'.
43 Grujić, 'Report'.
44 Mališa Atanacković, *Dnevnik 1915–1919* [Diary 1915–19], ed. Ilija Misailović (Užice: Historical Archive Užice, 2006). Atanacković was even permitted to visit the Western Front.
45 Stanislav Sretenović, *Francuska i Kraljevina Srba, Hrvata i Slovenaca, 1918–29* [France and the Kingdom of Serbs, Croats and Slovenes] (Belgrade: ISI, 2008), p. 79.
46 Dušica Bojić, *Srpske izbeglice u Prvom svetskom ratu 1914–21* [Serbian Refugees During the First World War, 1914–21] (Belgrade: Zavod za udžbenike 2007), pp. 448–9.
47 Bojić, *Srpske izbeglice*, pp. 230–1.
48 Bojić, *Srpske izbeglice*, pp. 154–5.
49 Bojić, *Srpske izbeglice*, pp. 155, 243.
50 Bojić, *Srpske izbeglice*, pp. 407–8.
51 Bojić, *Srpske izbeglice*, p. 401.
52 Bojić, *Srpske izbeglice*, pp. 166–7.
53 Bojić, *Srpske izbeglice*, p. 230.
54 Bojić, *Srpske izbeglice*, pp. 167–71, 180–90.

55 Bojić, *Srpske izbeglice*, p. 373.
56 Wilson, *In the Margins of Chaos*, p. 21.
57 'Srpska Kronika' [Serbian Chronicle], *Le Colombo*, 12 March 1916, p. 2.
58 Dejan Zec, Filip Baljkas and Miloš Paunović, *Sport Remembers: Serbian-British Sporting Contacts During the First World War* (Belgrade: Centre for Sport Heritage South East Europe, 2015), p. 176.
59 Vladimir Tomić, 'Belgrade in the Great War 1914–15: photographs', in Danilo Šarenac and Vladimir Tomić, *A City Surprised: Belgrade in the Great War 1914–15* (Belgrade: Muzej grada Beograda, 2015), pp. 25–9.
60 Ubavka Ostojić-Fejić, 'Obeležavanje Kosovskog dana u Velikoj Britaniji tokom Prvog svetskog rata' [Kosovo Day ceremonies in the UK during the First World War], *Istorija XX veka*, vol. 2 (1994), 19–23.
61 Sretenović, *Francuska i Kraljevina Srba*, pp. 80–1.
62 The estimates vary between 200,000, as officially claimed in the Serbian memorandum presented to the Peace Conference, and 20,000, according to general Milan Nedić.
63 Kosta Nikolić, *Istorija Ravnogorskog pokreta* [History of the Ravna Gora Movement], vol. 3 (Belgrade, 1999), pp. 303–4.
64 Zec et al., *Sport Remembers*, p. 172.

12

The refugee question in Bulgaria before, during and after the First World War

Nikolai Vukov

Introduction

Bulgaria stands out as a specific case in relation to population displacement during the First World War for several reasons. The migration of ethnic Bulgarians to Bulgarian territory took place on a very large scale prior to the First World War, reflecting the consequences of popular uprisings at the turn of the century, and especially the impact of the Balkan Wars in 1912–13, the second of which ended with a catastrophic defeat for Bulgaria and a mass exodus of Bulgarians from territories ceded to its neighbours (see Map 12.1). Bulgaria consequently had to cope with refugees from Eastern Thrace, Macedonia, Dobrudja and Asia Minor against the backdrop of a renewed military effort and mobilisation. The country's involvement in the First World War was driven primarily by the wish to reclaim these lost territories and achieve 'national' unification. Following its defeat and the disastrous conditions imposed by the Treaty of Neuilly in 1919, Bulgaria faced further dismemberment that triggered fresh population displacement during the 1920s.[1]

This chapter focuses on the circumstances of displacement, the reception and settlement of refugees, and the state's attempts to address the political, economic and social shock of accepting thousands of refugees from the lost territories. It outlines the centrality of the refugee issue to the development of the modern Bulgarian state, particularly after the Balkan Wars when it occupied a central role both internally and externally.[2] The chapter focuses on three main episodes: before 1912, when a quarter of a million refugees had already fled to Bulgaria, whose population was around 4.5 million in 1912; between 1913 and 1918, when 120,000 refugees settled in the country; and in the years 1919–25 during

Map 12.1 Bulgaria and its neighbours during the First World War.

which time Bulgaria witnessed the influx of an additional 180,000 refugees (the country's total population stood at 5.5 million in 1925).[3] Some consideration is given to prevailing social and economic conditions, such as the impact of refugees on urban and rural life in Bulgaria, and to the role of refugee relief organisations. Attention is also devoted to the international repercussions of the refugee crisis.

Bulgarian refugees before and after the First World War

In 1878, when the Treaty of Berlin was signed, ethnic Bulgarians were mainly to be found in one of three polities: the Principality of Bulgaria, the autonomous province of Eastern Roumelia, and in territories remaining under Ottoman rule.[4] The news that Macedonia and Thrace would be handed back to the Ottoman Empire led thousands of Bulgarians to flee these territories for the newly liberated Bulgarian Principality. The first significant wave of refugees from Macedonia reached Bulgaria after the suppression of the Kresna-Razlog uprising against the Ottomans in 1878–79. Thousands of refugees settled in the south-western part of the Principality. Hungry and destitute, they petitioned the western powers to help liberate their native lands from Ottoman rule. Within a year, their number had reached 40,000.[5]

This next massive influx of 30,000 Bulgarian refugees followed the defeat of the Gorna Djumaya uprising in 1902 and the brutal Ottoman suppression of the Ilinden uprising in Macedonia and Thrace in 1903. Although some people took advantage of an amnesty and returned to their towns and villages in 1904, most refugees stayed in Bulgaria around the Black Sea coast and the Danube River, in Burgas, Varna and Russe.[6] In any case, the Sultan issued an order in September 1904 stating 'as it is not in the interest of the Ottoman Empire to increase the Bulgarian population in Odrin [Edirne] area, we should not allow the Bulgarian refugees to return'.[7] Using the pretext of 'disarmament' and 'demilitarisation', the Ottoman authorities settled Muslims in their place, many of whom were themselves refugees from Bulgaria, having fled during or after the Russo-Turkish war of 1877–78 before settling in Thrace, often in newly created Turkish villages.[8]

Between the liberation of Bulgaria from Ottoman rule in 1878 and the First Balkan War in 1912, more than 200,000 Bulgarians from Macedonia and Thrace migrated to Bulgaria. Some estimates put the figure at 250,000.[9] Usually these refugees and other immigrants settled in compact groups in the sparsely populated parts of the country where they received farmhouses, land and livestock. The influx of refugees was manageable from an administrative and social point of view, and it stimulated a degree of national sentiment and compassion among the host population of Bulgaria.

The First Balkan War in 1912 opened a new chapter, triggering substantial migration in Macedonia and Thrace and causing significant ethnic changes. Some of these came about as a result of the destruction of Turkish villages by the combined Bulgarian, Greek and Serbian armies.[10] The end of the war and the London Peace Treaty (17 May 1913) created the conditions for resettlement across the newly defined borders, but territorial disputes between the former Allies and the Second Balkan War in June 1913 resulted in new military campaigns, loss of life and mass displacement. The situation was particularly dramatic in Bulgaria, now at war with its neighbours. In July 1913 Ottoman forces intervened and wreaked revenge, destroying Bulgarian villages, as reported in detail by the Carnegie commission of enquiry.[11] According to the prominent Bulgarian scholar L. Miletich, in 1913 and 1914 around one-third of the Christian Bulgarian population in Thrace were killed, and the remainder fled to Bulgaria.[12] A similar situation prevailed in northern and western Macedonia.[13]

During the Second Balkan War refugees again began to enter the country in large numbers, particularly after the treaties of Bucharest and Tsarigrad (Constantinople) in 1913, which ceded territories with a substantial Bulgarian population to Bulgaria's neighbours. In the summer and autumn of 1913, Bulgaria was faced with a mass influx of refugees from Thrace and Macedonia, from southern Dobrudja (seized by Romania), and from Asia Minor. According to incomplete lists prepared by the authorities, they numbered upwards of 140,000 people.[14] This was the situation confronting Bulgaria when it joined the Central Powers in September 1915 – struggling to cope with refugees, territorially crippled, and economically exhausted, but keen to seek revenge for the humiliation inflicted on it. Military action in Macedonia after 1915 and in Dobrudja in 1916 impoverished the population in these territories and created uncertainty. Many people there looked for greater security by moving far away from the front line.[15]

In total, according to a report issued in 1925 by the Bulgarian Red Cross, between 1912 and the end of the First World War at least 200,000 refugees came to the country.[16] It is difficult, however, to estimate the exact number of the refugees in Bulgaria because of the constant inflow and the scale of internal displacement. Given that around 250,000 refugees arrived before the Balkan Wars, the Bulgarian delegation to the Paris peace conference maintained that there were half a million refugees in Bulgaria as of summer 1919, namely 300,000 from Macedonia, 160,000 from Thrace and 40,000 from Dobrudja.[17] These figures may have been exaggerated but the overall number of refugees to Bulgaria is unlikely to have been below 350,000.[18]

One substantive difference between the situation before and after 1912 is that economic conditions had deteriorated in the interim. Insufficient arable land made life difficult for refugees, and the under-developed industrial base offered few opportunities for employment. The support provided by the state during the First World War was limited and largely symbolic.[19] Refugees frequently had to find accommodation themselves in badly damaged houses or in barns. The state prioritised other national tasks and lacked the means to support refugees, who pinned their hopes on being able to return to their homes after Bulgaria's victory in the war. But these hopes evaporated with Bulgaria's defeat and with the additional loss of territory in the aftermath of the First World War.

The Paris Conference and the Neuilly Treaty (27 November 1919) not only put an end to Bulgaria's attempts at national unification, but also deepened the political, economic and social problems in the country. Customarily termed by Bulgarian historians as the 'second national catastrophe' (after that following the Second Balkan War), Neuilly ceded territories with a substantial Bulgarian population to neighbouring states and imposed harsh reparations. The influx of refugees from territories beyond Bulgaria's border posed a heavy burden. As a leading reporter observed:

> The arrival of Bulgarian refugees, expelled from neighbouring countries, as a result of the First World War, continues incessantly in a long chain that adds to the difficult situation created by several hundred thousand miserable folk who escaped from Romania, Serbia, and chiefly from Thrace and Macedonia, and who found shelter in what for them was a foreign part of the fatherland, as a consequence of the events in 1903 and 1913.[20]

When the First World War came to an end, more than one million Bulgarians remained in the territories of neighbouring states. Many of them, threatened by violence and the prospect of forcible assimilation, left their native lands in Macedonia, Thrace, Dobrudja and the western borderlands and, together with the retreating Bulgarian army and administrative authorities, sought refuge and protection in Bulgaria. At least 200,000 came from Macedonia (now under the sovereignty of Greece and Serbia) and Thrace (under Ottoman and Greek rule).[21] More than 20,000 refugees fled from Romanian-administered Dobrudja. In 1919 Serbia which, in accordance with the Neuilly Treaty, occupied parts of western Bulgaria forced at least 10,000 refugees to flee to Bulgaria.[22] Many more came from Serbian-administered Strumitsa.[23] The situation was further complicated by the fact that Turkey expelled 30,000 Bulgarians from Asia Minor, giving an overall total of 260,000 refugees in the immediate post-war years.[24]

Parallel to the signing of the Neuilly Treaty, at the insistence of the Greek government the Bulgarian delegation was offered a Convention for the mutual and 'voluntary' exchange of population between Greece and Bulgaria, according to which the two states would allow ethnic, religious and linguistic minorities to migrate freely to the respective territories and to acquire the nationality of the country in which they settled.[25] After the defeat of the Greek army in Asia Minor in the autumn 1922, the government in Athens forgot about the 'voluntary' aspects of this Convention and forcibly expelled Bulgarians from Western Thrace. As a result, 22,208 families (100,653 people in all) settled in Bulgaria.[26] In contrast, only about 10,000 Greeks took advantage of the agreement before 1924, whilst 32,000 remained in Bulgaria.[27] The Convention thus led to a significant decrease of the Bulgarian population in Aegean Macedonia and Western Thrace.[28]

Regardless of the large number of its own refugees, the Bulgarian state also made considerable efforts to provide Armenian and Russian refugees with accommodation, subsistence, and schools for children.[29] It should be noted that for both these groups Bulgaria sometimes turned out to be a temporary destination: after the Balkan Wars many Bulgarians migrated to the USA, Canada and Australia.[30]

Whilst the constant inflow of refugees increased Bulgaria's population (reaching, according to some calculations, 14 per cent of the actual population)[31] economically and socially it posed a serious challenge to a state that was exhausted by wars, humiliated by international arrangements, and traumatised by the failure of its 'national' ideal. The arriving refugees had to be provided with accommodation, work and means of survival, but despite the efforts of governments and state institutions, the Bulgarian state did not have the necessary material and financial means to satisfy these needs. Reparations and military operations drained its resources. Refugees added to the large number of unemployed workers. Most refugees were peasants who were given land that belonged to large landowners and municipalities, and this created tensions between refugees and poor farmers who expected to be given priority.[32]

After the Second Balkan War the refugee issue was a major problem for Bulgarian society, and was the focus of attention for civil servants, political parties, mass organisations, economists and financial specialists. Refugees themselves established various organisations to defend their interests and participate in political life. Jobless, lacking property, and suffering exploitation, they became in the 1920s a fruitful ground for propaganda by the Bulgarian Communist Party.[33]

In terms of foreign affairs, the refugee issue played a central role in the external policy of the state, particularly relations with its Balkan neighbours. It was one of the key factors that guided Bulgaria's involvement in the First World War on the side of the Central Powers. It played a central role in all the international negotiations of the state during the interwar period. The demand to allow the refugees to return to their native places and to guarantee them there the rights of free human existence, by strictly observing the clauses of the post-war treaties for protection of the national minorities, was voiced explicitly by the Bulgarian government at the Genoa conference in April–May 1922 and kept on resonating during the state's participation at the Lausanne conference (1922–23), at the Council of the League of Nations, and at world congresses for international peace during the interwar period. Bulgaria aimed to improve the condition of Bulgarian minorities in the neighbouring countries and thus to reduce the influx of refugees. Most of these demands were, however, rejected by the victorious states in the war and particularly by Bulgaria's neighbours, who vehemently opposed any change to the status quo.

Statistical calculations of the size of the refugee population were bedevilled by the incessant influx and by a lack of technical expertise. In practice refugees managed to evade registration and observation, particularly when checkpoints were overwhelmed. Refugees often failed to make a declaration on entry or entered the country illegally via routes that were less accessible to officials.[34] Others lived with their relatives and reported to the authorities only in extremis. Deaths were under-reported.[35] Record keeping was not much better during and after the First World War.[36]

In the summer of 1915, on the order of the Ministry of the Interior and Public Health, the central commission for the refugees, established a year earlier to deal with refugee issues, compiled detailed statistics of Bulgarians who had been expelled after the Second Balkan War. The commission found that 25,766 families (120,690 people) had arrived in Bulgaria from Vardar and Aegean Macedonia, from Eastern Thrace, Dobrudja and Asia Minor. To this number the commission added at least 50,000 individual families and refugees, who lived with their relatives or chose to work by themselves in the major cities, and who did not figure in the official record. Nor of course did the overall number take into account people who were killed on their way to Bulgaria or the many thousands who died of exhaustion and sickness shortly after their arrival. The official figures likewise took no account of refugees who came to Western Thrace temporarily in 1913 before returning to their destroyed villages; their number was put at around 10,000 people.[37]

Many of the uncertainties around the actual numbers deepened further during the First World War. In reports issued by international organisations the number of refugees in Bulgaria was variously put at between 200,000 and 600,000.[38] One factor influencing the numbers game was the government's wish to highlight the scale of the refugee crisis and to emphasise the economic and social burdens that it had to face. The most thorough calculations were made at the end of 1924 after a law was passed on agricultural employment, and in May 1926 when a representative of the League of Nations completed his inquiry and concluded that 175,192 people (nearly 40,000 families) came to Bulgaria between 1912 and 1920. Bearing in mind, however, that many refugees fled without their families, that many widows with their children did not consider themselves as a family, and considering also the numerous unregistered refugees, this data too gave a misleading picture.[39]

The insecure and unsystematic data about the refugees was used by Bulgaria's neighbours to dismiss the validity of its claims, and influenced the decision of the League of Nations to provide minimal help to the refugees. Anti-Bulgarian propaganda used discrepancies in the statistics to claim that the Bulgarian government artificially inflated the number of refugees in order to secure a reduction of reparations and an international loan that would be used for other purposes.[40] Although there is some truth in these accusations, nevertheless the refugee crisis was certainly acute. Other dubious comments came from Greek officials who complained that refugees fled with plenty of cash. In fact most refugees were agricultural workers or hired labourers in farms, who had fled with few assets.[41]

Accommodation and resettlement on the eve of and during the First World War

As already remarked, the Balkan Wars of 1912–13 opened an entirely new page in the history of forced resettlements in the region. Whilst persecution and violent displacement of ethnic and religious groups was well known during the Ottoman period and was a customary feature of Ottoman rule, the extension of military action and the mutual extermination of different national communities were largely unseen until this time. In what would later be seen by some historians as a prototype to cases of ethnic cleansing during the twentieth century, the Balkan Wars led to considerable loss of life and to the forced resettlement of population groups.[42] The Balkan Wars and the decade of political rearrangements that followed highlighted the figure of the refugee as an object of persecution by military troops and administrative authorities and the symbol of territorial contestation, whose life had been disrupted and who was expected to resettle, often with little assistance.

The pattern of constant resettlement in the course of several years is nicely illustrated in an account about Bulgarians from a village in Thrace:

> In 1912 [...] political events compelled people from Pishmankyoy to leave their homes and seek shelter in two neighbouring villages – Boztepe and Tyurkmen that had been left by its previous inhabitants. Some people returned. Several months later they were forced to leave again, some of them being taken to Asia Minor. In Istanbul, a Russian diplomat intervened and they were sent to Bulgaria. For a short period, they were accommodated in Varna where they gathered with others from Pishmankyoy before deciding to return to their native village. The two groups left first for Gyumyurdjina [in Western Thrace]. In the Greek town of Maronya they stayed for two or three years. During the First World War Maronya was bombed by the British-US fleet and the people of Pishmankyoy left, resettling in the village of Subashkyoy, Dimotika area [Western Thrace]. Here their stay was short. They returned again to Bulgaria and settled in Stara Zagora, Harmanli region where they met with other refugees who advised them to settle in villages in Burgas. However, malaria compelled them to head for Pomorie, but they did not get along with the local population. In the location of 'Sokata', they, together with refugees from the villages of Enidjiya and Kavakliya, Lozengrad region [Eastern Thrace], founded the future village of Sarafovo, which numbered 144 houses until 1929 – 108 of them of people from Pishmankyoy, 30 of people from Enidjiya, and 6 of people from Kavakliya.[43]

This kind of odyssey was not unusual. The circumstances varied, but displacement was traumatising given the terror inflicted by Ottoman authorities in Eastern Thrace, persecution by Greek, Serbian and Romanian authorities in Western Thrace, Macedonia, western borderlands and Southern Dobrudja, the expropriation of property, as well as pressure to declare that exile was 'voluntary'. Leaving one's place of birth was the main choice open to them to avoid oppression, to preserve a sense of cultural identity, and – in many cases – to survive. The attempt to escape persecution was traumatic in itself:

> In school there were numerous refugees. We gathered together and went to Pazardjik [in central Bulgaria] where we stayed in a large room for three

months along with many other families. Then we learnt that the border would be opened and we moved to Nevrokop [south-western Bulgaria], to be closer to the border and to go back to our village, regardless of the fact that everything had been burnt down.[44]

Bulgarian refugees nurtured hopes of returning to their place of birth. For refugees from Eastern Thrace, such hopes grew with the Tsarigrad (Constantinople) Treaty of 1913, which stated that Bulgarians could keep their moveable and immoveable property in Thrace, and that those who fled during the Second Balkan War would be allowed to return within two years. A separate clause in the treaty stipulated an exchange of populations from villages along the border, but the Odrin agreement of 2/15 November 1913 stated that Bulgarians from Odrin and Lozengrad could not return. Not only were the refugees denied the possibility of returning to their homes, but even those Bulgarians who still lived in Thrace and Asia Minor were pressed to leave and to hand over their homes to Muslim refugees.[45] Ultimately the Ankara agreement of 1925 between Bulgaria and Turkey confirmed that refugees' property would remain with the Turkish state.[46]

A similar drama was played out in Western Thrace which passed successively from Ottoman to Greek rule, then to Bulgaria, subsequently to the Allies and finally to Greece. During the Second Balkan War many of the Bulgarian villages and neighbourhoods were destroyed and many Bulgarian families took over empty Greek and Turkish houses. When the Greek troops returned, many of the Greek families followed in their wake. The Turkish population also fled. As a newly incorporated part of Bulgaria in 1913 Western Thrace gathered Bulgarians returning from Western Thrace and those from Eastern Thrace, Dobrudja and Aegean Macedonia, and even Christians from Albania.[47] The situation changed drastically in 1919 when, fearing persecutions, the Bulgarian population fled despite the attempts of the French military to prevent this movement. (At this point in time the French promoted the idea of an autonomous Thrace. But with the ceding of Western Thrace to Greece in 1920 this idea came to an end.) In the years that followed, Bulgarians fled this region en masse, their homes being assigned to Greek refugees from Asia Minor.[48]

Several other points of comparison can be made between the pre-1912 refugees and those entering Bulgaria in 1913–19. Most of the refugees from Macedonia and Thrace before the Balkan Wars were not deprived of their rights and could either sell their properties or find a temporary occupant who could use the land until they returned. They were accommodated more easily as a compact group in places that they usually chose themselves and adjusted relatively quickly to the new living conditions. At this stage the possibilities still existed of acquiring land, livestock and houses that had been deserted or sold by Turks, although the state gave only modest financial credit to support those refugees most in need. In the first few weeks after their arrival refugees were also supported by churches, schools and charities. By contrast, the refugees who arrived after 1913 found accommodation and social support in short supply. There was not enough land; municipal pasture diminished, and this affected local people too. Most refugees did not have the means to purchase land and houses. They wandered from village to village.[49]

The specificity of the refugee waves during and after the Balkan Wars helps explain the difficulty of Bulgarian state institutions and society at large to respond to the refugee crisis. Both the Second Balkan War and its disastrous conclusion were largely unexpected. It took months for state institutions to organise themselves and to provide at least some support to refugees. The enormous influx at the end of the Second Balkan War was spontaneous and chaotic. Totally unprepared for such a situation, Bulgaria had to find ways to assist refugees who had travelled long distances, mostly on foot and under constant threat. They reached their destination hungry and exhausted, but government institutions were unable to provide proper help. Most of the immediate aid for the refugees came from people in the border regions and from charities that collected money through theatre performances and other campaigns. More substantial support was provided by the Bulgarian Red Cross, which gave thousands of blankets in the winter of 1913–14. The government appealed to the Bulgarian public to donate money.[50] Despite the wide resonance of these initiatives, the resources that were gathered could not alleviate the misery suffered by the refugees.

The accommodation provided to refugees reflected the need to help them survive the approaching winter before – it was hoped – they could return to their homes. During the Second Balkan War, the acceptance and sheltering of the refugees depended on the point at which they crossed the Bulgarian border. Refugees from Eastern and Western Thrace were accepted in the south, those from Macedonia in the south-west. The most numerous refugee groups were settled in Burgas region, where they numbered around 7,000 families, some 42,000 people in all. Those from Western Thrace (the main part of them around 2,330 families with more than 10,000 people), were accommodated temporarily mostly in Haskovo.[51] With the end of the war, when Western Thrace remained under Bulgarian rule and when refugees continued to arrive from Macedonia and Eastern Thrace (joined also by those from Southern Dobrudja), the Bulgarian authorities decided to settle them in the newly acquired territory in Western Thrace, Pirin Macedonia, and Malko Tarnovo. This was prompted by the belief that they could stay there temporarily until a better solution was found, and on the assumption that they would strengthen the Bulgarian ethnic component in this area.

In early spring 1914, the government undertook the reorganisation of the refugee commissions, destroying most of the previous ones. In the beginning of March it established a central commission with the task of taking care of the accommodation for the refugees in the newly gained territories and in the spring of 1914 'Temporary guidelines for the accommodation of refugees' was developed. This document clearly stated the plan to accommodate the refugees in the newly liberated territories, using for this purpose the lands deserted by Turks and Greeks, as well as properties without owners that previously belonged to the Ottoman state, to religious or waqf institutions. The local authorities explained to the refugees that 'nobody would be accommodated in the old territories of Bulgaria', whilst the accommodation in the so-called new lands was expected to provide shelter and to give refugees a chance to support themselves. The temporary guidelines stipulated that local commissions would house refugees in villages and towns similar to their native economic and climate conditions.[52] In addition to these measures, an emigration bureau was created by the Ministry of the Interior and Public Health and a special law was accepted in July 1914 to exempt from taxes the livestock, goods and household tools of the newly arrived refugees from Dobrudja and Eastern Thrace. The ministry used two additional external loans in 1914 to support the refugees from Macedonia and Thrace.

These measures did not do much to help. In fact, the refugees were either left to their own devices or obliged to rely on the generosity of local people. Financial help from the state was minimal, and available only at high rates of interest, and was targeted largely at the most impoverished refugees. Most refugees found themselves in a desperate plight. There was no unified office to direct the refugees to areas where their prospects might be better.[53] The situation was particularly complicated in Western Thrace, which was expected to accept refugees at this time, most of whom originated from disparate regions and who had travelled great distances. These people had lived in different climates, under different cultural and political conditions, and had different visions of their future. The refugees from Asia Minor came expecting to settle in Bulgaria permanently; they waited impatiently to receive land and get to work. Those coming from Eastern Thrace nurtured the hope of a revision of the border between Bulgaria and Turkey and expected to return to their villages when these passed to Bulgarian jurisdiction. People from Dobrudja who were settled in Western Thrace did not accept that they would live in a foreign land and hoped that Dobrudja would be returned to Bulgaria and that they would be able to go back to their native villages. Lastly, many of the people from Macedonia had participated actively in the fight for national liberation under the leadership of the Internal Macedonian Revolutionary Organisation – they were eager to continue the struggle and considered their stay in Western Thrace to be a temporary solution. In the end, the authorities had to change their plans and started settling refugees in the territory that Bulgaria had before the Balkan Wars.[54]

The mass, quick and poorly organised sending of the refugees to Western Thrace in 1914 created a critical situation for thousands of already tormented people. As the leading historian of these dramatic events Stayko Trifonov remarks, the entrance door for all refugees determined for settlement in Western Thrace was Dedeagatch (Alexandroupolis). During the winter, spring and summer of 1914, thousands of refugees arrived in this port from Aegean Macedonia. In the spring of 1914 some 6,000 people also came from Asia Minor. The Greeks who left this area after the Balkan Wars took with them all their moveable goods, in contrast to refugees from Macedonia, who were expelled by Greek authorities to Bulgaria without being allowed to take even clothes and blankets. The sheltering of refugees was hasty and chaotic – in barracks, schools and private homes, in houses deserted by Muslims and Greeks, and often in the fields. They lacked land, farm tools or draft animals, and threw themselves on the charity of local people, supplemented by the modest support provided by the state.[55]

Many of the worst fears of hunger were confirmed soon after the refugees' arrival. A notorious example was the newly founded village of Klimentovo in Western Thrace, which had 247 refugee families from Asia Minor. For a long period after their arrival, they had to live without any shelter, in the open, until they could build some wooden barracks. Due to hunger and diseases, many of the refugees had already died by the summer of 1914; the rest scattered throughout the area, in desperate attempts to survive. On 29 September, the village police inspector reported to Prime Minister Radoslavov: 'We found a terrible situation in the newly established village of Klimentovo. This is no longer a village, but a cemetery … There were around 250 families from Asia Minor.

Most of the families went to the neighbouring villages to seek food and subsistence, so now there remain 20 families, and these people will probably die by spring as they do not have any bread, water or wood'. A year later it was stated that 'there is no longer anyone left alive in the village, only 167 graves'.[56] Many similar letters were sent to government officials from refugees themselves, such as this one that found its way to the Prime Minister's desk:

> Our situation is desperate, because the means for subsistence are scarce, and the support that the state gives us is minimal. It is even worse for those of us who have no shelter and who are forced to spend these hard days in the open field. We lack shelter, blankets and food. Due to the deprivation, hunger and cold, we face imminent death. People are dying every day, and the land is covered by their graves.[57]

At the beginning of 1915 the situation of the refugees in Western Thrace (as well as all over the country) worsened seriously. To the hunger, cold and despair, was added the exploitation by more affluent people on farms, where some of the refugee men were hired.[58] The tensions in the area intensified further when the authorities allowed many rich Greeks to return – they went back to the occupied houses and demanded the money for the rents from the refugees who were sheltered in them.[59] The appeals of receiving land and financial support, or of being permitted to settle somewhere else in Bulgaria where there could be a better standard of life, were growing: 'We are really like arrested people – 520 refugee families wrote in their petition – because we are not given a chance to work the land and we have stayed in this town for months, without being able to go into the field'.[60]

The situation was much the same in other parts of the country. Since 1913, refugees had poured into Bulgaria in large numbers. Officials found it extremely challenging to co-ordinate relief efforts. Refugees moved from one village to another, sometimes getting separated from their relatives. Because of the unusually difficult conditions, it was impossible to distribute the refugees systematically, or to undertake a rational colonisation of them. Those from an urban background were settled in cities, and villagers likewise sent to the countryside, although a good many refugees from villages were compelled to move to the city. Thus many peasant farmers became propertyless day labourers, something that was to have profound implications for Bulgaria's social and political development during the interwar period.[61] The allocation of certain groups to different parts of the country was often accompanied with tensions among the local population – although many of the locals tried to help, they were themselves in need, and the arrival of these large groups of hungry people threatened their own survival. Particularly acute were the tensions in some villages along the Black Sea coast. Near Pomorie, for example, refugees fashioned modest shelters from reeds during the night, whereupon municipal officials promptly destroyed them in daylight on the grounds that refugees had no legal right of settlement. Officials aimed to keep the land free for local farmers to graze their cattle. Fights erupted between refugees and farmers until the police intervened and steps were taken to establish a new village for the refugees nearby.[62]

In terms of geographical distribution within Bulgarian territory prior to the Balkan Wars, refugees were settled in the valleys near the Danube and Maritsa rivers, as well as along the Black Sea coast. Most were accommodated in Burgas in south-east Bulgaria. The special place this region occupied in the history of the refugee question was determined by several factors: it was the largest and most sparsely populated place with a relative abundance of land. The other coastal region to the north, in Varna, was also a regular destination for refugees from the late nineteenth century, and it continued to play a central role in the settlement of refugees after the Balkan Wars. In the cities, the major concentration of refugees was in the capital Sofia, followed by Varna and Burgas. In practice, refugees settled in large numbers in all major Bulgarian towns. The migrants from Macedonia were scattered in cities and villages throughout the country; the Thracians were found mostly in southern Bulgaria and in the vicinity of Varna. Refugees from Dobrudja were settled mostly in Varna, Russe and Sofia. Already by this period, many towns in Bulgaria had developed separate refugee neighbourhoods, named after the territories of origin – Macedonian, Thracian, Dobrudjan. These neighbourhoods continued to grow as new groups of refugees arrived after the war.

Aside from specific legislative and administrative measures, after the Balkan Wars the state hardly addressed the refugee issue at all, the assumption being that refugees would probably soon go back to their native places. In fact, some of them tried to do so during the reoccupation of some of the lost territories by the Bulgarian army in 1915–18, but most of the refugees chose to wait until the end of the war. Usually explained by the state's lack of economic and financial capacities after the Balkan Wars, this relative neglect intensified when Bulgaria entered the First World War and when the government could no longer deal with the refugee issue. The government took decisions in favour of refugees only in very extreme cases. Thus, for example, on 26 February 1916, the

The refugee question in Bulgaria

National Assembly passed a law for providing financial support only to those refugees of the 1912 and 1913 wars who were adolescents, orphans and widows without work, or were very elderly or invalids. Among the newly arrived refugees, only those who were still without work could receive support. The one-off subsidies did not change the situation for most refugees; in sum, the war consumed enormous financial resources that could otherwise have been used for social purposes.[63]

The First World War shook the foundations of agricultural production in Bulgaria and hence sharpened the issue of malnutrition and physical survival. The national economy was deprived of almost 685,000 able-bodied peasants and this affected agricultural production for several years. Economic activity became the preserve of elderly men, women and children. Agricultural output fell, but food was regularly requisitioned.[64] The war also brought land redistribution to a standstill. The refugee question formed an important aspect of the agrarian problem in Bulgaria, in so far as refugees needed land. Whereas in 1913–14 this issue was largely overshadowed by the need to provide refugees with basic accommodation and first aid, by 1915 land distribution had become critically important, since only the provision of arable land could help guarantee their survival. Some initial steps were taken to assign land to refugees but this was done only on a local basis rather than as part of a systematic policy. Later on during the war the Ministries of Agriculture and Internal Affairs and Public Health developed a plan to accommodate some refugees on abandoned or uncultivated lands. But in the main the government anticipated that the end of the war would lead to a redrawing of international borders, enabling refugees to return to their place of origin or to be resettled permanently as part of an organised programme of internal colonisation. A project along these lines was submitted to the National Assembly. A project along these lines was submitted to the National Assembly, but the loss of territory after the war meant that it was never implemented.[65] Territorial losses and the forfeit of fertile land (particularly in Dobrudja and Thrace) led to an increase in population density. The agrarian crisis in the country deepened with the end of the war and the new refugee influx after 1918.

The refugee question in the aftermath of the First World War

Bulgaria's exit from the First World War, the Salonika agreement of 1918, and the Neuilly Treaty raised the stakes in relation to the refugee problem. Refugees fled in great numbers following the retreat of the Bulgarian army in Macedonia and Thrace, and the flow continued thereafter. The gloomy scenes of displaced people crowding at the Bulgarian borders surpassed even the drama of the Balkan Wars. The Bulgarian Red Cross Society and international observers described the resulting desperation:

> Even in this severe weather – November – endless lines of old people, of women and children, stiff from cold and dampness, silenced by their great sorrow for their lost homes, move with bowed heads toward unknown lands.[66]
>
> The streams of wretched refugees at stations and check-points, in open carts, frozen to death women and children, helpless young women, and corpses of old people who had not managed to survive the leaving of their native places.[67]
>
> I registered the deep misery of these poor people, many of whom, often expelled brutally and by force from their houses and with no possibility of taking their animals or agricultural tools so necessary to their agricultural work, which nourishes many Bulgarian refugees.[68]
>
> When we saw the miserable condition of the refugees in Bulgaria, we thought that we are in one of the circles of Dante's hell. This is a real European scandal, which cannot be tolerated any longer.[69]

In order to cope with the crisis, the Bulgarian government created central and regional committees whose job it was to house, feed and clothe the refugees. Three reception stations were opened on the Greek border, at Svilengrad in the Maritsa river valley (for refugees from Western Thrace), at Makasa in the Rhodope Mountains (for those coming from Aegean Macedonia) and at St. Vrach in the valley of the Struma River (for those coming from Vardar Macedonia and the western borderlands).[70] Refugees presented themselves at checkpoints, where they were registered by the police, examined by a doctor and offered the services of the Bulgarian Red Cross.[71] Most refugees were then directed to Burgas, Sofia, Petrich and Varna. The procedures were lengthy and complicated, and many refugees lost patience and made their own arrangement for onward travel and resettlement.[72] Observers wrote:

> At the end of 1924, at the most important checkpoint of Svilengrad, even basic provision for refugees was lacking [...] no shelter from rain and snow, two or three hundred families, many without the necessary clothing ... The refugees stayed there in the open for weeks and even months until they received an order of accommodation and settlement. They stayed without food and hungry for a long time, until the opening of a food distribution office by the Red Cross.[73]

The accommodation of new refugees after the First World War followed a familiar pattern, namely relocating them on abandoned or poor land or in neighbourhoods of the larger cities, and providing only minimal support. The situation was further complicated by hunger and epidemic disease. Tuberculosis was prevalent in Haskovo, malaria raged in Burgas, Varna, Plovdiv and Vidin in 1921. Two in three refugees in Burgas fell victim to hunger and malaria, which was widespread in the swampy terrain.[74] Infant mortality increased at a startling rate: around one-quarter of babies born in 1920 died before reaching their first birthday. Many women gave birth to babies while they were on the road, and the Svilengrad Red Cross opened a special facility. As Kramer reported, 'you cannot but feel horrified at the awful suffering and privation to which these innocent beings are exposed'.[75] Families were split apart and this added to stress and trauma. Many orphans did not survive.

The lack of food was a major scourge. Many refugees depended on local charity or on what they could scavenge. Kramer reported 'I saw them dragging themselves with difficulty and eating soft and indigestible dough made of corn, the only food they managed to produce'.[76] Many refugees died of hunger, children being again the primary victims.

In the early 1920s, international organisations and donors took initiatives to provide financial, medical and logistical support to alleviate this tragedy. The chief agency was the Bulgarian Red Cross, but various overseas charities also offered food, clothes and money to the refugees such as Near East Relief, the British Balkan Committee, Save the Children Fund, the British diplomatic mission in Solun, and the French College. By 1925, the Red Cross had cared for 1,300 orphans in extreme need.[77] Special nursing missions arrived from Germany, Belgium, Hungary, Italy and Sweden. Particularly useful were the social canteens that were opened at checkpoints and in the towns with a heavy concentration of refugees, such as Petrich and Nevrokop (Hungarian missions), Stanimaka (a German mission), Haskovo (a Belgian mission) Harmanli (a French mission) and elsewhere. Quakers managed canteens in villages in Topolovgrad. In the mid-1920s donations for Bulgarian refugees came from Spain, the USA, Finland, Lithuania, Norway, Sweden and even as far afield as Ecuador and Venezuela.[78]

The Bulgarian countryside underwent a significant change. New villages were created and old ones expanded. Sofia was surrounded by a wide belt of refugee settlements, although many refugees lived in railway wagons or barracks. The population of Plovdiv doubled after the war to 100,000 inhabitants. Burgas, Varna and Russe also grew rapidly.[79]

Mass immigration strengthened existing refugee organisations and led to the appearance of new ones. Organisations of Thracian and

Macedonian refugees emerged in the late nineteenth century and expanded after the Balkan Wars when new branches were established in most towns. After the First World War new organisations came into being at the behest of refugees from the western borderlands. These included female and youth groups. In many towns several such organisations existed: in Vidin, for example, the Macedonian emigration alone boasted four such organisations: Macedonian brotherhood society 'Gotse Delchev', the 'Ilinden' association, female immigrant association, and the youth association 'Gotse Delchev'.[80] These associations actively directed attention inside and beyond Bulgaria to the plight of refugees. Stimulated by the Bulgarian authorities, they maintained a range of political activities – organising public meetings, issuing protest declarations to international institutions and to the National Assembly, preparing petitions for the refugees' right of return to their ancestral lands, sending appeals for revising the peace treaties or at least recognising their minority rights. Resolutions and requests for support were sent to the League of Nations and to other international organisations by emigrant organisations of the Bulgarian diaspora in western Europe and North America. However, most of these attempts came to nothing.

Internally, the major problem of providing land for refugees continued to be of central importance. The post-war government of Alexander Stamboliiski promulgated an agrarian reform. One piece of legislation provided for an increase in state lands, another for the accommodation and welfare of refugees. A special land fund entitled refugees to receive between 50 and 120 hectares as well as timber. They were also entitled to travel free of charge to their new homes.[81] Some refugees received a credit that enabled them to construct small houses. The policy of the government was to reclaim swamps and wasteland, converting them to productive agricultural use. Despite various weaknesses – a lack of co-ordination, high interest charges, opportunities for abuse by non-refugees – between the end of 1920 and early 1923 the Stamboliiski government succeeded in rehousing more than 23,000 refugee families.[82]

The refugee issue and its various political, economic and social dimensions continued to resonate in Bulgarian society between the two world wars. Internationally it helped determine Bulgaria's relations with its neighbours and with other European states, and influenced the state's involvement during the Second World War, particularly in relation to Bulgarian administration of occupied territory in Greece and Yugoslavia and the attempts to resettle Bulgarian refugees from Macedonia and Western Thrace. Internal politics were profoundly affected by refugees and their associations, which maintained a presence in the political life of the country. Those on the right kept alive revanchist claims, while leftists demanded the abolition of the existing social order. Economically, the accommodation and welfare of the refugees necessitated heavy government expenditure. Successive Bulgarian governments were preoccupied by the refugee question for two decades. Despite numerous efforts to alleviate their condition many economic and social issues remained unresolved. Trauma, and the bitterness that resulted from being wrenched from one's native land, remained part of the collective memory of refugees and they persist among their descendants even today. They resonate in family stories and are evoked in the activities of various refugee organisations in Bulgaria nowadays, particularly the annual meetings and commemorative rituals that direct attention to traumatic events in the past.[83] Despite the passing of time, the 'refugee experience' continues to inform cultural identity. One may recall in this respect the statement of the prominent intellectual and socialist D. Hadjidimov in 1924:

> No settlement or accommodation, no alms can warm the refugees' hearts. The real complete and final solution of the refugee issue will happen when there are no longer refugees, when all or most of them can return freely to their homeland [...] and get rid once and for all time of their refugee status.[84]

Reflecting the prevailing hopes in post-war Bulgarian society, these remarks are also an illustration of the 'refugee world' beyond the specific context of the First World War.

Conclusion

Three major conclusions may now be drawn. The first is that despite being fairly remote from military developments in the rest of Europe, Bulgaria became an arena of intense population displacement. The disastrous consequences showed up in the movements of people in different directions across the peninsula, and in their resettlement. Taken together these movements represented the most significant demographic episode in the Balkans during the First World War. As this mass civilian displacement was taking place aside from the war fronts in Macedonia and Dobrudja, and in many respects completely unrelated to it, the experience of Bulgarian refugees during 1914–18 seemed like a parallel world, which did not immediately invite comparisons with the rest of Europe.

However, it provides an alternative picture to what the rest of the continent experienced in terms of human displacement.

The second conclusion is related to the extended chronological frame. Although the First World War is certainly associated with mass human displacement in a relatively short time span, the war itself was only one part of the story and by no means the most significant; on the contrary, the drama of displacement occurred as a result of the Balkan Wars and then as a consequence of the Treaty of Neuilly. The refugees who crossed the Bulgarian border after 1919 were a distant echo and a continuation of the waves of refugees who arrived in Bulgaria from the later nineteenth century and after the territorial rearrangements during the Balkan Wars. In this context, the First World War was a subsidiary event.

Lastly, the Bulgarian example not only reveals the failure of international efforts to prevent the flow of refugees, but also underlines the fact that displacement was also a direct consequence of decisions taken by the great powers. This geopolitical dimension was reflected at the Berlin Congress in 1878 and in the subsequent lack of international response to the numerous uprisings in the Ottoman Empire. It was further revealed in 1913 and 1919, when those responsible for the political remapping of the peninsula remained oblivious to the waves of refugees that this would create and were ignorant about their economic and social survival. In the post-war period, the anti-Bulgarian front of its Balkan neighbours and the support they received from France and Great Britain intensified the flow of refugees and produced a crisis of catastrophic dimensions. The League of Nations was also unable to fulfil its role as a guarantor of the rights of the Bulgarian minority in neighbouring states or to compensate refugees for the property they left behind. So far as refugees were concerned, we might conclude: 'once a refugee, always a refugee'.

Notes

1. Key works in English include R.J. Crampton, *Bulgaria, 1878–1918* (New York: East European Monographs, 1983); R.C. Hall, *The Balkan Wars 1912–1913: Prelude to the First World War* (London: Routledge, 2000).
2. See particularly G.V. Dimitrov, *Nastanyavane i ozemlyavane na balgarskite bezhantsi, 1919–1939* (Blagoevgrad: Pechatna baza na VPI, 1985); G.V. Dimitrov, *Maltsinstveno-bezhanskiyat vapros v balgaro-gratskite otnoshenia, 1919–1939* (Blagoevgrad; SU Kliment Okhridski, 1982); T. Kosatev, 'Politikata na pravitelstvoto na Balgarskia zemedelski naroden sayuz po bezhanskia vapros, 1919–1923', *Izvestiya na instituta po istoria*, 26 (1983),

44–79; *Selskostopansko nastanyavane na bezhantsite, 1927–1932* (Sofia, 1932); V. Vasileva, *Migratsionni dvizhenia na balgarite 1878–1941*, vol. 1 (Sofia: Universitetsko izdatelstvo Sv. Kliment Okhridski', 1993).
3 Figures from Dimitrov, *Nastanyavane*, p. 63.
4 All these had belonged to Bulgaria under the terms of the San Stefano peace treaty, signed in March 1878 at the end of the Russo-Turkish War
5 G.V. Dimitrov, *Balgarskata komunisticheska partia i bezhanskiyat vapros, 1920–1929* (Blagoevgrad; VPI, 1986), p. 11; G. Georgiev, *Bezhantsite vav Varnensko, 1878–1908* (VMRO, 1998), p. 5; Dimitrov, *Nastanyavane*, p. 13.
6 Georgiev, *Bejantsite*, p. 6; Dimitrov, *Nastanyavane*, p. 14.
7 A.S. Razboynikov and S.A. Razboynikov, *Naselenieto na Yuzhna Trakia s ogled narodnostnite otnosheniya v 1830, 1878, 1912 i 1920 godina* (Sofia, 1999), p. 227.
8 Dimitrov, *Nastanyavane*, p. 14; Dimitrov, *Balgarskata komunisticheska partia*, p. 13. Razboynikov and Razboynikov, *Naselenieto*, p. 216.
9 *Les Réfugiés et les conditions du travail en Bulgarie* (Geneva: Bureau international du travail, 1926), p. iv; *The Refugee Question in Bulgaria* (Sofia: The Bulgarian Red Cross Society, Executive Committee for Refugee Relief, 1925), pp. 14–15.
10 Razboynikov and Razboynikov, *Naselenieto*, p. 231.
11 *Carnegie Endowment for International Peace. Report of the International Commission to Inquire into the Causes and Conduct of the Balkan Wars* (Washington: Press of Byron S. Adams, 1914), pp. 123–35.
12 Staiko Trifonov, *Trakia. Administrativna uredba: politicheski i stopanki jivot, 1912–1915* (Sofia: Trakiiska fondatsiia Kapitan Petko voïvod, 1992), p. 163.
13 Dimitrov, *Balgarskata komunisticheska partia*, p. 13.
14 Trifonov, *Trakia*, p. 182; *Les Réfugiés*, p. iv.
15 Dimitrov, *Balgarskata komunisticheska partia*, p. 14.
16 *The Refugee Question in Bulgaria*, p. 15.
17 Dimitrov, *Balgarskata komunisticheska partia*, p. 15.
18 Dimitrov, *Nastanyavane*, p. 23.
19 Dimitrov, *Balgarskata komunisticheska partia*, p. 15.
20 L. Kramer, *Dneshnoto polojenie na balgarskite bejantsi* (Sofia, 1925), p. 1.
21 *The Refugee Question*, p. 25; Aleksandur Grebenarov, *Legalni i tayni organisatsii na makedonskite bejantsi v Balgaria, 1918–1947* (Sofia: Makedonski nauchen institut, 2006), p. 9.
22 *The Refugee Question in Bulgaria*, p. 15.
23 B. Keremidchiev, *Bolka, narechena Makedoni: Spomeni ot bezhanstvoto nyakoga v Gorna Djumaya. Zhivi razkazi* (Blagoevgrad: Strimon Pres, 2004), pp. 78–9.
24 In *Les Réfugiés*, p. iv, the overall number between 1918 and 1925 (not including the refugees from Asia Minor) is put at 180,000 people. Kramer calculated at least 250,000 refugees between 1921 and 1925. Kramer, *Dneshnoto polojenie*.

25 *Les Réfugiés*, p. 5.
26 Dimitrov, *Balgarskata komunisticheska partia*, p. 18.
27 *The Refugee Question in Bulgaria*, p. 16.
28 Dimitrov, *Balgarskata komunisticheska partia*, p. 17; Theodora Dragostinova, 'Navigating nationality in the emigration of minorities between Bulgaria and Greece, 1919-1941', *East European Politics and Societies*, 23, no. 2 (2009), 185-212; Stephen Ladas, *The Exchanges of Minorities: Bulgaria, Greece and Turkey* (New York: Macmillan, 1932).
29 *The Refugee Question in Bulgaria*, p. 15.
30 *The Refugee Question in Bulgaria*, p. 17.
31 *Les Réfugiés*, p. 6.
32 Dimitrov, *Nastanyavane*, p. 6.
33 Dimitrov, *Balgarskata komunisticheska partia*, p. 32.
34 Grebenarov, *Legalni i tayni organisatsii*, p. 8.
35 Georgiev, *Bejantsite*, p. 7.
36 N. Yakimov, *Bezhanskiat vapros v Balgaria: natsionalen komitet na makedonskite blagotvoritelni bratstva* (Sofia, 1925), p. 3-4.
37 Trifonov, *Trakia*, p. 212.
38 Yakimov, *Bezhanskiat vapros*, p. 5.
39 Kosatev, 'Politikata', pp. 52-3.
40 Yakimov, *Bezhanskiat vapros*, p. 5.
41 Yakimov, *Bezhanskiat vapros*, p. 9.
42 P. Mojzes, *Balkan Genocides: Holocaust and Ethnic Cleansing in the Twentieth Century* (New York: Rowman & Littlefield, 2011).
43 V. Sekiranova, 'Preselenieto' ili prehodat kym nova kulturna sreda – stereotip i adaptatsia', in Todor Mishev, *Istoriya na Sarafovo, 1913-1922* (Sofia: KorektA, 2007), p. 312.
44 Memoir of Atanas Todorov Vasilev, born 1904, in the village of Maglen, Syar region (Aegean Macedonia), in S. Paskova (ed.), *Po sledite na belia vyatar: Spomeni na egeyskite bezhantsi ot Dramska, Syarska i Zilyahovska okolia* (Blagoevgrad; Irin-Pirin, 2008), p. 85.
45 Dimitrov, *Balgarskata komunisticheska partia*, p. 16.
46 Razboynikov and Razboynikov, *Naselenieto*, p. 236.
47 Razboynikov and Razboynikov, *Naselenieto*, p. 237.
48 Razboynikov and Razboynikov, *Naselenieto*, p. 239.
49 Dimitrov, *Nastanyavane*, pp. 14-16.
50 Trifonov, *Trakia*, pp. 212, 215.
51 Trifonov, *Trakia*, pp. 182-3.
52 Trifonov, *Trakia*, pp. 191-2; Dimitrov, *Nastanyavane*, p. 19.
53 Dimitrov, *Nastanyavane*, p. 20.
54 Trifonov, *Trakia*, pp. 207-8.
55 Trifonov, *Trakia*, pp. 188, 199, 211.
56 Trifonov, *Trakia*, p. 206.

57 Trifonov, *Trakia*, p. 184.
58 Trifonov, *Trakia*, p. 210.
59 Trifonov, *Trakia*, p. 211.
60 Dimitrov, *Nastanyavane*, p. 18.
61 *The Refugee Question in Bulgaria*, p. 19.
62 G.M. Kazakov, 'Kratka istoriya na selo Pishmankyoy, Malgarsko do 1913 g.', in Mishev, *Istoriya*, pp. 346–413.
63 Dimitrov, *Nastanyavane*, p. 21.
64 *Selskostopansko nastanyavane*, pp. 17–18.
65 Dimitrov, *Nastanyavane*, p. 21; Dimitrov, *Balgarskata komunisticheska partia*, p. 15.
66 *The Refugee Question in Bulgaria*, p. 11.
67 *Selskostopansko nastanyavane*, p. 35.
68 Kramer, *Dneshnoto polojenie*, p. 3.
69 Kramer, *Dneshnoto polojenie*, pp. 1–2.
70 *The Refugee Question in Bulgaria*, p. 18.
71 *Les Réfugiés*, p. 7.
72 Yakimov, *Bezhanskiat vapros*, p. 16.
73 Yakimov, *Bezhanskiat vapros*, p. 14.
74 Kramer, *Dneshnoto polojenie*, p. 6; T. Kosatev, 'Nastanyavaneto na bezhantsite v Burgaski okrag (1919–1932)', *Istoricheski pregled*, no. 2 (1975), 57–69.
75 *The Refugee Question in Bulgaria*, p. 24.
76 Kramer, *Dneshnoto polojenie*, p. 5.
77 *The Refugee Question in Bulgaria*, p. 25.
78 *Selskostopansko nastanyavane*, pp. 32, 35.
79 *The Refugee Question in Bulgaria*, p. 19.
80 G. Valchev, *Iz istoriyata na grad Vidin: Makedonskite balgari vav Vidin* (Vidin: Izdanie na organizatsiyata na VMRO v grad Vidin, 2003), p. 18.
81 Kosatev, 'Politikata', p. 55.
82 Dimitrov, *Nastanyavane*, p. 60.
83 N. Vukov, 'Resettlement waves, historical memory and identity construction: the case of Thracian refugees in Bulgaria', in H. Vermeulen, M. Baldwin-Edwards and R. van Boeschoten (eds), *Migration in the Southern Balkans: From Ottoman Territory to Globalized Nation States* (Cham: Springer, 2015), 63–84.
84 D. Hadjidimov, *Bezhanskia vapros v Narodnoto sabranie: Rech, proiznesena na 3 yuli 1924* (Sofia, 1924), p. 10.

13

From imperial dreams to the refugee problem: population movements during Greece's 'decade of war', 1912–22

Emilia Salvanou

Introduction

The twentieth century came to be known as the century of the refugee, with the Great War marking the beginning of decades of forced human mobility.[1] Nevertheless, especially as far as the Balkans are concerned, population mobility had started much earlier. By the nineteenth century, with the prospect of a diffusing discourse of nationalism and an Ottoman Empire that was challenged by multi-leveled crisis, national movements had emerged across the Balkan region. Tensions and antagonisms culminated dramatically at the beginning of the twentieth century. The forces that later on belonged to two opposing sides of the Great War clashed openly for the first time and through this clash crystallised the shape of their national communities.

During the Balkan Wars and the Great War that followed, hundreds of thousands of Muslims left the Balkans, mainly for Anatolia, while a similar fate befell the hitherto cohabiting Christian populations of the region who moved in the opposite direction. Futhermore, through the nationalisation process of the late nineteenth and especially the early twentieth century, the undivided Christian community of the Balkans split into antagonistic ethnic groups. Such was the case with Greeks, Serbs and Bulgarians, especially after the Balkan Wars. After the end of the long period of war, the Greek and the Ottoman world had been drastically transformed by ethnic cleansing and population exchange. In place of the Ottoman Balkan territories, five new nation states had emerged: Greece, Bulgaria, Serbia, Albania and Turkey. The flourishing Greek communities in Russia were all deserted after the October Revolution and the civil war. In addition, according to the Lausanne Treaty, Greeks were forced to leave the Ottoman Empire with few exceptions and Muslims who had lived in the Balkans for centuries were required to follow the opposite route, towards Anatolia.[2] The dream of the 'Great Greece', of reconstituting the Byzantine Empire that was close to being realised with the Treaty of Sèvres, collapsed violently and traumatically, giving way to a comparatively small state, which since then struggled to balance the tension between the quest of modernisation and the memories of a glorious fate that never materialised.[3]

National narratives are usually formed *a posteriori*, so as to make the present meaningful, through an interpretation of the past that is aligned to the national identity – and vice versa. In this process, the dynamics and ambiguities of the past are often silenced or smoothed over.[4] The war decade, 1912–22 is narrated as if it concerned nation states that were already fully formed. Nevertheless, modern and interdisciplinary approaches of nationalism indicate the centrality of the notion of 'nationness', as introduced by Rogers Brubaker, in understanding the dynamics of the Balkan War decade and the way existing primordial identities were transformed into national ones. According to Brubaker, the nation should not be treated 'as substance but as an institutionalised form … not as entity but as contingent event'.[5] Furthermore, he underlines that the propensity of national practitioners to reify the nation as the protagonist in national struggles should be avoided, so as to bring to light the fluidity of identities during the process of state building and the forged character of national homogeneity, an aspect of which was the negotiation of identities at a grassroots, community level.[6]

This chapter is concerned with the construction of this homogeneity in the Balkan region and aims to underline the fact that the process of nation building was both dynamic and full of contested identities, especially within the Christian population. It therefore argues that population movements and refugee waves within the period around the Great War were not the result of a change of power balance concerning nation entities that were already established, but were part of the process that led to their establishment and to the consolidation of the content of national identity. More precisely, this chapter will explore these dynamics in the case of the modern Greek state. The first two decades of the twentieth century were crucial for its crystallisation and emergence as a modern state, not only because during that time its territory was more or less stabilised (with the exception of the Dodecanese that were added after the Second World War) but because it abandoned its imperial dreams and focused on elaborating a path towards modernisation. Part of this process was the shaping of the content of national identity, which could only materialise through the dynamic tension between antagonising nationalisms and nation-building processes that developed during that period.

The chapter is divided into three parts, each of which is connected with the appearance of an important refugee wave in the region. The first refers to the ferment in Ottoman society associated with ideas of nationalism during the nineteenth century and how this process caused the first important population mobility connected to an early attribution (or adoption) of a national identity and the forging of bonds among communities of the Ottoman population with different ethnic communities. The second part focuses on national antagonisms in the region during the early twentieth century and the turning point of the Balkan Wars. It is during this phase that antagonising nationalisms clashed openly for the first time, creating not only massive population mobility within the Balkans, but extended use of systematic violence connected to ethnic cleansing practices in the region. The third part will focus on the Great War and the eventual 'nationalisation' of the former Ottoman Empire. In this phase population mobility was part of a broader politics of state-building that culminated not only in the emergence of nation states but the consolidation of a 'refugee problem' that became an important part of the modernist condition during the interwar period.

The Balkans and its people during the nineteeth century

In the early nineteenth century a series of uprisings challenged the integrity of the Ottoman Empire (by Serbs 1804, 1815–17; Greeks 1821–30; in Bosnia-Herzegovina 1875; in Bulgaria 1876; in Crete in 1866–68 and again in 1896–97). Unlike preceding ones, these uprisings had, at least partially, not only social claims but national ones as well. The aim was the formation of sovereign nation states, even if the content of national identity remained to be defined.[7] Ethnic cleansing was an integral part of the process.[8] But who was considered 'the other' in such a fluid context?[9]

In the Balkans the emergence of a national discourse is to be understood as part of a transnational process that was unfolding at the intersecting of the communities with the diaspora. Communities established by Christian merchants outside the Ottoman Empire, around the Mediterranean, in the Russian Empire and in western Europe (such as, in the case of the Greek community, Vienna, Paris, Trieste, Odessa, London, Antwerp, Amsterdam, Marseille, Port-Mahon, Cairo and Alexandria to name only a few) were not only thriving economically, but were participants in the intellectual fermentations of their time.[10] Nations, societies or cultures, as Eric Wolf has put it, are not objects that are internally homogenous and externally distinctive and bounded.[11] Ideas cultivated in the diaspora reached the masses through its popularised version. Local elites in the Ottoman Empire cultivated national identities in a rather broader context that was aligned with the emergence of discourse of modernism. However, the situation differed in rural areas, where locals were unwilling to renounce the mixture of social, cultural and ethnic elements that gave rise to various shades of identity.

During the Greek Revolution, the dividing line between who was considered to be a potential member of the nation and who was excluded was religion. When the war was over, Muslims had fled to Anatolia and no longer lived in the region that became the Greek Kingdom. On the other hand, hundreds of thousands of Greeks had left their homelands in Anatolia and fled either to Greece or to the communities of the diaspora, so as to avoid the suffering and violence that was then inflicted collectively against the Christian subjects of the empire. In the course of the decade that the revolution lasted, but even later, during the first years of the independent Greek state, the national belonging of these refugees was a challenge for the state. As early as 1825 the issue of where and how the refugees would settle in Greece and whether they would be compensated for their properties was recurring in parliamentary discussions, although not always with much effectiveness.[12] In 1828 a situation resembling a humanitarian crisis emerged, and food (mainly rice and flour), that reached Greece through philanthropic initiatives of US Greeks, was distributed to over 50,000 refugees in Rumelia and Moria.[13]

Refugees should not be seen only as passive subjects in need of intervention. They were rather actors that contributed to the shaping of the new condition. The founding of the harbour city of Hermoupolis on Syros by Anatolian refugees in 1825 was one such example; Hermoupolis played a key role in the country's industrialisation during the nineteenth century.[14] Similar was the case in Macedonia, although still Ottoman in that period. During the late eighteenth century and the first half of the nineteenth century, extended population movements took place, mainly by Albanian and Vlach populations, due to the tensions provoked by the Greek revolution and the conflict between Ali Pasha and the Sublime Porte. The refugees founded dozens of new villages (some collectively named as 'Katsaounika' – the villages of those who had fled) or settled within existing communities. The memory of these population movements and the antagonisms that emerged between newcomers and locals were still fresh when the war over Macedonia started.[15]

Population uprooting in the Balkans at the turn of the nineteenth century

The demographic image of Anatolia and the Balkans had drastically changed over the nineteenth century, so that at the dawn of the twentieth century it no longer resembled that of the early nineteenth. Ethnic Greeks had fled to the Anatolian coast not only due to fear of inflicted violence over the course of the wars (mainly the 1770 uprising, the politics of Ali Pasha and the Greek Revolution), but due to economic reasons as well: the shrink economy of the Greek Kingdom was too suffocating compared to the opportunities Ottoman cities (and networks) offered. Smyrna, Ayvali and Trabzon are just some examples of such cities that concentrated the interest of Greek bourgeois. Moreover, especially since the end of the nineteenth century, the railway connection of Smyrna with the Anatolian inland led to a process of emigration of Greek populations towards the inland, and therefore to the demographic strengthening of Greek communities there. On the other hand, the demographic consistency of Muslims had also changed. After the uprooting of the Muslim population from the Greek Kingdom territory in the first decades of the nineteenth century, Muslims immigrated from the Balkans to Anatolia in three major waves. The first wave arrived mainly in Anatolia from Russia in the mid-1860s, a population that counted over 236,000 Circassians; the second wave in the mid-1870s, when thousands of Muslims fled the Balkans to Anatolia after the crisis of 1875–78; and the third wave occurred at the end of the nineteenth century and concerned Muslims that fled Crete towards the Asia Minor coast.[16] The Crete issue involved population movement in the opposite direction as well, since the issue expanded beyond the island and climaxed in the Greek-Turkish war of 1897, in which Greece was defeated. Following this defeat, at the northern borders of the country, ethnic Greek communities of the Ottoman Empire followed the retreating army and fled south in their thousands, fearing that after the war they would suffer at the hands of the Turks.[17] Additionally, smaller waves of Muslim emigration occurred during this period, such as the almost 40,000 Muslims that left Thessaly towards the Asia Minor coast – especially Smyrna from 1881 (when the region was annexed to Greece) until 1911.[18] Moreover, since the 1880s, Christian nationalisms (Greek, Serb and Bulgarian) had started to systematically claim Macedonia and Thrace, initially by putting forward projects to nationalise its people.

During the Ottoman regime, Macedonia and Thrace was not a distinct administrative entity. They had been organised in different provinces since the administrative reorganisation of 1878. They were populated by a mosaic population, as the rest of the Balkans, with variety occurring not only between Christians and Muslims, but among the Christian population and Muslim population as well. Identities and populations were more or less intermingled, with terms that today are inscribed in national contexts (such as Bulgar or Turk) being used in totally different (and predominately social) conceptual frameworks.[19]

The rise of nationalisms in the region further complicated the situation. After 1878 Christians were divided between two Orthodox millets, the Greek Orthodox and the Bulgarian Exarchate (although the first break in the unity of the millet had already occurred in 1833 with the foundation of the Greek national church). The division between these two groups became the core around which the fight over Macedonia and Thrace evolved. Although from a top-down perspective, belonging to a group meant adopting a clear national identity (whether Greek or Bulgarian), the population of Macedonia did not adhere to such a rigid division in their everyday lives, to the great disappointment of national agents. Christians were Slavic and Greek speaking without an established alignment between the language and the loyalty to one of the two Orthodox millets. Neither language nor ecclesiastical loyalty could serve as a safe criterion of identification, as both became fluid and interchangeable because of local and communal antagonisms and economic reasons. Identities were connected to locality and social stratum rather than nationalism, at least within each millet. Christians clashed during that period not due to pre-existing national identities, but as part of the process that those identities emerged.[20] As late as 1907 Stylianos Gonatas, serving at the consulate of Edirne, reported to Athens that 'the villagers are in a miserable condition of national neutrality, to the point that many of them are content with the religious differentiation between Christians and Muslims or Jews and do not care or do not know the national differentiation between Greeks and Bulgarians or Russians'.[21]

National propaganda was systematically practised by all sides, by a complex network of sympathetic churches, schools and teachers, ambassadors and secret agents – practices that were more or less orchestrated by committees and societies based in the relevant nation states.[22] Language, geography and history education were among the main tasks pursued by the nationalist campaigns during this period, in order to 'nationalise' the identities of the locals and connect them with the national centre.[23] Greek, Serbian and Bulgarian patriots claimed historical and cultural rights to the land and denied the existence of a Macedonian nationalism. Practices of map-making and statistical record keeping were recruited in the war to prove national rights in Macedonian territory.[24] Moreover, since the end of the century, Balkan governments encouraged the dispatching of irregulars to the region, who presented themselves as brigands but at the same time had the economic, political and diplomatic support of the government and its diplomatic mechanism. Brigands in this case were used as a cover for state-induced violence.[25]

While these nationalisms were antagonising to one another and irregulars caused minor problems to those considered national enemies, especially in the countryside, the struggle over the nationalisation of Macedonia and Thrace did not involve the extensive and systematic use of violence before the Ilinden uprising in 1903. It was after this point that violence became not only systematic but strategic, and it was used to shape the population's political behaviour.[26] As far as the Greek case was concerned, the aggressive turn in irredentism since the late nineteenth century meant that irregulars were systematically sent to the Ottoman Balkan territories, especially Macedonia, under the leadership of officers who usually came from upper-class families and held a romanticised perception that they would be liberating compatriots. Nevertheless, despite the violence, there was not a considerable population movement in this period – except for the fact that prior refugees from Macedonia were among the recruits of the irregulars that reached the region.

The war was not fought only in the rural areas by irregulars, though. It was equally fought in the cities. The anti-Greek episodes in Bulgaria in the summer of 1906 (especially in northern Thrace), although not exceptional, were indicative of the situation of widespread enmity between different ethnic groups during this period. During the summer, extended pogroms against the Greeks were carried out by the Bulgarians, who regarded them as their main national enemies. They took the form of mob violence, looting and even of systematic destruction of the city by fire, as was the case at Anchialos. As a result, over 20,000 Greeks were urged to leave Bulgaria during that turbulent summer. Emigration waves started after the looting of Plovdiv on 16 July 1906 and were not initially destined towards Greece, but towards neighbouring Greek communities in Romania (Constantza/Constanța) and the Ottoman Empire (Edirne and Istanbul); neither did they involve the whole population, but mainly affluent individuals. Nevertheless, emigration became generalised after the fire of Anchialos. After that point, Greeks were not only fleeing Bulgaria in fear for their lives, but because of the economic destruction of their cities and cultural oppression (i.e. the forbidding of the Greek language). The Greek state supported the emigration movement, established a central commission to co-ordinate relief, provided accommodation, and granted citizenship to the refugees. The flight of the population acquired political connotations, as it was linked to the state's ability to protect its co-nationals abroad. Relocation attempts begun in 1910, after the problems of the underdeveloped Greek state to effectively accommodate the refugees escalated, both economically and concerning public health issues. Until 1911 almost 5,000 refugees returned to Bulgaria, while others relocated in the Ottoman Empire, Egypt or the United States.[27]

The Balkan Wars

Even this pogrom could not compare to the extended population movements that had taken place since the Balkan Wars, continued throughout the Great War and reached their zenith with the Greek-Turkish exchange of population in 1922–23. The Balkan Wars were part of this new condition of nationalising the territory, in the sense that they were the continuation of the antagonism between states rather than within the states. Although the Balkan Wars did not last long, the consequences were crucial for the region. Warfare during the Great War resembled that of the Balkan Wars, especially in the Eastern Front and the Balkans. Endemic diseases, mass fatalities and atrocities towards enemy civilians were widespread, and propaganda was widely used by all parties.[28] Atrocities and massacres that took place in the Balkans between 1912 and 1913 systematically appeared as headlines in major European newspapers.[29]

Population movements were a crucial part of the Balkan Wars, as populations followed the constant change of the borders at the region.[30] The Muslim population suffered most during the First Balkan War at the hands of Greek, Serbian and Bulgarian troops and irregulars, while their villages were in many cases burnt down by their Christian neighbours. Thousands of refugees sought shelter in cities like Thessaloniki (Salonika) and Istanbul.[31] In the period between 1878 and 1913 about 1.7–2 million Muslims were displaced from the Balkans to Anatolia and Eastern Thrace.[32]

In the Second Balkan War, Greek civilians in particular suffered at the hands of Bulgarians and were forced to leave their villages in Macedonia and Thrace – from Meleniko and Strumnitsa alone, 5,000 of them fled towards Greece. Many of them were compelled to take Bulgarian nationality. Others lost their lives: in the region of Edirne, thousands of Greeks civilians were killed during July 1913.[33] After the Bucharest Treaty, Bulgarians from the Greek part of Macedonia resettled in the Bulgarian-held Western Thrace from which 40,000 Greeks had already fled in the opposite direction.[34] In all, according to the report of the Carnegie Commission, around 156,000 people took refuge in Greece, 104,000 in Bulgaria, and more than 200,000 Turks fled to Anatolia.[35]

It is important to add that a protocol attached to the peace agreement signed in Constantinople (September 1913) provided for a mutual, reciprocal and voluntary limited population exchange between the Bulgarian and Ottoman governments.[36] The protocol was designed to improve the position of those refugees who had already fled Bulgaria and the Ottoman Empire respectively. It established a mixed commission to assess and liquidate the property left behind by the refugees. This voluntary agreement was never carried out because the Great War began shortly afterwards.[37] Nevertheless, it heralded the first in a series of population exchange agreements during the twentieth century.

Defeat at the Balkan Wars struck the Ottoman Empire to its core, as it shook the heart of the state and the unity of its civilians. The loss of Macedonia had deeply affected the Young Turks, since it was homeland for a number of them. Kemal Atatürk, for example, was born in Thessaloniki, a city lost to the Greeks during the Balkan Wars. Part of the blame for the defeat was put on the Christian recruits at the Ottoman army, while in addition, economic help from the Christian communities to the Balkan states was suspected.[38] Moreover, refugee waves of Muslim migrants from the Balkans to Anatolia only intensified the distrust and anger between Turks and the 'others'.

The emergence of the Turkish nationalistic project in 1913, according to which Anatolia was to become homeland to ethnic Turks exclusively, set in motion a series of ethnic cleansing programmes based on the perception that non-Turkish communities of the Ottoman Empire, especially where these were dense and flourishing, had a close affiliation to nation states that claimed them as co-ethnics. Violence inflicted on populations considered as 'internal enemies' could either take the form of economic boycotts and mob violence or deportation to regions where these groups were considered incapable of doing any harm. The numerous deaths en route formed part of this process. Attempting to avoid such a fate, many members of the targeted communities opted to migrate to Greece, Egypt or elsewhere.

Persecutions against Ottoman Greeks started well before the Great War, in the spring of 1914. At that point, politics favouring the Turkification of Anatolia became mainstream among the Committee for Union and Progress, as the Ottoman Empire, slowly recovering from the defeat at the Balkan Wars, was questioning the loss of territories, especially that of the Aegean Islands. As a result, its relations with Greece were deteriorating and a new war was visible on the horizon.[39] The target was to ethnically homogenise Anatolia so as to become a homeland for the Turks that were losing the Empire. In order to do so, the plan was to drive Ottoman Greeks out of sensitive Ottoman territory, such as Thrace, Istanbul and the Anatolian Coast and replace them with Muslim refugees from the Balkans and Crete.[40] The strategy followed towards this end was twofold: on the one hand to encourage or impose population mobility through deportation, expulsion or population exchange agreements, and on the other to practise an undercover war against the unwanted populations. Boycotts, visits by Turk irregulars, job dismissals, even graffiti on the walls were among the first measures undertaken against the Ottoman Greeks. But terrorising practices expanded even further: thefts, attacks on homes and killings become an everyday fear for the Ottoman Greeks in the summer of 1914. Such acts were implemented by a mixture of grassroots anger against the 'unbelievers' and official enforcement of the boycott by state agents, who punished Muslims who failed to follow.[41]

Episodes were focused where the Greek population was denser, namely at the west coast of Anatolia and Eastern Thrace, at harbour-cities and across the railway line. Deportations started from Eastern Thrace, where Greek-Ottoman communities were economically thriving next to the empire's capital. Edirne, Rodosto, Kirk Kilisse, Samokovo, Malgara, Bunar Hisar, Kessani and the surrounding villages were among the sites that suffered in this phase by the implementation of the new policies. As early as 1913, when the Turks were reoccupying Thrace from the Bulgarians, the Greek villagers of Krithia (a village in Eastern Thrace) were ordered to leave the village. A similar fate befell the villagers of Aigialoi, a village occupied by the Bulgarians in 1912 and reoccupied by the Turks in 1913. The villagers, aware of the massacres taking place by the Turks in neighbouring villages, deserted the village before the troops arrived in other cities of Eastern Thrace where the Bulgarian army was still present, such as Tyroloi and Tsento. When they returned after almost a month, they found the village destroyed. During the Great War, they were conscripted into labour battalions, after which only 25 survived.[42] Such practices were so extensively used that the Ecumenical Patriarchate issued a report complaining to the Sublime Porte about the violent acts against Greek civilians, including massacres, deportations and the looting of villages.[43] Reportedly, in 1914 alone 150,000 Greeks were deported from the western coast of Anatolia and another 50,000 marched towards the interior of Anatolia.[44]

As a result of this extended violence, an agreement of mutual population exchange, on the pattern of the Ottoman-Bulgarian one, was pursued between the Ottoman Empire and Greece in May 1914. During the previous period, in the course of what has been described as a 'campaign of threats and intimidation', over 200,000 Orthodox (of 450,000) had been forced to leave the Asia Minor coast, especially from the area of İzmir, because of the fear of violent acts against them.[45] The Ottomans, who already resented the loss of Rumelia, pursued putting into action a plan of social engineering that would solve the national question and create Anatolia as an ethnically homogenous homeland for the Turks.[46] In this context, they sought to make the situation of the reduced Greek population in Anatolia permanent, and proposed, in May 1914, a plan of mutual population exchange to the Greek Prime Minister Eleftherios Venizelos, based on the pattern developed in the case of Bulgaria. Venizelos accepted, on the condition that it would remain voluntary. The exchange, primarily concerning the Greeks of İzmir region and the Muslims of Macedonia, would be overseen by a specially established committee that would guarantee the just disposal of properties. Nevertheless, the plan never materialised because the Great War broke out and the situation took a new turn.[47]

The Great War

The Ottoman Empire entered the Great War in November 1914, on the side of the Central Powers. Greeks, Armenians and Pontics still lived in the empire, mostly at the western and the northern coast of Anatolia and at the Balkans. When the Ottoman Empire entered the war in autumn 1914, the authorities gathered all male citizens between 20 and 45 for conscription. This proved to be a major issue for the non-Muslim Ottoman subjects, who brought to the fore their multi-layered and often contested loyalties. Mobilisation during the Great War re-shaped and redefined state–society relations in the gradually nationalising Ottoman Empire.[48] Mutual distrust between the authorities and the non-Muslim communities created a tense atmosphere. Practices of trying to avoid conscription were often held by non-Muslim Ottoman subjects, either by hiding or by acquiring a foreign passport.

Everyday life was on the edge of collapsing: abnormality, in the form of house confiscation or open violence, became part of the regular agenda. Of course, tensions between the Greek-Orthodox community and the Ottomans existed well before the Great War, in periods when peaceful coexistence was challenged. Nevertheless, the scale of the persecutions that took place during the Great War was unprecedented.[49] Fear was so intense, that thousands of Greeks fled their homes from Asia Minor towards the Greek Aegean Islands, mainland Greece and even towards Europe and the USA. Forced relocation of Greek communities, especially near the battlefields, should be added to the ethnic cleansing programme practised by the Ottoman authorities. Greeks, for example, were deported from the Marmara region in 1915, when Turkish and Allied forces fought for the control of the Dardanelles straits.

The expulsion of the Greeks from the Aegean region continued between 1916 and 1918. These expulsions were part of the Turkification programme as well, but in this case military reasons were stronger than the economic ones. For example, the entire Greek population of Ayvali was exiled to inner Anatolia, following directions given by the German general Liman von Sanders, in order to achieve security in the region. Throughout this period, large numbers of the Greek communities were gathered and forcedly made to relocate into the less vulnerable regions of central and eastern Anatolia. The transfer involved long-distance marches across rough terrain in extreme weather conditions and without provisions, during which hundreds of thousands lost their lives. If Ottoman Greeks did not meet the fate of Armenians and Syrians, it was mainly because an 'external power' could support them and therefore regulate and limit the politics of exclusion.[50]

The Pontus region experienced such wide-spread violence because it was a battlefront with the Russians and therefore considered sensitive. Although many Pontics lost their lives in the marches, many took the weapons and fled to the mountains, fighting a partisan war against the Muslim troops. The situation changed in 1916, when Russians troops entered the region. During the period 1916–18 Eastern Pontus was administrated by a semi-autonomous government at Trabzon, under the Rum bishop Chrysanthos, who retained balance between Muslims and Christians in the region. That was the reason why, in 1918, after the Russian troops withdrew from the region, the official direction given to the Turkish army was not to destroy the Christian villages. Nevertheless, the situation was out of control, since Muslim and Christian bandits looted the area and created conditions of intense insecurity. During this period, the Pontic guerrilla war intensified mostly by the population of the inlands, while at the same time the urban Rum population fled to Russia, following the Russian troops.

In 1916 thousands of Greeks fled Bulgaria as well, a population movement that followed the opposite route of that in 1913. After Bulgarian occupation, ethnic cleansing was in part practised in the occupied region of Macedonia and Thrace, although mostly affected the leaders of Greek nationalism. About 36,000 Greek inhabitants were deported by Bulgarian officials from the Bulgarian occupied Aegean Macedonia and in their place 39,000 Bulgarians were settled, many of them refugees from the Balkan Wars. In 1917, when Greece officially entered the war on the side of the Allies, persecutions intensified. According to the descriptions of the Inter-Allied Commission, at least 42,000 Greeks were deported during this period, while famine made the death toll for Greek civilians even higher.[51] After 1918, when the Bulgarian administration evacuated the area of Aegean Macedonia and Western Thrace, Bulgarians who had settled in the area in previous years fled back to Bulgaria, while Greeks who had fled in 1913–14 returned to their homelands.[52]

The widespread violence against ethnic Greeks in Anatolia in 1914 resulted in the first large-scale flight of Ottoman Greeks to Greece during the twentieth century. Irredentist rhetoric became more resonant. At the same time, signs that ethnic Greeks who arrived from the Ottoman Empire were already being perceived as 'second-class' co-nationals appeared in the way the Greek state conducted the administrative organisation of the 'New Lands' (i.e. the territories acquired gradually after 1832). This amounted to a kind of colonial governance.[53] Nevertheless, the arrival of thousands of refugees in the territory of the state in 1914 made the division more apparent, given the political tension between Prime Minister Venizelos and King Konstantinos that was already growing at the time.

The first tension to appear referred to the development of requests for national preference in the workers' union, aiming to limit the occupation of refugees, favouring local workers. Although complaints that ethnic Greeks from the Ottoman Empire were taking jobs from Greek nationals seemed to have been appearing since 1912 in Athens, they were not wide-scale and were rather limited within certain vocational communities. In 1914 though, such complaints became widespread, appeared in the daily newspapers, and resulted in the submission of a memorandum by the Workers' Centre of Athens to the government, according to which 'refugees receive an allowance from the state and should not be allowed to take the jobs of local workers because this is to take bread from the mouths of the very people who will be their future liberators'. In this discourse, although refugees are not excluded from the national imaginary, they are marginalised from the civil community, which is connected to the sacrifices made for the nation – in this case, military service and going to war.[54]

Not much later, in 1916, in the shadow of the National Schism, discourses that excluded the refugees from the nation appeared. Refugees became an easy target for the supporters of King Konstantinos.[55] Hostility towards the refugees can be understood only as part of the tense relation between Prime Minister Venizelos and King Konstantinos. To the supporters of the King, Venizelos, who favoured Greece's participation in the war on the side of Entente, should be held accountable for the refugees' presence in the country. As was the case with the workers' union, the equation between military service and participation in the civil community was once more apparent: 'Episratoi', a royalist paramilitary organisation formed in the context of the National Schism, blamed refugees who, having supported the war at the outset, 'when they are called to arms, in a cowardly and dishonest manner, claim to be Ottoman subjects'.[56] Opposition culminated during the episodes of November 1916, when Greece was already a divided state with two governments (the King at Athens and the Prime Minister in Thessaloniki). The British and the French navies imposed a blockade at Piraeus so as to put pressure on the government in Athens to participate in the war. At the same time, in Athens, opponents of Prime Minister Venizelos conducted a large scale pogrom against his supporters in Athens, and especially against the refugees, who were accused of being spies for the French and British and were executed, without trial, that night. Although the numbers of the victims have probably been exaggerated by scholarship favouring Venizelos, nevertheless the perception of the refugees as spies (and therefore as national 'aliens') is telling about how identities and understandings of who, and on what basis, was part of the national community were still under development.[57]

Conclusion

By 1912 over five million ethnic Greeks (most of them Ottoman subjects) lived outside the territory of the Greek nation state, in the Ottoman Empire and Russia.[58] Similarly, ethnic Bulgarians and ethnic Turks were dispersed in the southern Balkans and Anatolia.[59] In the years that followed, population movements were regulated through three major population exchange agreements, two of which were voluntary, while the last was obligatory: the aforementioned Treaty of Constantinople (1913) between Bulgaria and the Ottoman Empire; the Convention between Bulgaria and Greece (signed with the Neuilly Treaty, 1919); and the Convention Concerning the Exchange of Greek and Turkish Population (attached to the Lausanne Treaty 1923). The last of these concluded a process of ethnic cleansing that had started at least a decade earlier. After the end of the war decade, in 1923, this world of diasporic communities had ended, giving its place to nation states that had included those who were perceived as co-nationals. Nevertheless, a great deal of work remained to be done, this time within the states, aiming to nationally homogenise old and new citizens.[60] Of course, warfare between co-religious communities gradually shattered the common identity that was rooted in religion and gave its place to the emergence of national identities, which became more rigid and intolerant, according to the cultural proximity of the other. Violence that was previously connected to massacres, deportations, burning of villages and so on, now took the form of a race over the formation and control of memory. Renaming landscapes, erasing the memory of the Ottoman past and creating a Greek national memory by erecting monuments and devising rituals formed part of this process.

Refugees held a key role in the formation of the memory of the war decade and the shaping of a new understanding of the content of nationality. Because their experience was excluded by the official narrative of the war decade that focused on the territorial expansion of the Balkan Wars and the military defeat at the Greek-Turkish War, intellectuals of refugee origin undertook the task of serving as interlocutors of memory for their communities. In a process that lasted almost 40 years, through a series of historical writing and historical practices these intellectuals shaped and disseminated a homogenous narrative of displacement, albeit with regional characteristics. By the 1960s the trauma of population displacement that had until then been a cultural trauma for refugees had become a collective trauma of the nation, to a point that the Asia Minor catastrophe has since emerged as one of the most important sites of memory of national history.

Notes

1. On the emergence of the 'refugee' as a political and social figure connected to modernity in the course of the twentieth century, see Peter Gatrell, *The Making of the Modern Refugee* (Oxford: Oxford University Press, 2013).
2. Apostolos Karpozilos, 'The Greeks in Russia', in Richard Clogg (ed.), *The Greek Diaspora in the Twentieth Century* (Basingstoke: Macmillan, 1999), pp. 137–57; Onur Yildirim, *Diplomacy and Displacement. Reconsidering the Turco-Greek Exchange of Populations, 1922–1934* (London: Routledge, 2006); Renee Hirschon (ed.), *Crossing the Aegean: an Appraisal of the 1923 Compulsory Population Exchange Between Greece and Turkey* (Oxford: Berghahn Books, 2003).
3. On the intense balance between imperial dreams and modernisation, see Dimitris Stamatopoulos, *Byzantium after the Nation: the Problem of Continuity in Balkan Historiographies* [in Greek] (Athens: Alexandria, 2009).
4. Antonis Liakos, 'For the repair of plenary and unity: the construction of national time' [in Greek], in *Scientific Meeting in the memory of K. Th. Dimaras* (Athens: Institute for Neo-Hellenic Research, 1994), pp. 172–99.
5. Rogers Brubaker, *Nationalism Reframed: Nationhood and the National Question in the New Europe* (New York: Cambridge University Press, 1996), p. 16.
6. Rogers Brubaker, *Ethnicity Without Groups* (Cambridge, MA: Harvard University Press, 2004), p. 17.
7. Nikos Theotokas, 'Tradition and modernity: comments on the Greek War of Independence' [in Greek], *Historica*, 17 (1992), 345–70; Padelis Lekas, 'The Greek War of Independence from the perspective of historical sociology', *The Historical Review/La Revue Historique*, 2 (2005), 161–83.
8. Benjamin Lieberman, *Terrible Fate: Ethnic Cleansing in the Making of Modern Europe* (New York: Rowman and Littlefield, 2006).
9. Paschalis Kitromilides, '"Imagined communities" and the origins of the national question in the Balkans', *European History Quarterly*, 19, no. 2 (1989), 149–94.
10. Maurizio Isabella and Konstantina Zannou, 'The sea, its people and their ideas in the long nineteenth century', in Isabella and Zannou (eds), *Mediterranean Diasporas* (London: Bloomsbury, 2015), pp. 1–23.
11. Eric R. Wolf, *Europe and the People without History* (Berkeley, CA: University of California Press, 1982), pp. 6–7.
12. *Geniki Efimerida tis Kyvernisis* [General Newspaper of the Government] [in Greek], 4 February 1828, p. 40.
13. On population movements during the Greek War of Independence, see A. Vakalopoulos, *Refugees and the Refugee Issue During the 1821 Revolution* [in Greek] (Thessaloniki: 1939) and E. Protopsaltis, 'Refugees during the Greek revolution', *Nea Estia*, 44 (1948), 1154–7, 1237–41, and 1298–1303.

14 Andreas Drakakis, *History of the Settlement of Hermoupolis, Syra, Volume A, 1821–1825* [in Greek] (Athens: 1979); E.Y. Kolodny, 'Hermoupolis-Syros, birth and development of a Greek island city' [in Greek], *Epetiris Etaireias Kykladikon Meleton* 8 (1969-70), 249–86; Ch. Loukos, 'La petite ville face a la grande: le cas d' Ano Syraau XIXe siecle', *Ariadni*, no. 7 (1994),151–64.

15 Vasilis Gounaris, 'Ethnic groups and political parties in Macedonia during the Balkan Wars' [in Greek], in K. Svolopoulos et al. (eds), *Greece During the Balkan Wars, 1910–1914* [in Greek] (Athens: ELIA (Hellenic Literary and Historical Archive), 1993), pp. 189–202.

16 Dimitris Stamatopoulos, 'Asia Minor expenditure: the human geography of the Catastrophe', in Antonis Liakos (ed.), *1922 and the Refugees: a Fresh Look* [in Greek] (Athens: Nefeli, 2011), p. 58.

17 Lieberman, *Terrible Fate*, pp. 31–3.

18 Justin McCarthy, 'Muslims in Ottoman Europe: population from 1800 to 1912', *Nationalities Papers*, 28, no. 1 (2000), 29–43 (here p. 32); Yannis Glavinas, *Muslim Populations in Greece (1912–1923): From Incorporation to Exchange* [in Greek] (Thessaloniki: Stamouli Publications, 2013), p. 16.

19 On the population mosaic of the nineteenth-century Ottoman Empire and the conceptual connotations of the terms used, see Martin Baldwin-Edwards, Riki van Boeschoten and Hans Vermeulen, 'Introduction', in Baldwin-Edwards et al. (eds), *Migration in the Southern Balkans* (Berlin: Springer Open, 2015), pp. 1–29.

20 Even attitudes towards the uprisings differed according to ethnic, cultural and religious characteristics of the community that eventually comprised the Greek nation. These differences were later effaced. See Christine Philliou, 'Breaking the Tetrarchia and saving the Kaymakam: to be an ambitious Ottoman Christian in 1821', in Antonis Anastasopoulos and Elias Kolovos (eds), *Ottoman Rule and the Balkans, 1760–1850: Conflict, Transformation, Adaptation* (Rethymnon: University of Crete, 2007), pp. 181–94.

21 St. Gonatas report on Thrace, December 1907 (Ministry of Foreign Affairs Archives, 1908 21.2).

22 In the case of Macedonia, the most important ones were the Bulgarian Cyril and Methodius Committee (1884), the Serbian Saint Sava Society (1886), and the Greek National Society (1894). For the role of schools and associations in diffusing national discourses, see Bernard Lory, 'Schools for the destruction of society: school propaganda in Bitola, 1860–1912', in Nathalie Clayer, Hannes Grandits and Robert Pichler (eds), *Conflicting Loyalties in the Balkans: the Great Powers, the Ottoman Empire and Nation-Building* (London: I.B. Tauris 2011), pp. 46–63.

23 Theodora Dragostinova, 'Speaking national: nationalizing the Greeks of Bulgaria, 1900–1939', *Slavic Review*, 67, no. 1 (2008), 154–71; Christina Koulouri, *History and Geography in Greek Schools, 1834–1914* [in Greek] (Athens: Geniki Grammateia Neas Genias, 1988); Emilia Salvanou, 'Aspects

of the modernizing process in the Greek-Orthodox communities of the late Ottoman Empire', unpublished PhD thesis, University of the Aegean, 2006.
24 Spiros Karavas, *Secrets and Tales from the History of Macedonia* [in Greek] (Athens: Vivliorama, 2010).
25 Mark Mazower, *The Balkans* (New York: Modern Library, 2000), p. 45.
26 Mark Biondich, *The Balkans: Revolution, War, and Political Violence since 1878* (Oxford: Oxford University Press, 2011), pp. 68–9.
27 Theodora Dragostinova, *Between Two Motherlands: Nationality and Emigration among the Greeks of Bulgaria, 1900–1949* (Ithaca: Cornell University Press, 2011).
28 Alan Kramer, *Dynamic of Destruction: Culture and Mass Killing in the First World War* (Oxford: Oxford University Press, 2007), p. 136.
29 Kramer, *Dynamic of Destruction*, pp. 137–8.
30 The way the Carnegie Endowment Report refers to these population movements is indicative of their extent: 'The population, warned by the glow from these fires, fled in all haste. There followed a veritable migration of peoples, for in Macedonia, as in Thrace, there was hardly a spot which was not, at a given moment, on the line of march of some army or other. The commission encountered this second fact everywhere. All along the railways interminable trains of carts drawn by oxen followed one another; behind them came emigrant families and, in the neighborhood of the big towns, bodies of refugees were found encamped'. Carnegie Endowment for International Peace, *Report of the International Commission to Inquire into the Causes and Conduct of the Balkan Wars* (Washington 1914), 151.
31 D. Akyalçin-Kaya, 'Immigration into the Ottoman territory: the case of Salonica in the late nineteenth century', in U. Freitag, M. Fuhrmann, N. Lafi and F. Riedler (eds), *The City in the Ottoman Empire: Migration and the Making of Urban Modernity* (London: Routledge, 2011), pp. 177–89.
32 Mazower, *The Balkans*, p. 11.
33 Carnegie Endowment, *Report of the International Commission*, pp. 106–35, 155–7.
34 Dragostinova, *Between Two Motherlands*.
35 Kramer, *Dynamic of Destruction*, p. 139.
36 Fikret Adanir, 'Non-Muslims in the Ottoman army and the Ottoman defeat in the Balkan War of 1912–1913', in Ronald G. Suny, Fatma Göçek and Norman Naimark (eds), *A Question of Genocide: Armenians and Turks at the End of the Ottoman Empire* (New York: Oxford University Press, 2011), pp. 113–25.
37 Erik-Jan Zürcher, 'Greek and Turkish refugees and deportees 1912–1924', Turkology Update Leiden Project Working Papers Archive. Department of Turkish Studies, Universiteit Leiden, www.transanatolie.com/English/Turkey/Turks/Ottomans/ejz18.pdf (January 2003) [accessed 2 August 2016].

38 Nicholas Doumanis, *Before the Nation: Muslim-Christian Coexistence and its Destruction in Late Ottoman Anatolia* (Oxford: Oxford University Press, 2012), p. 148.
39 Doumanis, *Before the Nation*, p. 151.
40 Mattias Bjørnlund, 'The 1914 cleansing of Aegean Greeks as a case of violent Turkification', *Journal of Genocide Research*, 10, no. 1 (2008), 41–57.
41 Doumanis, *Before the Nation*, p. 179.
42 Konstantinos Vakalopoulos, *Persecution and Genocide of Thracian Hellenism* [in Greek] (Thessaloniki: Stamoulis, 2000), p. 203.
43 Alexander Papadopoulos, *Persecution of the Greeks in Turkey Before the European War* (New York: Oxford University Press, 1919), pp. 27–9.
44 Michael R. Marrus, *The Unwanted: European Refugees in the Twentieth Century* (Oxford: Oxford University Press, 1985), p. 48.
45 Erik-Jan Zürcher, *Turkey: a Modern History* (London: I.B. Tauris, 2004), p. 126; Erik-Jan Zürcher, *The Young Turk Legacy and Nation Building* (London: I.B. Tauris, 2010), p. 140.
46 On social engineering and the creation of a Turkish nation state see Erol Ülker, 'Contextualising "Turkification": nation-building in the late Ottoman Empire, 1908–1918', *Nations and Nationalism*, 11, no. 4 (2005), 613–66; Uğur Ümit Üngör, 'Seeing like a nation state: Young Turk social engineering in eastern Turkey', *Journal of Genocide Research*, 10, no. 1 (2008), 15–39; N. Sigalas and A. Toumarkine, 'Ingénierie démographique, génocide, nettoyage ethnique: les paradigmes dominantes pour l'étude de la violence sur les populations minoritaires en Turquie et dans les Balkans', *European Journal of Turkish Studies*, 7 (2008), http://ejts.revues.org/2933.
47 Ellinor Morack, 'The Ottoman Greeks and the Great War, 1912–1922', in Bley Kremers (ed.), *The World During the First World War* (Essen: Klartext, 2014), pp. 215–30; Ryan Gingeras, *Sorrowful Shores: Violence, Ethnicity, and the End of the Ottoman Empire 1912–1923* (Oxford: Oxford University Press, 2011); Yiannis Mourelos, 'The 1914 persecutions and the first attempt at an exchange of minorities between Greece and Turkey', *Balkan Studies*, 26, no. 2 (1985), 389–413; Ayhan Aktar, 'Homogenising the nation, Turkifying the economy', in Hirschon (ed.), *Crossing the Aegean*, pp. 82–4.
48 Mehmet Beşikçi, *The Ottoman Mobilization of Manpower in the First World War: Between Voluntarism and Resistance* (Leiden: Brill, 2012).
49 Vangelis Kechriotis, 'Experience and action in a transforming political field: the Greek-Orthodox community of Smyrna at the beginning of the twentieth century' [in Greek], *Deltio Kentrou Mikrasiatikon Spoudon*, 17 (2011), 61–105 (here p. 105).
50 On the argument about nation-building policies and their relation to the way 'non-core groups' are supported or not by 'external powers', see Harris Mylonas, *The Politics of Nation-Building: Making Co-Nationals, Refugees, and Minorities* (Cambridge: Cambridge University Press, 2012).

51 Lieberman, *Terrible Fate*, p. 87.
52 Dragostinova, *Between Two Motherlands*.
53 The first debate as to whether ethnic Greeks of the Ottoman Empire should be considered co-nationals and have civil rights took place in 1843 when Greek speaking and/or Orthodox Christian Ottoman communities were acknowledged as ethnic Greeks, part of the nation's population, and potentially unredeemed. See Elli Skopetea, *The Exemplar Kingdom and the Great Idea: Aspects of the National Problem in Greece, 1830–1880* [in Greek] (Athens: Polytypo, 1988).
54 Regarding the antagonism between local and refugee workers in Greece during the Great War and the way the right of participating in civil society was conceptualised, see Nikos Potamianos, 'Local stuff!' The claim of "national/ethnic preference" and the strategies of market control by the workers' unions of Athens and Piraeus in the early twentieth century' [in Greek]. Paper presented at the 7th Historical Conference, Athens, 20–21 May 2011, http://historein-historein.blogspot.com/2011/05/blog-post_14.html [accessed 9 November 2016].
55 On the National Schism see Giorgos Mavrogordatos, *1915: the National Schism* [in Greek] (Athens: Pataki, 2015), and Augusta Dimou, *Entangled Paths Toward Modernity: Contextualising Socialism and Nationalism in the Balkans* (Budapest: Central European University Press, 2009), chapter 6.
56 *Nea Imera*, 18 August 1916, cited in Mavrogordatos, *1915: the National Schism*, pp. 226–7.
57 On the episodes of November 1916 and the possible exaggeration of numbers, see Mavrogordatos, *1915: the National Schism*, pp. 276–7.
58 N. Petsalis-Diomidis, *Greece at the Paris Peace Conference, 1919* (Thessaloniki: Institute for Balkan Studies, 1978), p. 15.
59 For the case of Bulgarians, see Raymond Detrez, 'Refugees as tools of irredentist policies in interwar Bulgaria', in Vermeulen, Baldwin-Edwards, and van Boeschoten (eds), *Migration in the Southern Balkans*, pp. 47–62.
60 See the chapter by Nikolai Vukov.

14

Becoming and unbecoming refugees: the long ordeal of Balkan Muslims, 1912–34

Uğur Ümit Üngör

Introduction: the Balkan Wars as a watershed

The twin Balkan Wars of 1912–13 truncated the Ottoman Empire and sparked more than a decade of population politics in the region. Serbia, Greece and Bulgaria wrested large territories from the Ottomans and expelled hundreds of thousands of Muslims from those lands. As the conflicts escalated into total warfare, defenceless civilians were assaulted by all sides: Muslims under Bulgarian and Greek rule, and Christians under Ottoman rule. Bulgarian, Serbian, Greek and Ottoman forces all committed acts of violence. The violence resulted in unprecedented refugee streams, especially of Muslims to the Ottoman Empire. This chapter will discuss the consequences of these atrocities, in order to address the overarching question of how Muslim refugees during the Balkan Wars experienced their flight and arrival in the Ottoman Empire. This chapter examines the expulsion of Ottoman Muslims in the Balkans and their ordeal in the rump Ottoman state. It discusses how their experiences as refugees influenced them, how they were received by the host population, and which social problems they faced as refugees.

Although there were clear distinctions between combatants and non-combatants, as the skirmishes unfolded into total warfare none of the armies respected this distinction. Atrocities were committed by all sides in the conflict, but contemporary journalists and victims accused the Bulgarian army in particular of the systematic maltreatment of civilians.[1] The forces commanded by the Bulgarian generals Ivan Fichev (1860–1931), Vladimir Minchev Vazov (1868–1945) and Radko Dimitriev (1859–1918) embarked on the large-scale destruction and arson of villages, beatings and torture, forced conversions, indiscriminate mass killing, and mass expulsion of Ottoman Muslims.² Leon Trotsky, reporting for the *Kievskaia Mysl'*, singled out Dimitriev as having been responsible for campaigns of ethnic cleansing and massacre, describing him as someone 'deeply animated by those features of careerism including careless zeal and moral cynicism'. When stubborn Ottoman defences frustrated his ambition to conquer as much territory as possible and as quickly as possible, Dimitriev ordered his troops to take no more prisoners and to execute all prisoners of war, including the wounded.³

On 10 November 1912 Bulgarian *komitadjis* (irregular forces) destroyed the villages of Maden, Topuklu and Davud, killing most inhabitants. The conservative Ottoman newspaper *Hikmet* expressed outrage: 'Will civilised Europe not notice savagery of this extent?'⁴ In the following days, the carnage continued and gradually became more participatory. To begin with, Bulgarian civilians who refused to participate in the violence were pressured and threatened by Bulgarian soldiers, who burnt farms around the town of Çorlu.⁵ But popular participation in the expulsions and killings of Muslims increased when the Bulgarian authorities announced that Muslim properties, including farmland, would be distributed among the Bulgarians. This led to a significant increase in popular participation in violence and flight.⁶ The Serbian authorities, too, encouraged 'local police officers, secret agents and lawyers to terrorise the Muslims and to make a calm life for them impossible'.⁷ According to an Ottoman gendarmerie report from Ezine, the Serbian authorities confiscated 16,000 *kurush* worth of property and livestock in Priština from four individuals. The Bulgarian authorities confiscated a total of 395,060 *kurush* in the towns of Ipsala, Babaeski and Malkara from just thirteen individuals.⁸

War crimes were another form of mass violence that sent terrified refugees fleeing the carnage. According to one contemporary account, whenever Bulgarian forces captured Ottoman prisoners of war, they would frequently set the Christians free but execute the Muslims among them.⁹ The violence also came to target cultural activities and property. When the Greek army occupied Salonika, it prohibited all publications in Ottoman Turkish for an indefinite period of time.¹⁰ Upon entering the town of Drama, the Bulgarian army converted all mosques into churches and took down all signs of Islamic culture.¹¹ Since the fez was widely seen as a sign of Ottoman culture and allegiance to Istanbul, inhabitants were not allowed to wear it. As it was also an ethnic marker for Muslims, when the Bulgarian and Serbian armies invaded their home towns, Muslims hid their fezzes and wore hats instead, for example in Varna and Salonika.¹²

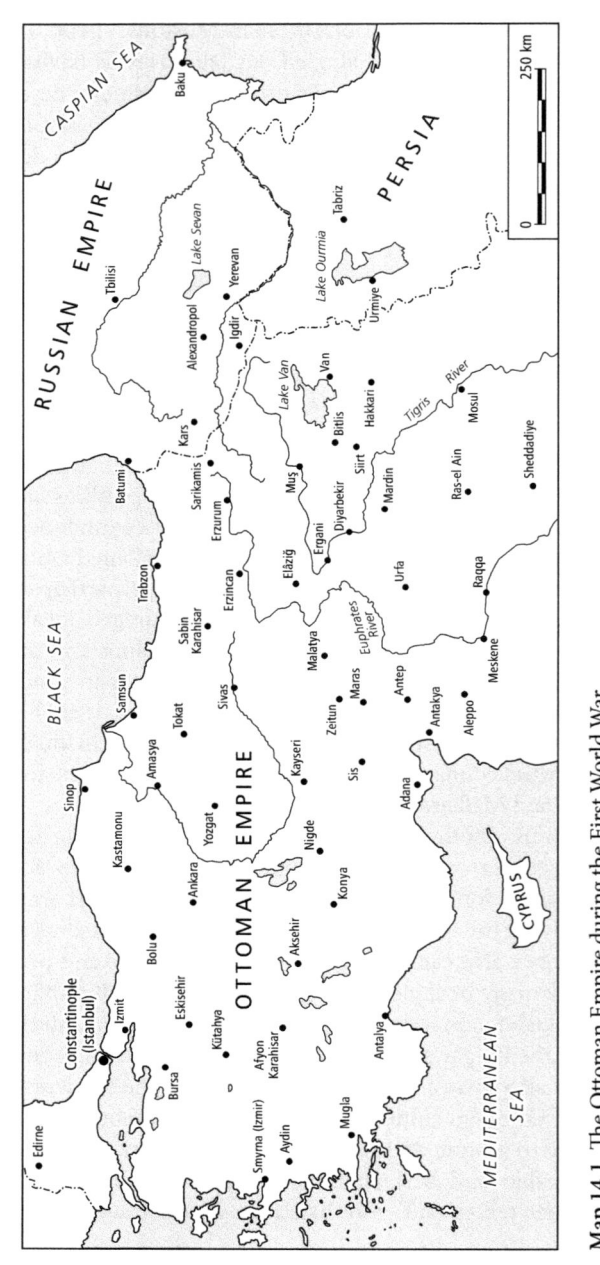

Map 14.1 The Ottoman Empire during the First World War.

The Ottoman government then set up the 'Association for the study of oppression' (*Tetkik-i Mezalim Cemiyeti*), headed by the journalist Ahmed Cevad Emre, whose team had the task of documenting the atrocities. In Edirne it took a multi-ethnic form, comprising four Muslims, two Greeks, three Armenians and a Jew. The committee produced reports that Ahmed Cevad Emre compiled, edited and published as 'The blood that flows in the Balkans' (*Balkanlarda Akan Kan*).[13] The plan backfired to some extent when radicals began using the content as propaganda for revenge acts. Victimised groups who fled to their 'ethnic brethren' with stories of terror helped to inspire retaliation against populations that they associated with their victimisers. Thus, whereas Bulgarian army units ignited a campaign of terror and ethnic cleansing, the response by Greek and Ottoman forces against Bulgarian villages could be at least as violent.[14]

The territorial erosion of the Ottoman Empire in the Balkans and in the Caucasus during the nineteenth century was a process that produced humiliation and large refugee flows.[15] But the total and permanent loss of the Balkan Peninsula in 1913 marked a watershed that affected the Empire's very existence. The effect of the Balkan Wars on Ottoman society was nothing short of apocalyptic, and the proud Ottoman elite found unbearable the loss of many major Ottoman cities, property and human life. The helplessness of the imperial army provoked dismay and compounded the sense of humiliation. The shock of the war would have a severe and lasting impact on Ottoman society, culture and identity. After 1913, hardliners on both sides of the political spectrum no longer regarded as feasible the hitherto viable umbrella Ottoman identity. Recent research on the Young Turk *coup d'état* on 23 January 1913 reveals a radical and activist Turkish-nationalist core around Dr Bahaeddin Shakir (1874–1922), Dr Mehmed Nâzım (1872–1926), Mehmed Talaat (1874–1921) and İsmail Enver (1881–1922), who definitively gave up hope of the ideal of Ottoman unity and inclusive citizenship as a result of the Balkan Wars. Without their experience of war, this radicalisation would not have seemed possible.[16]

The refugee crisis

The most immediate repercussion of the war was an acute refugee crisis. In the first half of 1913, Istanbul was bursting with hundreds of thousands of refugees.[17] Newspaper articles provided vivid descriptions of the condition of the refugees:

> Refugees from the areas of Macedonia and Kosova are flocking here ... It is reported that another group of 6,000 people has set out from Salonica. Every ferry from Salonica brings 1,200–1,500 refugees. Most of them do not own anything other than the clothes on their backs. These poor souls were forced to flee the calamity and tyranny without a stitch.[18]

If Istanbul was entirely overstretched with refugees, other cities too shared some of the burden. For example, many refugees from Salonika arrived by boat in İzmir on the Aegean coast. When the city became overcrowded in the summer of 1913, 6,000 refugees were shipped onwards to Antalya province on the Mediterranean coast.[19] The same also happened with refugees from the area of the Rhodope mountains: 3,000 embarked on a ship in Salonika and sailed to İzmir where they briefly moored before finally reaching Iskenderun on the Syrian coast. Within a matter of weeks, these people had crossed not only seas but entirely civilisations: from the 'cool Balkans' to the 'hot Levant'.[20]

As if the sight of these refugees were not bad enough, the stories and trauma they brought to the capital added fuel to the fire. Their horror stories were met with disbelief and rage by the Ottoman press. One commentator on the refugees' fate bewailed how 'our motherland was trampled on by the muddy boots of the poorest enemies. Our co-religionist brothers and compatriots were slaughtered in the thousands like sheep'.[21] The feminist and nationalist author Halide Edib (1884–1964) wrote:

> The spectacle of Moslem refugees, men and women and children, fleeing from the fire and sword of the enemy; the slaying of prisoners of war, their mutilation and starvation; atrocities and massacres perpetrated on the civil population – the first of their kind in twentieth-century warfare – inflicted wounds far deeper than the defeat itself.[22]

The British consul in Salonika witnessed the process of forced migration and reported as follows:

> The result of the massacre of Muslims at the beginning of the war, of the looting of their goods in the ensuing months, of the settling of Christians in their villages, of their persecution by Christian neighbours, of their torture and beating by Greek troops, has been the creation of a state of terror among the Islamic population. Their one desire is to escape from Macedonia and to be again in a free land ... They arrive in Turkey with the memory of their slaughtered friends and relations fresh in their minds, they remember their own sufferings and the persecutions of which they have been victims, and finding themselves without means or resources, encouraged to some extent by their own government, they see no wrong in falling on the Greek

Christians of Turkey and meting out to them the same treatment that they themselves have received from the Greek Christians of Macedonia.[23]

A major part of the refugee crisis was the catastrophic effect of the war upon the female population. Bulgarian forays into the Thracian countryside and the Bulgarian occupation in general spelled persecution and terror, frequently accompanied by rape.[24] Indeed, the large-scale victimisation of Ottoman Muslim women, on dual grounds of being Muslim and female, gradually became widely known among the public. For example, Ömer Seyfeddin wrote an essay based on interviews with refugees about the behaviour of the Bulgarian Major Radko Balkaneski, a graduate of Galatasaray Lycée in Istanbul and the Sofia Military Academy. Radko raided the town of Serres, disarmed the Muslim population, and ordered his men to gather the prettiest Turkish girls. A dozen girls were brought in from the nearby villages of Cuma and Osenova and stripped naked in front of him. Two girls were 'pretty' but they were famished and had contracted malaria. The other girls 'were real village girls, with thick arms, legs and hips'. Radko fed them wine and brandy and distributed them to their men, who raped the girls until they were deemed to be no longer of use. Due to feelings of shame and guilt, the surviving women often committed suicide.[25]

Those women who did make it to Istanbul awaited a difficult future including impoverishment, homelessness and sexual exploitation. The Ottoman government wanted to make sure that girls' rights were respected and issued an order on 13 November 1912 stipulating 'in no way should girls be taken as housemaids under the pretext of adoption'.[26] Yet it is certain that Ottoman Muslim women suffered very serious social consequences as a result of the Balkan Wars. Whether the inability of Ottoman men to protect their womenfolk gave rise to a crisis of masculinity remains a subject for future study. As for the children, Eyal Ginio convincingly argues that the Ottoman elites' concept of childhood changed as a result of the violence of the Balkan Wars. If we follow this logic, both developments go a long way to explain the fate of women and children during the Great War as both symbols and targets of violence.[27]

The emotions of Young Turk elites expelled from their ancestral lands included humiliation, helplessness, anger, loss of dignity, lack of self-confidence, anxiety, embarrassment and shame: a toxic mix that, combined together, contributed to the growth of collective hate and destruction fantasies in the years that followed. Besides these objective effects, the subjective perception of the tragedy in the minds of the Young Turks merits perhaps even more attention. For them, the loss of power and prestige shattered the conventional myth of an Ottoman identity and Islamic superiority. One contemporary commented that for the Young Turks 'it was especially difficult to be forced to live under the rule of their own former subjects after having been the dominant element for hundreds of years'.[28] The fear of being ruled by historical enemies was a theme even before the Balkan Wars, when the Young Turk press published widely read articles with a deeply defeatist tone:

> Serbia, Bulgaria, Montenegro, Bosnia-Herzegovina, and Crete were lost. Right now the grand [dear] Rumelia is about to be lost and in one or two years Istanbul will be gone as well. The holy Islam and the esteemed Ottomanism will be moved to Kayseri. Kayseri will become our capital, Mersin our port, Armenia and Kurdistan our neighbours, and Muscovites our masters. We will become their slaves. Oh, is it not shameful for us! How can the Ottomans who once ruled the world become servants to their own shepherds, slaves, and servants?[29]

The young Ottoman journalist Falih Rıfkı Atay had been through the Balkan Wars and later became a secretary to Minister of Navy Cemal Pasha. In the aftermath of the Balkan Wars, he recorded in his diary:

> When they took Belgrade from us, the enemy delegations also wanted Niš. The Ottoman delegation stood up: 'That's it, what, you want Istanbul too?' For our forefathers Niš was so close to Istanbul. We thought that the Turkish people would not survive if we abandoned Vardar, Tripoli, Crete and Medina. I did not know Turkey, when I took the train from Haydarpaşa to the most distant provinces … Our illusions about Istanbul, Cairo, Jerusalem, Damascus, Aleppo and Baghdad were being abandoned and we began to worry about our own lives. I always wondered, will they also enter Istanbul?[30]

The 1914 opening address of parliament was equally rancorous and emotional: 'Do not forget! Do not forget beloved Salonika, the cradle of the flame of liberty and constitutional government, do not forget green Monastir, Kosovo, İşkodra, Yanya and all of beautiful Rumelia'. The emotional deputies exclaimed: 'We shall not forget!'[31]

Hardship

The refugees faced immense hardship when they arrived, with trials and tribulations around health, housing, security and public hostility to the fore. As the Ottoman state had depleted its public funds, non-governmental organisations quickly took over some major tasks of the state. This outsourcing of public functions was not only necessary, but also efficient: all tasks could now be covered by an intelligent division of labour.

During the late autumn and winter of 1912, epidemics broke out among the refugees. In October alone, for example, 2,549 cases of cholera were diagnosed, of which 1,479 people died.[32] As the mayor of Istanbul, Dr Cemil Topuzlu (1868–1958) wrote:

> A few days after the declaration of war, refugees came into our city. But what an arrival! All of them were miserable and forlorn (*sefil ve perişan*). These ill-fated people, packed together in clippers and trains, disembarked at Sirkeci train station hungry and unclothed. And then there were those who had taken the road on oxcarts from their villages and towns. Although Istanbul's Directorate for Refugees would send some of the Balkan War refugees bit by bit to Anatolia, despite this, we could not prevent there being a permanent group of forty or fifty thousand sick and ragged people in our city.[33]

To cope with the epidemic, Topuzlu convened the municipal 'high commission for matters of healthcare' (*Umûr-u Sıhhiye Meclis-i Ali*), which allocated funds for the establishment of new hospitals.[34] But the truth was that the state was hopelessly overstretched in its attempt to cover the refugees' needs. The Ottoman government had to allocate enormous resources to transport, house, feed, educate, equip, employ and clothe them. As a result, civic organisations began taking over some of the tasks. Philanthropic associations such as the Red Crescent or the Association for Muslim Refugees from the Balkans provided relief for the refugee community. For example, the Red Crescent converted barracks and sheds into improvised hospitals. It also rented an Ottoman governor's summer house in Parmakkapı district, and on 8 February 1913 completed its conversion into the 'refugees' hospital' with a capacity of up to 100 beds.[35]

Healthcare was bad, but housing was a true disaster. The government therefore took full emergency measures by requisitioning hotel rooms, empty dachas and warehouses for the refugees, many of whom were otherwise sleeping in the streets or in Istanbul's train stations. The government saw no other choice than to temporarily transform mosques into shelters. In Istanbul more than 90 mosques were initially furnished as sanctuaries. By the end of October 1913 the large Nuru Osmaniye Mosque was already full to the brim.[36] According to the Ottoman Red

Crescent, refugees were mainly housed in mosques, for example 125 families in the Edirnekapı mosque, 107 families in the Sultan Selim mosque, and 86 families in the Murad Pasha mosque. Nor were prominent mosques spared, such as the Aya Sofia and the Sultan Ahmed (the Blue Mosque). Initially, another 643 families (2,798 people) were sheltered in makeshift huts on the outskirts of Istanbul.[37] The government responded to these unexpected setbacks by issuing a policy aimed at regulating what had become known as the 'refugee question' in Ottoman political discourse. Thus was born the 'refugee village' (*muhacirköy*), a generic name for many villages, neighbourhoods and urban settlements founded for the refugees across the Ottoman Empire. These villages are quite easy to identify and find even now: some prospered, whilst others were abandoned after a few years, but all were inhabited by Balkan refugees.

The idea of building villages from scratch sprang from the pre-existing 'regulations for housing of refugees' (*İskân-ı Muhacirîn Nizamnâmesi*). Issued on 22 January 1906, the regulations foresaw a comprehensive policy of housing, subsistence, education, health care and social integration. In the first place, empty plots of land had to be found, and if this were not sufficient refugees would be placed temporarily in rented property. Their settlement would be determined by a commission, whose delegations would travel anywhere with municipal housing engineers and for exploratory visits. After the explorations and approval by the commission, the construction of settlements would begin rapidly. Since most refugee families were peasants, plots for agriculture would also be determined in advance. According to the regulations, a refugee village was to comprise at least 20 households; 20 villages would in turn constitute a township. Meadows and marshes needed for each village would also be specified. The refugees would first be settled in empty villages, on vacant land and abandoned plots. Each household, consisting of a population between one and five, would be given a plot of land between 50 and 100 acres. The commission was entrusted with the task of allocating land for mosques and schools. Villages were to be set up along mail routes, near forests and close to a source of water, and steps were taken to avoid building villages near dangerous places. The newly established model villages would be named after the house of Osman, especially 'the great sultans', and the commission would communicate such requests to the provinces. As a result, the villages took the names Mesudiye, Muradiye and Osmaniye.[38] Existing villages were likewise Ottomanised in this manner. After the establishment of the Turkish Republic they were changed in favour of secular Turkish names.

Meanwhile, those refugees who stayed in Istanbul encountered a restless imperial capital with all the ugly social problems a modern metropolis could have. Crime added insult to injury, and plagued the hapless villagers who often had little awareness of the pitfalls of urban life. Some naive refugees, thinking they would be safe with their fellow Muslims in Istanbul, strayed or were led into desolate warehouses in the seedy Sirkeci district and promptly robbed.[39] Profiteers waited for the refugee columns at the city's boundaries and tried to swindle them by telling them they would not be able to feed their livestock and were better off selling it – and then swiftly buying the animals scandalously below market value.[40] Since imams had to register refugees as new parishioners, one imam in Fatih district requested a cut of the refugees' subsistence fee, leading first to complaints and then to his arrest. The crowds of refugees were also an ideal place to hide for army deserters and all kinds of 'vagrants' (*serseri*) who took advantage of free housing.[41] Indeed, some locals passed themselves off as Balkan refugees to get free benefits such as bread and housing. Some bakers tried to palm off the worst loaves of bread to the refugees, such as the baker on Balıkpazarı Street in Istanbul's Pera district.[42] When the authorities caught wind of these scams, they asked the refugee commission to investigate these and other abuses, as a result of which inspectors were assigned to monitor the distribution of goods and see to the orderly conduct of refugee affairs.[43] The municipal authorities also promised severe punishment for those who abused the refugees, even threatening profiteers and swindlers with court-martial.[44]

In order to organise themselves in a social movement, the refugees established the newspaper *Muhacir*, which organised various forms of relief, ran a missing persons column, and advertised jobs for the refugees. The chaos in the aftermath of the Balkans catastrophe led to a great tangle of missing persons – often children lost in the dust of war. Letters such as these abound in refugee newspapers:

> It is implored, in the name of humanity (*insaniyyet nâmına*), that any information relating to the 13-year-old Recep, son of the late Haci Selimzâde and his stepmother Emine, both from Selimiye town in Drama district in Salonica province, who migrated at the beginning of the war and of whom no information has been received ever since, is sent to the below address. Signed: Brother of the missing person, Arif bin Hacı Selim, residing with Tiğlizâde Hakkı Efendi in Eğirdir town in Isparta province.[45]

Children, with or without parents, became a major concern of the government. Near the Tophane barracks, 60 poorly clad children were provided with shirts, socks, fezzes, handkerchiefs, robes and overalls, as well as alphabet books and religious manuals for their education.[46] The Committee for Union and Progress (CUP) instrumentalised childhood during the crisis by assigning symbolic and practical roles to children. The children's victimisation was seen as a baptism of fire through which they would become 'future Turks', members of a future nation hardened by the violent struggle for existence.

Finally, hostility from the Anatolian population compounded the refugees' sense of frustration and rejection. The Ottoman archives are littered with requests by Anatolian Muslim communities to remove the refugees. Tension between the local populations and the refugees was nothing new: refugees from earlier wars had not always been warmly welcomed. In some areas such as Biga and Midilli, district governors had refused to settle vulnerable refugees in the settlements for reasons of finances and social stability.[47] Bosnian refugees in Gönüllü village complained that the district governor failed to give them any help at all, and that only the local mosques provided clothing and bedding. People succumbed to dysentery, as a group of refugees argued in an opinion piece, lamenting: 'Were the refugees, who left their homelands to take refuge in a place of safety, supposed to be left in this state? Is leaving them to sleep on cold stones, hungry, and without medicine, meant to be a bosom of protection?'[48]

Local people reacted to refugees with a mixture of admiration and resentment. On the one hand, there were widespread rumours among Anatolians that Rumelians were hard-working, frugal and productive people, and some locals indeed took pity on the vulnerable refugees. An Armenian man from Istanbul, Armenag Badalian, witnessed a refugee who wanted to buy bread in the central Beyoğlu district, and wrote angrily about the situation: 'with just a compass in their hands, these wretched people arrive at bakeries to buy bread … Why do the municipal officials, sitting just 50 yards away, not see this? If they are treated like this close to municipal offices, imagine what is happening further away'.[49] On the other hand, many Anatolians resented the 'preferential treatment' the Rumelians ostensibly received. The Ottoman government's social policies fed into suspicions that the Ottoman elite, who themselves were mostly from the Balkans, cared for their 'own' people much more than they ever did for neglected, dusty Anatolia. As a result, not all Ottomans were happy to receive and shelter refugees. A Greek man, Mikhail Grigoriadis, wrote a letter of complaint to the government to protest the settling of Balkan refugees in his farm in the Sivrihisar district.[50] But many Muslims too resented the refugees, even though they shared their ethno-religious identity. Refugees expected to encounter Muslim solidarity, and its absence became a source of profound disillusionment. In the Muslim villages where they settled, refugees were called names, such as 'lousy refugee', 'dirty refugee' and 'naked refugee'. According to Köker and Keskiner's oral-history research in western Anatolia, some locals cursed the refugees, wishing that their ships had sunk so they would not have landed in Anatolia.[51]

The First World War and the settlement of the refugees

The consequences of massacre and expulsion on the Balkans strained the relationship between the refugees and the residual Ottoman Muslims, but also and especially that between Muslims and Christians in general. In the critical period between the end of the Balkan Wars in May 1913 and the outbreak of the First World War in August 1914, ethno-religious polarisation intensified from the political elites down to ordinary people on the ground. Young Turk radicals broadcast propaganda with the aim of spreading fear and hatred towards Ottoman Christians. Social interaction diminished between Muslims and Christians in major cities, provincial towns and villages. The extremists also targeted moderate Muslims, intimidating and silencing the political centre.[52] The Young Turks' perception that the catastrophe of the Balkans should not be repeated on the remaining territories of the Ottoman Empire, especially the eastern provinces, would give birth to unprecedented forms of violence.[53] Some Ottoman intellectuals foresaw the looming cataclysm. In his 1913 book on the Balkan Wars, the Armenian journalist Aram Andonian (1875–1952) wrote that 'the principle of nationality' had spelled disaster in the Balkans and was utterly untenable in the eastern provinces where most Armenians lived.[54] Andonian had planned to write a second volume to his book. He never did, because in April 1915 he was deported from his home city of Istanbul.

On 2 August 1914, one day after the German declaration of war against Russia, Germany and the Ottoman Empire signed a written agreement on closer co-operation and mobilisation. On 29 October 1914, without a formal declaration of war, Enver Pasha ordered the Ottoman navy to bombard the Russian port city of Sevastopol. Ottoman battle cruisers destroyed oil tanks and sank fourteen vessels.[55] The *fait accompli* triggered declarations of war by the Triple Entente powers. From 11 November 1914 the Ottoman Empire was officially at war with Russia, France and Britain.[56] The First World War did not happen incidentally to the empire; rather, powerful cadres in the CUP's nationalist wing consciously headed towards armed confrontation, though not with one particular state. Entry into the war formed 'part of a strategy to achieve long-term security, economic development and, eventually, national recovery'.[57] In other words, by participating in the war the CUP hoped to solve the perceived problems of the empire in a radical fashion.

One such problem was the refugee crisis. To cope with such large numbers of refugees the CUP created a 'Directorate for the Settlement of Tribes and Immigrants' (*İskân-ı Aşâir ve Muhacirîn Müdüriyeti*, İAMM). This bureaucratic apparatus served to settle and provide accommodation for homeless Muslim refugees, expelled from the lost territories.[58] It would later be expanded to constitute four branches, namely settlement, intelligence, transport and tribes.[59] Talaat assembled the CUP leaders and asserted that 'Anatolia is a closed box for us', arguing that they had to 'get to know the contents' in order to operate on it. After Talaat had spoken, Turkish-nationalist ideologue Ziya Gökalp took the floor and declaimed:

> We have made a political revolution ... But the biggest revolution is the social revolution. The revolutions we can spark in our social body [*içtimaî bünyemiz*], in the field of culture, will be the largest and most productive. This will only work if we get to know the morphological and physiological structure of Turkish society ... In order to research these structures let us send comrades with scholarly ability to open this box.[60]

These metaphors heralded a fundamental ethnic reorganisation of the Ottoman Empire, in which Armenians, Kurds, Greeks and Balkan Muslims found themselves as the targets of wartime population politics.

From April 1915 onwards, the CUP began to deport Armenians, beginning with male community elites and increasingly expanding this target category to finally encompass all Ottoman Armenian civilians. The İAMM was entrusted with the task of deportation. Alongside the deportation of Armenians from their historic homeland, the CUP also ordered Turks to be resettled in that region. This two-track policy would expedite the demographic 'Turkification' process. Most settlers were Bosnian Muslims, Bulgarian Turks and Albanian Muslims who had fled the war and persecutions in the Balkans. These refugees were filtered out for immediate settlement in Armenian villages. At first the settler-deportees were lodged in mosques and seminaries, where other poor and miserable citizens were temporarily housed as well. Ultimately they were to be housed in the empty Syriac and Armenian villages, mostly the fertile and large ones near city centres, such as Muş, Diyarbekir and

Mardin. Beginning in the summer of 1915, this settlement policy continued until the end of the war. Muslims who had been expelled from or fled the Balkans now became pawns in a government-sponsored scheme of demographic warfare. To the CUP regime, they were only useful as a counterweight against Armenians and Kurds, who lived mostly in the eastern provinces. In other words, the CUP leadership exploited the refugees' ethnic identity for its own purposes.

Thus the settlers compulsorily resettled in historic Armenian towns and villages were Muslims who had sought asylum in the Ottoman Empire after the Balkan Wars. Many of them had lived in Istanbul in shabby dwellings, impoverished and traumatised. When war broke out in 1914, the CUP activated its plans for the ethnic reorganisation of the empire; the settlers were mobilised and expected to play their part in it. Albanians comprised one group to be deported and settled. In June 1915 the İAMM ordered their 'scattered settlement in order for their mother tongue and national traditions to be extinguished quickly'.[61] Albanian and Bosnian refugees were to be settled all over the empire, especially in formerly Armenian villages.[62] On 30 June 1915 the İAMM ordered 181 Bosnian families temporarily residing in Konya to be deported to Diyarbekir province and settled in its 'empty villages' – a pithy euphemism for Armenian villages.[63] Orders for the deportation and settlement of ethnic Turks from Bulgaria and Greece were issued the next day.[64]

In the meantime, the genocidal persecution of the Armenians raged in full force. While they were being massacred throughout the summer of 1915, the Balkan settlers were on their way. However, preparations were still needed in the Armenian villages in order to lodge the settlers successfully. On 17 June 1915 the İAMM reiterated its request for economic and geographic data on the emptied Armenian villages of several eastern provinces. In order to send settlers to the province, its capacity to absorb immigrants had to be determined.[65] A week later the İAMM ordered educational resources to be provided for the settlers:

> It is necessary to appropriate the schools of the towns and villages that have been emptied of Armenians for Muslim immigrants to be settled there. However, the present value of the buildings, the amount and value of its educational materials needs to be registered and sent to the department of general recordkeeping.[66]

This national order constituted a warrant for the seizure of all Ottoman-Armenian schools and their conversion into Ottoman-Turkish schools. The Commission for Abandoned Properties was assigned the task of allocating school benches, blackboards, bookcases and even paper and pens to the prospective settlers.[67]

The CUP intended the deportation and settlement of Balkan Muslims to be a one-way trip. The settlers were expected to 'Turkify' the non-Turkish regions. The CUP reiterated the point that the settlers should remain in those regions. On 9 November 1916 the İAMM warned the provincial authorities of Diyarbekir 'to prevent by all means the Turkish settlers in the province being moved to other regions'.[68] Four days later it repeated the order 'with special emphasis'.[69] Even after the Russian army had imploded and retreated in 1917 and the Ottoman army swept forward all the way to Baku, the refugees were not allowed to leave anywhere. The order was repeated in March 1918 and in April 1918.[70] The German official Von Lüttichau observed that settlers who secretly attempted to return to their native regions 'died in their hundreds, because they had no bread (*unterwegs zu Hunderten umkamen, weil sie kein Brot hatten*)'.[71] An assessment of the settlement of these Balkan Muslim communities in the formerly Armenian villages would produce ambivalent results. On the one hand they met with hardship as they had difficulties acclimatising to the eastern Anatolian climate, which was different from the Balkans. On the other hand they were protected and well-provided for by the Ottoman government, and later by the Turkish Republic. In any case, the First World War did not signal the end of their ordeal.

The early Turkish Republic

The establishment of the Turkish Republic in 1923 accompanied one of the most formative events in the episode of Ottoman collapse, namely the Greek-Turkish population exchange, the largest one of its kind before the Second World War. It was prefaced by the Greek-Turkish war of 1919–22, which razed parts of Western Anatolia and laid waste to the cosmopolitan Aegean port city of Smyrna (İzmir). When Greece and Turkey signed the Treaty of Lausanne in February and March 1923, the treaty institutionalised and legalised a huge population transfer in which 1.5 million Greek-Orthodox Ottomans were exchanged for 500,000 Greek Muslims. Many of the former spoke a Turkish dialect and many of the latter had Greek as their mother tongue. But following the Ottoman *millet* system, religious identity took precedence over linguistic identity.[72] The influx of so many refugees had a profound demographic, political and cultural impact on both societies. It also generated acute social problems, of which the land settlement issue constituted the major problem.[73]

Throughout the 1920s and 1930s, the Turkish government prepared the colonisation of those villages that were planned to be depopulated. Two important settlement laws, in 1927 and in 1934, foresaw deportations of Kurds from their homeland and settlement of Turks in their stead. The fact that it was possible for settlement plans to predate deportations might conceivably denote that the deportations were but a pretext for clearing out high-quality living quarters on behalf of Turkish settlers, but there is no definite evidence for this claim. Whatever its timing, the eastern provinces needed to be prepared to receive a large influx of settlers. For example, in May 1927, the vice-governor of Diyarbekir reported to the Ministry of the Interior that preparations were being made to receive the settlers. Of the 75 households of settlers from Yugoslavia, around half had already gone to various regions. The provincial authorities settled refugees from the Macedonian towns of Kumanovo and Veles/Köprülü in 'empty houses' in the province. According to the governor, since these people had suffered 'destitution and misery', they should be compensated with additional immovable and movable property.[74]

Reports suggested that the settlement campaign did not always seem like an easy affair either. Eyewitness reports were often sceptical. Travelling through eastern Turkey in the late 1920s, the author Harold Armstrong came across a refugee who was in the process of being resettled:

> His language was Greek and he could as yet only speak a little broken Turkish with a thick Greek accent, though his ancestors had come from Constantinople. The Turkish and Greek Governments had been exchanging Christians and Moslems, he told me. He had been forcibly rooted up and sent here. He bemoaned his fate. In Crete he was happy and well off. His great-grandfather's father had owned the farm he had inherited, but the Greeks would only have Greeks in Greece. In the village, he said, were refugees from all parts: from Western Thrace, Greece proper, Salonika, Macedonia and even from Cyprus. They had tried to start life again, but they had no capital; the land was not theirs and at any moment they might be moved, so they had patched the houses just sufficiently to live in, and did only just enough work on the land to make it produce. The fruit was beginning to ripen in the gardens and the vineyards; the country was full of foxes and thieves, so that if they did not watch they might be ruined in one night. He was like a child, helpless, lost, pathetic, homeless.[75]

The Kemalist regime did not regard the long-term well-being of the settlers as their primary concern. So long as the settlement campaign increased the demographic ratio of Turks in the eastern provinces, it continued unabated.

The 1934 Settlement Law was more encompassing and draconic than the 1927 one. The entire country was divided into two zones: one zone for 'people who are culturally Turkish', and another one for those that were not. People from the former zone would be transferred to the latter zone, and vice versa. This is where the three demographic policies overlapped with each other: the destruction of the Armenians, the deportation of the Kurds, and the settlement of the Balkan Muslims. If there were still Armenian villages, the refugees could be settled there; otherwise they could be settled in Kurdish villages, but where there was no more capacity, villages would be constructed from scratch. The government confiscated another two hundred houses from Kurds and assigned them to the settlers. To a great extent the resources emanated from the Armenian genocide and the various confiscations from Kurdish elites – some of which were also formerly Armenian goods.[76] Following the promulgation of the 1934 law, government commissions aimed to build three to five Turkish villages with one hundred houses apiece annually. When the settlers finally arrived, the inspector-general of the eastern zone argued that 'This way our progressive nation can assimilate the backward nation' and establish 'economic dominance in a Turkish centre'.[77] According to official sources, between 1928 and 1938 a total of 1,988 migrants were sent to Diyarbekir province. In 1938 another 2,143 households were expected to settle there. Because the Republican province of Diyarbekir was much smaller than its Ottoman predecessor, to this number we should add some of the settlers sent to Elazığ province in the north. There, from 1932 onwards, a total of 1,571 households were sent, numbering 6,045 settlers from Yugoslavia, Bulgaria, Greece and Syria. As all the settlers were peasants, they were settled in the rural areas.[78]

Official propaganda texts portrayed the settlement of Turks in Armenian and Kurdish villages as an unequivocal success. One brochure published by the governorship of Diyarbekir boasted that it worked hard to 'attract our Turkish brothers from beyond our national borders, settle them in the homeland, and turn them into productive people truly connected to the superior ideal of the nation'.[79] Here, the distinction between the ethnic 'Turkish brothers' versus 'Turkish citizens' is vital for understanding the government's views on nationhood and citizenship. The local authorities in Diyarbekir acclaimed the settlement of the Turks in the same discourse as national directives: 'three beautiful and brand new villages have been established near Diyarbekir city for our brothers from Bulgaria and Romania ... the settlers have now passed into a state of being fully productive people'.[80] Another official wrote in the same vein: 'the attention given to the settlers is considerable. After having provided for their maintenance, farm animals, ploughs, seeds, and land have also been supplied. Their sick are being taken care of by the state. The Bulgarian and Romanian immigrants work hard and have rapidly transformed into productive people'.[81]

Internal correspondence and oral-history suggest otherwise. In his 1935 report İnönü remarked in an uneasy tone:

> there have been efforts to settle immigrants from everywhere. A population of about fifteen hundred toil on very fertile and water-rich terrain. There are three groups of immigrants with a gap between them of three to five years ... Almost all of them complain to government officials about their condition ... The people are needy and destitute, the fields have not yet been productive. The pastureland has been distributed poorly. They are complaining.[82]

The issues that vexed the settlers included non-economic concerns. One elderly Turkish settler remembered that even though his parents were allotted plenty of property by the government, they decried their arid eastern village as 'this accursed place', and longed for their estate in Thessaloniki.[83] Another family of settlers faced a culture which, in their own words, they 'never understood'. They were overwhelmed by the 'cut-throat' economic rivalry and higher levels of everyday violence. They also felt intimidated by their Kurdish neighbours, who envied and despised them for their connections and preferential treatment at government offices.[84] The deportations and settlements also sowed the seeds of conflict among local Kurds and Turkish settlers. For these settlers, the climate did not alleviate their lives either, even though the Settlement Law clearly included a clause that the Turks should be settled 'according to suitable living and climatic conditions'. Although the law promised to take into consideration the acclimatisation of the peasants from the Balkans, who were used to green hills with plenty of precipitation, some of them fell ill in the scorching, arid Tigris valley and died.[85] Much like the Kurdish deportees in western Turkey, many Turkish settlers in eastern Turkey likewise felt alienated and regretted having been resettled.

Conclusion

The implosion of the Ottoman Empire between 1912 and 1923 constituted the *Urkatastrophe* of the modern Middle East. The violence of the two Balkan Wars, the ensuing population exchanges and expulsions, the

First World War, the Armenian Genocide, the Greco-Turkish War, and the 1923 great population exchange occurred within one decade. Greece and Turkey especially had become veritable refugee societies, since the refugees would not be returning according to the Lausanne Treaty. Three issues dominated the agenda surrounding the refugees: collective trauma, difficult inter-group relations, and disempowerment.

After so much violence in the Ottoman territories, it was only logical that hundreds of thousands of people were physically wounded and psychologically traumatised – the modern academic term would be 'post-traumatic stress disorder'. Demobilised soldiers came home with frightening stories of mass death; entire neighbourhoods had been emptied; families had lost their male populations; refugees were begging by the roadside; and miserable orphans were roaming the streets naked. War, displacement and flight had thoroughly scarred all actors and caused lasting damage to the psychological development of the refugee community at large.[86] The Turkish government overestimated the settlers' resilience and willingness to stay in their settlements, and underestimated the tenacity of Kurds and Armenians to return. Much like Palestinians after the 1948 war, 'Armenia' or 'Kurdistan' had become an abstract, imagined but emotive space to which Armenians and Kurds longed to return.[87] And the Armenians and Kurds were not the only ones longing. Balkan Muslim culture profoundly infused Turkish culture. Balkan songs and popular culture revolve around the loss of homeland and express the desire to return, such as the famous Macedonian song 'The Vardar Valley' (*Vardar Ovası*):

The reeds growing on Mayadağ	*Mayadağ'dan kalkan sazlar*
White girls with red shoes	*Al topuklu beyaz kızlar*
My lover's heart is aching	*Yarimin yüreği sızlar*
I cannot stay, I cannot linger	*Eylenemem aldanamam*
I cannot stay in these places	*Ben bu yerlerde duramam*
The Vardar valley, the Vardar valley	*Vardar ovası Vardar ovası*
I could not gain a piece of the homeland.	*Kazanamadım sıla parası*[88]

A century after the Armenian genocide and the settlement of refugees, most Balkan Muslim settlers may have assimilated in Turkey and become 'modern' Turks, but few ever forgot their community's painful history.[89]

The mass trauma was not allowed to become a 'collective trauma' because the Turkish Republic's memory politics of the violent decade diverged from popular memories. In March 1922, Mustafa Kemal denounced the 'atrocities' of the Greeks and decried their acts of 'destruction and

Becoming and unbecoming refugees

aggression ... irreconcilable with humanity ... impossible to cover up and deny'.[90] But after the establishment of the Republic the tide turned and the accusatory tone of this moral indignation disappeared from view. The 1930s witnessed a diplomatic rapprochement between Turkey and Greece as relations improved with the signing of several agreements and conventions. By the time the Greek Premier Panagis Tsaldaris (1868–1936) visited Turkey in September 1933, the same Mustafa Kemal now spoke of the Greeks as 'esteemed guests' with whom contact had been 'amicable and cordial'.[91] Throughout the 1920s and 1930s, the Turkish and Greek nations were portrayed as having coexisted perennially in mutual respect and eternal peace.[92] Friendly inter-state relations in the service of Turkey's acceptance and stabilisation into the nation state system took precedence over old grief, without any serious process of closure or reconciliation in between. The refugee community was disappointed, but it acquiesced in the Kemalist regime's portrayal of their recent history.

Finally, the wartime humiliation and post-war disempowerment of the refugee community drove a disproportionate number of them to embrace radical Turkish nationalism. These survivors of persecution crossed borders and became attracted to right-wing politics in the receiving society. Many of them sought a means of escape from their low social status and found it in chauvinistic causes. The Turkish government's security and intelligence agencies were well aware of this and readily enlisted the refugees, who were over-represented among those organisations in modern Turkish history.[93] The movement of traumatised and victimised refugees from one society to another can have a dual impact: it can destabilise, polarise and radicalise the domestic political cultures in a significant way, and it can produce opportunity structures for political elites to enlist the uprooted in various nationalist causes. It might go too far to attribute to the refugees a certain 'Stockholm syndrome', but their exploitation by the then Turkish government is beyond doubt.[94] By enlisting in those organisations, the refugees attempted to shed their victim identity and 'unbecome' refugees.

Notes

1 George F. Kennan, *The Other Balkan Wars: a 1913 Carnegie Endowment Inquiry in Retrospect with a New Introduction and Reflection on the Present Record* (Washington, DC: Carnegie Endowment for International Peace, 1993), pp. 109–35; Richard C. Hall, *The Balkan Wars, 1912–1913: Prelude to the First World War* (London: Routledge, 2000), pp. 136–8. For an analysis

of the Ottoman involvement in the Balkan Wars from a military perspective, see Edward J. Erickson, *Defeat in Detail: the Ottoman Army in the Balkans, 1912-1913* (Westport, CT: Praeger, 2003).

2 Momchil Yonov, 'Bulgarian military operations in the Balkan Wars', in Béla K. Király and Dimitrije Djordjevic (eds), *East Central European Society and the Balkan Wars* (Boulder, CO: Social Science Monographs, 1987), pp. 63-84.

3 Leon Trotsky, *Die Balkankriege 1912-13* (Essen: Arbeiterpresse Verlag, 1995, transl. Hannelore Georgi and Harald Schubärth), pp. 296-7.

4 *Hikmet*, 11 November 1912, p. 4.

5 *Hikmet*, 14 November 1912, p. 1.

6 *Ikdam*, 5810, 25 April 1913, p. 3.

7 Katrin Boeckh, *Von den Balkankriegen zum Ersten Weltkrieg: Kleinstaatenpolitik und ethnische Selbstbestimmung auf dem Balkan* (München: Oldenbourg, 1996), pp. 165, 199.

8 Ahmet Halaçoğlu, *Balkan Harbi Sırasında Rumeli'den Türk Göçleri (1912-1913)* (Ankara: Türk Tarih Kurumu, 1995), p. 43.

9 Ahmed Cevad, *Balkanlarda Akan Kan* (Istanbul: Şamil, n.y.), pp. 118-19.

10 *Ikdam*, 5668, 30 November 1912, p. 2.

11 *Ikdam*, 5689, 21 December 1912, p. 2.

12 Abdürrahim Dede, *Rumeli'nde Bırakılanlar* (Istanbul: Otağ Matbaası, 1975), pp. 151-70.

13 Cevad, *Balkanlarda Akan Kan*.

14 Elçin Kürşat-Ahlers, 'Die Brutalisierung von Gesellschaft und Kriegsführung im Osmanischen Reich während der Balkankriege (1903-1914)', in Andreas Gestrich (ed.), *Gewalt im Krieg: Ausübung, Erfahrung und Verweigerung von Gewalt in Kriegen des 20. Jahrhunderts* (Münster: Lit-Verlag, 1995), pp. 51-74.

15 For an introduction see Justin McCarthy, *Death and Exile: the Ethnic Cleansing of Ottoman Muslims, 1821-1922* (Princeton, NJ: The Darwin Press, 1995), pp. 1-22.

16 M. Şükrü Hanioğlu, *Preparation for a Revolution: the Young Turks, 1902-1908* (Oxford: Oxford University Press, 2001), pp. 173-81.

17 The best study on the Muslim refugees remains: Halaçoğlu, *Balkan Harbi Sırasında Rumeli'den Türk Göçleri*.

18 *Alemdar*, 10 January 1913, p. 2.

19 *İkdam*, no. 5934, 28 August 1913, p. 3.

20 *Babalık*, no. 214, 5 September 1913, p. 3.

21 Ali İhsan Sâbis, *Balkan Harbında neden Munhazim Olduk?* (Istanbul, 1913), p. 95.

22 Halide Edib, *Conflict of East and West in Turkey* (Delhi: Jamia Press, 1935), p. 80.

23 Quoted in Mark Mazower, *Salonica, City of Ghosts: Christians, Muslims and Jews, 1430-1950* (London: HarperCollins, 2004), pp. 338-9.

24 *Rumeli Mezâlimi ve Bulgar Vahşetleri* (Istanbul: Rumeli Muhâcirîn-i İslâmiyye Cemiyeti, 1913), p. 49.
25 Nesime Ceyhan, *Balkan Savaşı Hikâyeleri* (Istanbul: Selis, 2009), pp. 217–20.
26 *Takvim-i Vekayi*, nu: 584, 31 Tesrin-i Evvel 1912, 13 November 1912, p. 3.
27 Uğur Ümit Üngör, 'Orphans, converts, and prostitutes: social consequences of war and persecution in the Ottoman Empire, 1914–1923', *War in History*, 19, no. 2 (2012), 173–92.
28 Bayur, *Türk İnkılabı Tarihi*, vol. 2, part III, p. 250.
29 Quoted in Nader Sohrabi, 'Global waves, local actors: what the Young Turks knew about other revolutions and why it mattered', *Comparative Studies in Society and History*, 44, no.1 (2002), 45–79 (here p. 64).
30 Falih Rıfkı Atay, *Zeytindağı* (Istanbul: Dünya, 1957), p. 10.
31 Tunaya, *Türkiye'de Siyasal Partiler*, vol. 3, p. 465.
32 *Alemdar*, 25 October 1912, p. 3.
33 Cemil Topuzlu, *İstibdat-Meşrutiyet-Cumhuriyet Devirlerinde 80 Yıllık Hatıralarım*, Hüsrev Hatemi and Aykut Kazancıgil, eds (Istanbul: İstanbul Üniversitesi Cerrahpaşa Tıp Fakültesi Yayınları, 1982), p. 124.
34 *İkdam*, 18 November 1912, p. 5.
35 *Osmanlı Hilâl-ı Ahmer Cemiyeti 1329–1331 Salnâmesi* (Istanbul: Ahmed Ihsan ve Şürekâsı Matbaacılık Osmanlı Şirketi, 1915), p. 138.
36 *Alemdar*, 27 October 1912, p. 3.
37 *Osmanlı Hilâl-ı Ahmer Cemiyeti 1329–1331 Salnâmesi*, pp. 220–5.
38 After Sultan Mesud I of Ghazni, Sultan Murad I, and Sultan Osman I, respectively.
39 *Hikmet*, 7 November 1912, p. 4.
40 *İkdam*, 10 November 1912, p. 2.
41 *İkdam*, 10 December 1912, p. 5.
42 *Alemdar*, 19 February 1913, p. 3.
43 *Alemdar*, 28 March 1913, p. 3.
44 *İştirâk*, 27 October 1912, p. 4.
45 *Babalık*, no.184, 7 April 1913, p. 4.
46 *İkdam*, 22 September 1913, p. 4.
47 See e.g. *Muhacir*, no. 54, 25 June 1910, p. 4; *Muhacir*, no. 73, 31 August 1910, p. 4.
48 *Muhacir*, no. 64, 30 July 1910, p. 2.
49 *Alemdar*, 19 February 1913, p. 3.
50 *Başbakanlık Osmanlı Arşivi* (Ottoman Archives, Istanbul), DH.İD 85/41, 18 January 1913.
51 Tolga Köker and Leyla Keskiner, 'Lessons in refugeehood: the experience of forced migrants in Turkey', in Renee Hirschon (ed.), *Crossing the Aegean: an Appraisal of the 1923 Compulsory Population Exchange between Greece and Turkey* (New York: Berghahn, 2003), pp. 193–208.

52 George W. Gawrych, 'The culture and politics of violence in Turkish society, 1903–14', *Middle Eastern Studies*, 22, no. 3 (1986), 307–30.
53 For a useful overview, see Mark Levene, 'Creating a modern "zone of genocide": the impact of nation- and state-formation on Eastern Anatolia, 1878–1923', *Holocaust and Genocide Studies*, 12, no. 3 (1998), 393–433.
54 Aram Andonian, *Balkan Savaşı* (Istanbul: Aras Yayıncılık, 1999, transl. Zaven Biberian).
55 Paul G. Halpern, *A Naval History of World War I* (Annapolis, MD: Naval Institute Press, 1994), p. 76.
56 John Keegan, *The First World War* (New York: Vintage, 1998), p. 217.
57 Mustafa Aksakal, *The Ottoman Road to War in 1914: the Ottoman Empire and the First World War* (Cambridge: Cambridge University Press, 2008), p. 191.
58 *İkdam*, 29 December 1913, p. 3.
59 Cengiz Orhonlu, *Osmanlı İmparatorluğu'nda Aşiretlerin İskânı* (Istanbul: Eren, 1987), p. 120.
60 Nejat Birdoğan (ed.), Baha Said Bey, *İttihat ve Terakki'nin Alevilik-Bektaşilik Araştırması* (Istanbul: Berfin, 1995), p. 8.
61 *BOA*, DH.ŞFR 54/216, İAMM to Konya, 28 June 1915.
62 *BOA*, DH.ŞFR 54/246, İAMM to Diyarbekir, 6 June 1915.
63 *BOA*, DH.ŞFR 54/246, İAMM to Konya, 30 June 1915.
64 *BOA*, DH.ŞFR 54/246, İAMM to Diyarbekir, 1 July 1915.
65 *BOA*, DH.ŞFR 54/39, İAMM to Diyarbekir, 17 June 1915.
66 *BOA*, DH.ŞFR 54/101, İAMM to provinces, 22 June 1915.
67 *BOA*, DH.ŞFR 54/331, İAMM to Diyarbekir, 7 July 1915.
68 *BOA*, DH.ŞFR 69/219, AMMU to Diyarbekir, 9 November 1916.
69 *BOA*, DH.ŞFR 69/248, AMMU to Diyarbekir, 13 November 1916.
70 *BOA*, DH.ŞFR 85/262, AMMU to Diyarbekir, 28 March 1918; *BOA*, DH.ŞFR 86/46, AMMU to Third Army Commander, 13 April 1918.
71 Uğur Ümit Üngör, *The Making of Modern Turkey: Nation and State in Eastern Anatolia, 1913–1950* (Oxford: Oxford University Press, 2011), p. 119.
72 For a concise overview, see Stavroula Chrisdoulaki, *Greek-Turkish Exchange of Population* (Norderstedt: GRIN Verlag, 2010).
73 Bruce Clark, *Twice a Stranger: the Mass Expulsions that Forged Modern Greece and Turkey* (Cambridge, MA: Harvard University Press, 2006).
74 Üngör, *The Making of Modern Turkey*, p. 146.
75 Harold Armstrong, *Turkey and Syria Reborn: a Record of Two Years of Travel* (London: John Lane, 1930), pp. 124–5.
76 Şeyhmus Diken, *İsyan Sürgünleri* (Istanbul: İletişim, 2005), pp. 36, 51, 98, 220, 239.
77 Hüseyin Koca, *Yakın Tarihten Günümüze Hükümetlerin Doğu-Güneydoğu Anadolu Politikaları* (Konya: Mikro Yayınları, 1998), pp. 495–7.
78 Hurşit Nazlı, *Elazığ ilinin coğrafi, zirai, ticari, tarih, nufus ve jeolojik durumu* (Ankara: Zerbamat Basımevi, 1939), p. 51.

79 *Cumhuriyetin 15inci yılında Diyarbakır* (Diyarbakır: Diyarbakır Matbaası, 1938), p. 106.
80 Usman Eti, *Diyarbekir* (Diyarbakır: Diyarbekir Matbaası, 1937), p. 44.
81 Eti, *Diyarbekir*, p. 51.
82 Saygı Öztürk, 'İsmet Paşa'nın Kürt Raporu', *Hürriyet*, 8 September 1992, p. 7. In his memoirs, İnönü denied the ethnic component of the deportation-and-settlement campaigns, justifying them as a matter of filling a thinly populated area. See İsmet İnönü, *Hatıralar* (Ankara: Bilgi, 1987), vol. 2, p. 270.
83 Interview conducted in Diyarbekir with Kerim B., 14 August 2007.
84 Interview conducted in Diyarbekir with A.S., 15 August 2007.
85 Şevket Beysanoğlu, *Anıtları ve Kitâbeleri ile Diyarbakır Tarihi* (Diyarbakır: Diyarbakır Büyükşehir Belediyesi, Kültür ve Sanat Yayınları, 1996), vol. 3, *Cumhuriyet Dönemi*, pp. 1026–9.
86 For an excellent oral-history study on post-war trauma among refugees see Aynur İlyasoğlu and Gülay Kayacan (eds), *Kuşaklar, Deneyimler, Tanıklıklar: Türkiye'de Sözlü Tarih Çalışmaları Konferansı* (Istanbul: Tarih Vakfı, 2006).
87 Nicola Migliorino *(Re)constructing Armenia in Lebanon and Syria: Ethno-cultural Diversity* (New York: Berghahn, 2008), pp. 31, 69; Juliane Hammer, *Palestinians Born in Exile: Diaspora and the Search for a Homeland* (Austin, TX: University of Texas Press, 2009), pp. 62–3.
88 Cahit Öztelli, *Evlerinin Önü: Türküler* (Istanbul: Özgür, 2002), p. 776.
89 A recent, candid memoir of an Ottoman civil servant includes many explicit and implicit references to trauma. Figen Taşkın and Mustafa Yeni (eds), *Bahaeddin Demir Aydın, 'Muhacir Olmak da Varmış': Rumelili Bir Kalem Efendisinin Anıları* (Istanbul: İş Bankası Kültür Yayınları, 2013).
90 Nimet Arsan (ed.), *Atatürk'ün Söylev ve Demeçleri* (Ankara: Türk Tarih Kurumu, 1959–1964), vol. I, p. 241.
91 *Cumhuriyet*, 6 and 9 September 1933; Arı İnan, *Düşünceleriyle Atatürk* (Ankara: Türk Tarih Kurumu, 1991), p. 162.
92 For a study of Turkish-Greek rapprochement after 1923, see Damla Demirözü, *Savaştan Barışa Giden Yol: Atatürk-Venizelos Dönemi Türkiye-Yunanistan İlişkileri* (Istanbul: İletişim, 2007).
93 Ryan Gingeras, *Sorrowful Shores: Violence, Ethnicity, and the End of the Ottoman Empire, 1912–1923* (Oxford: Oxford University Press, 2009), chapter 3.
94 The most striking example of such a process was post-war Hungary, which was flooded with refugees from former Habsburg territories who became the most radical elements of society. See István I. Mócsy, *The Uprooted: Hungarian Refugees and their Impact on Hungary's Domestic Politics, 1918–1921* (New York: Columbia University Press, 1983). Another excellent example is Hutu refugees from Burundi, driven into exile in Tanzania after the failed 1972 insurrection against the Tutsi dictatorship. See Liisa H. Malkki, *Purity and Exile: Violence, Memory, and National Cosmology among Hutu Refugees in Tanzania* (Chicago: University of Chicago Press, 1995).

Index

Albania 240, 242, 244–5, 284
Aleppo 3
Algeria 251, 252
Allgemeine Jüdische Zeitung 163
Alsace-Lorraine 23
Altona 32–3
American Joint Distribution
    Committee 12
American Relief Administration 16
Anatolia 2, 3, 287, 293, 295
    Muslim refugees 11, 284, 287, 288,
        293, 304–27
Andonian, Aram 315
Andrić, Jelisije 242
Antwerp 198–9, 202
Arabazhin, Konstantin 56
Argentina 21
Armenia
    Armenians in Turkey 314, 316,
        317, 320
    refugees 3, 4, 7, 14, 16, 20, 265
    Soviet Republic of 14–15
Armstrong, Harold 319
Arras 222–3
Asia Minor 260, 263, 264, 266
Askew, Claude and Alice 239, 257
Assyrian refugees 3, 14–15, 16
Atanković, Mališa 249
Atatürk, Kemal (Mustafa Kemal) 292,
    322
Atay, Falih Rıfkı 310

Australia 265
Austria-Hungary, 91, 109, 122, 123,
    130, 136, 151, 159, 170, 179,
    180, 182, 237
    Austrian Republic 150, 188
    deportations 131, 134, 179
    Ministry of the Interior (Austrian)
        135, 138, 145, 160, 163
    Ministry of War 135
    minorities 4
    as occupying country 18
    refugees 9, 13–14, 17, 129–55
        Bosnian Serb 4, 133
        Italian 185–191
        Jewish 3, 6–7, 8, 11, 14, 136, 138,
        150, 156–76
    see also Galicia; Gmünd;
        Ruthenians

Babiański, Aleksander 79
Baku 318
Balkan Wars 6, 236, 239–40, 260, 263,
    265, 267, 271, 272, 280, 284,
    291–4, 304–5
Balkelis, Tomas 46, 55
Baltic Germans 45–6, 47–8, 49, 50, 51,
    52, 55–6
Baltic States 12–13, 14, 52
    see also Estonia; Latvia; Lithuania
Baranovichi 69, 70, 71, 93
Bartoszewicz, Joachim 81

Index

Batocki, Adolf von 24, 26–7, 28, 36, 37
Bártfa (Bartfeld, Bardejov) 158
Basly, Émile 221, 226
Belarus 69, 74, 77
  refugees 54, 72, 79, 89, 91, 99, 122
Belgium 197, 206, 212
  German occupation 36, 197–8, 212, 221
  government in exile 207
  refugees 5, 7–8, 9, 10, 11, 12, 197–214
    in Britain 20, 198, 199, 200–2, 204, 205, 207, 210, 211
    in France 199, 201, 204, 206, 207, 210, 211
    in the Netherlands 198–9, 201, 202, 203, 204, 209, 211
    relief measures 200–4
    repatriation 210–12
Belgrade 241
Belostok *see* Białystok
Belskii Gostinets (newspaper) 89
Berger, John 1, 3
Berlin 31, 32, 39
  treaty of 262
Białystok (Belostok) 54, 69, 89, 94
Bischoff-Culm, Ernst 34
Bobruisk 71, 93
Bohemia 159, 162, 169, 179, 188
Bolzano 177
Boppe, Auguste 239
Bosanquet, Robert Carr 247
Bosnia 129, 133
  refugees 314, 316
Bourgeois, Léon 221, 226
Brackmann, Albert 24
Brest-Litovsk, treaty 46, 52, 101, 109, 121
Briansk 94
Brubaker, Rogers 285
Bruck an der Leitha (camp) 7, 136, 142
Bucharest 263
Budapest 156, 158, 159, 162, 163, 164
Bukovina 129, 133, 139, 164
Bulgaria 238–9, 241, 260, 262, 264, 265–6, 274, 275, 278, 284, 290
  Communist Party 266
  irregular forces 305
  Ministry of Agriculture 275
  Ministry of Interior and Public Health 266, 271, 275
  population exchange 265
  refugees 16, 260–83, 296
    political activity 278
    relief measures 270, 271, 275, 278
  see also Balkan Wars

Canada 265
Caporetto 12, 183, 185, 190
Cassin, Raoul 227
Caucasus 2, 15, 307
Chełm (Kholm) 69, 89, 91, 114
Constantinople, treaty 263, 269, 292
Corfu 246, 249, 250
Courland, refugees from 45–65
  see also Latvia
Crete 288
Croatia, refugees 143, 147
Czapka, Paula 142
Czechoslovakia 150
Czernowitz (Chernivtsy) 134

Daugavpils 55, 56
Davidović, Ljuba 250
diaspora 12, 157, 278, 286
Dimitriev, Radko, 304–5
Djilas, Milovan 244
Dobrudja 260, 263, 264, 266, 272
Dowbor-Muśnicki, Józef (general) 68

East Prussia 4, 25
  deportations 29
  Jews 28, 33–34
  refugee commission 27–8
  refugees 6, 7, 11, 12, 13, 23–44
    relief measures 31–2, 40
    repatriation 36–9
  Russian occupation 29
Edib, Halide 308
Edirne 289, 290, 292, 293
Egypt 291, 293
Ekaterinoslav (Katerynoslav) 75, 113, 116, 121, 124

Index

Emre, Ahmed Cevad 307
Emtsev, Timofei 120
Estonia 47, 52

Fiume 177–8
Folks, Homer 2–3, 14, 22
France 180, 216, 223–4, 229, 230, 249, 256
  evacuation 218
  German invasion and occupation 216, 218
  Ministry of the Interior 218, 225
  refugees 3, 8, 9, 10, 11, 215–35
    as citizens 225–6, 227
    letters from 227, 228–9
    newspapers 221–2
    relief measures 224, 225, 226, 228, 229
    social identity 220–3, 228, 229, 231
    see also Serbia, refugees
Frankfurt 31
Fridenson, Patrick 224

Galicia 9, 66, 71, 81, 108, 122, 129, 133, 141, 147, 157, 158–9, 164
  Russian occupation 66, 73, 156, 168
Gatrell, Peter 47, 112, 231
Gause, Fritz 24
Genoa, conference 266
Germany 16, 23, 31–4, 41, 91, 109, 122, 123, 197
  refugees 15, 16, 24, 29–30, 41
  see also East Prussia; Latvia; Lithuania; Russia
Gerson, Stéphane 229
Gesemann, Gerhard 241, 242
Gies, Ludwig 35
Ginio, Eyal 309
Glinka, Władysław 67, 68, 69
Głaz, Alicja 73
Gmünd (camp) 7, 9, 129–30, 131, 139–49
Gonatas, Stylianos 289
Gouda 7, 203
Gökalp, Ziya 316
Grabski, Stanisław 79

Grabski, Władysław 71, 72, 78
Greece 13, 269, 285, 288, 293, 295, 297, 323
  Pontic Greeks 295–6
  population exchange
    with Bulgaria 265, 298
    with Turkey 16, 285, 294, 298, 318
  refugees 269, 284–303
  war with Turkey (1897) 288
Grodno 53, 54, 89, 90, 93, 114
Grujić, Slavko 247, 248
Guépratte, Émile 252
Gumbinnen, battle 24

Habsburg Empire *see* Austria-Hungary
Hadjidimov, D. 279
Hanebrink, Paul 171
Hermoupolis 287
Hindenburg, Paul von 24
Hoover, Herbert 16
Horne, John 230
Hrushevsky, Mikhail 108
humanitarianism 118, 126, 160, 200
Hungary 16, 156–7, 159, 161, 165, 170–1
  Ministry of the Interior 162, 163, 164, 166, 167, 169
  refugees after 1918 16, 170
  see also Austria-Hungary

Imber, Mózes 168
Inglis, Elsie 253
Irkutsk 48
Istanbul 307–8, 311, 313
Italy 12, 177–80, 183, 246
  civilians interned 181
  Ministry of the Interior 179, 182, 183, 191
  refugees 5, 9, 12, 14, 177–96
    letters from 188–9
    relief measures 6, 182, 184
  see also Austria-Hungary
Ivanov, Nikolai (Russian general) 66
İzmir *see* Smyrna

Index

Jałowiecki, Bolesław 79
Jewish Relief Committee (Vilnius) 51
Jewish World Relief Conference 57
Jews *see under individual countries*
Joffre, Joseph 246

Kaluga 10, 11, 12, 88, 93, 96, 98
Karadjordjević, King Peter I 241, 255
Karadjordjević, Prince Regent Alexander 245
Katzenau (camp) 186
Kaunas (Kovno) 7, 47, 48, 49, 50, 96
Kharkiv (Khar'kov) 112, 114, 117, 122, 124
Kherson 113, 120
Kholm *see* Chełm
Kiev (Kyiv) 69, 75, 78, 79, 81, 82, 108, 116, 122, 124
Klimentovo 272
Klinger, Heinrich 167–8
Kobrin 71
Konstantinos, King 296, 297
Kölm, Lothar 24
Königsberg 24, 28, 30, 32, 34, 38
Korwin-Kossakowski, Michał S. 69, 70, 75–6
Kosovo 239–43
Kossert, Andreas 24
Kovno *see* Kaunas
Kożuchowski, Józef 71
Kraków (Krakau, Cracow) 130
Kraljevo 239
Kuizinas, Stanislovas 58
Kudrinskii, F. A. 89, 90, 91, 93
Kurds 316, 319, 320
Kursk 88
Kuszłejko, Jacek 81

Lausanne, conference (1923) 266, 298
Latvia 45, 49, 52, 53, 125
  German occupation 46, 60
  independence 55, 56, 59
  refugees 21, 45–65, 99, 122
  Russians in 56
Latvian Committee for Refugee Relief (Ekaterinodar) 55

Latvian Provisional National Council 52
Latvian Riflemen 53
League of Nations 3, 15, 266, 267, 278, 280
Le Bon, Gustav 241
Lednicki, Aleksander 79
Lević, Avram 247
Lipschitz, Shaul 47, 48
Lipschütz, Alexander 52
Lithuania 9, 15, 45, 51, 125
  communities in the Russian Empire 29, 112
  German occupation 46, 47, 48, 50, 53
  independence 51, 55, 57, 58–9
  Jews 45–6, 48, 50, 55, 57, 58, 124
  Ministry of Jewish Affairs 57
  refugees 15, 45–64, 79, 99
Lithuanian Society for War Relief (Vilnius) 51
Liulevicius, Vejas 50
London, treaty 263
Łopaciński, Stanisław 79
Lublin 69, 91
Lubomirska, Maria 67
Ludendorff, Erich von 25
Lüdinghausen, Bernd von 31, 39
Lviv (Lemberg) 79, 130, 134
Lyck 29, 34

Macedonia 239, 240, 260, 262, 263, 264, 270, 271, 287, 289, 294, 319
  Internal Macedonian Revolutionary Organisation 272
Marjanović, Rista 253
Mayeur, Jean-Marie 229
Memel 41
Mevorah, Moša 241, 245
Mihailović, Dragoljub 255–6
Miletic, L 263
Minsk 69, 72, 93
Mittendorf (camp) 7, 145, 147, 149
Mogilev 69, 75
Moldenhower, Jerzy de 71
Montenegro 241, 243–4

Index

Moravia 159, 162, 169, 179, 188
Moreno, Jakob Levy 149
Moscow 9, 75, 125
Moskalevsky, Stanislav 122
Muhacir (newspaper) 313
Munich 31
Mussolini, Benito 12

Najdus, Walentyna 72
Nedić, Milan 246
Near East Relief 17, 277
Neuilly, treaty 260, 264, 275, 280, 298
Nicholas II 90
Niš 238, 239
Niva (newspaper) 89
Nivet, Philippe 216
Nunspeet (camp) 7, 203
Nušić, Branislav 242-3

Obeliai 15, 55, 56-7, 59
Obrenović, Duke Miloš 242
Odessa 109, 122
Oltmer, Jochen 143
Omsk 94
Orel 88, 98
Orsha 47
Ottoman Empire *see* Turkey

Paris 218, 220, 252
   peace conference 263, 264
Partridge, Bernard 253
Pašić, Nikola 247, 253, 256
Patai, József 157, 171
Peć 241, 242
Petrograd 9, 75, 79
Petrović, Rastko 236, 239, 244
Podolia 69, 122
Poland 122, 125
   independence 71, 81, 89
   nobility 46
   refugees 9, 12, 66-87, 96, 112, 124
      Central Citizens' Committee of the Provinces of the Kingdom of Poland (CKO) 70, 71, 72, 78
      national identity 75, 80-2

newspapers 81
relief measures 71, 72, 73, 78-80, 82
war with Lithuania 53
war with Soviet Russia 53, 82
Polish Refugee Relief Committee (Vilnius) 51
Poltava 113, 116, 118
Pottendorf (camp) 139, 140, 144, 148, 154
Prague 157
Priedite, Aija 46
prisoners of war 23, 108, 129, 131, 138, 146, 148, 238, 242, 243, 305
Prokuplje 240

Quakers 17, 277

Radoslavov, Vasil 272
Rappaport, Bruno 67, 70, 73, 76, 77
Red Army 53, 101
Red Crescent 311
Red Cross
   American 14, 17, 248
   Bulgarian 263, 270, 276, 277
   Egyptian 7
   German 15
   International Committee 29
   Russian 69
   Swedish 125
Reder, Josef 148
refugees
   camps 7-8, 9, 17, 116, 137, 139-50, 186, 187, 202-4, 246, 252
   categorisation 5, 95, 130, 136, 180-2, 217
   children 33, 70, 115, 118, 120-1, 143, 148, 199, 209, 248, 313-14
   commemoration 13, 89, 212-13, 238, 255, 279, 298
   cultural life 8, 13-14, 81, 96, 140, 145, 207, 221, 322
   deaths 70, 148, 187, 266, 277
   economic activities 10-11, 77, 98, 117, 144-5, 165, 167, 204-6, 224, 249, 250

eyewitness accounts 27, 36, 48, 67, 68–9, 70, 71, 89, 91, 93–4, 99, 102–3, 110, 114, 116, 120–1, 147, 168, 185, 215, 264, 268–9, 272–3, 276–7, 301, 308, 311, 319
health 54, 55, 91, 117–18, 123–4, 147–9, 158, 161, 166, 277, 311, 322
letters 188–9, 227, 228–9, 273, 313
national and local identity 9, 12, 80–2, 95–6, 220–2
photographs 29–30
relief and welfare 8, 30–2, 51, 78–80, 95–8, 111, 116, 130, 135, 182, 187, 200–4, 226, 270, 313
religious beliefs and practices 77, 118–19, 208
repatriation 3, 13–15, 36–9, 46, 51–2, 53–9, 82, 101–2, 121–5, 130, 131, 149–50, 169, 210–12, 232
sexual abuse 309
statistics 3, 4, 19, 26, 27, 32, 34, 49, 50, 55, 71–3, 88, 89, 98, 102, 109, 113, 130–1, 158, 162, 165, 183, 185, 198–200, 217, 240, 260–1, 262, 263–4, 265–7, 291–2, 308
women 11, 29, 33, 114, 115, 119–20, 208, 309
see also diaspora
Rennenkampf, Paul von 24
Riazan 88, 93, 98, 99
Riga 49–50, 51, 99
Risser, Nicole Dombrowski 231
Rogachev 91
Romania 7, 15, 162, 165, 263, 290
refugees 19, 113
Roslavl 69, 71, 93
Russia 45, 130
civil war 46
deportation policy 45, 47–8, 110
Duma 95, 106
February Revolution 8, 100, 108

German settlers 4, 15, 49, 89, 90
Greek settlers 284
High Command 4, 5, 67
invasion of East Prussia 25–6, 28
Jews 47, 90
Ministry of the Interior 91, 93, 95
October Revolution 12, 14, 48, 80, 82, 100, 102
Provisional Government 80, 100
refugees, pre-October 1917 5–6, 7, 11, 17, 45–65, 74–8, 88–107, 110
Iugobezhnets 93, 105, 111
Jewish 12, 47, 90, 99
national committees 12, 91, 95–6
relief measures 95–8
Severopomoshch' 93, 105, 111
Special Council for Refugees 73, 80, 95–6, 97, 110, 112
Tatiana committee 49, 72, 73, 80, 90–1, 94, 95, 97, 98, 110, 111, 118
refugees, post-October 1917 3, 72, 100–2, 265
Tsentroplenbezh 101–2
Union of Towns 93, 111
Union of Zemstvos 93, 111, 116
Zemgor (All-Russian Union of Towns and Zemstvos) 97
Russo-Turkish War 262
Ruthenians 5
refugees 4, 129, 133, 138, 139, 143, 146, 148, 149, 150

Salandra, Antonio 177, 181
Salonika (Thessaloniki) 237, 250, 252, 275, 291, 292, 305, 308
Samsonov, Aleksandr 24
Sanders, Liman von 295
Sandes, Flora 248
Save the Children Fund 53, 56, 59, 277
Scholtz, Friedrich von 26
Scottish Women's Hospitals 17, 253
Second World War 13, 41, 211, 213, 231, 255, 278, 285

Index

Serbia 238, 250, 253, 264, 305
  French military mission 246
  great retreat 237, 239, 241, 242, 243
  High Command 236, 242, 245
  Ministry of the Interior 252
  refugees 12, 13, 16, 236–59
    in Britain 250, 251
    in France 250, 251, 256
    international support 247, 248, 253
    Roma 239
  see also Balkan Wars
Serbian Relief Fund 247, 249, 253
Seton-Watson, Robert 250
Seyfeddin, Ömer 309
Sèvres, treaty 285
Shkoder 245, 246
Siberia 9, 25, 77, 94, 101
Simonović, Milenko 241
Skoropadsky, Pavlo 109
Skowronneck, Richard 31, 38
Slaviansk 114
Slovenia
  refugees 2, 4, 11, 143, 147, 150, 190, 191
Smolensk 69, 72, 93
Smyrna (İzmir) 288, 294, 308
Sonnino, Sidney 177
South Tyrol 129, 133, 139, 186
Stade 32
Stamboliiski, Alexander 278
Steinklamm (camp) 7
Stettin 33, 34
Stojadinović, Milan 238–9
Strumitsa 264
Stulginskis, Aleksandras 51
Styria 150
Sweden 124
Switzerland 180, 217
Światopełk-Czetwertyński, Seweryn 78
Świda, Adolf 82

Talaat, Mehmed 307
Tannenberg, battle 24, 25
Tarasiuk, Dariusz 82

Tatiana committee *see* Russia, refugees
Tchernoff, Samson 253
Thalerhof (camp) 148
Thorpe, Julie 8, 9
Thrace 262, 263, 264, 270, 271–2, 289
  Eastern 260, 266, 268–9, 293
  Western 265, 267, 269, 271, 272, 273
Topuzlu, Cemil 311
Tratnik, Fran 11
Trentino 129, 133, 179, 185–91
Trifonov, Stanko 272
Trotsky, Leon 305
Troubridge, Enrest 246
Tsaldaris, Panagis 323
Tula 88, 93, 96, 98
Turkey 262, 286, 294, 314, 318, 323
  Armenian population 4, 316, 317, 318
  Committee for Union and Progress *see* Young Turks
  Directorate for the settlement of tribes and immigrants (İAMM) 316, 317, 318
  Greek population 293–4, 296, 314, 316
  Muslim refugees 262, 304–27
    letters 313
    relief measures 313
  Ottoman rule 286–7
  population exchange with Greece 16, 285, 318
  refugee villages 312, 320
  Settlement Law 320, 321
  see also Balkan Wars; Kurds; Young Turks

Uden (camp) 203
Ukraine 69, 74, 111
  Central Rada 108–9, 121, 125
  independence 3, 109, 115, 124
  Ministry of the Interior 123
  refugees 53, 99, 108–28
    Jewish 15, 57, 112, 116
    national committees 112, 115–16, 122

relief measures 113, 115, 116
repatriation 113, 121–6
Soviet Socialist Republic 109, 125
Ungarisch Hradisch (Uherské Hradiště) (camp) 158, 159, 160, 162, 164
USA 12, 265, 291

Venizelos, Eleftherios 294, 296, 297
Vienna 13, 136, 140, 157, 158
Vilnius (Vilna) 47, 48, 50, 51, 54, 69, 89, 93
Volhynia (Volyn') 69, 108, 114, 120, 122
Volkov, E. Z. 88
Voronezh 28, 88, 96, 98
Vystavkina, E. 17

Wagna (camp) 7, 131, 141, 142, 147, 148

Warsaw 54, 67, 79
 Citizens' Committee 67
 evacuation 91
Wasilewski, Zygmunt 70, 71, 72, 73, 74, 81
Watson, Alexander 29
Weber, Eugen 229
Wéber, Koloman 160, 161
Windheim, Ludwig von 24, 26
Wilson, Francesca 22
Wojciechowski, Stanisław 78, 82
Wolf, Eric 287
Wójtowicz, Ryszard 70, 76, 77

Young Turks 293, 307, 310, 314, 315, 316–17
Yugoslavia 13, 253, 255, 319

Zinuk, Jan 93
Żabko-Potopowicz, Antoni 72
Żukowski, Władysław 79

EU authorised representative for GPSR:
Easy Access System Europe, Mustamäe tee 50,
10621 Tallinn, Estonia
gpsr.requests@easproject.com

www.ingramcontent.com/pod-product-compliance
Ingram Content Group UK Ltd.
Pitfield, Milton Keynes, MK11 3LW, UK
UKHW021842210426
5322IPUK00022B/425